# Studying Religion

# Studying Religion

## An Introduction Through Cases

### Gary E. Kessler

*California State University, Bakersfield*

Boston   Burr Ridge, IL   Dubuque, IA   Madison, WI   New York
San Francisco   St. Louis   Bangkok   Bogotá   Caracas   Kuala Lumpur
Lisbon   London   Madrid   Mexico City   Milan   Montreal   New Delhi
Santiago   Seoul   Singapore   Sydney   Taipei   Toronto

*McGraw-Hill Higher Education*

A Division of The *McGraw-Hill* Companies

1 2 3 4 5 6 7 8 9 0 FGR/FGR 0 9 8 7 6 5 4 3 2

**Library of Congress Cataloging-in-Publication Data**

Kessler, Gary E.
    Studying religion : an introduction through cases / Gary E. Kessler.
        p. cm.
    Includes bibliographical references and index.
    ISBN 0-7674-2227-9
    1. Religion—Case Studies.   I. Title.
BL48.K47 2002
200—dc21

2002026525

Publisher, Ken King; sponsoring editor, Jon-David Hague; production editor, Holly Paulsen; manuscript editor, Judith Brown; design manager, Sharon Spurlock; art editor, Emma Ghiselli; text designer, Susan Breitbard; cover designer, Claire Seng-Niemoeller; illustrator, Joan Carol; photo researcher, Holly Rudelitsch; production supervisor, Rich DeVitto. The text was set in 10.5/13 Weiss by G & S Typesetters, and printed on acid-free 45# New Era Matte, by Quebecor World Fairfield.

Cover image: Coptic funerary cushion (textile c. 5th–6th century). Musée Historique des Tissus, Lyon, France. © SEF/ArtResource, NY

**Photo Credits**

p. 1 British Museum, London, UK/Bridgeman Art Library; p. 74 © Arvind Garg/ CORBIS; p. 51 Amelia, Umbria, Italy/Bridgeman Art Library; p. 128 © CORBIS; p. 148 © Colin Hoskins, Cordaiy Photo Library Ltd./CORBIS; p. 339 © Gianni Dagli Orti/ CORBIS; **Part I chapter icon** Courtesy of Dover Pictorial Archive Services; **Part II chapter icon** Ashmolean Museum, Oxford, UK/Bridgeman Art Library; **Part III chapter icon** © CORBIS

www.mhhe.com

*To all who practice compassion*

# Preface

*Islam* means "submission" to the will of Allah, and comes from an Arabic word meaning "peace." This peace refers to individual contentment and to social harmony, both gained by submitting to the will of God. When I explain the meaning of *Islam* to my students, the shock of September 11, 2001, shatters historical consciousness. What is going on here? How could people commit such an act of barbaric terrorism in the name of a religion that teaches peace?

Such horrific events challenge students of religion to find explanations. The events of September 11 must somehow be interpreted so that they make sense, and their strangeness must be made familiar. The process of making the strange familiar in order to understand also involves the parallel process of making the familiar strange. Students raised in Christian traditions can search for possible parallels in the horrors of Christian crusades and the immense popularity of stories about Christian martyrs eager to die for their faith. Students raised in other religious traditions can begin to explore their own traditions for possible parallels. If, as some have claimed, one of the primary goals of religious studies is to make the strange familiar and the familiar strange, then this book can provide students with some of the tools that will help them achieve that goal.

*Studying Religion: An Introduction Through Cases* initiates readers into the academic study of religion and leads them on a journey through some of the history, beliefs, and practices of various religious traditions from around the world. It can serve as a textbook in introductory religious studies courses, and may also be appropriate for methods or other courses. The general reader will find this book a convenient way to learn about the academic study of religion as it is currently practiced in most public and many private colleges and universities.

I wrote this book for three primary reasons. First, the study of different religious traditions can be both fascinating and exciting, and it is important for the generally educated person to understand the significance of religion in shaping people's lives and behaviors. Second, it is important to teach students how to engage in the academic study of religion, and the case study approach facilitates this process. Third, no book that I know of presently on the market uses extended cases to teach students how to approach religious studies from an academic viewpoint. Most books explain what other scholars have learned about the religious traditions of the world, but do not take the next step of inviting students to participate in the academic activity of studying religions and showing them the basics of how to undertake such a study.

## COVERAGE

A glance at the contents will reveal the topics I discuss. Students will learn about many of the major ideas of the field of religious studies, some of the problems associated with defining religion, and some of the methods employed by scholars. They will also learn about diverse religious beliefs and practices. Topics covered include (among others) sacred power, myths and rituals, religion and art, religious experience, the problem of evil, and the relationship between religion and morality. Each topic is illustrated by case studies drawn from several historical periods and religions. I have selected the cases from religious traditions that have influenced (and are still influencing) large populations by shaping and reshaping their identities, communities, and values.

*Studying Religion* includes discussions of religious diversity and of questions regarding religious claims to truth that arise from the existence of a wide variety of religious viewpoints. In addition, this book pays attention to issues of gender and religious institutionalization. Many of my students claim to be spiritual, but do not belong to a specific religious organization. Religion for them is a private affair, having to do with their inner thoughts and feelings. The text invites students to reflect on the ways in which the processes of secularization, so characteristic of the modern and postmodern periods, have contributed to the privatization of religion or, as some might call it, the spiritualizing of religion.

Religious violence and cultic activity make headline news, and the very real and deadly conflicts that are often associated with religion need to be addressed when introducing students to the study of religion. Accordingly, one of the cases I analyze is Jonestown, and I also discuss the many meanings of Islamic *jihad,* going well beyond the oversimplified newspaper accounts.

## PEDAGOGICAL FEATURES

I have designed this book to address some of the typical problems instructors encounter when introducing students to the academic study of religion. One central problem is teaching students how to recognize, acknowledge, and control their religious biases. Because bias cannot be escaped, the question is how to effectively deal with it when striving for academic objectivity in the study of religion. Another problem mentioned at the beginning of this preface is in helping students recognize that something seemingly strange can be more familiar than they at first realize, and conversely that what is familiar can be something others find strange. To help solve these problems, I address in the first chapter how we can cultivate qualities that help us become better students of religion.

The following list highlights some of the pedagogical features included in *Studying Religion: An Introduction Through Cases* that aid beginning students to develop an understanding of religion from an academic perspective. This book

- invites readers to analyze and compare cases through specific questions and examples
- provides examples drawn from various religious traditions and different times and places
- emphasizes the development of descriptive, comparative, interpretative, and explanatory skills
- includes suggestions for further readings
- provides information on Internet resources
- contains a combination glossary/index with definitions of key terms and concepts

## ORGANIZATION

*Studying Religion: An Introduction Through Cases* is divided into three parts: "Preliminaries," "Liminaries," and "Postliminaries." I use this terminology in order to make clear an analogy between being introduced to the academic study of religion and the stages of a rite of passage. Rites of passage, both religious and secular, have three general stages. The preparatory stage takes place "before the threshold," that is, pre (before) *limen* (threshold). To prepare students for a rite of passage involving their thinking about religion, in Part I, "Preliminaries," I describe the qualities required of the student of religion, the field of religious studies, methods and approaches, and the meaning(s) of the concept of religion. The information and argumentation in these first three chapters reorients student thinking about religion from an insiders' perspective to an outsiders' perspective.

The threshold is crossed in Part II, titled "Liminaries," indicating the place of separation from preliminary thinking. In this new intellectual space I introduce students to specialized scholarly knowledge about broad topic areas in religious studies and scholarly practices of description, interpretation, comparison, and explanation.

Each of Chapters 4 through 12 opens with two cases and with summaries of some of the scholarly work relating to the topic of the chapter. These same chapters close with a research case, which invites students to think about a particular example by answering a series of questions.

Part III, "Postliminaries," focuses on the implications of religious pluralism for the issue of religious truth. After initiation into scholarly thinking about religion, students are left with a variety of questions relating to the legitimacy of their new knowledge and its implications for questions relating to religious truth. I encourage them to carry these questions into public discourse about religion, to avoid premature closure, and to continue their thinking about religion beyond the confines of this book.

## ACKNOWLEDGMENTS

No one writes a book alone, and I am indebted to many people. Among them are publisher Ken King, who first encouraged me to undertake this project, and my sponsoring editor Jon-David Hague, who saw it through. My production editor Holly Paulsen and manuscript editor Judith Brown have been most helpful. My partner Katy helped me clarify my ideas in numerous discussions. I have, over the years, learned much about both teaching and religion from my students in ways they would probably never guess.

I also wish to thank my colleagues who reviewed drafts of this book. The following individuals provided critical assessments and suggestions that have been most helpful:

William L. Power, University of Georgia
Micki Pulleyking, Southwest Missouri State University
Barry Sang, Catawba College

I hope the readers of this book will not only learn something about religion that they did not know before, but also something about what it means to be human in an often troubling, changing, and sometimes strange world.

# Contents

# Chapter 8 Religious Experience   153

# Chapter 9 Evil   189

# Chapter 10 Human Existence and Destiny   218

## Chapter 11  Religion and Morality    259

## Chapter 12  Institutionalized Religion    292

## PART III  Postliminaries   339

### Chapter 13  Religious Diversity and Truth   341

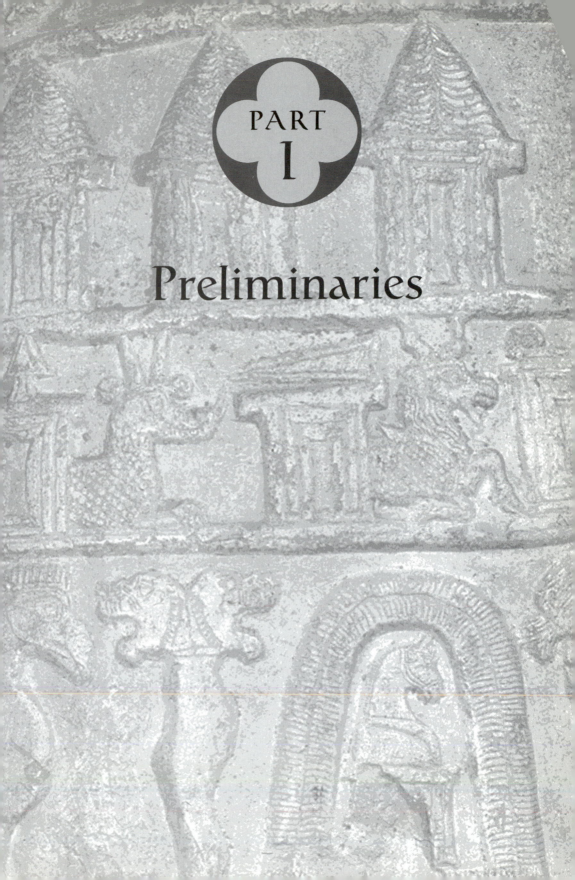

# PART I

# Preliminaries

CHAPTER  1

# Thinking about Being a Student of Religion [1]

IT IS TEN O'CLOCK ON A Sunday morning in Toronto. A girl is beginning her Sunday school lesson. On Saturday, some Jewish boys in Florence were debating the meaning of commentaries on Genesis at a synagogue. In Philadelphia, Islamic students gathered at a mosque on Friday to pray and to recite the Quran. In Bangkok, a thirteen-year-old boy is memorizing some Buddhist scriptures in preparation for taking monastic vows.

## 1.1  INSIDER'S AND OUTSIDER'S PERSPECTIVES

Like the people I have just described, those of us who have read the Bible in Sunday school or synagogue school, or have recited the Quran in a mosque or Buddhist scriptures in a temple, have encountered religion from an insider's point of view. The **insider's view** is that of the participant in a religious tradition. The insider's approach presupposes religious commitment and promotes an understanding that will lead to greater commitment. It promotes the interests and furthers the causes of a specific religious organization.

3

There are numerous religious traditions, including Hinduism, Buddhism, Daoism (Taoism), Confucianism, Judaism, Christianity, Islam, Jainism, Sikhism, Parsi, Chinese popular religion, and many more. All of these constitute the subject matter of religious studies, or religion studies, as some prefer to call it.

The academic study of religion is different from the insider's approach. It is study done from the **outsider's view**. The student stands outside all religious traditions and studies religions using the methods and standards associated with the academic disciplines of the secular university. The outsider's viewpoint does not presuppose any kind of religious commitment, although it does presuppose a commitment to the standards associated with the secular academy. Its goal is neither to increase nor to decrease an individual's religious faith, although it may have profound effects on that faith.

For the insider, the study of religion is itself a religious activity. For the outsider it is not, at least not in a sectarian sense. The difference between the two perspectives is like the difference between speaking a language and studying how a language is spoken. Studying is a **second-order activity** because it stands outside the actual **first-order activity** (speaking) that it seeks to understand. The academic study of religion is a second-order activity; it will not call on you to worship, but to observe those who do worship.

The controversial ruling of the U.S. Supreme Court (*Abington v. Schempp,* 1963) on prayer in public schools noted the difference between the insider's and outsider's perspectives by making a distinction between the **teaching of** versus the **teaching about religion**. The teaching of religion involves sectarian indoctrination, while teaching about it provides information without supporting any particular sect. Nothing, according to the Court, in the ruling prohibiting prayer in public schools, should be understood to forbid teaching *about* religion in public schools. What the public schools must avoid is the promotion of the viewpoint of a particular religious sect or group. If students in public schools come from a variety of religious backgrounds and if the United States is serious about the doctrine of the "separation of church and state," as stated in the First Amendment to the Constitution, then the public schools cannot promote one religious group over another.

If I were to ask you to list the advantages and disadvantages of the viewpoints of the insider and outsider, it would not take you long to create a list. On the one hand, the outsider's viewpoint provides a greater hope for achieving objectivity, which is particularly valuable when studying many different religions. On the other hand, the insider's viewpoint offers a greater hope for sympathetic understanding of one particular religious tradition. The insider can appreciate nuances and feelings that the observer can easily miss.

The situation is like the relationship between you and a psychological counselor. You know yourself from the inside, as it were, and hence have an advantage like no one else when it comes to self-knowledge. However, your very intimacy can lead to self-deception, distortions, and blind spots that an outside, trained observer like a counselor can detect almost immediately. For example, it may take me a while to realize that I tend to be a defensive person, but a good counselor can probably detect my defensiveness within ten minutes of an initial interview.

There can be considerable conflict between the insider's view and the outsider's view. The values that each holds appear to be opposed. The outsider appeals to such values as critical reason, disinterested and unemotional judgment, impersonal observation, and detached analysis. The insider's approach certainly involves the use of reason, but it is tempered by a personal, sometimes passionate, religious commitment. At its worst the outsider's approach can lead to a radical depersonalization of the subject matter, taking the vitality out of religions by reducing them to factors far removed from living reality. For example, some scholars claim that religion originates in fear of unseen powers—that religious faith is just another form of fear. This hardly seems plausible given the richness and diversity of religions, even if fear does play a role in religions.

At its worst the insider's approach can become so defensive and so prejudicial that it ceases to be honest, distorting facts and ignoring or suppressing evidence. For example, some insiders regard all religions other than their own as the "work of Satan." This kind of attitude reduces the academic study of religion to a combination of **apologetics** (a defense of an individual's own religion) and polemics (an attack on the religion of others). It is, of course, quite appropriate to defend your religious viewpoint. But this is not the task of the academic study of religion. Its goal is not to defend religion or to attack it, but to understand it.

I have identified the academic study of religion with the outsider's viewpoint in contrast to the insider's viewpoint. However, the picture I have painted is distorted. None of us is completely inside or outside in our viewpoints. Even if we practice no religion, religious traditions and values have so permeated our cultures and societies that, like fish, we live in a sea already containing religious currents. There is no view totally outside everything and no view totally inside. These extremes are "ideal types." They characterize the ends of a continuum. The real situation is more complex. The outsider can be as prejudiced as the insider, although in a different direction, and a plausible case can be made that the outsider is as much committed to promoting the interests of the academic "church of reason" as the insider is committed to promoting the interests of her or his church.

Are you beginning to see the challenges presented by the academic study of religion? It requires a scrupulous self-consciousness about how fairly we are treating others, others who may have very different values and beliefs from our own. To some extent the "other" is always threatening, and the "religious other" can be extremely threatening, because he or she is often a good person who believes in his or her way of life as sincerely as we believe in our own. It is difficult in such a situation to sustain the belief that other people are totally wrong religiously.

## 1.2 QUALITIES WORTH HAVING

The academic study of religion challenges the student of religion to develop certain qualities—qualities that aid in promoting fairness and sympathetic understanding of other people's faiths. In cultivating an outsider's perspective that treats religions fairly, we need to develop, among other things, the qualities of openness; honesty; critical intelligence; careful observing, reading, and listening; and critical tolerance. We will examine each of these qualities in turn.

It is conventional to use the generic singular *religion* instead of *religions* in such phrases as "the academic study of religion" and "the student of religion," and I will follow that convention. However, the use of the singular runs the danger of being misleading in two senses. First, it suggests there is some sort of *essence* to all the different religions, when there may not be such an essence, and second, it obscures the fact that the student must be the student of religion_s because comparative studies are such an important part of the academic study of religion(s).

### 1.2.1 Openness

To be open in the academic study of religion is to be prepared for surprises. Openness is a willingness to regard as tentative the categories, classification systems, labels, and names used to pigeonhole religious phenomena. Classification systems are incomplete and can be revised. Openness is not a refusal to draw conclusions, nor is it a noncommittal willingness to entertain anything and everything. To be open is to recognize that however helpful classification systems, explanations, and theories can be, they may be wrong and in need of revision as additional evidence comes to light. As students of religion we should welcome, as do students of physical science, evidence that we might be wrong, because if we are wrong and it can be shown, we have learned something new and thereby come that much closer to understanding.

Open-minded people recognize the fallibility of their beliefs. They realize that they might be wrong. Contrast this with closed-minded people, who fail to recognize this fallibility. They tend to be dogmatic and assume an air of infallibility. People can be open minded or closed minded with regard to many different things, not just religion. However, some people tend to be more closed minded with respect to religion than to other matters because religion is so important to human existence. A threat to religious convictions can cause people to close their minds and refuse to think further about threatening matters. The same is true of a threat to someone's favorite antireligious convictions. Theists may embrace stories of miracles too quickly, and atheists may reject them out of hand. Remaining open minded takes effort and a deliberate resolve to follow the evidence wherever it may lead.

### 1.2.2 Honesty

Honesty involves responsibility to others, to the subject matter, and to ourself. By responsibility I mean the ability to respond in a nonprejudicial way to what we learn. To be prejudiced is different from being biased (although the words are often used interchangeably). *Prejudice* means prejudgment. *Bias* means a particular slant, outlook, or perspective. Even the honest person is biased (has a perspective) because human beings existing in time and space see, of necessity, what they take to be real from a certain viewpoint. There cannot be a view from nowhere, just as there cannot be a view from everywhere. However, the honest person understands his or her biases and is mindful of them, thereby attempting to overcome whatever limitations those biases might impose. Using the analogy of studying a language, honesty can be characterized in terms of the ability to responsibly study the "language" of religion and at the same time to be aware of the perspective embedded in the second-order language used to describe religion.

Honesty requires eliminating prejudices and taking responsibility for biases. It also requires a willingness to understand the sources of prejudices and biases. How do we acquire them? Why do we find them useful? How do they protect us? How do they influence what we do and believe? Mindfulness and self-knowledge are the keys to finding answers to these sorts of questions.

Acknowledging a prejudice and its influence on us can be painful. It is frequently easier to hide behind the veil of objectivity than to examine our biases. However, we cannot progress very far down the road of the academic study of religion until we confront as honestly as we can our prejudices and examine as carefully as we can our biases. The openness described earlier and the critical intelligence examined next can aid in the process of becoming academically honest.

### 1.2.3 Critical Intelligence

Some may associate the word *critical* with a negative approach or an unfavorable judgment. However, I do not mean to indicate something exclusively negative by that term. To criticize is to evaluate by exercising careful judgment. Critical intelligence implies an effort to see things clearly so judgment can be rendered fairly. Evaluations may be positive or negative, but in an important sense the goal of all fair criticism is positive. We benefit by knowing when our judgments are right and when they are wrong.

Critical intelligence involves a number of different intellectual skills, including both analysis and synthesis. In analysis we seek to take things apart, to break wholes into more basic elements. Just as we might take a clock apart in order to see what makes it tick, engaging in the academic study of religion challenges us to take apart religious practices and beliefs to see what makes them work.

When analyzing a belief or practice, we seek to identify key elements that make up the whole. These elements depend on underlying assumptions. Finding the elements and their underlying assumptions is no easy task. For example, we might seek to identify the religious roles people play and uncover the assumptions of power on which those roles are based. This requires careful analysis of such matters as gender relations, privilege, and traditional patterns of submission and dominance.

There is more to critical intelligence than analysis. Synthesis—putting things back together again—is also required. This means being alert for the discovery of previously unseen relationships and for the sudden insight that what we took to be contradictions are reconciled in a greater harmony. Our tasks as academic students of religion are not only to analyze religion, but also to synthesize its various parts so that underlying and often unexpected relationships come to light. The elements of a belief or practice always stand in relationship to other elements. Understanding how the elements work together is as important as understanding what the elements are. For example, if we know the priestly role in a certain rite is to mediate divine grace, then how that element functions in conjunction with other elements such as gestures of blessing and sprinkling holy water helps us grasp the meaning of the rite as a whole.

At the heart of critical intelligence is the critical pursuit of truth. Although we live in an age of relativism, when phrases like "the pursuit of truth" sound outdated, such a pursuit cannot be given up, even when we are uncertain there is any truth to be found. Criticism, be it positive or negative, is essential to any scholarly program of study.

To look for truth in the study of religion necessitates criteria regarding what is going to count as truth. The task of articulating such criteria is by no means easy. However, there are generally accepted critical standards available (for example, consistency, use of good evidence, valid arguments) for what is to count as true; and the student of religion, as the student of biology, ought to employ these standards and, at the same time, seek to improve them.

Arguments supporting a particular conclusion must be carefully examined to see if the premises are true and the conclusion actually follows from the premises. If someone claims that near-death experiences *prove* there is a life after death, we must ask if that is so. What do such experiences actually prove? How much can we safely infer from a near-death experience about an after-life? What is the difference between *prove* and *provide evidence for*?

Consistency in theory and its application is a hallmark of the pursuit of truth. Evidence must be carefully examined for reliability. If I claim that fear is the essence of religion and explains the desire to be blessed by a priest, then I must also check for possible counterevidence and counterexamples, such as the incredible sense of joy and release experienced by those who feel forgiven. Claims need to be appropriately qualified and modified in light of evidence. Rigorous experiments such as the kind found in the physical sciences are sel-dom possible in the academic study of religion, but that does not mean that all checking procedures are impossible.

We also need to check the precision of our terms. What do we mean by *religion*, and by *fear*? Can these terms be defined precisely enough to be useful? We do not know whether the admonition of some religions to "fear God" counts as evidence for the claim that fear is the essence of religion unless we know that the fear we are talking about and the fear they are talking about mean the same thing. We do not know whether the joy of forgiveness that people experience is a good counterexample to claims about fear residing at the heart of religion until we know how joy and fear might be related. Does the joy of forgiveness require the fear of damnation?

Crucial to the search for truth is the ability to question. Most of us are too easily satisfied with superficial answers and stop questioning too soon. The willingness to continue to raise questions even when we think we understand and to pursue alternative answers is an indispensable tool in the quest for truth. Moreover, there is an art to questioning. It is not enough just to question. Rather, we ought to carefully examine our questions, seeking to find out whether they are correctly formulated and lead in fruitful directions. As stu-dents of religion, we must remember that questioning is not an end in itself; rather, its purpose is to lead the way to answers.

## 1.2.4 Careful Observing, Reading, and Listening

Developing the quality of careful observing, reading, and listening sounds simple enough. Doesn't every student observe, read, and listen? My experience has been that while I think I am observing, reading, or listening, I am not al-ways doing so. As a professor I am used to students asking questions. The more I teach the more I become accustomed to certain kinds of questions. This has lulled me into not listening fully. The student may be in the midst of a ques-tion or comment, and I find myself already formulating a reply in my mind. I sometimes become so preoccupied with formulating my reply that I cease to listen.

Actions, comments, questions, and textual materials are often deceptive. The actions or words say one thing, but the person behind the actions or words may be saying something else. Learning to see, to read, and to listen for the hidden meanings is especially important when dealing with religious art and religious texts. **Sacred** writings and art of all varieties contain many different levels of meaning. We can train our eyes and ears to become sensitive to as many different levels of meaning as possible. There is great joy in studying religions when a new level of meaning in some familiar saying or ritual action surprises us. Religious rituals and experiences contain a symbolic richness that will unfold for the student who observes, reads, and listens carefully.

Careful observing, reading, and listening require sympathetic imagination. Imagination is one of our greatest assets. As children it was through imagination that we began to chart that vast unknown world of the experiences of adults. Playing teacher or astronaut is a way of trying to see what the world is like from the perspective of someone who is different from us. Through imagination we can project ourselves, at least partially, into the worldview of a **shaman** doing magical healing, a yogi in meditation, a prophet proclaiming a judgment, and a Christian or a Muslim at prayer.

The ability to imagine—to play, to make believe—is invaluable as we struggle to comprehend cultures, beliefs, practices, and experiences that seem different and strange. Sympathetic imagination requires projecting ourselves into the viewpoint of others and trying to see the world from their perspective. Insofar as we all share in a common humanity and a common world, such a projection is possible and valuable.

At the same time, beware of the limits of imagination. Projection can easily lead to distortion. For example, some early scholars, following missionary leads, equated the Lakota Sioux notion of Wakan Tanka, which they translated as "Great Spirit," with the idea of a monotheistic god as understood in the Jewish, Christian, and Islamic traditions. Wakan Tanka is better translated as "Great Mysteriousness." It is a collective name for a number of different *"wakan* (powerful and sacred) beings" (see Chapters 4 and 6). To identify Wakan Tanka with the monotheistic god of nonnative religious traditions obscures important and instructive differences.

### 1.2.5 Critical Tolerance

Those who study and teach about religions hope to promote religious tolerance. Religious tolerance is a culturally approved, public virtue that allows all of us to get along in greater harmony than does religious intolerance. Religious tolerance not only permits, but also encourages the free expression and practice of diverse religious traditions. In a diverse society in which a vast variety of religious traditions exist side by side, the alternative to religious tolerance appears to be bigotry and strife.

No one who studies the history of religious warfare and conflict would seriously advocate religious intolerance. We are so accustomed, however, to thinking of religious tolerance as a public good, that we often fail to address difficult underlying issues. We tend to think of religious tolerance superficially as a kind of happy acceptance, if not approval, of religious differences.

A superficial view of toleration ignores two underlying problems. First, there are religious traditions of which people disapprove whether we think they ought to or not. If we could accept everything about a religious group, there would be no reason not to join if asked. Second, there are religious beliefs and practices of which we think people ought to disapprove. Few of us would advocate neglecting the medical needs of a child, even if religious reasons are given. Few of us would approve of physical mutilation, even if it is a long-standing practice in one or another sacred tradition. Few of us would support the Taliban's denial of human rights to women in Afghanistan, even if they argued that it is Islamic law (which, by the way, it is not).

Students of religion cannot be content advocating an uncritical religious and moral tolerance. Rather, they must seek to develop a **critical tolerance** that endorses freedom of religion but does not automatically approve of any and all religious beliefs and practices.

Sympathetic imagination and keeping an open mind are indispensable in studying religion, but they need to be balanced by critical intelligence. Sympathetic imagination and openness promote tolerance for those who are different, and critical intelligence promotes a tolerance tempered by evaluation. We can and should come to understand religious tragedies such as Jonestown (see Chapter 12), where people committed mass suicide, or Waco, Texas, where David Koresh and his followers were plunged into a fiery and deadly encounter with the U.S. government, but we cannot condone mass suicide and violence.

Sometimes it is easy to know where to draw the line between understanding and tolerance. At other times it is more difficult. We can understand why some religions sacrificed humans and thought it was right to do so, and we have no difficulty condemning such a practice should it occur today. However, what should we say about the sacrifice of animals, which still takes place in religious settings? Should it be tolerated or condemned? Should we tolerate sects that advocate the use of physical punishment in order to discipline children? When does physical punishment become physical abuse "in the name of God"?

As these questions indicate, there is no simple way to balance sympathetic understanding and critical intelligence in all situations. Although this is no easy task, it is a challenge worth meeting. Studying religion challenges us to examine the limits of toleration. Openness demands a willingness to suspend what might be our immediate moral and religious disapproval in order to understand more deeply.

We cannot, however, suspend our disapproval forever and in all cases. Sometimes, as our understanding deepens, our disapproval will lessen. Eventually it may seem to us just plain silly to condemn certain religious beliefs and practices. Do we really want to fight religious wars over how someone is baptized? Sometimes, however, even after we have understood as deeply as we can, we find ourselves unable to condone, let alone support, certain religious beliefs and practices. Do we really want to support the denial of equal religious rights to women? Perhaps we can do little more than advocate the right of those who are oppressed by a religious group to leave that group if they should so desire. Forcing people to accept ideas and practices they find oppressive is incompatible with human dignity and worth. However, respect for difference and the right to be different requires that we be careful in religious matters. Critical tolerance is necessary, but not easy.

---

**Qualities Worth Having**

1. Openness
2. Honesty
3. Critical intelligence
4. Careful observing, reading, and listening
5. Critical tolerance

---

## 1.3 WHY STUDY RELIGION?

Many of you are taking an introductory course in the study of religion because it fulfills some sort of general education requirement. You are reading this book in conjunction with that course and, perhaps, wondering what this course has to do with getting a job and making money after graduation. Many people believe that if it "bakes no bread" it's useless.

Some of you may not be thinking along those lines. You may be thinking that college education is more than vocational training, and it is worthwhile to study subjects that may have no immediate or obvious practical application. You may be thinking that the *study of religion helps us understand a force that influences, for good or for ill, the lives of practically everyone who is alive.*

So much of human history and culture remains a mystery if we cannot comprehend the role religion has played and continues to play in the development of human institutions, values, and behavior. American culture, for example, cannot be fully understood without knowing something about the role that Christianity played in shaping its political, judicial, and educational institutions, not to mention its role in establishing such values as individual freedom and human rights. In America, religious ideas were used both to promote the destruction of indigenous peoples and to end it, to promote slavery and to stop it.

In addition to helping understand the role religion has played and continues to play in human history, studying religion, especially the religions of others, helps us overcome our all-too-comfortable ethnocentric attitudes and achieve a more global and multicultural perspective. *Developing a global perspective* is particularly important at a time when advanced technologies make it possible to travel to places and communicate with peoples about which past generations could only read. National borders are increasingly porous as people immigrate from one country to another. As multinational corporations rapidly create a global economy, we cannot avoid beginning to see ourselves as citizens of the world, or *cosmopolitans* (as the Greeks would say), in addition to members of different cultures and ethnic groups. It is as likely that someday some of us may be living and doing business in China or the Middle East as living and working in the United States, Mexico, or Canada. Mosques spring up down the street from Christian churches, and Hindu temples find their place in communities that once knew only synagogues and churches.

The idea of developing a global perspective is closely tied to yet another reason for studying religion: *the development of a comparative perspective.* Comparison is an indispensable tool for the student of religion. It is, however, more than just an academic tool that increases our knowledge. It also develops understanding, not just of others but of ourselves as well. Just as we learn more about our own languages and cultures by studying the languages and cultures of others, so we learn more about our own religion and values by understanding them in contrast to the religions and values of others. F. Max Müller (1823–1900), an influential linguist and historian of religions, liked to apply to the study of religion what Johann von Goethe applied to the study of language, "he who knows one . . . knows none."[2] Comparative understanding enriches our lives and aids in the search for a more humane way to live together on an increasingly overcrowded, violent, and polluted planet.

As a young student of religion, having been schooled in the Lutheran tradition of Christianity, I recall thinking, when I began the study of the Buddhist concept of "letting go of attachments," that I now understand more deeply what Martin Luther, one of the sixteenth-century founders of the Protestant Reformation, meant when he claimed that the heart of the Christian gospel is justification by faith, not by works. Luther counseled that we should give up trying to work our way into heaven. We cannot make it on our "own power." Buddhists would say we need to "let go" of that attachment.

In addition to expanding our understanding of the significant role religion plays in shaping human history and aiding us in developing a global and comparative perspective, the study of religion opens up a space in our busy lives where we can pause and *reflect on the meaning and purpose of our lives.* It provides an occasion for us to think, in a comparative setting, about what constitutes the good life. By comparing and evaluating what others have said about how humans should conduct themselves, we are in a better position to develop a reflective philosophy of life. Most of us are too busy living our lives to give much thought to how we *should* live. Although the academic study of religion cannot provide answers to the "big questions" about the purpose of human existence, it can help us understand the answers different religions have given to where we came from, how we should live, and where we are going. Studying religion provides a space in which to compare what we have been taught by our own religious traditions with what other traditions say.

Finally, I would add that it is not entirely true that the study of religion "bakes no bread." Most of you will not go into vocations that directly involve the use of expertise about religion, but some of you will. The academic study of *religion does prepare you for a career* if you become professionally interested in the field. It also aids in preparation for other kinds of careers. A wide variety of employers are looking for people who are tolerant of diversity, are able to learn from others, are adaptable to new situations, and have knowledge of history and international affairs. Studying religion can help you cultivate the qualities many employers find attractive.

The study of religion will certainly increase your understanding of something that has been and is enormously influential in human history. But more than that, it will develop within you a global and comparative perspective that will help you discover who you are and how you may wish to conduct your life as you move deeper into the twenty-first century.

---

### Why Study Religion?

1. To satisfy a requirement for general or liberal education
2. To discover the important role religion plays in the development of history and culture
3. To develop a global perspective
4. To develop a comparative perspective
5. To have an occasion to reflect on the meaning of the good life
6. To prepare for a career in the field of religious studies and other fields

---

## 1.4 PLAN OF THE BOOK

I have divided this book into three parts, each marked with a boundary stone from a different culture, corresponding to the three phases of the rites of initiation found in many religions. It seems appropriate that a book introducing the academic study of religion should be thought of as a process of initiation. Though the initiation is not religious, but academic, it is no less of an initiation.

*Limen* is the Latin word for "threshold." A threshold marks a doorway, which in turn marks a division among three spaces and times: before the threshold, inside the threshold, and beyond the threshold. The notion of *limen* is used by anthropologists to designate three phases of a **rite of passage**. These rites mark passages or transitions in the life journey. A marriage ceremony, for example, is a rite of passage: Prior to the threshold (phase 1), you have a certain social status (unmarried) involving appropriate rules of behavior. During the threshold time (phase 2), that unmarried status is suspended, and you are initiated into the knowledge and lore appropriate for a new status. For example, you are usually told during a marriage ceremony about the new rights and responsibilities that you are expected to assume as a married person. After the ceremony (phase 3), a new social status (married) emerges on the other side of the threshold. People now treat you differently than they did before you were married.

Part I of this book, entitled "Preliminaries," literally means "prior to the *limen.*" This part treats such topics as the qualities appropriate for the student of religion (Chapter 1), the field of religious studies (Chapter 2), and the definition of religion (Chapter 3).

Part II is coined "Liminaries" to indicate the threshold stage of the initiation, a stage that follows the preliminaries. The initiate will find chapters (4 through 12) dealing with different categories useful for comparing religious traditions: sacred power, sacred story, sacred action, sacred space and time, religious experience, evil, human existence and destiny, religion and morality, and institutionalized religion.

I have invented the word "Postliminaries" (compare the English *subliminal*) to mark Part III. The initiation here moves into its third phase. I deal with only one of many possible topics—the question of religious truth in the face of religious diversity (Chapter 13). This postliminary phase continues long after we have finished the last chapter. We will have learned to think about religion differently than we thought about it before. Even if some of you reject much or most of what I have to say, that very rejection will change the way you think. Your intellectual world will be different after initiation into the academic study of religion.

## 1.5 SUMMARY

We began this chapter by distinguishing the insider's perspective from the outsider's. The academic study of religion promotes the values of the outsider's viewpoint while recognizing the values of the insider's viewpoint. In part that means cultivating qualities of openness; honesty; critical intelligence; careful observing, reading, and listening; and critical tolerance. These qualities are the same as those necessary for the academic study of most topics. They require a willing suspension of belief, a moderate dose of skepticism, a keen awareness of how wrong we often are (fallibilism), and a healthy dose of respect for the difficulties involved in the study of a topic over which people continue to fight wars.

There are many reasons for studying religion. It increases our understanding of important factors that shape our lives, helps us develop a global and comparative perspective, and provides an opportunity to reflect on the meaning and purpose of our existence. It may even lead to a career.

The study of religion can be as difficult and as exciting as learning to understand and appreciate another human being, another culture, another way of life. At its best, the study of religion can show us how to see what the world is like through the eyes of another. It can disclose the depths of human suffering and the heights of human joy. The simple act of a prayer, a sacrifice, lighting incense, or eating a humble meal can reveal richness of meaning, a sense of proportion and grace, a feeling of awe and mystery that enlarges our souls.

## EXPLORATIONS

Near the close of the first three chapters I will pose questions to ponder. These "explorations," as I call them, invite you to think more deeply about key issues. Jot down your answers. Compare your answers with those of your classmates, and make a sincere effort to think beyond what I have said.

1. Alasdair MacIntyre, a philosopher, wrote an essay entitled "Is Understanding Religion Compatible with Believing?" Imagine that you have been asked to write an essay with the same title. What would you say, and what reasons would you provide to support what you say?
2. Wilfred Cantwell Smith, a historian of religion and Islamic scholar, once said that no statement made by a scholar of religion is valid unless a religious believer could accept it as correct. Do you agree? Why or why not?
3. Is it morally right to tolerate and hence permit what you sincerely believe to be morally wrong? Why or why not?
4. Is "teaching about" religion just another form of indoctrination?

## SUGGESTIONS FOR FURTHER READING

In addition to the material found in the notes, the reader may wish to consult the following for more information.

Braun, Willi, and Russell T. McCutcheon. *Guide to the Study of Religion*. London: Cassell, 2000. This book is a collection of essays dealing with a variety of topics (ritual, ethnicity, gender, etc.) often encountered by the student of religion.
Browne, M. Neal, and Stuart M. Keeley. *Asking the Right Questions: A Guide to Critical Thinking*. 5th ed. Englewood Cliffs, NJ: Prentice-Hall, 1997. The authors include, among other things, a good discussion of the importance of being open minded.

Carman, J., and S. Hopkins, eds. *Tracing Common Themes: Comparative Courses in the Study of Religion*. Atlanta: Scholars Press, 1991. This book includes essays on the value and importance of the academic study of religion.

Holm, Jean. *The Study of Religions*. New York: The Seabury Press, 1977. Although out of date in some respects, this little book is a useful guide for those who are just beginning the academic study of religion.

McCutcheon, Russell T. *Critics Not Caretakers: Redescribing the Public Study of Religion*. Albany, NY: State University of New York Press, 2001. McCutcheon argues that the scholar of religion must be a critic of cultural practices rather than a caretaker of religious tradition.

——, ed. *The Insider/Outsider Problem in the Study of Religion: A Reader*. London: Cassell, 1999. This book contains a useful collection of writings on issues relating to the academic study of religion.

Reynolds, F., and S. Burkhalter, eds. *Beyond the Classics? Essays on Religious Studies and Liberal Education*. Atlanta: Scholars Press, 1990. The essays in this volume will take you deeper into the issues of how the study of religion relates to liberal education.

## INTERNET RESOURCES

Always remember that information on the World Wide Web must be used with caution, as does information from other sources. Don't believe everything you see or read on the Web. One thing to check for is whether the information is from an insider's or outsider's perspective. You can learn from both perspectives, but be critical of both. Check for bias.

http://www.aar-site.org/   Here is the site for the American Academy of Religion, the primary professional organization for scholars and instructors in religious studies. Once there, try the links for more information.

http://www.ccsr.ca/   This will take you to the homepage for the Canadian Corporation for Studies in Religion, a "virtual community for the academic study of religion in Canada." Links to Canadian academic societies for the study of religion can be found here plus much more.

http://www.adherents.com/   At this site you will find statistical and geographical information on the religions of the world. It is packed with interesting information.

## CHAPTER 2

# The Field of
# Religious Studies

IN THE FIRST CHAPTER WE discussed some of the personal qualities that are useful in the study of religion: openness; honesty; critical intelligence; careful observing, reading, and listening; and critical tolerance. These qualities come into play as we learn to engage in the academic study of religion. Along with explaining what the academic study of religion is, I wish to show beginning students something about how to practice it. It is worthwhile not only to learn how others have engaged in the academic study of religion, but also to begin to learn how to do such study yourself. This chapter will help you accomplish these goals by describing the field of religious studies, how people engage in the academic study of religion, and what methods they employ.

## 2.1 A SIMPLE MAP OF THE FIELD

Before discussing methods directly, let's look at a brief disciplinary outline of the field of religious studies as it is presently practiced in many colleges and universities in the United States and elsewhere:

I. History of religion
   A. Developmental studies
   B. Comparative studies

II. Social scientific study of religion
   A. Anthropology of religion
   B. Sociology of religion
   C. Psychology of religion
III. Philosophy of religion
   A. Analytical
   B. Critical

This outline does not include areas that cut across these divisions, such as feminist studies, literary studies, and scriptural studies, but it will do as a starting point.

Developmental historical studies (**history of religions**) employ the theories and methods of history to study how a religion, religions, or part of a religion have developed through time. Religions that are living traditions have changed and are changing, because nothing that survives can do so without adapting to its changing environment. Those that have ceased to change are dead religions of the past, although parts may have survived in other religious forms. An example is the spring fertility rituals using painted eggs that have been incorporated into Christian Easter celebrations of the resurrection of Christ. Developmental historians are interested in how religions have changed and what factors are at work that cause change. They are also interested in continuities, because not everything changes completely. A basic assumption of the developmental approach is that religions are complex and dynamic historical processes exhibiting both change and continuity.

Comparative studies focus primarily on comparing different religious traditions. The concern is less with the changes that religions undergo and more with structures or types (although there is no reason why a comparative study of changes could not be done). The comparativist arrests time by taking snapshots of different religious phenomena and comparing them. The comparativist may select one of the many dimensions of religion, such as ritual, and do a comparative study of certain types of ritual activities in, say, Islam and Judaism. One basic assumption of comparative studies is that there are certain analytical categories (belief, ritual, morality, and so on) that are useful for cross-cultural comparison. Ideally, the comparativist should balance the description of similarities and differences, but often, differences are submerged or overlooked in the rush to find similarities.

Social scientists use the current methods and theories of their fields to understand and explain religion within a larger setting. A basic assumption for social scientists is that insofar as religion is a human activity, it can be explained by cultural, social, or psychological factors, just as any human phenomenon can be explained by such factors. The anthropologist (**anthropology of religion**) is particularly concerned with religion in relation to culture. Although the concept of culture is vague and can have a variety of meanings, here, it refers to the sum total of the symbols humans produce in order to convey information, make sense of experience, and order relations within human groups. Cultures need symbol systems to convey information. Language, art, religion, philosophy, science, technology, manners, and morality are examples of significant cultural symbol systems that convey information and create the meaning necessary for human groups to cope successfully with their environments.

Anthropologists interested in the study of religion pay particular attention to the nature and function of religious symbol systems. One of the most influential definitions of religion derives from the work of cultural anthropologist Clifford Geertz. According to Geertz, religion is "(1) a system of symbols which act to (2) establish powerful, persuasive, and long-lasting moods and motivations in men by (3) formulating conceptions of a general order of existence and (4) clothing these conceptions with such a aura of factuality that (5) the moods and motivations seem uniquely realistic."[1]

Geertz's definition indicates one way to approach the study of religion. Following his lead, the student of religion would seek to uncover some of the ways in which religion functions to motivate humans and order social life by means of symbols. For example, some religions have symbol systems that deal with life after death in terms of heaven and hell. Symbols of heaven and hell can powerfully affect human behavior. In some cases they can motivate extreme behavior, such as suicide bombings, inquisitions, and holy wars. These kinds of symbol systems create a this-worldly/otherworldly framework for thinking about life. Life in this world is preliminary to an afterlife in another world. Symbols of the afterlife can be powerful enough to convince people that what they cannot see is real. Indeed, these symbol systems can convince people that they have genuine information about the future. People who live in a culture filled with symbols of the afterlife live in anticipation of a future yet to be. The best (or the worst) is yet to come.

For sociologists (**sociology of religion**), the operative category is society. As used here, society is a narrower category than culture. It encompasses the particular ways groups within cultures organize themselves. Sociologists are particularly interested in the social functions of religion. Many sociologists see religion as a kind of "social glue" that binds groups together. It helps to provide group identity and thereby differentiate one human group from another. Religion can also split groups apart and rearrange an old grouping into a new social order. The sociologist seeks, among other things, to discover how religions promote social solidarity and contribute to social change.

For example, a sociologist might be interested in studying how belonging to a religious group provides people with a sense of identity. Having an identity is fundamentally important to human existence. If asked who they are, people might include in their response, "I am a Muslim," or "I am a Hindu." Establishing such identities not only tells people who they are, it also tells them who they are not: "I am Hindu, and they are not." Identities imply complex sets of beliefs, values, and behaviors. So they might think, "Hindus practice this ritual and Muslims practice that ritual, and since I am a Hindu I too must practice as Hindus do and not as Muslims do."

Psychologists (**psychology of religion**) are usually more individually oriented than sociologists and anthropologists. Rather than focusing on religion as a cultural symbol system or on its social functions, psychologists often focus on how religion expresses repressed feelings or universal psychic tendencies. Psychologists might ask how religion shapes character development. Or they may be concerned with the relationships among religious commitment, deviant behavior, mental illness, and moral development. There is little doubt that religious experiences play important roles in people's lives, and psychologists are particularly interested in the experiential aspect of religion. They seek to find out what kind of religious experiences occur and how to best understand such experiences.

I divide **philosophy of religion** into two categories: analytic and critical. This is somewhat artificial, however, because in practice they are often combined. Elsewhere I have defined philosophy of religion as "the rational attempt to formulate, understand, and answer fundamental questions about religious matters."[2] The philosophical quest for formulating, understanding, and answering fundamental questions demands both careful analysis of religious beliefs and actions and a critical response (negative or positive) whose goal is a deeper rational understanding of religious matters. Exactly what is rational and what are fundamental questions are subjects of intense debate. A basic assumption of this discipline is that if there is such a thing as religious truth, careful philosophical criticism and analysis should be able to uncover it. So philosophy of religion is typically concerned with arguments for God's existence, the reasonableness of notions about life after death, whether religious experiences provide evidence of some religious reality, whether the existence of evil in the world is incompatible with the existence of God, or other questions arising out of religious belief and practice. Historians and social scientists usually refrain from offering judgments about the truth or falsity of the religious beliefs and actions they study, but philosophers are often concerned with questions of truth. Philosophers want to know if religions are bearers of truth.

I have not listed theology as part of the field of religious studies, and some may find that odd. **Theology,** according to St. Thomas Aquinas (1225–1274), is the study of the divine, and its goal is knowledge of God. For St. Thomas, a Roman Catholic Christian, God is at the apex of a triangle that includes humans and nature; hence theology is the queen of the academic sciences, while humanities (the study of humans) and natural science (the study of nature) assume subordinate positions. Historically, religious studies evolved out of theology, and, while theology is no longer considered the queen of the sciences, both religious studies and theology find a place among the numerous academic pursuits found in modern universities.

If we think of religious studies as an activity of the outsider, then theology, as traditionally understood, is an insider activity. It is true that theologians interpret their faith traditions using critical tools, which are often the same critical tools used by the outsider. But theology is not just an act of critical interpretation, it is a confession of faith. Doing theology usually presupposes a commitment to religious truth, whereas religious studies do not. For example, some Buddhists affirm that the Buddhist experience of "enlightenment provides the ultimate criterion of interpretation."[3] Likewise many Christian theologians claim that theology must be rooted in faith. The widely accepted formula of "faith seeking understanding" often characterizes the Christian theological approach.

If religion has to do with a reality that transcends the world of ordinary experience, then theology can be characterized as an attempt to directly study transcendence; to give us, following St. Thomas, "knowledge of God." The focus of religious studies, however, is not on transcendence per se, but on believers and how they experience and interpret what they take to be transcendent. Theology, understood as the interpretive practice of the insider, is one more aspect of the subject matter with which religious studies concerns itself. Theology is the scholarly language *of* religion, and religious studies are the scholarly language *about* religion. Although some may see theology and religious studies as opposed (if not antagonistic) and others as complementary, one thing is clear: they are different, and the student of religion can learn much by reflecting on how they are different.

There is much more to say about the historical, social scientific, and philosophical fields that make up religious studies. As you become more deeply initiated into the complexities of the academic study of religion, these beginning characterizations will become more refined. For now, they will serve as a beginning road map.

## 2.2 UNDERSTANDING AND EXPLAINING

There is considerable scholarly debate about what methods and approaches are most appropriate for understanding religion. One major debate centers on a distinction between *understanding* and *explanation*. These terms are vague and are often used in different ways (understanding can even be thought of as one type of explanation). But in this debate, understanding usually means reconstructing meanings from the "agent's point of view." This is equivalent to a type of interpretation that many scholars find most appropriate to academic studies in the humanities.

In contrast to understanding, explanation, in this debate, is frequently restricted to a causal account that treats religion like any other social phenomenon. Why do humans do the things they do? Why do they behave in some particular way? We can ask such questions about political and economic behavior, and there is no reason why we cannot ask such questions about religious behavior. The theories that help us answer these questions in one area of human life (politics, for example) should also be able to help us answer these questions when it comes to religion.

According to one of the camps (usually called **phenomenology of religion**) in this debate about understanding and explanation, it is most appropriate for the scholarly study of religion to seek understanding of the agent's point of view because religion is *sui generis* (self-generated). That is to say, religion is based on something irreducibly religious, and hence religious actions cannot be explained or at least not completely explained in nonreligious terms. The phenomenologists (so called because they claim to focus on only what appears, or phenomena) maintain that the academic study of religion is properly made up of one and only one discipline. This discipline is appropriate to the study of the *sui generis* nature of religion, which they sometimes refer to as "the sacred," or "the holy." According to phenomenologists, the student of religion must describe and interpret what appears (religious phenomena), but should not explain or evaluate what appears by standards foreign to religion. Religions are the appearance of the sacred in different times and places. The scholar of religion comes to understand the sacred by comparing all of its different appearances.

Phenomenologists sometimes call what they do "history of religion" or "comparative religion." They shun social scientists as hopelessly prejudiced (although they often use information gathered by anthropologists) because they think that social scientists project their own nonreligious theories into religious phenomena. Phenomenologists accuse social scientists of being "reductionistic" because they explain religious behavior in terms of social causes (economic, cultural, and psychological) and not in terms of manifestations of the sacred.

Social scientists and philosophers generally see the field of religious studies as multidisciplinary and multimethodological. There are many different ways of studying religion, and each has something of value to offer. There is no good reason to exclude nonreligious causes of religious events if in fact they were causes of some event, and, at least for the philosophers, there is no good reason to refrain from asking whether what some religions claim is true, is in fact true. Phenomenologists typically want to bracket, or set aside, the question of truth because while human scholarship is capable of understanding religious claims to truth, it is not capable of settling disputes about such claims.

The debate about **reductionism** can be illustrated by taking a brief look at Karl Marx's famous claim that religion is the opiate of the people. Marx

(1818–1883) writes, "Religion is the sigh of the oppressed creature, the heart of a heartless world, just as it is the spirit of a spiritless situation. It is the opium of the people."[4] Religion, in other words, is a coping mechanism. It is a way for oppressed peoples to get along in a cruel and heartless world. Marx goes on to remark that religion becomes a tool in the hands of the wealthy, used to keep the poor content with their lot in life. It promises "pie in the sky by and by" if people mind their manners now and accept things as they are. Religious behavior is explainable as a function of certain economic conditions of oppression. Whatever the agents may think they are doing when they pray for salvation, what they are really doing is coping as best they can with a miserable situation. Marx would urge them to get off their knees and take to the streets in revolutionary protest if they really wish to effectively change their lot in life.

From the phenomenological viewpoint, Marx has reduced religion to economic factors. He fails to take into account the point of view of the agent, and hence he misses the religious meaning of the act of praying for salvation. Praying for salvation is a uniquely religious act that needs to be understood on its own terms. It is a sacred or holy activity that involves special and often intense feelings of sin, guilt, hope, awe, and sometimes even despair. Explaining it in nonreligious terms amounts, from the phenomenological perspective, to "explaining it away."

## 2.3 GOALS AND METHODS

We will have many occasions in this book to revisit this debate about reductionism in one form or another. For now, let us assume that the goals of religious studies, whether historical, social scientific, or philosophical, are very much like the general goals of all academic disciplines—namely, to describe, interpret, explain, and evaluate certain phenomena. Given the preceding discussion, it is clear that phenomenologists would be suspicious of trying to explain and evaluate religious phenomena using nonreligious standards. Having noted this suspicion, however, we will move on to distinguish the activities of describing, interpreting, explaining, and evaluating and see how they are done. Let's begin with descriptive methods.

### 2.3.1 Description

There is no such thing as pure description because every description is already an interpretation; but for the moment I will artificially isolate it and characterize it as gathering and stating the facts of the case. Just as in a court of law a case cannot proceed without knowing the facts, so the study of religion cannot proceed without knowing the data. In the field of religious studies, there is an enormous amount of information in a variety of different languages and cultures, ranging from archeological artifacts, pictures, coins, statues, and the like, to sacred scriptures, commentaries on sacred scriptures, and many other kinds of writings. The range is great, and I have not yet mentioned rituals, rites, oral traditions, and extraordinary experiences of transformation and revelation.

Gathering this information requires mastering a variety of technical skills such as learning different languages. Presenting the information fairly and accurately is not easy. Mistakes can easily creep in, especially when dealing with gestures, customs, games, and rites from vastly different cultures.

In order to facilitate the collection and presentation of data, students of religion use classification schemes. These schemes can be very general, referring to religious traditions as a whole (for example, Buddhism, Islam, Christianity), or they can be more specific, referring to aspects of different religious traditions (for example, beliefs, myths, symbols, scriptures, experiences, morality, rituals, and organization). Whatever classification scheme is used, scholars create it by reflecting on information at hand and then use it to gather and organize additional information. Generally this sort of **description** involves classifying $x$ under a category according to some property $(p)$ of $x$. Suppose $x$ is the Islamic belief that asserts Allah is the one and only God $(p)$. As students of religion, we might categorize such a belief as monotheistic because **monotheism** is a category that includes all beliefs that share the property of claiming there is only one God. We now know a fact about Islam that allows us to describe it as a monotheistic religion. This also allows us to compare this monotheistic belief with beliefs about the divine found among other religions.

Developing classification systems requires that we identify prototypes. A **prototype** is an ideal exemplar of the type or category in question. Other things are matched to this prototype. The closer the match, the more likely we are to describe something (bowing the head and folding the hands) as a member of the class in question (praying). If the match is not very close, we are unlikely to describe some action (slashing oneself with a knife in grief) as praying.

**Typologies** are schemes of classification. They organize data into different types. For example, after studying the data, we might conclude that there are two primary types of praying: supplication and thanksgiving. This typology can then be used to organize new data. The advantage of typologies rests primarily in their ability to organize vast amounts of data, but there are disadvantages as well. Typologies are often incomplete—prayers exist that do not neatly fit in one category or another—or they obscure other important features of the data. Why not create a typology of praying by classifying prayers as formal and informal, or as silent and spoken, or as communal and solitary? Lurking within every typology is a degree of arbitrariness. Sometimes typologies reveal more about the creator's biases than they do about the data.

How do we select prototypes, identify the relevant properties, and create useful typologies? We learn how to do it based on study, experience, reasoning, comparison, and intuition. I began by stating that pure description is not possible because it simply is not possible to describe without classifying, and every classification scheme reflects a comparative interpretation.

### 2.3.2 Interpretation

What does the described data mean? That is the central problem for **interpretation**. The first question is "mean to whom?" To the insider, meaning is part of the descriptive data. To the outsider, meaning reflects the best understanding an outside observer can arrive at given the data, the methods of interpretation, and the theories available.

Methods of interpretation are often called hermeneutical. **Hermeneutics** is the "science of interpretation," although the word *science* is used here in a very broad sense. To interpret is to see *x* as a *sign* of *y*. We interpret when we assign a particular referent (the signified) to a sign (the signifier). Signs can be letters, words, pictures, sounds, musical notes, physical gestures—the list is almost endless because practically anything can be taken as a sign, from trees and cloud formations to flags and buildings. Hence hermeneutics is part of a more general study called **semiotics**—the study of signs.

Hermeneutical studies can focus on any aspect of religion (beliefs, rituals, experiences), but I will describe it briefly by focusing on the interpretation of written texts. The first rule of hermeneutics is that meaning is *context dependent*; that is, what a text means depends on a variety of contexts both immediate and remote. Just as words have different meanings in different contexts, so texts have different meanings in different contexts. If I said, "I am going to the bank," you would not know the exact meaning of the word *bank* until I went on to specify, "in order to fish." The context of fishing rather than the context of cashing a check lets you know what I mean—that is, what the sign *bank* signifies (edge of a body of water).

One way to uncover context is to discover what the Germans call the **Sitz im Leben** (situation in life) of a text. Where and when was it written? By whom and to whom was it written? What is its purpose or function? Knowing the situation in life reveals much about the meaning of a text (or any other sort of sign for that matter).

There are also certain formal features of a text that provide information about its meaning. What type of writing is it? Is it a letter, poem, narrative, scripture, or commentary? What is its surface structure, that is, its organization, style, and themes?

In addition to surface structure, there is also a "deep" structure that is more difficult to discern. Deep structures are the hidden rules governing what is said, much like the structure of language is determined by the hidden rules of grammar. In order to get at this hidden structure, scholars distinguish between the text (what the author writes) and the subtext (either explicit asides by the author about what he or she writes or indirect meanings such as irony). Scholars look at what is *included* in a text, but they must also be aware of what is *excluded*. Social rules about inclusion and exclusion determine, in part, what is said. For example, I have excluded certain words from my account of hermeneutics because they are deemed inappropriate in textbook writing or I have judged them to be misleading.

**Comparison** is implicit in the activities of determining the type of text and in determining structure and function. The remote context of religious phenomena can be uncovered by comparing different examples and discerning the similarities and differences. A story of a saint in Christianity can be illuminated by comparison with a story of a saint in Buddhism, even if the stories are very different and unrelated culturally and historically.

Comparison involves selecting significant examples and then looking for similarities and differences among them. No attempt should be made to determine whether one example is "better" than another in the sense of truer or morally superior. (Avoid judgments such as the Christian saint is really a saint, and the Buddhist saint is a fraud.) One example might be judged more typical or less typical of the type under discussion (stories about saints), but even that judgment is tricky. As you can see, there is much room for prejudice and unconscious bias to enter the selection process. Why is one story rather than another selected as "typical"?

Developing a comparative perspective is essential to learning about others. Religion is one of the most enduring and vital traits of human societies. We learn much of value about being and becoming human from studying the similarities and differences among religions as fairly and sympathetically as possible.

### 2.3.3 Explanation

The student of religion seeks not only to collect and describe information and to interpret it by employing hermeneutical and comparative methods, but also to explain what is going on.

The word **explanation** can mean several different things. To some, it means an understanding gained by discovering the meaning of religious phenomena. In other words, interpretation is one type of explanation. To others, it means finding and describing the cause or causes of some religious phenomenon. This requires a direct and explicit appeal to some theory.

Description and interpretation are influenced by theory, but explanation is the most clearly theory-laden activity. This can be explained most easily by an example. In physics the event of a falling apple is explained by subsuming it (along with many other examples of falling things) under the theory of gravity. So a religious event like a sacrifice might be explained by subsuming it under a general theory about the causes of violence.

Historical and social scientific explanations, however, are not always causal in the sense of the occurrence of one set of events necessarily resulting in another set of events. Sometimes explanations are functional, such as Marx's explanation of religion functioning as an opiate. This explanation of religion is in terms of its effects (what it does), not its causes (what produced it). Other explanations are structural in nature. For example, Marx also explains religious behavior in terms of class differences between rich and poor. Social structures like a class system are not events, and if causes must be events, then social structures cannot be causes.

An important question to ask when studying any human behavior is, who benefits (*cui bono*)? In whose interest is it that certain rites are performed in certain ways? Who benefits from the way power is distributed in a religious group? Do certain worldviews benefit one social class more than another? All beliefs are not equal; some benefit certain people more than others. Although much religious morality speaks of the virtue of being altruistic or unselfish (and this is something we should not ignore), much human behavior is selfish, even when people claim otherwise. When trying to explain why humans do the things they do, the answer to the *cui bono* question reveals much.

The student of religion will encounter different kinds of explanation. Some will be causal, some functional, and still others structural. All, however, will appeal to some theory about religion, and hence the study of theory is unavoidable.

### 2.3.4 Evaluation

For an explanation to make sense, the theory that gives rise to it must be correct. How can we find that out? Physical scientists can check their theories by controlled laboratory experiments, but in religious studies such checking procedures are seldom possible. What is possible is to check the fruitfulness of a theory by measuring it against many different examples to see if it makes sense of all or most of them. Does a detailed and careful study of ten examples of religious movements selected at random from the world's religions make more sense when viewed from Marx's theory rather than some other theory? For example, Marx's theory implies that religion is primarily a conservative force working against social change. But is that always the case? Haven't religious movements also fostered social change? Religious groups and leaders have been in the forefront of promoting social change. Martin Luther King, Jr., and the civil rights movement come immediately to mind. Is Marx's opiate theory adequate to explain that movement?

**Evaluation** has many different levels. We might evaluate the accuracy of someone else's description by checking it against our own reading of the original data. We might question the value of someone's interpretation by checking on how rigorously the hermeneutical method was employed. We can evaluate a theory by checking its explanatory power against other possible theories. In this sense of evaluation (what I call second-order evaluation), one scholar is evaluating the work of another against such criteria as logical consistency, strength of evidence and argument, compelling counterexamples, and alternative explanations.

What about evaluating religious claims themselves? Can we engage in first-order evaluation? Indeed, should we do first-order evaluation? Many scholars acknowledge that the methods of history, the social sciences, and philosophy are limited to natural explanations. There is, they assert, no human way to evaluate supernatural claims. Was Jesus truly the Son of God, or did he and others just think so? That he made that claim or did not make it, that others made it, and what it meant—these are things that are possible to check, provided enough information survives. But the theological claim that Jesus is the Son of God—how could we check that?

Some philosophers and theologians might think we can check it just like we check other metaphysical claims—that is, is it logically consistent with everything we know about other kinds of things? Given what we know about history, about the physical universe, about human behavior, about other religions, about the effects on people's lives of believing Jesus is God's Son, is it plausible that Jesus is truly the Son of God? You can imagine the arguments on both sides, and you can imagine arguments claiming that such questions fall outside the range of questions that can be asked (let alone answered) in the academic study of religion. We shall return to this issue in the last chapter.

---

### Goals and Methods of Religious Studies

1. Description
   a. Prototype
   b. Typology
2. Interpretation
   a. Hermeneutics
   b. Comparison
3. Explanation
   a. Causal
   b. Functional
   c. Structural
4. Evaluation
   a. First-order
   b. Second-order

---

## 2.4 SUMMARY

The academic study of religion seeks to describe, interpret, explain, and evaluate religious data. It draws on the specific methods of different disciplines —history, social science, and philosophy—in order to do this. Some very general methods involve the collection and classification of data, applying hermeneutical tools, and using techniques of comparison.

Generally, phenomenologists want to limit religious studies to description and to understanding the agent's interpretation because they think anything else involves projecting the bias of the scholar into the phenomena. They also believe that religion is *sui generis,* and its uniqueness will be overlooked if it is treated like any other human phenomenon. They are suspicious of theories imported from other academic disciplines.

Others claim that explanation and evaluation are legitimate activities of the scholar. Whatever else it may be, religion is a human phenomenon, and like any other human phenomenon, it is understandable by the application of the normal methods of history, social science, and philosophy. There is nothing particularly sacred about religion or about its claims that demands the scholar politely leave her or his critical toolbox at the door of the temple.

Describing, interpreting, explaining, and evaluating are practices, and like any practices, we learn them by doing them. I invite you to engage in these practices, and as we proceed, this invitation will be issued with respect to specific examples of religious beliefs and practices. Reading about studies of religions done by others is exciting, but engaging in that study ourselves is still more exciting.

Studying something involves learning how to ask and answer questions. There are multitudes of questions a scholar can ask. Our brief look at goals and methods provides a place to begin. We can ask and seek to answer such questions as these:

Descriptive: What is said or done?
Interpretive: What does it mean?
Explanatory: Why was it said or done?
Evaluative: First-order—is what is said or done correct? Second-order—is what is said about what is said or done correct?

## EXPLORATIONS

1. Bruce C. Lincoln, a scholar of religion, writes, "Reverence is a religious, not a scholarly virtue. When good manners and good conscience cannot be reconciled, the demands of the latter ought to prevail." Do you agree? Why or why not?
2. Do you think there is something unique about religion that historians, social scientists (anthropologists, sociologists, psychologists), and philosophers cannot understand or grasp? If so, what?
3. Suppose you came across a strange inscription in a strange text. Once deciphered it reads, "May Yecovib help us." What would you make of this inscription? How would you interpret it? How would you explain it? What else would you need to know in order to understand the inscription?

## SUGGESTIONS FOR FURTHER READING

In addition to the material found in the notes, the reader may wish to consult the following for more information.

Benson, Thomas L. "Religious Studies as an Academic Discipline." In *The Encyclopedia of Religion*, vol. 14, edited by Mircea Eliade, 88–92. New York: Macmillan, 1987. This article provides a brief history of the development of religious studies in the academy.

Capps, Walter H. *Ways of Understanding Religion*. New York: Macmillan, 1972. Although somewhat dated, this collection of essays on theories and methods from a variety of disciplines (anthropology, history, psychology, philosophy, and more) is still useful.

Connolly, Peter, ed. *Approaches to the Study of Religion*. London: Cassell, 1999. This collection of essays discusses different ways of studying religions, ranging from anthropological to theological approaches.

Kessler, Gary E. "The Study of Religion: One Field, Many Methods." In *Presence and Promise: Religious Studies in the University*, edited by John Hatfield and Benjamin Hubbard, 27–33. Long Beach, CA: Institute for Teaching and Learning, 1992. Here I present an argument for recognizing the unity of the field of religious studies while acknowledging its methodological pluralism.

Martin, Luther H. "Comparison." In *Guide to the Study of Religion*, edited by Willi Braun and Russell T. McCutcheon, 45–56. London: Cassell, 2000. The author critically reviews different theories about how best to undertake the comparative study of religions.

Penner, Hans H. "Interpretation." In *Guide to the Study of Religion*, 57–71. Penner reviews present understandings of interpretation and makes a "radical" proposal for a new account.

———. "The Study of Religion." In *The HarperCollins Dictionary of Religion*, edited by Jonathan Z. Smith and William Scott Green, 909–917. New York: HarperCollins, 1995. A clear and concise account of the nature of theory and basic approaches (sociological, phenomenological, psychological, historical, etc.) to the study of religion, along with a critical discussion of functional theories.

Sharpe, Eric J. "Methodological Issues." In *The Encyclopedia of Religion*, vol. 14, 83–88. Sharpe provides a discussion of different methodological issues such as value judgments, translation, and insider and outsider perspectives.

Smith, Jonathan Z. "Classification." In *Guide to the Study of Religion*, 35–44. Smith provides a helpful account of how classification works in religious studies.

Stone, Jon R., ed. *The Craft of Religious Studies*. New York: St. Martin's Press, 2000. Leading scholars present their views on "doing" religious studies in this collection of essays.

## INTERNET RESOURCES

http://www.chass.utoronto.ca/~bsalton/method/links.html   This site provides links to tons of information on anthropology, sociology, psychology, history, phenomenology, and philosophy of religion.

http://www.oup-usa.org/isbn/0195105036.html   At this site is a brief description of Russell T. McCutcheon's book *Manufacturing Religion,* in which the author argues that the category *sui generis* is suspect and the study of religion is properly cross-disciplinary.

http://www.cba.uc.edu/faculty/leean/herm.htm   Allen S. Lee has prepared a guide to selected references on hermeneutics.

CHAPTER 3

# On Defining Religion

THE QUESTION "WHAT is religion?" is deceptively simple. Most people think they know what religion is. You can look it up in a dictionary and find what is called a lexical definition. If I asked you to write a one-sentence definition, you could do so after a little thought. So, what is the problem with defining religion?

## 3.1 MARKS OF A GOOD DEFINITION

For the student of religion, not just any sort of definition will do. In order to engage in the academic study of religion, we need a definition that is analytically useful. That means it should be

- useful for the purposes at hand,
- as precise as possible without being too narrow in scope,
- and as free from bias as possible.

### 3.1.1 Usefulness

Definitions are not necessarily true or false, but more or less useful. They tell us how to use words effectively depending on the situation and what we are trying to communicate. For example, historians who wish to study religious beliefs and practices (such as rites, moral behavior, aesthetic or artistic creations) that characterized people in China two thousand years ago may find one kind of definition useful for their purposes. A sociologist who wishes to describe social influences on religious practices in contemporary England may find another kind of definition useful.

Suppose sociologists or psychologists were interested in measuring religiosity, that is, the degree to which someone is religious. They would need a definition of religion that could be empirically tested (operationalized) by asking specific questions whose answers could be statistically measured. If they defined religion as "belief in God," they could operationalize this definition by creating questions about what people believe, such as "Do you believe in God?" This would be a *unidimensional* measure because only one dimension, the belief or intellectual dimension, is central to the definition.

A questionnaire based on this single dimension would be of limited use because there is more than one way to be religious. Someone might believe in God, but never pray to God, offer devotion to God, strive to live a godly life, or participate in any way in organizations that promote such beliefs. Would the researchers want to call such a person "religious"? Then again, some people might be uncertain about whether they genuinely believe in God, but they might pray, read religious literature, and strive to live a moral life as they think God requires. Would such people be called "irreligious" because they did not score very high on the belief dimension?

It is clear that the definition of religion as "belief in God or gods" is not very useful when it comes to measuring religiosity. What is needed is a *multidimensional* approach that measures, in addition to belief, religious practice, experience, devotion, knowledge, and more. Hence a more complex definition of religion is required if it is going to be useful to social scientists interested in creating measures of religiosity.

For scholarly purposes, definitions should stimulate further investigation and thought. Different academic disciplines—history, sociology, psychology, anthropology, literature, philosophy—will find different definitions more or less useful, depending on their perspective. Given these circumstances, the quest for one universal definition of religion that can be useful for all academic disciplines appears misguided.

You might be thinking that what I have just said does not sound quite right. What if the definition the historian uses and the definition the sociologist uses are totally different? How could we be sure that they were both studying religion rather than two very different things? That is a good question and leads directly to a discussion of precision.

## 3.1.2 Precision

The purpose of definitions is to draw boundaries and thereby limit a field of study. If everything fell under the category of religion, the study of religion would become quite impossible to manage. Definitions can be too precise, however, and boundaries drawn so narrowly that they exclude some things that ought to be included. For example, the above definition of religion as "belief in God or gods" leaves out too much of importance, such as religious practices. Religions are more than belief systems; they involve **ritual** practices, moral codes, various types of social organizations, and much more. In addition, religions that deny that ultimate reality is divine (some types of Buddhism), or those that center on beliefs in spirits, would be unjustifiably excluded.

The other side of the coin is drawing boundaries too broadly. Some scholars have favored definitions that involve the use of terms like *ultimate concern* or *sacred*. Unless carefully specified, these terms are so vague that practically anything can fit within their boundaries. Are capitalists, who devote their lives to the pursuit of wealth, religious because money and the power it brings have become their ultimate concern? Are socialists, who devote their lives to the equal distribution of wealth, religious because economic justice is a sacred cause for the socialist?

The questions and problems associated with precision are closely tied to two very different theories of the nature of definition. Some scholars hold to a theory of essentialism. For them, the purpose of definitions is to state the essence of something. The **essence** is a universal quality or set of qualities that makes something what it is and not something else. For example, the essence of a table is whatever characteristic(s) it must have in order to be a table and not a chair. The essence of a human being is whatever qualities or characteristics humans must have in order to be human and not a tree or a rock.

Those who pursue essential definitions of religion usually favor either a **substantive definition** that states what religion *is* or a **functional definition** that states what religion *does*. For example, if we defined religion as "belief in the supernatural," we would be stating what we think it is, or what its nature is. This substantive definition distinguishes religious belief from other sorts of belief in terms of objects. According to this definition, religious belief differs from other types of belief because its object is the supernatural. That is its essence, or substance. If we defined religion as a "set of beliefs that give meaning and purpose to human life," we would be stating what religion does, or how it functions. Its function is to provide meaning and purpose to human life. According to this definition, the essence of religion is in what it accomplishes. This example of a functional definition differentiates religious beliefs from other beliefs by stating what they do (provide meaning and purpose to human life), which is, presumably, different from what other sorts of beliefs do.

There are problems with both substantive and functional definitions. Substantive types often turn out to be too narrow because of the vast diversity of religious beliefs and practices, and functional types often turn out to be too broad because different things can often function in the same way. For example, political beliefs as well as religious beliefs can give meaning and purpose to human life.

A very different theory of definition rejects the idea of essences. According to this theory, we should look for a cluster of characteristics that makes something part of a certain family. **Cluster definitions** are based on an analogy with families. Families are made up of many members who have many different traits or qualities. Some are blue-eyed, and some brown-eyed. Some are tall, and some are short. Yet, in spite of these differences, they are all members of the same family. There may be no set of traits that are essential, but there are traits that allow us to group them into the same family. There are, to borrow Ludwig Wittgenstein's term, "family resemblances."

Perhaps religion is like a family. There are many members with many different characteristics but no set of characteristics that captures some essence. Those who favor cluster definitions of religion readily acknowledge that the boundaries between religion and other things, such as politics, are fuzzy. There is no sharp line of demarcation, but a kind of fading away of qualities until there are not enough to fit into the "family" of religion.

William P. Alston, a contemporary philosopher of religion, offers a cluster definition consisting of nine "religion-making" characteristics. No single characteristic, including belief in supernatural beings, constitutes some sort of essence. In other words, there can be religions that do not posit a supernatural reality. Here are Alston's nine characteristics:

1. Belief in supernatural beings (gods).
2. A distinction between sacred and profane objects.
3. Ritual acts focused on sacred objects.
4. A moral code believed to be sanctioned by the gods.
5. Characteristically religious feelings (awe, sense of mystery, sense of guilt, adoration), which tend to be aroused in the presence of sacred objects and during the practice of ritual, and which are connected in idea with the gods.
6. Prayer and other forms of communication with gods.
7. A worldview, or a general picture of the world as a whole and the place of the individual therein. This picture contains some specification of an overall purpose or point of the world and an indication of how the individual fits into it.
8. A more or less total organization of one's life based on the worldview.
9. A social group bound together by the above.[1]

Alston calls these characteristics religion-making because they contribute to making something a religion. Precision, he admits, is not possible. For example, we cannot say that for x to be a religion, the first two plus three other characteristics must be present. Nor can we say that before x qualifies as a religion, it must exhibit five of these nine traits. The most we can say is that when enough of these characteristics are present, we have a religion.

What is enough? That must be an informed judgment made by scholars who are familiar with a wide range of religions. Cluster definitions avoid the problems of being too narrow or too broad that plague essential definitions. However, they do so at the price of precision. Still, they are not so imprecise that they cease to be useful for scholarly purposes.

### 3.1.3 Freedom from Bias

As I said in the first chapter, useful definitions of religion should be as free from bias as possible. None of us can totally escape our biases because we must necessarily study the subject matter from some perspective. However, we can become aware of our biases. This awareness allows us to correct for bias when we formulate definitions.

*Western Bias*　One common bias can be called the Western bias. It is very subtle (as many biases are), and to unmask it will take careful analysis. The English word *religion* comes from the Latin word **religio**. Latin scholars are not certain about the etymology of *religio*. Some believe it stems from the root *leig*, meaning "to bind," while others think it comes from roots meaning "to reread" or "to be careful." In early Roman Latin usage, *religio* was a cultic term referring primarily to the careful performance of ritual obligations. This sense survives in the English adverbial use of *religiously* in such sentences as, "She walks her dog every morning religiously."

Early Latin Christians used the word *religio* to distinguish true worship from false. For them, *religio* did not refer to the world religions as it does today, but to genuine and sincere worship. In the Middle Ages, *religio* was not widely used, but when it was, it often referred to "the religious," that is, those who chose the monastic life. Hence *religio* distinguished the monastic life from the life of the laity.

With the dawn of the modern age, when knowledge of and encounters with religions different from Christianity increased, the word *religion* began to be used to refer to the various religious traditions of the world. So, for example, we often speak of the world's religions, meaning such traditions as Judaism, Christianity, Islam, Hinduism, Buddhism, and Daoism—to mention only a few.

The word *religion* is also used in many other ways in English, but we are not concerned with all of them here. Given the close association the word *religion* has with the development of Western culture, it is not surprising that some scholars have proposed dropping the use of the word altogether for scholarly purposes. It is tied, they argue, too deeply to Western biases and has such a wide variety of meanings in common speech that precision is impossible.

Benson Saler, an anthropologist, summarizes this view when he writes, "the practitioners of a mostly Western profession (anthropology) employ a Western category (religion), conceptualized as a component of a larger Western category (culture), to achieve their professional goal of coming to understand what is meaningful and important for non-Western peoples."[2]

Correcting for the ethnicity of the idea of religion is not easy. If we do not use the word *religion*, what word should we use? Are *faith* or *tradition* any more free from a Western bias? Probably the best we can do is recognize that ethnocentric ideas are starting points (we have to start from our own culture, whatever it may be), but ethnocentrism should not be a stopping point. If it is, it shows we have not learned anything about our biases.

**Value Bias**   Complicating this ethnocentric bias is a value bias. Definitions reflect how the people creating them value religion. If their attitude is positive, the definition will be positive. If their attitude is negative, the definition will be negative, and if their attitude is mixed or uncertain, their definition will reflect that too. For example, if I defined religion as an illusory hope for a better future, you would immediately detect a negative attitude in my definition.

We can correct our value biases by adding qualifying words like *allegedly*, *presumably*, or *maybe*. Thus I might revise my definition of religion to "the hope for a better future, a hope that may or may not prove to be an illusion." Once you become sensitive to value biases, rewording with appropriate qualifications often does the trick.

**Theory Bias**   Every definition of religion is part of a more general theory of religion. A definition is "theory-laden," to use the technical term. Behind every definition is some theory about what religion is and how it functions. This is not a bad thing, and indeed it is unavoidable. However, we need to be aware of the ways (some obvious and some not so obvious) that theory influences definition. For example, some theories hold that there is something irreducibly "religious" about religion. Religion is unique and can only be understood on its own ground. Other theories claim that religions are like any other human phenomena and can be understood in cultural, historical, sociological, or psychological terms. According to these theories, there is nothing uniquely religious about what humans believe or do. General psychological theories of human behavior, for example, can explain quite well why people act in religious ways. These two divergent theories of religion generate very different definitions as well as arguments over reductionism (see Chapter 2).

**Gender Bias**   Still another subtle bias that slips into both theory and definition is gender bias. Historically, males have dominated religions, and when people think about religion they often take as the implicit model traditional patriarchal religions. Theories and definitions are then constructed under the influence of these models, and gender bias is the result. Even the word *God* implies for many a male figure. Gender bias inclines people to think of religions as having to do with belief in God or gods, rather than belief in goddesses. One unfortunate social and cultural effect of this is to encourage people to think of males as rulers and leaders. As the feminist theologian Mary Daly says, "if God is male, then the male is God."[3]

*Confusion of Religion and Spirituality*    Another bias that slips into definitions is the confusion between spirituality and religion. Consider these two statements:

1. A person can belong to a religion and not be religious.
2. A person can be religious and not belong to a religion.

The key term is "belong to." If "belong to" means being an official member of some organization, then statement 1 seems obviously true. The second statement is more problematic because a case could be made that the truly spiritual person will seek membership in some religious organization because religious organizations try to foster spirituality and provide an opportunity for spiritual fellowship. It is undoubtedly true that religious organizations present themselves as a path, or way, that fosters growth in spirituality, but there seems to be no good reason why someone could not foster spiritual growth in ways other than belonging to some religious organization.

Crucial to this debate about **spirituality versus religion**, is a clear distinction between the two. If defining religion is difficult, defining spirituality is even more difficult. The situation is complicated by the fact that use the adjective *religious* is used interchangeably with *spiritual*. To be spiritual is to be deeply and genuinely religious. But how can someone be religious without religion?

There have been various attempts to define spirituality. The psychologist of religion William James (1842–1910) suggested that it is a quest for a transformation from a state of perceived wrongness to a state of perceived rightness by making contact with some higher power or powers (see Chapter 10). The contemporary philosopher John Hick thinks of spirituality as a transformation from a selfish and egocentric state to an unselfish and caring state. However, all of these terms are vague and notoriously difficult to make precise. Nevertheless, I think it is important not to confuse religion and spirituality as if they amounted to the same thing. When we do, we are tempted to transfer whatever negative qualities we may associate with religious organizations to people who sincerely seek to make a better life for themselves and others.

The two statements I asked you to consider earlier (a person can belong to a religion and not be religious; a person can be religious and not belong to a religion) presuppose that spirituality or religiousness is best thought of as a personal quality—a characteristic or set of characteristics that some people have. They also presuppose that religion refers to an organized group of people. This organized group presents itself as an effective way to nurture the personal quality of spirituality, but it is always possible that it fails to do so or, at least, fails to satisfy the spiritual desires of those who join. The problem of how religion and spirituality are related is, to some extent, a product of how we conceptualize them.

Something close to our distinction between spirituality and religion is the ancient Roman distinction (derived from the Greeks) between *cultus* and *pietas*. *Cultus* refers to religion as a cultural system consisting of things like creeds, moral codes, rites, and an organized group. *Pietas* refers to religion as a personal quality of devotion. However, in the ancient world, the modern notion that someone could be spiritual (*pietas*) and not belong to an organized group (*cultus*) would be unthinkable. In the modern world religion is becoming less public and more privatized due to a number of factors that I will talk about in more detail in the last chapter.

---

### Some Possible Biases

1. Western ethnocentric bias
2. Value bias
3. Theory bias
4. Gender bias
5. Confusion of spirituality and religion

---

### 3.1.4 Should We Start with Definitions?

I have discussed some of the many problems involved in the deceptively simple task of defining religion. Finding a useful definition that is precise and free from bias is no easy task. There is another problem as well. Should we define religion before we study religion or only afterward? Some might argue that it is not fair to define the subject matter before we actually look and see what is there. Others might argue that without some idea of where to look (and a definition gives us an idea of where to look), we will be looking in vain. This is a variation of the chicken and the egg problem. However, rather than being a problem about which came first (obviously religion did), it is a problem of which should come first—definition or observation? I think this problem is not too difficult to solve. Definition and observation must go hand in hand. We need to start with working definitions that tell us where to look, and as we look, we need to revise and refine our definitions.

## 3.2 TWO DEFINITIONS

In our discussion about defining religion, we have discovered there are some typical problems with different types of definitions. We can put our discoveries to work by critically analyzing two important and influential definitions. I want you to assume the role of analyst and critic. We learn to do religious studies by engaging in its practice, and part of that practice is the critical analysis of definitions. I will prompt you, but you need to do the work.

Paul Tillich (1886–1965), a Christian theologian and philosopher, defined religion as "the state of being grasped by an ultimate concern, a concern which qualifies all other concerns as preliminary and which itself contains the answer to the question of the meaning of life."[4]

What kind of definition is this—essential or cluster? Is Tillich concerned with the substance or the function of religion? Is his definition too broad or too narrow? Do you detect any bias? Think about these questions, and before you continue reading, take a moment to write brief answers.

. . . . . .

While Tillich's definition captures something important about religion, I wonder (and you may have wondered too) what Tillich means by "ultimate concern." Some critics have pointed out that the term is ambiguous. The word *ultimate* might qualify the state of being concerned, or it might refer to the object of some concern. Tillich plays on this ambiguity when he defines idolatry as an ultimate concern about what is less than ultimate.

Another question arises when we consider whether someone might have more than one ultimate concern. Certainly people have major concerns in their lives and perhaps, from time to time, some dominant interest, but do they have a single ultimate concern that "qualifies all other concerns as preliminary"? Tillich seems to suggest that there can be only one, but there seems to be no good reason why there cannot be several. Perhaps Tillich's monotheistic bias shows through here. If willingness to die for something is a test of having an ultimate concern, then some people might be willing to die for several different things, such as country or family, as well as some deity that they worship. Could not supernatural beings, people, places, nations, wealth, pleasure, art, science, and politics become religious objects—that is, objects of ultimate concern?

Suppose someone has the nation as an ultimate concern. Does that mean we should count nationalism and patriotism as religions? People are willing to die for their countries, and if the willingness to give your life for a cause is a sign of an ultimate concern, then national and political commitments appear to be as much religions as do traditions such as Christianity and Islam. Is Tillich's definition hopelessly broad?

We turn now to an influential definition by the contemporary anthropologist Melford E. Spiro. According to Spiro, religion is "an institution consisting of culturally patterned interaction with culturally postulated superhuman beings."[5] Is this definition functional or substantive, essential or cluster, too broad or too narrow? How does Spiro's reference to "superhuman beings" compare to Tillich's use of "ultimate concern"? Substitute the word *politics* for *religion*, and reread Spiro's definition. Does it make sense as a definition of politics? If not, why not? What makes the cultural institution of politics different from the cultural institution of religion?

Compare Tillich's definition with Spiro's definition. How are they similar, and how are they different? Do you detect any biases? If you did not know that Tillich was a Christian theologian and Spiro is an anthropologist, could you tell that from these definitions? How could you tell? Which of these definitions is more useful? Once again, briefly answer these questions before proceeding.

· · · · · ·

It seems to me that Tillich's and Spiro's definitions are very different. Tillich locates religion in a subjective state (feeling?) that differs from other human states because of the ultimacy or unconditionality of its concern, a concern that gives life meaning and purpose. This captures something of importance about religion, or at least about how some people feel about religious objects. It also reflects the notion that the human capacity to be religious stems from the human capacity for self-awareness or self-transcendence that gives rise to the quest for meaning and purpose (see Chapter 10). Spiro locates religion in cultural institutions that postulate superhuman beings. Spiro's definition makes religion subordinate to culture in a way that Tillich's definition does not, and this too captures something of importance about religion. Religions and cultures are closely connected. Spiro also thinks of religion as an institution, while Tillich appears to think of it more in terms of spirituality.

As mentioned above, in Tillich's definition "ultimate concern" is ambiguous. However, Spiro's "superhuman beings" is vague. If we regard "ultimate" as restricted to the quality of a concern, then if I had a concern about golf that was ultimate, I would, according to Tillich, be religious. However, if I had a concern about God that was less than ultimate, I would not be religious. This seems odd. What or who are Spiro's superhuman beings? Are they supernatural beings or simply beings with more power than humans, but still a part of nature? If a lion does not count as a superhuman being, why not?

## 3.3 SUPERSTITION, MAGIC, AND RELIGION

We all know what superstitions are. They are things like the belief that walking under a ladder will bring bad luck, or the idea that breaking a mirror will bring seven years of bad luck, or the hope that rubbing a rabbit's foot will bring good luck. To study superstitions, take a trip to Las Vegas, where gamblers can share with you a bewildering array of lucky charms.

Why do we think that such beliefs are superstitious? What makes them superstitious? You might say that they involve false beliefs about connections between events and are motivated by fear. There is no real connection between lucky charms and good fortune. People only think there is or hope there is because they are afraid. Is the same true of activities we sometimes call religious? People believe that baptism takes away sin, that praying to saints will help in a crisis, that miracles happen, that what you do affects your next life, that going to church is beneficial, that the cross will ward off evil, that pilgrimages will curry divine favor, and much more. How do such beliefs differ from superstitious beliefs? How can we objectively distinguish false from true causes and right from wrong motivations?

**Superstition** is a judgmental term that implies a negative evaluation. Traditionally, dominant religions like Christianity used it to denigrate (portray in a negative light) other religions, especially so-called primitive (itself a negative term) religions. The adherents of some particular religious orthodoxy often label those who think differently as superstitious. So Protestant Christians labeled Catholic Christians as superstitious. The ancient Romans regarded the "new cult" of Christ as superstitious. The anthropological perspective says that people define superstition in opposition to their culture's concept of true religion. Hence the term is not really descriptive, but evaluative. It is inevitably pejorative.

The student of religions is interested in tracing the history of the concept of superstition and studying how the concept is used in different ages and different places. Superstition is part of the vocabulary of religions and cultures. It is part of the language we, as students of religion, study. However, it is not an analytically useful term for describing what people believe or do. It is not a category that can be used to pick out certain beliefs and practices for the purposes of distinguishing them from religious beliefs and practices. Students of religion have no objective measures by which they can survey the world's religions and say with authority that this is superstition and that is not.

While you might find this argument for the descriptive uselessness of the term *superstition* plausible, you might also be thinking about **magic**. Isn't magic superstition? Of course you don't mean stage magic and card tricks, but real, honest-to-goodness magic like casting spells, summoning the dead, fortune telling, and practicing witchcraft. Surely we can distinguish magic from religion, and if magic is superstition, we can distinguish superstition from religion.

Like superstition, magic is a loaded term. It too is often used pejoratively. Yet scholars of religion, especially anthropologists, have found magic to be an analytically useful category. It does, many believe, pick out something distinctive and something unlike religion in important ways. Therefore, to understand how magic and religion differ increases our understanding of religion as well as magic. I would like you to think further about this issue by asking yourself two questions.

Do you think that one important difference between magic and religion is that magic involves attempts to control the divine, and religion involves asking the divine to freely respond to a request? The magician commands· and casts a spell that will work automatically by compelling the gods or spirits to deliver. The priest asks and does a ritual that may or may not work, depending on the will of the gods.

Do you think that another important difference between magic and religion centers on communal involvement? Magicians act alone. They have no church or community. Individuals come to them as clients. Priests and pastors are part of a wider community. They have congregations, not clients.

If you think that these are important differences—commanding versus asking and individuality versus community—you are not alone. These distinctions were popularized by early anthropological studies of the relationship between magic and religion. Magicians, it is widely thought, seek to bend superhuman powers to their will by spells that make demands and are formulated as commands. Those who believe in magic often think the spells work automatically. Hollywood has capitalized on these ideas and struck fear in the hearts of its audiences with many a movie about the struggles between the sinister power of evil magicians working "black" magic and the beneficial power of good wizards (note the change of terms) working "white" magic. Both the wise wizard and the black magician are often pictured as lone individuals, working by themselves on the fringes of the community in caves or castles casting spells that automatically work.

However, there is evidence to indicate that these conceptions distort reality. As early as 1937, Edward Evans-Pritchard's anthropological work on witchcraft in Africa (*Witchcraft, Magic and Oracles among the Azande*) showed that all magical formulas used against witches took the form of requests, not commands. The historian Keith Thomas, in his massive study *Religion and the Decline of Magic* (1971), showed that, at the popular level, the medieval Christian Church was saturated in magical ideas.[6] Sacraments were thought to work automatically (it was even debated whether a mouse who ate the host [bread] would be saved), merely attending a Mass was thought to bring blessings, and pilgrimages to shrines of saints were widely believed to provide miraculous cures. Priests were thought to have special superhuman powers that could accomplish things ordinary humans could not. Levi-Strauss, the brilliant French anthropologist, effectively argued that magical practices and accusations of witchcraft have as one of their important purposes the reinforcement of a society's belief system.[7] So, for example, in Puritan New England the practice of magic and witchcraft was condemned as the "work of the devil" at the same time that its reality was defended. After all, if magic and witchcraft, however evil, exist, then their very existence demonstrates the reality of the invisible and supernatural world of the divine. Far from operating on the lunatic fringes

Magical style                                                                                    Nonmagical style

FIGURE 3.1  The continuum from magical to nonmagical style.

of communities, magic can reinforce some of the primary and central beliefs of the dominant community.

As the customary distinctions between religion and magic confronted strong counterevidence, scholars have been forced to rethink the relationship between religion and magic. Some of the more interesting thinking in this regard has come from the anthropologist Mary Douglas. In her book *Purity and Danger* (1966), Douglas argues that magic should be conceptualized as a religious style.[8] Some religions, by emphasizing miracles and rituals, tend to be magical in style, and others that downplay such beliefs and practices tend not to be magical in style. One of these religious styles is not better than the other, just different. These two religious styles, the magical and the nonmagical, are a matter of degree (Figure 3.1). No religion, for example, is completely devoid of magiclike ritual activity. However, in some, it plays a greater role than it does in others.

You might object to Douglas's blurring of the distinction between magic and religion on the grounds that religion primarily involves the worship of superhuman personal powers thought to be intrinsically worthy of our attention, and that magic primarily involves the manipulation of superhuman impersonal powers for selfish purposes. Thus magic, unlike religion, is concerned with limited areas of human life: finding lost articles, healing, preventing disease, finding a lover, gaining revenge, identifying witches, and the like.

There is some validity to this objection, but again it seems to be a matter of degree. Some religions focus on personal forces, and some focus on impersonal powers. While religions show primary interest in larger goals such as salvation, most also offer more limited benefits. Prayers for the healing of physical disease or for help during some crisis like a drought are commonplace in many religions. Limited utilitarian goals exist alongside larger purposes.

## 3.4  TOWARD A WORKING DEFINITION

At this point in introductory textbooks, it is customary for the author to offer his or her one-sentence "working definition" of religion. I prefer to keep the issue of definition open, not only because this more accurately reflects the fact that, at present, there is no consensus among scholars on how best to define religion, but also because there seems little point in adding yet another definition to the many hundreds that already exist. We have examined enough definitions to orient us, and, no matter what formal working definition I might offer, you will most likely continue to rely on your intuitions (although I hope with a greater critical awareness) about what religion is and does.

I do think, however, that Alston's way of talking about religion-making characteristics is important to keep in mind. His list of nine items (see Section 3.1.2) is a good starting point, although it needs to be refined and amended. For example, not all the superhuman powers with which religions are concerned are supernatural, nor, for that matter, are they all gods. (Spirits, ancestors, heroes, kings, and much more need to be included.) These are refinements that we can make as we, following Wittgenstein's advice, "look and see."

Alston's approach has the distinct advantage of allowing us to focus on features that are undeniably present in clear cases of religion (such as Christianity, Judaism, Islam, Hinduism, and the like) and to compare, when useful and illuminating, these clear cases with less clear cases (such as political movements) without being overly concerned with locating precisely the border between religion and nonreligion. It also has the advantage of multidimensionality. It allows us to focus on the various dimensions of religion without reducing religion to a single dimension. Thus we can talk about the *intellectual dimension* of religion (beliefs, worldviews, philosophies, theologies), the *practical dimension* (ritual activities, moral behavior), the *experiential dimension* (feelings like awe, adoration, forgiveness), and the *social dimension* (organizations, institutions) without singling out any one of these dimensions as primary, the way Tillich and Spiro do.

Although I prefer Alston's approach to the problem of definition, there is value in thinking about religion the way both Tillich and Spiro do. Religions function to provide meaning and purpose to human life by connecting humans to alleged superhuman powers and realities. Discovering exactly how they perform that function and examining the sorts of connections they establish between the human and the alleged superhuman is, in part, what religious studies is about and what we will be learning to do in the chapters that follow.

## Dimensions of Religion

1. Intellectual
2. Practical
3. Experiential
4. Social

So where does this leave us? I left the question of a working definition open in part because, at present, there is no adequate scholarly definition of religion that has received widespread acceptance in the field of religious studies.

An optimistic conclusion is to hope that sometime in the future such a definition may emerge. If you decide to pursue the academic study of religion seriously, you might play a role in finding that definition. On a more pessimistic note, it is possible that the field of religious studies will always be hopelessly imprecise and uncertain about its subject matter.

I cannot predict the future. But I think it is fair to conclude that given the variety and richness of what is studied and the many different perspectives from which it is studied, there will continue to be a variety of definitions for the foreseeable future. We need not regret this situation, but we must be more aware of how we, and others, use the word *religion*.

## 3.5 SUMMARY

We began by pointing out that the student of religion requires a useful, precise, and bias-free definition of religion. Definitions are not necessarily true or false, but more or less useful for the purposes at hand. Our discussion of precision led to distinctions between substantive and functional definitions as well as essential and cluster definitions. Problems relating to scope (what is included and what is excluded) emerged as we looked at different kinds of definitions. Alston's definition lists several characteristics of the members of the family called *religion*. We uncovered several sorts of biases that frequently creep into definitions of religion, including cultural, theoretical, and gender biases, along with confusion between spirituality and religion. We traced a brief history of the word *religion* in Western culture and illustrated some of the many different ways it has been and is used.

We tested our skills of critical analysis by looking at two different definitions of religion offered by Tillich and Spiro. Tillich's definition appears to be geared toward the idea of spirituality because it locates the heart of religion in a subjective, personal state called "ultimate concern." Spiro is more concerned with religion in the sense of some kind of cultural institution. Each of these definitions has some positive features, but neither is totally problem free.

We looked at the ideas of superstition and magic in relation to the idea of religion. The concept of superstition is not helpful to the scholar of religion because it is not analytically useful. Magic is an important category, but precisely how it is to be differentiated from religion remains problematic. Some contrast magic and religion in terms of command versus asking, individuality versus community, and the manipulation of impersonal powers for limited ends versus the worship of personal powers for unlimited ends. Mary Douglas suggests that magic is one kind of religious style, and the boundary between religion and magic is a matter of degree.

We concluded that although there is a lack of agreement on a definition of religion, this only serves to stimulate further thought on the richness of the concept of religion.

## EXPLORATIONS

1. What would you identify as clear examples of religion? Why do you think they are good examples? How do your examples differ from what you would call magic?

2. Sir James G. Frazer, an early anthropologist of religion, claimed that religion is "a propitiation or conciliation of powers superior to man which are believed to direct and control the course of Nature and of human life."[9] What do you think of Frazer's definition? Is it a good definition or not? Why?

3. Which of the following are substantive definitions, and which are functional? Why did you identify them one way or another? Check your answers with a classmate and discuss any differences.

   a. "Religion is a complex form of human behavior whereby a person (or community of persons) is prepared intellectually and emotionally to deal with those aspects of human existence that are overwhelming, critically threatening, and beyond control." (William Calloley Tremmel, *Religion: What Is It*, 1997)

   b. "Religion is the recognition of all our duties as divine commands." (Immanuel Kant, *Religion within the Limits of Reason Alone*, 1960)

   c. "Religion is that system of activities and beliefs directed toward that which is perceived to be of sacred value and transforming power." (James C. Livingston, *Anatomy of the Sacred*, 1998)

   d. "Religion . . . [is] a means toward an ultimate transformation." (Frederick J. Streng, *Understanding Religious Life*, 1985)

   e. "The service and adoration of God or gods as expressed in forms of worship." (*Webster's New Collegiate Dictionary*, 1956)

4. Do we have a right to use our definition of religion to classify beliefs and activities in cultures other than our own? Is it possible to escape starting with an understanding of religion that reflects our cultural heritage? If not, does this pose a problem for the scholarly study of religion?

## SUGGESTIONS FOR FURTHER READING

In addition to the material found in the notes, the reader may wish to consult the following for more information.

Arnal, William E. "Definitions." In *Guide to the Study of Religion*, edited by Willi Braun and Russell T. McCutcheon, 21–34. London: Cassell, 2000. This is a discussion of the problems associated with substantive and functional definitions along with a critical analysis of Geertz's definition. Arnal, pessimistically, concludes, "there is no such thing as 'religion'." It is an abstraction created by scholars, but not a concrete reality.

Idinopulos, Thomas, and Brian C. Wilson, eds. *What Is Religion? Origins, Definitions, and Explanations*. Leiden, Netherlands: Brill, 1998. Many of the articles are useful, but

Wilson's article, "From the Lexical to the Polythetic: A Brief History of the Definition of Religion," is particularly helpful.

King, Winston L. "Religion." In *The Encyclopedia of Religion*, vol. 12, edited by Mircea Eliade, 282–293. New York: Macmillan, 1987. This is a discussion of different definitions and some of the problems associated with defining religion.

O'Neal, Mary R. "Superstition." In *The Encyclopedia of Religion*, vol. 14, 163–166. New York: Macmillan, 1987. O'Neal discusses the different ways in which the word *superstition* has been used.

Smart, Ninian. *Worldviews: Crosscultural Explorations of Human Beliefs*, 2nd ed. Englewood Cliffs, NJ: Prentice-Hall, 1995. Smart argues that we should subsume the category religion under the even broader category of worldviews, and we should think of and compare worldviews in terms of six dimensions: doctrinal or philosophical, mythic or narrative, ethical or legal, ritual or practical, experiential or emotional, social or institutional.

Smith, Jonathan Z. "Religion, Religions, Religious." In *Critical Terms for Religious Studies*, edited by Mark C. Taylor, 269–284. Chicago: University of Chicago Press, 1998. This useful discussion reminds us that the concept of religion is a Western anthropological notion.

Streng, Frederick J. *Understanding Religious Life*, 3rd ed. Belmont, CA: Wadsworth Publishing, 1985. The first chapter, "The Nature and Study of Religion," treats with insight some of the themes and topics I have discussed in this chapter and in the first chapter.

## INTERNET RESOURCES

http://camden-www.rutgers.edu/dept-pages/philosreligion/resource .html    Here you will find links to a great variety of information on different religions.

http://dir.yahoo.com/society_and_culture/religion_and_spirituality/ This will take you to the Yahoo! Religion and Spirituality Index. Use with care.

http://www.religion-online.org/    The aim of this site is to develop an extensive library of links to sites that treat religion from the "perspective of sound scholarship." Try the link "Search Religion Online." This allows you to type in your topic of interest, and the search will be automatically made for you.

# PART
## II

# Liminaries

CHAPTER **4**

# Sacred Power

WITH THIS CHAPTER, we enter the "liminaries"—a land betwixt and between the preliminary phase and postliminary phase. In our first encounter (many more will follow) during this threshold (*limen*) stage, we will meet a bewildering variety of superhuman beings. Some merely claim superiority, and others claim to be ultimate. We start with two case studies from different times, places, and religions, then survey some of the forms sacred power takes. We close with our first research case, which affords an opportunity to interpret one of the many manifestations of sacred power.

## 4.1 TWO CASE STUDIES

### 4.1.1 Dao (Tao)

Daoism (Taoism) is a Chinese religion that today numbers over 20 million adherents. After severe persecution by the Chinese Communist government, it survives in two important schools known as the Heavenly Masters Sect and the Perfect Truth Sect. Daoism has had enormous influence on Chinese and East Asian culture, most notably in the fields of traditional medicine and science.

Once upon a time (some say as early as the sixth century B.C.E.), the western border guard of China saw an old sage approaching, riding on an ox. The Old Master named Laozi (also spelled Lao-tzu and pronounced "lou-dzuh") was leaving a China whose society, in his view, had become corrupt. The border guard, so the story goes, would not let him leave until he wrote down his

> ### A Note on Translation
>
> There are different ways to transliterate Chinese characters
> into English letters. One is called Wade-Giles, which has been
> common in the West for a long time. The other is the Pinyin
> system, which is preferred in China and is now starting to be
> used extensively in the West. I will use the Pinyin spelling be-
> cause I think it is often closer to how the Chinese word sounds
> than the Wade-Giles spelling. When Pinyin spelling differs from
> Wade-Giles, I will put the Wade-Giles spelling in parentheses.

wisdom. The resulting book, variously known as the *Daodejing* (*Tao-te-ching*),
the *Laozi*, and *The Five Thousand Character Classic*, became one of the foundation
texts of Daoism in particular and Chinese religion in general.

There is no firm historical evidence that Laozi ever lived, let alone au-
thored the *Daodejing*. Historians date the book from the mid–fourth century
B.C.E. Among other things, it offers political advice to rulers by praising those
who gain voluntary respect and cooperation from their people by setting a virtuous example. Historians refer to the time when the book first appeared as the
Warring States Period (463–222 B.C.E.) because the heads of different states
engaged in war with each other, seeking wealth, territory, and power.

A new class of political advisors emerged during this period, and the *Daodejing* may well be a product of their attempt to influence the course of political
affairs. The book claims that the good ruler sets the tone for his people by cultivating the qualities of competence, concern, and care. The people live best
who follow the ways of nature and avoid the corrupting influences of society.

The book itself is a collection of individual sayings that once circulated in-
dependently. These sayings have a proverbial quality, offering bits of wisdom
about how to live the good life. The sayings are organized into two parts: the
first contains sayings dealing with the **Dao** (Way), and the second contains
sayings focused on *de* (power). As traditionally organized, the chapter that
opens the text is its most famous and one of its most obscure. In one of its
many translations, it reads in part:

> The Dao that can be told of is not the eternal Dao;
> The name that can be named is not the eternal name.
> The Nameless is the origin of Heaven and Earth;
> The Named is the mother of all things.[1]

The opening lines distinguish two Ways. One is the Way that can be told
or named. And the other is the Way that cannot be told or named. The named
Way is the "mother of all things." The nameless Way is the "origin of Heaven

and Earth." We are told that the named Way (mother of all things) of which we can speak is not the eternal Way (origin of Heaven and Earth) of which we cannot speak. To be eternal is to be without beginning or end. So the "origin of Heaven and Earth" is without beginning and end, but the "mother of all things" has a beginning and an end because it is not eternal.

The word *Dao* means "way" or "method" and, by extension, "process" or "rule of life." According to Isabelle Robinet, an authority on Daoism, the word *Dao* takes on the meaning of "ultimate truth" for the first time in the *Daodejing*. This ultimate truth is "one and transcendent, is invisible, inaudible, imperceptible, not usable, not nameable, an unmarked trail that one must travel to know."[2] In the final analysis, there are not two different Ways, a named and an unnamed; there is only one Way, the Way of all ways.

> We look at it and do not see it;
> > Its name is the Invisible.
> We listen to it and do not hear it;
> > Its name is The Inaudible.
> We touch it and do not find it;
> > Its name is the Subtle (formless).
>
> These three cannot be further inquired into,
> And hence merge into one.
> Going up high, it is not bright, and coming down low it is not dark.
> Infinite and boundless, it cannot be given any name;
> It reverts to nothingness. (Chapter 14)

What can we say about the Nameless Dao? Traditionally, Daoists call it the Way of Nature and regard it as the balance or harmony between two opposite, yet complementary, cosmic powers: the active and aggressive called *yang* and the passive and yielding called *yin*. The goal of life is to live in harmony with the Dao, in part, by practicing *wu-wei* or "nonaction" (sometimes translated as "actionless action"). The power or excellence (*de*) of the Dao resides in its accomplishing things naturally, without forceful action (*wu-wei*). It acts like the emptiness of a bowl that allows it to be filled simply by being receptive. It acts like the doors and windows of a room that make it useful by doing nothing. Those who permit nature to take its course are those who live rightly.

> Dao invariably takes no action, and yet there is nothing left undone.
> If kings and barons can keep it, all things will transform spontaneously.
> If, after transformation, they should desire to be active,
> I would restrain them with simplicity, which has no name.
> Simplicity, which has no name, is free of desires.
> Being free of desires, it is tranquil.
> And the world will be at peace, of its own accord. (Chapter 37)

As the Daoist religion developed, many came to believe that living in harmony with the Dao was the key to immortality. Daoists developed elaborate rituals, diets, and meditation practices in the hope of becoming immortal. The focus here, however, must remain on the Dao itself. If the Dao is ultimate truth, why call it Nameless?

The answer, I think, can be found in the idea of linguistic transcendence. That is to say, Dao goes beyond the capacity of human language. Human language can be used to name things. But how can it be used to name something that is not a thing? The eternal Dao is not a thing among other things that can be picked out and differentiated by a name. It is not like a tree or a cat.

> There was something undifferentiated and yet complete,
> Which existed before heaven and earth.
> Soundless and formless, it depends on nothing and does not change. (Chapter 25)

"But," you may well ask, "Isn't the Dao a name?" In an important sense it is not. It does not, like most names, refer to something specific. In a way, we can say it refers to nothing (no-thing) because the Nameless Way transcends every-thing. We can say what it is not—invisible, inaudible, imperceptible, without beginning and end—but we cannot say what it is. Ultimate truth eludes mere mortal thought.

> It may be considered the mother of the universe.
> I do not know its name; I call it Dao.
> If forced to give it a name, I shall call it Great. . . .
> Therefore Dao is great.
> Heaven is great.
> Earth is great.
> And the king is also great. . . .
> Man models himself after Earth.
> Earth models itself after Heaven.
> Heaven models itself after Dao.
> And Dao models itself after Nature. (Chapter 25)

For the Daoist, the way of nature is the ultimate mystery. It is a sacred power. The word *sacred* refers to what is extraordinary, and for the Daoist, nature is extraordinary. We humans often miss that in our attempts to domesticate nature, make it ordinary, and bend it to our will. Try as we might, we will never fully understand or fully control such an awesome force as nature. That is one of the many mysteries of ultimate truth that continually escapes us.

### 4.1.2 Anselm on God

We transition from ancient China to medieval Christian Europe, moving from a Daoist sage riding an ox, to a Christian monk in dispute. Christianity is a world religion that today numbers nearly 2 billion adherents and exists in a profusion of churches, denominations, and sects. Its major organizational forms include Nestorians, the Coptic Church, Eastern Orthodox, Roman Catholics, and Protestants. The influence of Christianity on world culture is immense due to the colonial and postcolonial impact of European and American societies.

For medieval Christian theologians of the Roman Catholic Church, the truth about nature was given by biblical revelation, not sages riding an ox. However, a major problem arose: how do we know that revelation is true? Do we know it by faith? Do we know it by reason? Monks, theologians, and philosophers took sides, and the disputes enchanted students and disturbed clergy.

Peter Damian, an eleventh-century Christian monk famous for his **ascetic** lifestyle, claimed that human reason was incapable of properly understanding divine revelation. Reason expresses itself in language, which is dependent on grammar. But human grammar is finite and hence inappropriate for the discussion of an infinite, eternal divine reality.

Lanfranc, the Italian prior* of the Benedictine Abby of Bec in Normandy, did not share Damian's pessimistic view of human reason. He argued that humans are created in God's image, and hence must have some divinely bestowed abilities to grasp something of divine reality. Of course divine revelation is authoritative for faith, but human reason can understand it, and we would be wasting God's great gift if we did not try to understand it.

A monk named Anselm (1033–1109), later to be made a saint for the miracles he allegedly performed, became Lanfranc's disciple. He entered the debate over reason and revelation, declaring that human reason and divine revelation lead to the same conclusions. Among his letters, prayers, meditations, and sermons are two books of interest here. The first is titled *Monologion*, and the second is titled *Proslogion*. In *Monologion*, Anselm claims that the "supreme nature" (one of his terms for God) is the ultimate truth.[3] It has neither beginning nor end. This supreme nature is unchangeable and unknowable. This means that the divine essence is "ineffable" (beyond speaking). Nevertheless, we can know something of God, even if we cannot know the divine essence.

In *Proslogion*, Anselm offers one of the most famous "proofs for God's existence" in the history of Western culture. He begins with a prayer asking God to help him understand Psalm 14:1, which claims that someone who declares that God does not exist is a fool. Anselm asks, why is it foolish to say God does not exist?

Anselm argues, in the so-called **ontological argument**, that God cannot be thought of as nonexistent because God is a being "than which no one greater can be thought." Anselm invites us to think about this conception of God. If

---

*A *prior* is a supervisor of a religious house who is second in command to the abbot.

the being of which we think when we think of God is indeed the greatest possible being that anyone can think of, then this being must exist in our understanding, or mind, as well as outside our mind. Anselm writes

> clearly that than which a greater thing cannot be thought cannot exist in the understanding alone. For if it is actually in the understanding alone, it can be thought of as existing also in reality, and this is greater. Therefore, if that than which a greater thing cannot be thought is in the understanding alone, this same thing than which a greater cannot be thought is that than which a greater can be thought. But obviously this is impossible. Therefore, there certainly exists, both in the understanding and in reality, something than which a greater thing cannot be thought.[4]

It might help us follow what Anselm says if we substitute "absolutely perfect being" for "that than which a greater thing cannot be thought." We can now interpret the above quotation in the following way: "If an absolutely perfect being exists in the *understanding alone,* then we can think of a more perfect being that is greater than the absolutely perfect being, namely one that exists *in* the mind and *outside* of it. But how can we think of something more perfect than an absolutely perfect being? How can we think of something greater than the greatest?" The answer Anselm wants us to come up with is, "We cannot." The conclusion he wants us to draw from this line of reasoning is that God, rightly understood, must exist both in and outside of our minds.

If this argument is so powerful, why do some people believe that God does not exist? Anselm argues that only a fool can say in his heart that God does not exist because only a fool can think an absolutely perfect being is merely a mental construct, a passing idea in the minds of mortals.

There is another way of saying all of this (although scholars often regard it as a second version of the argument). If God were merely a passing thought or idea only in people's minds, God would be like all other things we know of, a *contingent* being or a being whose existence is conditional insofar as its existence is dependent upon the mind that thinks it. But God is not a contingent being whose existence is dependent on other things, God is a *necessary* being whose existence is unconditional. Now Anselm asks you, how can a being whose existence is necessary not exist?

Anselm's reasoning is difficult to follow, and, while this line of dense reasoning has often been construed as a proof for God's existence, some scholars have claimed that his reasoning was not a proof in the strict sense of the term. It is an intellectual exploration into the nature of the divine. His faith in divine revelation had already convinced him that God existed. He had no doubt about that. But he wanted to understand what that meant. His faith needed to be understood by his reason, and the result is this meditation on God's nature as the greatest possible for thought and hence on God's existence as necessary and unconditional.

Anselm's fellow monk and critic, Gaunilo, also firmly believed in God's existence. But he did not trust Anselm's reasoning in this matter. When Gaunilo read Anselm's *Proslogion*, he found the reasoning absurd. He counterargued that we might as well admit, using the same logic as Anselm, that an absolutely perfect lost island exists somewhere in the vast uncharted seas. If this lost island is perfect, and if we can think of no greater island than this perfect lost one, then we must have every confidence, if Anselm's reasoning about God is correct, that it exists and set sail immediately to find it.

Anselm was undeterred, responding that if his line of reasoning truly applied to perfect, lost islands, he would find that "lost island, not to be lost again." However, lost islands, no matter how perfect, are one thing, and God is quite another. Islands are conditioned, limited sorts of things, but God is not. God's existence is necessary, and the existence of islands is contingent. This is to say that God's existence is dependent on nothing other than God, but the existence of islands is dependent on all sorts of things.

## 4.2 COMPARISON

What are we to make of these two views—one from ancient China and the other from medieval Europe—of ultimate reality? How are they the same, and how are they different? It is obvious that different people in different times and places wrote the texts used in our case studies. They also come from different religions, which have different histories and practices, not to mention beliefs. There are many significant contextual differences that affect Laozi's and Anselm's conceptions of what is ultimate, and a complete, careful comparison would need to pay attention to these contextual differences. Here, we will briefly focus on just three factors: language, text, and social status.

In order to provide a precise linguistic comparison, we would have to know ancient Chinese and medieval Latin quite well. However, assuming the translations I have selected are good ones, we can do a linguistic comparison based on the translations with some confidence (although not complete confidence) that reasonably accurate similarities and differences will emerge.

The language Laozi uses is metaphoric, relying heavily on analogies with ordinary things and natural processes. The Dao is compared to the hollow of a bowl, the doors of a house, and, in passages I did not quote, to the lowliness of a valley and the flow of water. Most importantly, the Dao is said to be the Nameless. It is beyond human reason, definition, and thought. The Dao does not seem to be personal. It is not like a person, but most like the processes of nature.

The language of Anselm is theological, philosophical, and abstract. And while Anselm recognizes that human thought cannot completely penetrate the divine mystery, he is quite confident that human reason can not only think

God, but also draw important conclusions based on that thinking. Human reason can confidently conclude that God must exist, given Anselm's conception of God as the greatest possible for human thought. God, for Anselm, is not nameless and not impersonal. He offers his thoughts to God as a kind of contemplative prayer, asking God to help him understand more deeply.

Laozi's text is not argumentative, or at least not explicitly argumentative. It is poetic, evocative, and stimulates our wonder by proverbs and cryptic aphorisms. Anselm's text is both prayerful and argumentative. He wants to understand why someone who thinks God does not exist is a fool as the Bible says, and he wants to draw reasoned judgments about God's existence based on a certain understanding of God. He draws conclusions and provides reasons to support his conclusions. It is not surprising that his text invites a counterargument from someone like Gaunilo.

Although there are important differences between Laozi's and Anselm's thinking about what is ultimate, both recognize that it functions as a notion that limits our thinking. For both, human life and thought need to be grounded in something absolute—some final, unlimited truth that humans would be well advised to acknowledge if they wish to live rightly.

Note that both Laozi and Anselm represent the educated elite of their day. Their ideas were probably not even known to the majority of people alive at the time they were writing (although the *Daodejing* became a more popular text than anything that Anselm ever wrote). Most people living in ancient China offered sacrifices in honor of their sacred ancestors and evoked a variety of deities to insure good crops and marriages that would produce sons to work the fields. Most people living in medieval Europe offered prayers to various saints, martyrs, and Mary, the mother of Jesus, for good crops and sons to plant and harvest. For most, religion was more a matter of dealing with superhuman powers that impinge on everyday existence than with thoughts about the ultimate origins of heaven and earth or the nature of the divine.

Only the educated elite of any society have the time to speculate. The peasant must earn a living. It is important to remember this because social conditions and status influence both religious thought and action. The religion of the elite is often different from the religion of the nonelite. Or to put it another way, religion on the street is different from religion in the books.

## 4.3 FORMS OF SACRED POWER

Power is a basic religious category. The universe is filled with many kinds of powers that require humans to do different sorts of things in order to get along in life and prosper. According to the Romans, some of these things are to be done "outside the temple," and hence they called them *profane* (in front of the *fanum*, or temple). Other things are to be done "inside the temple," and hence they called them *sacred* (derived from the sacrifices that occurred in the temple). While the sacred and profane are often sharply contrasted and the sacred defined as that which is set apart from the profane, both have to do with power.

In many ways, profane power is easier to deal with. In our daily affairs, we can often deal with ordinary profane power in fairly straightforward ways, using the technology available to plant the corn, harvest the crops, get to work, and start the computer. Sacred power, however, is extraordinary, not ordinary. Like the Dao, it is invisible and inaudible. We are never quite sure how, where, and when it will manifest itself. Perhaps it could manifest itself as a being whose existence is unlimited, unconditioned, and necessary, thereby reminding us of our limited, conditioned, and contingent existence. Sometimes sacred power will be strong, active, and aggressive, creating and destroying whole universes. Sometimes it will be weak, passive, and yielding, yet accomplishing all that is necessary without effort. In whatever forms humans believe they have encountered sacred power, it is experienced as something beyond—to some extent—human control, and something especially important to the well-being of humans. Religions teach that human existence and welfare depend upon sacred power. It gives life and it takes life.

The Bhagavad Gita, one of the most important sacred books of Hinduism, provides an example of sacred power when Arjuna (a warrior chief) has a vision of Lord Krishna (one of the incarnations of the divine). Picture Arjuna's vision as you read what he says:

> I see no beginning
> Or middle or end to you;
> only of boundless strength
> in your endless arms,
> the moon and sun in your eyes,
> your mouths of consuming flames,
> your own brilliance
> scorching this universe.
>
> You alone
> Fill the space between heaven and earth
> and all the directions;
> seeing this awesome,
> terrible form of yours,
> Great Soul,
> The three worlds [heaven, earth, and sky]
> tremble. (11:18–20)[5]

Sacred power takes many forms in the religions of the world. Laozi's Dao and Anselm's Perfect, Necessary Being are only two. In some ways they are the least typical because both express the sacred as ultimately unconditioned yet conditioning all else as its creator or source. Most of the many forms of the sacred express notions of powers and beings that are superior to humans in many ways but are not necessarily ultimate. Often their existence, like human existence, is conditioned and limited.

### 4.3.1 Spirits, Ancestors, and Totems

**Animism** refers to religious practices and beliefs centering on the notion that spirits or souls inhabit and animate most, if not all, natural phenomena. A British anthropologist, E. B. Tylor (1832–1917), introduced the term in 1871 to characterize the religions of so-called primitive societies. According to Tylor, our prehistoric human ancestors, in thinking about what was going on when they dreamed, fainted, and saw others die, came up with a plausible explanation. There must be, they reasoned, an inner spirit or soul that, when it left the body during faints or in death, rendered the body immobile. This same spirit might appear in dreams, and when we wandered about in our own dreams, it was our soul wandering about. If humans have such spirits, surely other things (animals, stones, trees, etc.) do as well. Tylor located the origin of all religion in animistic belief. He argued that from this early animism more complex views, such as **polytheism** and monotheism, gradually evolved. Laozi's Dao and Anselm's God can be seen as the end product of a long evolutionary history beginning with animism.

Most scholars reject Tylor's theory. It lacks supporting evidence. Many also reject animism as a useful term for cross-cultural comparison. Nevertheless, many people, be they ancient or modern, appear to believe in some type of soul or spirit. This soul/spirit is usually represented as a quasi-material force, and not a completely separate, immaterial reality. It is often linked with the breath, shadow, image, or blood. Its primary function is to animate a body, but it is often thought to be the seat of personality and character.

Although, according to animism, trees, stones, woods, valleys, lakes, mountains, deserts, birds, bears, snakes—indeed anything and everything—can and do have spirits whose power concerns us, the vital force that animates humans and links them together even after death is of greater concern. The spirits of the deceased ancestors are particularly powerful because they can help or hinder the living. Offering prayers and sacrifices to the spirits of ancestors is commonplace in many Asian, African, and Native American religious traditions. In the Celtic Samhain—pre-Christian Halloween—the spirits of the dead were honored each autumn with food and gifts, lest they cause trouble for the living. These rites are not ancestor worship; rather, they are ways of linking the living and the dead into a single functioning community.

In Ojibwa, a Native American language, *ototeman* means "he is a relative of mine." A **totem** is another example of a superhuman force, usually (although not always) an animal that embodies the spiritual essence of a group. Often it is said to be the "first ancestor." Clan totems such as turtle, panther, and bear are typical in North America, and most tribal societies exhibit some form of totemism. Secular and profane totems survive in animal symbols for states (California is the bear state) and athletic teams (the Tigers).

Emile Durkheim (1858–1917), one of the pioneers of sociology, thought that the totemism found among Australian Aborigines held the key to the origin of religion. Noting that the totem symbolized a social group like a clan, Durkheim argued that all sacred powers (totems, ancestors, gods) are symbols for the social power of the group to control and shape the individual. Humans recognize that survival depends upon the strength of the group to which they belong. The spirit of the group is embodied in the totem or the sacred ancestor. To worship it, is to worship, in symbolic form, the social power that makes life possible.

Scholars no longer accept Durkheim's theory about the origin of religion. However, they do recognize that totems play an important role in classifying differences among social groups. Totems stand for opposing social categories and regulate such important social affairs as marriage between clans, inheritance, warfare, and ritual obligations.

Spirits, ancestors, and totems may not be thought of as ultimate in the sense that Laozi views the Dao and Anselm views the Perfect God, but they are superhuman powers thought to be of immense importance to human well-being.

## 4.3.2 Goddesses and Gods

Polytheism, the belief in many deities, is a widespread and persistent form of religion. There are thousands of gods and goddesses, and they have always been difficult to organize.

There is Thor, the Scandinavian god who loves mead (beer) and drives a chariot drawn by goats. This warrior-god crushes the powers of chaos by slaying the giant Thryn. There is also Freya, the most important Scandinavian goddess of desire, whose Greek counterpart is Aphrodite, goddess of beauty and passionate love.

We have all heard of Zeus, the greatest of Greek sky-gods, who hurls his thunderbolts to guard law, order, and justice. Hera, his long-suffering wife, is the goddess of women and matrimony. We must not forget Zeus's daughter, Athena, who springs in full armor from her father's forehead. She is goddess of wisdom and war, who is the eternal virgin defending the state against its enemies with her shield and lance. The owl is her bird.

The gods and goddesses of ancient Egypt crowd center stage, looking for attention and worship. Ra, the sun-god, crosses the heavens in his boat, spreading light over the land and defeating Apophis, the dragon, who seeks to prevent Ra's life-giving journey each dawn. Osiris, set upon by his brother Seth, is killed and dismembered. Isis, his wife, reassembles him and brings him to life, thereby assuring continuing fertility of the land and resurrection from the dead for all the faithful.

The scene shifts to Africa, where Nzambi, great god of the Bakongo, creates humans and punishes those who violate his prohibitions. The Yoruba of West Africa worship the orisha deities such as Ogun, the god of iron and of war, Oko the god of farming, and Eshu, a trickster god who must be appeased to maintain "peace in the market place."

Turning to the Native American religions of North America, we find, among the Oglala Sioux, Wakan Tanka, the Great Mysteriousness. J. R. Walker, a Sioux medicine man explains:

> Every object in the world has a spirit and that spirit is *wakan*. Thus the spirits of the tree or things of that kind, while not like the spirit of man, are also *wakan*. *Wakan* comes from the *wakan* beings. These *wakan* beings are greater than mankind in the same way that mankind is greater than animals. They are never born and never die. They can do many things that mankind cannot do. Mankind can pray to the *wakan* beings for help. There are many of these beings but all are of four kinds. The word *Wakan Tanka* means all of the *wakan* beings because they are all as if one. *Wakan Tanka Kin* signifies the chief or leading *Wakan* being which is the Sun. However, the most powerful of the *Wakan* beings is *Nagi Tanka*, the Great Spirit who is also *Taku Skanskan*. *Taku Skanskan* signifies the Blue, in other words, the Sky . . . Mankind is permitted to pray to the *Wakan* beings. If their prayer is directed to all the good *Wakan* beings, they should pray to *Wakan Tanka*; but if the prayer is offered to only one of these beings, then the one addressed should be named . . . *Wakan Tanka* is like sixteen different persons; but each person is *kan*. Therefore, they are only the same as one.[6]

The deities and spirits can be organized by cosmic regions: the sky, the earth, and the underworld. There appears to be a deity for every place, if not a place for every deity. They have been related in elaborate **pantheons**— divine family trees of mothers, fathers, sons, daughters, aunts, uncles, and cousins. They personify natural forces; so they might be organized by wind and storm, flood and rain. They are **anthropomorphic** beings, described as being like humans but with more power. But are they all one, as J. R. Walker suggests? Do they all manifest a single divine, sacred power pervading the heavens and the earth?

It is perhaps best to continue an analogy between gods and humans. Just as humans form a single human species, but are different persons, so the gods and goddesses form a single superhuman species, but are different deities. It is even possible to recognize the existence of many gods, but worship only one (**henotheism**). The first of the Ten Commandments from the Hebrew Bible hints at henotheism when it says that the "Lord God" who brought the Hebrews "out of the land of Egypt" commands, "You shall have no other gods before me" (Exodus 20:3).

The deities provide comfort, help, protection, and security. However, superhuman powers are not always good. We have yet to mention the bad **demons** (some demons are good), devils, and dangerous deities that also populate the religious landscape. Sacred power can be good, but it can also cause harm. Often the gods of the conquered become the demons of the conquerors. So the Greek god Pan, half-human and half-goat, became the model for Christian images of Satan, the fallen angel and adversary of God. In Japanese mythology, demons are fierce, ugly, and foul smelling. They prey on young children and inhabit lonely places.

Demons, in many religions, are not actually deities, but superhuman forces midway between humans and gods. Nor are they always bad. In Bali there are good demons that work for the benefit of humans. Sometimes demons are merely merry pranksters, causing trouble and playing tricks. Even superhuman powers can have fun.

### 4.3.3 Monotheism and Deism

Monotheism refers to the belief that there is only one God, and certain practices are associated with that belief. It comes in several varieties. **Unitarianism** is the view that the nature of this God is an absolute unity. Unlike other beings, God has no parts. Judaism, Islam, and some forms of Christianity and Hinduism are monotheistic in the unitarian sense.

The second of the "Thirteen Principles" of Moses Ben Maimon, a medieval Jewish theologian and philosopher, states, "I believe with perfect faith that the Creator, blessed be his name, is a Unity, and that there is no unity in any manner like unto his, and that he alone is our God, who was, and is, and will be."[7] The Islamic scripture called the Quran declares, "Allah: there is no god but Him, the Living, the Eternal One . . . He is the Exalted, the Immense One. . . . Allah is One, the Eternal God. He begot none, nor was He begotten. None is equal to him" (Surahs 2 and 112).

**Trinitarianism** is the view that the nature of the one and only God is a triunity. This is the major form of monotheism found among Christians who hold that God is three persons in one divine nature. The persons are called Father, Son, and Holy Spirit. The Father creates and sustains the universe, the Son redeems humans in the person of Jesus the Christ, and the Holy Spirit sanctifies (makes holy or sacred), teaches, and inspires.

Controversies about God's nature abounded among early Christians, and the Roman Emperor Constantine, hoping to have a unified religion to support a unified empire, called bishops (leaders) of various Christian groups to gather in a council at Nicea in 325 to formulate a confession of faith (creed) to which all might agree. According to this Nicene Creed, all Christians should confess:

> I believe in one God the father almighty, maker of heaven and earth, and of all things visible and invisible. And in one lord Jesus Christ, the only begotten son of God, begotten of his father before all worlds, God of God, light of light, true God of true God, begotten, not made, being of one substance with the father, by whom all things were made. Who for us men, and for our salvation came down from heaven, and was incarnate by the Holy Spirit of the Virgin Mary,

and was made man, and was crucified also for us under Pontius Pilate. He suffered and was buried, and the third day he rose again according to the scripture, and ascended into heaven, and sits on the right hand of the father. And he shall come again with glory to judge both the living and the dead; whose kingdom shall have no end. And I believe in the Holy Spirit, the lord and giver of life, who proceeds from the father (and the son), who with the father and the son together is worshipped and glorified, who spoke by the prophets. And I believe in one universal and apostolic church, I acknowledge one baptism for the remission of sins, and I look for the resurrection of the dead, and the life of the world to come. Amen.[8]

As you might guess, the Nicene Creed did not settle matters or produce the unity Constantine desired. Exactly how the three persons of the Trinity are related was, and has been ever since, a focal point of often bitter and divisive controversies among Christians. One of the many hotly debated issues concerned the question of whether the Son was "one substance" with God or of a "similar substance." Much of the debate centered on the Son, the second person of the Trinity, because if Jesus, the incarnate Son, were not fully divine and fully human, how could he have the power to save humans from sin and death? But how could a being be both fully divine and fully human? The answers represent different divisions of Christianity.

Nestorian Christians claim that Jesus is two distinct persons, one divine and one human. Monophysite (Coptic) Christians maintain he is one person with only one divine nature. Eastern Orthodox, Catholic, and most Protestant theologians maintain the Christ is one person with a divine *and* a human nature. Eastern Orthodox theologians, however, reject the notion that the Holy Spirit proceeds from *both* the Father and the Son. They think that such language implies a subordination of the Holy Spirit as less divine than either the Father or the Son.

The division among these groups involved more than theological quibbles. Political, linguistic, and cultural factors contributed to the division and, even today, keep many Christian groups apart. As sociologists remind us, when groups become more complex and need to show how they are different from competing groups, the need for ever more precise definitions of key ideas and teachings arises. However, the more definitions formulated and the more precise the formulations, the greater the risk. Splinter groups develop who do not agree with the definitions, and the hoped for unity through careful definition evaporates.

Speculation about the nature of God is not confined to Christians. The Hindu notion of *trimurti* (three forms of the divine) is another example. Hinduism is a name for a wide variety of religions associated with India, whose devotees number well over half a billion. Among Hindus the *trimurti* is very old. In Hindu iconography, the gods Brahma, Vishnu, and Shiva are combined into one figure with three different faces. Brahma creates a universe, Vishnu sustains or preserves it, and Shiva destroys it. I say "a" universe, because within the belief structure of Hinduism, universes are infinite. We live in only one phase of an infinite number.

Brahma, the creator, is not much worshiped today in India. Also, Hindus often say another god, such as Vishnu or Shiva, creates him. Hindus recognize that all "forms of divinity" are significant, but often claim that whatever form of deity they worship, be it Vishnu or Shiva, is the one who is the creator, maintainer, and destroyer of universes. Like the Christian focus on Jesus as the incarnation of God's Son, the incarnations of Vishnu (such as Lord Krishna) play a large role in devotion.

From a sociological and historical view, two factors are important in these examples. First, as peoples become more united socially and politically, the gods of each group tend to merge into one divine power. Second, as the one divine power (or one of its aspects like the Father or Brahma) becomes more abstract and distant from the everyday concerns of people, other divine beings (and/or saints) concerned with specific areas of life become more important in devotional life. People want their gods accessible and nearby.

However, not all people want personal divine power close at hand. In the eighteenth century, both in Europe and the American colonies, **deism** became popular among the educated elite. Deism is a type of unitarian monotheism based on the belief that God created the universe, but no longer has anything to do with it. The universe runs according to the physical laws discovered by Newton, and to think, as traditional monotheism does, that miracles occur or God intervenes directly in worldly affairs is to indulge in anthropomorphic fantasies.

The deists argued that without a divine First Cause, the universe remains unexplainable. Out of nothing, nothing comes. There must be a cause that is not the effect of any prior cause, and so they accepted, on what they took to be purely rational grounds, the traditional monotheistic view of the **aseity** of God. God is, unlike other beings, self-existent, necessary, and without a prior cause.

Once the universe has been created by this divine First Cause, it runs according to natural laws much like a clock keeps running after it is started. Praying to God for help, as well as most religious devotional activities, makes little sense to a deist, because it would be irrational of the deity to interrupt the chain of cause and effect started so very long ago in order to attend to your or my momentary needs. To think otherwise is selfishness on a truly cosmic scale.

### 4.3.4 Dualism Divine

Zoroastrianism, the ancient religion of Persia (Iran), was founded by Zarathustra (also called Zoroaster), perhaps as early as 1000 B.C.E. Today, there are about half a million Zoroastrians, now known as Parsi. According to tradition, Zarathustra received a revelation from Ahura Mazda (later called Ohrmazd), the supreme God and "Wise Lord of Light." Based on this revelation, Zarathustra set about reforming Persian polytheism, claiming that when Ahura Mazda created the world, he gave humans freedom to choose between two competing spirits. Spenta Mainyu is the good and holy spirit of Ahura Mazda, who is constantly challenged by Angra Mainyu, the evil and satanic spirit. According to the *Gathas* (hymns written by Zarathustra), "the two primal Spirits, who revealed themselves in visions as Twins, are the Better and the Bad in thought and word and action—between these two the wise one chose right, the foolish not so."

Zarathustra did not teach a strict dualism between good and evil divine powers because he believed that, in the fullness of time, the good spirit, Spenta Mainyu, would destroy the evil spirit, Angra Mainyu. Centuries later, however, when Ahura Mazda and his good spirit Spenta Mainyu were transformed into Ohrmazd, and the evil spirit Angra Mainyu had become Ahriman, the Evil One, people began to recognize that these forces were coequal. So in the Zoroastrian priestly text called *Vendidad* (ninth century), Ohrmazd is pictured as the creator of all that is good and Ahriman as creator of all that is evil.

Human beings, like other beings, do not like to suffer. One of the most important functions of religion (a consolation unavailable, as far as we know, to nonhuman animals) is to help us cope with suffering. Monotheistic religions cannot blame a perfectly good divine being for suffering and evil. They must find a scapegoat either in human failures like sin or ignorance or in some satanic force of limited power, which the all-powerful, good divine being cannot, for some reason, completely control right now.

In contrast to monotheism, dualistic religions like Zoroastrianism have the advantage of ascribing evil to an evil superhuman source. Given this dualistic hypothesis, the world in which we all live, a world with a mixture of good and bad, is understandable if it can be seen as the result of moral and cosmic battle between good and evil. The disadvantage of the dualistic view centers on how secure we may feel living in a universe whose moral outcome is uncertain. If we do not know who will win the battle between good and evil, how secure can we be about our future? Then again, the uncertainty may inspire us to make every effort to secure the victory of good by doing good to our fellow creatures (see Chapter 9).

### 4.3.5 Pantheism and Monism

The word **pantheism** comes from Greek and literally means "all god." Some use this term for any belief or theory that holds that the essence of the universe is divine. Others use it to refer to views asserting that the sum total of the universe is divine. However it is understood, pantheistic ideas deny that there is a deity greater than the universe. In other words, the transcendence of the divine is denied, along with the idea that the divine has some sort of personality.

Some claim that Daoism, with which we opened this chapter, is pantheistic, or at least closer to pantheism than monotheism. I think it is misleading to think of the Dao as some kind of god. Nevertheless, it is clear that according to Daoist philosophy the "Way of Nature" is the ultimate truth.

Stoic philosophers like the Roman Emperor Marcus Aurelius (121–180) and the Roman statesman Cicero (106–143) were pantheists because they subscribed to the view that God is identical to the rational order of the universe, which the Greeks called the *logos*. This identification of God with the universe's rational order influenced the Dutch philosopher Benedict Spinoza (1632–1677). Spinoza was of Jewish origin, but abandoned traditional Jewish monotheism because both science and philosophical reason convinced him that there is only one substance. Everything else is but a mode or quality of this one substance. When asked to name this substance, Spinoza said we can call it God or we can call it Nature. However, this one substance, unlike traditional Jewish monotheism, creates no universe out of nothing, hears no prayers, and does not act in the unfolding of history.

Some views of sacred power are monistic. Plotinus (204–270), a Neoplatonic philosopher, represents one kind of **monism.** He argued that there was one ultimate reality from which all other principles emanate (similar to rays emerging from the sun). He called this ultimate reality the One, as well as God. Notice that this One does not *create* the world out of nothing, but somehow *emanates* it out of itself.

In the Hindu context, monism often refers to the claim that there is no difference between the essence of consciousness (called Atman) and the essence of the universe (called Brahman). In the *Chandogya Upanishad*, an early Indian text, a father teaches his son, Shvetaketu, the relationship between his individual self and the Atman. The father says, "The finest essence here—that constitutes the self of this whole world; that is the truth; that is the self (atman). And that is how you are S'vetaketu" (6.9.4).[9]

Shankara (ca. 788–820), an important member of the Advaita (nondualistic) Vedanta school, developed this Upanishadic insight into the nature of human consciousness. Shankara preferred the term nondualism to monism because human language is limited. We can say what ultimate reality is not, but we cannot say what it is. Shankara distinguishes between a lower and a higher knowledge. According to lower knowledge, the divine appears to humans as a personal lord called Ishvara (the Sanskrit word for "lord"), but according to the higher knowledge, the divine essence is revealed as Atman/Brahman, the one true and only reality. Atman is often translated as "Self," but it is best to think of it as "Pure Consciousness," that is, consciousness purified of all individual elements. It is neither my individual consciousness nor yours, but consciousness as such.

It is difficult to translate Brahman by a single English word; perhaps the "Divine Essence" or "True Reality" is the best we can do. So, when Shankara argues that Atman is Brahman, he is asserting that Pure Consciousness is True Reality. He is also asserting that everything else that appears to us to be real is just that, only an appearance. Beyond Atman/Brahman nothing genuinely real exists. It as if we are living now in a dream, and we think there are many different things because we dream many different things. When we wake up from the dream, we will realize that all those things were just dream images. There is only Atman/Brahman, and that is how we all are.

Monotheism attempts to preserve both the transcendence of God as a reality independent of the universe and God's immanence within the created order we call the universe. Pantheism abandons transcendence in favor of immanence. God is, according to the pantheist, the creative power found within the universe, not outside of it. Monism rejects any sort of divine pluralism, and in that sense it is like monotheism. But the One of the monists is usually thought of as nonpersonal and as the only thing that truly is. This is unlike monotheism, which asserts that the divine is personal and is not the only thing that is real.

---

**Different Views of Sacred Power**

1. Animism, ancestors, and totems
2. Goddesses and gods
3. Monotheism and deism
4. Dualism divine
5. Pantheism and monism

---

## 4.4 AGNOSTICISM AND ATHEISM

Differing conceptions of sacred power, such as animism, totemism, polytheism, monotheism, and pantheism, presuppose that humans are in a position to know something about superhuman realities. **Agnosticism** refers to the claim that humans cannot know about divine matters, in particular, whether any divine powers exist or not.

Agnostic arguments often presuppose a particular theory of knowledge called *evidentialism*. According to evidentialism, it is wrong to believe any statement true on the basis of inadequate evidence. William K. Clifford (1845– 1879), a British mathematician, wrote a famous and influential article titled "The Ethics of Belief." Clifford argued that "it is wrong, always, everywhere and for anyone to believe anything upon insufficient evidence." He gives the example of a ship owner who, believing his ship seaworthy, sends it out to sea without checking on its safety. Whether the ship sinks or not, Clifford argues, the owner is morally responsible for holding a belief in the safety of the ship without sufficient evidence. "He had," Clifford writes, "no right to believe on such evidence as was before him."

For Clifford, nonempirical (not available to our senses), superhuman entities like gods or God are beyond the reach of our minds. We simply are in no position to get the sort of evidence required to justify believing in some divine reality. Any such belief must be a leap of faith based on insufficient evidence. It is as morally wrong for humans to make such a leap as it is for the ship owner to believe his ship seaworthy without sufficient evidence.

**Atheism,** the claim that there is no God, is often based on a particular sort of analysis and explanation of religion. Ludwig Feuerbach (1804–1872), for example, maintained that a careful analysis of religion shows that humans project their highest and best virtues into a spiritual realm and create a being called God. God is a projection of idealized humanity. We create our gods in our own images.

Feuerbach's atheism is, odd as it may seem, religiously motivated. He saw himself as a second Martin Luther (1483–1546). Just as Luther had given birth to the Protestant Reformation in Germany, thereby creating a new form of Christianity, so Feuerbach hoped to give birth to a new form of Christianity, a form he called "realized Christianity."

Feuerbach argued that a correct analysis of religion shows that it amounts to a symbolic and mythical expression of an unconscious self-estrangement. Humans are divided selves. There is a division between our actual selves and our idealized selves (recall the cartoons with a devil on one shoulder and an angel on the other, whispering advice). Religion reflects this division between the real and the ideal. On the one hand, we project our idealized selves (what we ought to be) as a divine being (God), and on the other, we project our own existence as one of sin in comparison with this God. When this "hidden truth" of religion is made plain, then humanity will be freed from its estrangement and freed for a "realized Christianity"—a humanized religion that has at its core the love of neighbor, not the love of an illusory God.

Feuerbach's critique of religion and his atheism have a religious significance. Although he was well aware of the differences among different religions, he believed that in all the so-called higher religions there is a common core of teaching, best exemplified in Jesus' teaching about love. However, this common core of moral teaching has been obscured by supernaturalistic elements. Thus, for example, in Christianity, the teachings about a supernatural God, the Trinity, Christ's divinity, and the like have deflected human love from its true object. Feuerbach's atheistic humanism had as its goal nothing less than to remove these supernaturalistic smoke screens and redirect human love to its proper object, humanity itself:

> Religion is the dream of the human mind. But even in dreams we do not find ourselves in emptiness or in heaven, but on earth, in the realm of reality; we

only see real things in the entrancing splendour of imagination and caprice, instead of in the simple daylight of reality and necessity. Hence I do nothing more to religion . . . than open its eyes, or rather to turn its gaze from the internal towards the external, i.e., I change the object as it is in the imagination into the object as it is reality.[10]

## 4.5 SUMMARY

We began with two case studies. The first focused on the Nameless Dao or Way of Nature, and the second focused on the ontological argument by St. Anselm concerning the existence of a being "than which nothing greater can be conceived." A comparison of the ideas of both Laozi and St. Anselm revealed that for both there is an ultimate truth, although their understandings of the nature of that ultimate truth differ in important ways.

Our discussion of sacred and profane power indicated how central sacred power is to the religious consciousness. Looking at a variety of beliefs about spirits, ancestors, and totems provided more concrete examples of sacred power. An early anthropologist of religions, E. B. Tylor, proposed that all religious beliefs about sacred power, no matter how complex, originated in early animistic beliefs.

A brief survey of polytheistic conceptions of sacred power in different religions showed how important gods and goddesses are to overcoming chaos, making food grow, and offering the possibility of eternal life. Human life depends on some sort of regular order in the universe, and hence, for many, it also depends on those powers (gods and goddesses) responsible for that order.

Monotheists divide between unitarians and trinitarians, but they all agree there is only one God who transcends the universe as its creator and is immanent within the created universe, sustaining and preserving its order. Deists find the idea of divine immanence implausible. A divine power actively involved in the day-to-day running of the universe is mere superstition, although they agree with monotheists that there is only one creator God responsible for the origin of the universe and the laws according to which it runs.

With dualism we encounter sacred power divided between good and evil forces locked in combat for control of the world order. In a universe full of suffering and misery, some people find comfort in attributing evil to an evil deity rather than a perfectly good divine power. If a perfectly good divine power is responsible for evil, than what hope do mortals have?

Pantheistic views frequently identify the divine with the universe. There is no sacred power transcendent of the universe. Whatever sacred force exists, it is found within the universe in which humans live. We need to learn to respect the divine in other humans, as well as in the trees, waters, and nonhuman animals. God and nature are one and the same.

Monistic views are closely associated with pantheism, but usually identify consciousness itself, one of the most powerful forces in the universe, with the ultimate reality. At its deepest level, consciousness in itself or consciousness per se is ultimate.

An examination of agnosticism and atheism demonstrated that agnostics have legitimate moral concerns about believing beyond the evidence, and atheism can have a profound religious significance. Organized religions may support morality in a variety of ways, but they may also hinder it. Feuerbach argued that emphasizing beliefs and practices associated with some alleged supernatural reality turns human attention away from the moral effort to realize the religious ideal of loving one's neighbor as oneself.

Peter L. Berger, a sociologist, remarked that "religion is the audacious attempt to conceive of the entire universe as being humanly significant."[11] The gods and goddesses who populate the human imagination, while sometimes evoking fear and even terror, also make the universe a home. Even more abstract, impersonal notions like ultimate truth and perfect being assure us that there is a foundation on which mere mortals can rely.

There is much to ponder in these rich and varied views about sacred power. We will conclude with a research case focusing on a particular manifestation of the sacred, followed by questions to help you make sense of it.

## 4.6 RESEARCH CASE—GANESHA

In spring 1999 a 650-pound black granite statue of a human body with an elephant head arrived in Orange Park, Florida. In September of the same year, this statue was the focal point of a three-day installation ceremony, which, according to Daya J. Patel, president of the Hindu Society, will "instill cosmic energy into the idol, so that God will come into it."[12]

The "idol," or image, is Ganesha ("guh-nay'shuh"), one of the most worshiped gods in all of India. He is the lord who removes obstacles and brings success. He is worshiped by the devotees of other Hindu deities as the god who starts them either on a spiritual path or on the road to worldly success. By some he is worshiped as the supreme deity and the creator of the universe. He operates on all levels of the Hindu pantheon, from the level of subsidiary gods to that of the supreme God, and his worship crosses the boundaries of different sects. It also crosses borders. He has worshipers in Tibet, China, Japan, and elsewhere in Asia. He even crosses religions, finding a place in the Buddhist pantheon of gods.

You have probably seen pictures of him. He has the head of an elephant and the body of a short human or chubby child with a potbelly. Sometimes he is pictured sitting on a throne with a crown, and sometimes he is seated in meditation. Sometimes we see him with multiple arms, sometimes riding on an

The Hindu God Ganesha

elephant, and sometimes he carries an axe, noose, sweet cakes, and a tusk. Often he has one tusk broken off. His image frequently graces the entrance to temples and shrines.

In the *Puranas*, a collection of Indian sacred stories, we encounter tales of Ganesha's birth, his beheading, his family, and his exploits. We are told he is the son of Parvati, wife of the god Shiva, destroyer of worlds. Parvati conceives Ganesha by herself because she wants a son to keep her company and guard the door to her bath, and Shiva, who is practicing asceticism and thus retaining his "seed," will not have sexual intercourse with her. When Shiva regains interest in Parvati and tries to enter her bath, Ganesha attempts to prevent him. Shiva, not knowing who Ganesha is, beheads him, much to the sorrow of Parvati. In order to comfort his wife and bring peace to his household, Shiva replaces the severed head with an elephant head, restores Ganesha to life, and adopts him as his own son.

Robert L. Brown offers an interpretation:

> In the Indian context, Ganesha is the liminal god of transitions: he is placed at the doorway of temples to keep out the unworthy, in a position analogous to his role as Parvati's doorkeeper, and he can set up, as he did for his father, obstacles to the successful completion of goals. His parents' ambivalent relationship, founded on the opposing concerns of asceticism and sexuality, places Ganesha in between. He is created by Parvati as a result of Shiva's asceticism and refusal to have children, but is annihilated due to Shiva's sexual interest in Parvati, only to be restored, transformed, as a bond between the two. He is here fulfilling his transitional role as a means to integrate opposing elements.[13]

In a frequently repeated myth, Ganesha has gorged himself on sweet cakes and begins his ride home at night on his rat vehicle. A snake frightens the rat, who shies, causing Ganesha to fall, breaking open his belly and spilling the cakes. In anger, Ganesha breaks off one of his tusks and throws it at the moon, which causes the moon to disappear. Ganesha restores the moon, but to this day it continues to wax and wane. This is also why Ganesha is often pictured with only one tusk.

The sanctification rite I mentioned at the beginning of this case also marked an overcoming of obstacles. More than 800 Hindus live on the northeast coast of Florida, and, in holding its first installation of Ganesha, this community begins the process of surmounting a problem faced by other immigrants to the United States—how to keep their religious traditions alive and well in an often hostile society. In pulling the Hindu Society of Florida together and bringing Ganesha to American shores, the immigrant Indians have become far more involved in their faith than they would have been in India. Most immigrants become "more religious" here than at home simply because there are fewer of them to keep the faith and culture alive. After traveling all over Asia, Ganesha is now alive and well in America.

## QUESTIONS ON THE CASE OF GANESHA

1. What sort of additional information about Ganesha would you like? Be as specific as you can, and say why you want that information. (You may wish to review the section "Goals and Methods" in chapter 2 to get some ideas about the kinds of questions to ask.)
2. How would you classify the worship of Ganesha? Is it polytheistic, henotheistic, monotheistic, deistic, or pantheistic? Why do you classify it as you do?

3. Do you agree with Brown's interpretation of the Ganesha birth story? Why or why not? What would you add?
4. Compare Ganesha to the Dao and to Anselm's perfect being. How are they the same and how different?
5. How do you think worship of Ganesha can help the Indian immigrant community in the United States overcome obstacles?

## SUGGESTIONS FOR FURTHER READING

In addition to the material found in the notes, the reader may wish to consult the following for more information.

Armstrong, Karen. *A History of God: The 4000-Year Quest of Judaism, Christianity and Islam.* New York: Alfred A. Knopf, 1994. This is a highly readable account of how the idea and experience of God evolved among the monotheistic faiths of Judaism, Christianity, and Islam.

Clifford, William K. *Lectures and Essays*, vol. II. London: Macmillan, 1897. This volume contains the essay "Ethics of Belief."

Csikszentmihaliji, Mark, and Philip J. Ivanhoe, eds. *Religious and Philosophical Aspects of the Laozi.* Albany, NY: State University of New York Press, 1999. Leading scholars carefully examine important religious and philosophical aspects of the *Daodejing.*

Fiorenza, Francis Schüssler, and Gordon D. Kaufman. "God." In *Critical Terms for Religious Studies,* edited by Mark C. Taylor, 136–159. Chicago: University of Chicago Press, 1998. This is a careful study of the many different ways the word *God* is used.

Holm, Jean, ed. *Picturing God.* London: Pinter Publishers, 1994. This collection of essays covering views about the divine in all the major religions contains much useful information.

LaFargue, Michael. *The Tao of the Tao Te Ching: A Translation and Commentary.* Albany, NY: State University of New York Press, 1992. A careful but controversial application of hermeneutical principles to Laozi's famous book.

MacIntyre, Alasdair, and Paul Ricoeur. *The Religious Significance of Atheism.* New York: Columbia University Press, 1966. In these Bampton Lectures of 1966, the authors examine, from very different perspectives, the crisis of faith that began in the nineteenth century.

Mbiti, John. *Concepts of God in Africa.* New York: Praeger Publishers, 1970. This is a classic study of notions of deity in Africa.

Neville, Robert Cummings, ed. *Ultimate Realities: A Volume in the Comparative Religious Ideas Project.* Albany, NY: State University of New York Press, 2001. This collection of essays explores notions of the ultimate in Chinese religion, Buddhism, Hinduism, Judaism, and Christianity, with essays on the difficulties of using the comparative method.

Niebuhr, H. Richard. *Radical Monotheism and Western Culture.* New York: Harper, 1960. This is a classic and widely influential study.

O'Flaherty, Wendy Doniger. *Hindu Myths*. Baltimore: Penguin Books, 1975. O'Flaherty presents a collection of classic stories about Hindu gods and goddesses.

Owen, H. P. *Concepts of Deity*. London: Macmillan, 1971. This is a study of Western theistic notions of the divine, such as monotheism and pantheism.

## INTERNET RESOURCES

www.cix.co.uk/~ganesh/ganesha.htm    This site provides a good image of Ganesha with quotations from the *Mudgala Purana* on the philosophical significance of Ganesha's form and a collection of stories about his origin. There are links to many other sites.

www.chinapage.com/laotze.html    This site provides a complete text of the *Daodejing* in both English and Chinese.

www.utm.edu/research/iep/a/anselm.htm    The material you will find here is from the *Internet Encyclopedia of Philosophy*. It provides background on Anselm's life and times, along with a clear summary of his ontological argument.

# CHAPTER 5

# Sacred Story

THE ENGLISH WORD *myth* comes from the Greek word *mythos*, which means "story." In common usage the word has come to mean a false story. In the scholarly study of religions, **myth** has a technical meaning. It refers to a particular type of story, a story some people regard as sacred (that is, an extraordinary narrative radically different from profane stories). If a story is thought to be sacred, its truth is beyond question for those who so regard it. Believers in sacred stories may argue whether their stories are literally or symbolically true, but true they must be for the believer, because such stories reveal something of great importance about the meaning of human life and about the universe in which we live and die.

Although myths are sacred stories taken to be true in some sense by believers, other people's sacred stories—other people's myths—are often thought to be false. The myths by which we live seem so obviously true, that we are shocked when others question them; yet the falsity of the myths of others seems obvious to us.

In this chapter, we shall explore some sacred stories and some scholarly theories about them. After examining two case studies, we will review some of the many different types of myths and some of the many ways myths function to provide meaning for humans. A discussion of different scholarly theories about how we should best understand myths will lead directly to an examination of the relationship between myth and science. A research case brings our study to a close by focusing attention on the primal, or first, man from whom, some have claimed, this whole, vast universe is derived.

## 5.1 TWO CASE STUDIES

### 5.1.1 *Enuma elish*

Our first case comes from the ancient religion of Babylon (located in what is now Iraq). Babylonian religion did not survive the fortunes of history, but it did have significant influence on religions that have survived. Echoes of its creation myth can be heard in the scriptures of Judaism, Christianity, and Islam. Its tale of a primal combat between the forces of order (good) and the forces of disorder (evil) is a cultural universal.

*Enuma elish* ("ay-noo'mah ay'leesh"), "When on high," are the opening words of a very old myth honoring Marduk, the chief God of Babylon. The myth takes its title from these words, and a written copy was discovered in the ruins of King Ashurbanipal's (668–626 B.C.E.) library at Nineveh. It was probably composed in the reign of Nebuchadrezzar I (1125–1104 B.C.E.) but circulated much earlier in oral form. Some of the gods mentioned are Sumerian, who were predecessors of the Babylonians in the Mesopotamian region of the Tigris and Euphrates rivers.

The *Enuma elish* is a poem of more than a thousand lines, divided into seven parts. In the introduction (Part 1), the gods emerge from chaotic waters, and tension mounts between old and young gods. The scene opens:

> When [on high] there was no heaven,
> no earth, no height, no depth, no name,
> when Abzu was alone,
> the sweet water, the first begetter; and Tiamat
> the bitter water, . . .

> When sweet and bitter
> mingled together, no reed was plaited, no rushes
> muddied the water,
> the gods were nameless, natureless, futureless, then
> from Abzu and Tiamat
> in the waters gods were created, . . .[1]

The poem continues by recounting how "discord broke out among the gods although they were brothers." Mummu, the primordial mist and the "dark counselor," advises Abzu to kill his offspring. And, although Tiamat, the "Old Hag, the first mother," suggests they wait until the gods have grown up some, Abzu will not be detoured. In the ensuing conflict, Ea, the god of wisdom, kills Abzu along with his hopes to subdue the unruly divine children.

Victorious Ea, god of wisdom and son of Anu, "the empty heaven," fathers Marduk whose "body was beautiful; when he raised his eyes great lights flared; his stride was majestic; he was the leader from the first." We are told Marduk is the tallest and strongest god, and lightning played around him crying, "My son, my son, son of the sun, and heaven's sun."

Tiamat, seeking revenge for her husband's death, "mothers a new brood." This time the brood is composed of monsters, not gods, and led by the demon Kingu. Four times in the course of the poem we are told (as if the author is seeking to justify the fate that awaits Tiamat):

She made the Worm
the Dragon
the Female Monster
the Great Lion
the Mad Dog
the Man Scorpion
the Howling Storm . . .

This "new brood" plots, growls, roars, and ruts, getting ready to be led by Kingu against Ea, his son Marduk, and the rest of the gods. The clouds of battle loom.

The second and third parts of the poem recount the story of Marduk's testing by the other gods, his receiving magical aids, and his final selection to champion the cause of the younger gods against the dreadful "new brood" of monsters and demons. He demands, if he wins, to be "set over the rest" and allowed to "decide the world's nature."

The long-awaited battle unfolds in Part 4 as Marduk mounts the storm, "his terrible chariot" drawn by Killer, Pitiless, Trampler, and Haste, who know the arts of "plunder" and have "skills of murder." Marduk is armed with powerful weapons and a magic word "clenched between his lips." He confronts Tiamat and shouts, "Mother of all, why did you have to mother war?" Tiamat, the bitter waters of chaos, is killed by Marduk and slit in two. The upper part of her body becomes the vault of the sky and lower part becomes the earth.

Part 5 tells how Marduk sets about creating cosmos (cosmos is the Greek word for "order") out of chaos using parts of Tiamat's body. Tiamat's eyes give rise to the mighty Euphrates and Tigris rivers on which Babylonian civilization depends. Marduk builds Babylon and its temples as his city and a home for all the gods. We are told, in Part 6, how Marduk creates humans from the blood of the demon captain Kingu for the purpose of serving the gods. These human servants of the gods are told they "must remember" whose creatures they are and sing the "Hymn of the Fifty Names of Marduk." The hymn continues in Part 7, lauding Marduk as "King of Kings, and Lord of Lords, Almighty God, Deliverer, and King of the Cosmos." An epilogue enjoins us mortal servants of the gods to remember the names of Marduk and to celebrate his defeat of Tiamat.

This story, sacred to the Babylonians, is a radical revision of traditional Mesopotamian belief. Prior to the rise of Marduk, the pantheon of Mesopotamian gods had a different leadership. As Babylon grew in power and influence, its city-god Marduk, once a minor deity, takes over leadership of the traditional pantheon. The myth dramatizes and celebrates the political history of Mesopotamia as it moves from warring communities, to city-states, and finally to empire. If, among gods, order emerges out of chaos by means of conflict, battle, and war, so too must order emerge out of chaos among mortals. This myth validates the history of the rise of Babylon by giving it a cosmic foundation. As the *Enuma elish* says, there is to be "a likeness on earth of what he [Marduk] did in heaven."

Some scholars have argued that the myth contains a dim memory of the overthrow of matriarchal rule by males, thus establishing patriarchy. Tiamat is a goddess, and the "Mother of All." Marduk is a male warrior-god who slays her. While we should be cautious about inferring historical events and social arrangements from mythic narratives, it is important to note the gender roles and relationships in this or any myth.

## 5.1.2 Moses

The second case comes from Judaism (although it can also be found in Christian and Islamic scriptures). Judaism today numbers over 15 million adherents, and its contemporary major organizational forms include Reform, Conservative, Orthodox, Hasidic, and Reconstructionist. The influence of Judaism on human culture, with its contributions to art, music, science, and literature, are beyond measure.

One of the great heroes of the Jewish **Torah** (the first five books of the Hebrew Bible) is Moses (in Hebrew, *Mosheh*, in Arabic, *Musa*), who led Israel out of Egypt and transmitted divine commandments. He is celebrated as a great prophet in a Jewish hymn called "Yigdal" and in the Quran, the holy scripture of Islam. The Jewish rabbinic tradition claims that "Moses, our rabbi" (*rabbi* means "teacher") not only handed down the written Torah, but also an oral Torah that became the basis for later rabbinic commentaries. Even Disney has celebrated his life and exploits in a full-length, popular cartoon movie.

Moses is an Egyptian name, perhaps from the root "to be born," and the biblical text links him closely to Egypt by indicating he was adopted by a daughter of the Pharaoh. The story of Moses that we find in the Torah is a composite picture. Some scholars think there may have been as many as four "Moses" figures, each associated with one of four major themes: (1) exodus from Egypt, (2) revelation at Mt. Sinai, (3) wilderness wandering, and (4) entrance into the Promised Land. Editors of the Torah used the "Moses" character we find in the text as the central figure holding these originally separate themes together. I will concentrate on the composite Moses as we find him after the editors have done their work. However, a more complete scholarly study would have to try to identify the component parts and their sources.

Some scholars argue that the story, or at least parts of it, has a firm historical base and can be dated from about 1350–1200 B.C.E. Other scholars dispute the historicity of much of the story, pointing out that Egyptian records make no reference to Moses, the Israelite slaves, or the exodus events. Whatever its historical base, there is little doubt that the story of Moses has become sacred to Jews, Christians, and Muslims alike. And, like the *Enuma elish*, it is a foundation story linking the identity and development of a unified people—a nation—with divine activity.

The Moses story opens in Egypt where the Hebrews are enslaved. We are told a woman from the priestly tribe of Levi bore a son, a "goodly child," and hid him because the Pharaoh had decreed that "every son born to the Hebrews you shall cast into the Nile" (Exodus 1:22). When she could no longer hide her son, she made a bulrush boat, put him in it, and cast him adrift. A daughter of Pharaoh found the boat and "took pity" on the Hebrew baby, eventually naming him Moses and raising him at the Egyptian court.

One day, when he is an adult, Moses witnesses an Egyptian beating a Hebrew slave. He kills the Egyptian and then flees to the land of Midian because Pharaoh seeks to kill him. By a well in Midian, Moses defends the daughters of Jethro, "the priest of Midian," from shepherds and eventually marries one of the daughters, named Zipporah. One day, while tending sheep, he sees a burning bush that is not consumed by the fire. Drawing close to the burning bush, he hears his name called and is told, "Do not come near: put off your shoes from your feet, for the place on which you are standing is holy ground" (Exodus 3:6). He does as instructed, and the voice from the burning bush continues by identifying itself as the Elohim (Hebrew for "gods," although usually translated "God") of Moses' ancestors. The Elohim tells Moses that he has seen the affliction of "my people," and commands Moses to return to Egypt and lead his people out of Egypt to a "land flowing with milk and honey, the land of the Canaanites" (present-day Israel and Palestine).

Moses does not want to go back to Egypt, so Elohim promises him a sign. Then Moses asks what he should say if the people ask the name of the Elohim that sent him. The voice in the burning bush replies, "I AM WHO I AM (**YHWH**) . . . say this to the people of Israel, I AM has sent me to you" (Exodus 3:14). YHWH was probably pronounced "Yahweh" (not "Jehovah," as some translations have it), but the name is considered so sacred that Jews do not say it. Instead, they say "Adonai" (Lord) whenever they encounter YHWH in the text.

Moses is still reluctant, complaining he cannot speak very well; so the Elohim named YHWH gives him several dramatic signs and a magic rod. Moses finally returns, and his natural brother Aaron meets him and speaks to the Israelite slaves on Moses' behalf, convincing them to follow Moses. However, the Pharaoh will not let the people go because YHWH has "hardened his heart." So YHWH sends a series of plagues—frogs, gnats, flies, boils, hail, locusts, darkness—culminating in YHWH's promise to kill all the "firstborn" of Egypt. However, his "angel of death" will pass over houses of the Hebrew slaves on whose doors the blood of a sacrificial lamb has been smeared. The people are instructed to "observe this rite forever."

After the horrible death of all the firstborn of the Egyptians, the Hebrew slaves were set free and driven out. They left in such haste that the dough did not have time to rise, so they had to eat unleavened cakes. As he had done so many times in the past, Pharaoh changed his mind, pursued the escaped slaves, and Moses had to use his magic rod to part the sea, allowing the Hebrews to pass safely. When the Egyptian army pursued them into the dry seabed, the waters came rolling back, destroying "the chariots and the horsemen and all the host of Pharaoh that had followed them into the sea" (Exodus 14:28).

The liberated Hebrews wander in the Sinai dessert, led by Moses and Aaron. They are fed and protected by YHWH. They camp at Mt. Sinai where Moses first encountered the burning bush. YHWH instructs Moses to climb to the top of the mountain (see Chapter 7 for more on sacred mountains), and the Lord descends with "thunders and lightning, and a thick cloud upon the mountain." A "very loud trumpet blast" is heard, and the people "trembled." On the mountaintop, YHWH gives Moses the Ten Commandments or Decalogue (Exodus 20:1–17). These include the commands to have no other gods before YHWH, not to make idols or "any likeness of anything that is in heaven above, or that is in the earth beneath, or that is in the water under the earth," not to take YHWH's name in vain, to remember the sabbath day "to keep it holy," and to honor one's parents. The commands continue (20:13–17):

> You shall not kill.
> You shall not commit adultery.
> You shall not steal.
> You shall not bear false witness against your neighbor.
> You shall not covet your neighbor's house; you shall not covet your neighbor's wife, or his manservant, or his maidservant, or his ox, or his ass, or anything that is your neighbor's.

The people want Aaron to make a golden calf to worship while Moses is gone on the mountaintop, and Moses, when he sees it, breaks, in his wrath, the tablets of stone on which the laws were written. Once the people have been chastised for worshiping idols, YHWH in his mercy makes another set of stone tablets on which YHWH rewrites the law.[2]

The Hebrews continue to wander in the Sinai desert, and finally YHWH permits them to enter the promised land of Canaan. But Moses is not allowed to enter that land "flowing with milk and honey." He dies after seeing it at the age of 120 years, and we are told "when he died; his eye was not dim, nor his natural force abated."

I think you can see in this sacred story that Moses is portrayed as both a "culture hero," who brings great cultural benefits to the Hebrews, and a "spiritual hero," who establishes the foundations of Israel's faith. I think you can also see some of the themes typical of hero tales: the remarkable birth of the hero, a situation that needs correcting, the hero told to go somewhere where he or she receives a commission and magical aid, conflict with an adversary, and a final victory.

There is a rich variety of details in the Moses story, but we will confine our discussion to the big events. They are the liberation from slavery, the revelation of the divine name, and the giving of the law. These three events leave an indelible mark on the Jewish faith. To a large extent they define the heart of Judaism—a religion that celebrates freedom from bondage, the revelation of the true divine but mysterious name of the one and only God, and the law by which people ought to order their lives.

The story of Moses inspired further mythologizing on the part of the Jews. In Jewish folklore, the Mt. Sinai episode gets magnified. We are told that God "bent the heavens, moved the earth, and shook the bounds of the world, so that the depths trembled, and the heavens grew frightened."[3] Even the kings of the whole earth trembled, and neither they nor the earth itself calmed down until they heard the first words of the Decalogue. In an interesting twist, this folk elaboration goes on to indicate that Mt. Sinai rose into the heavens, touched the "feet of the Divine Throne," and there appeared "twenty-two thousand angels with crowns for the Levites, the only tribe that remained true to God while the rest worshiped the Golden Calf." The Levites are the tribe from which the Jewish priests come, and Moses' mother is said to be a Levite. Aaron becomes the first priest. Who do you think might benefit from such a tale?

## 5.2 COMPARISON

On the surface, these two myths seem very different. One is a story about the creation of the world out of the body of the first mother, Tiamat. The other is a story about the adventures and deeds of a culture hero. While it is true that the *Enuma elish* is often treated as a creation myth, the central character in that story is also a hero, Marduk, and it can be persuasively argued that the story is more about the hero Marduk than it is about creation. The typical themes of hero myths noted in the case of Moses can also be found in the Marduk story: a remarkable birth, a situation that needs correcting, the hero told to go somewhere where he receives a commission and magical aid, conflict with an adversary, and a final victory.

Marduk is a god. Moses is a human being. This is a major difference between the two myths. Further, the *Enuma elish* contains an account of creation that the Moses story does not. Nevertheless, both stories are about beginnings. Marduk is responsible for the beginnings of cosmic order, human beings, and Babylon, including its buildings, laws, rites, religion, and political structure. Moses is responsible for the beginnings of the Hebrew nation and its laws.

However, the ways in which the two heroes are responsible differ. Marduk, once he is commissioned by the council of gods, proceeds to manifest his own power in bringing about these important events. Moses, while commissioned by YHWH to lead the Hebrews out of Egypt and through the Sinai wilderness, often manifests weakness and reluctance to follow his calling. We get the overwhelming impression that YHWH remains in control of events throughout. He is the real leader and real author of the law code given at Sinai. Moses, unlike Marduk, is a transmitter, a go-between, and a servant of a higher power. Marduk, once given authority to act by the other gods, is his "own man."

It might be more appropriate to compare Marduk to YHWH than to Moses. Both are divine beings, both engage in conflicts, both form a nation, and both give laws. Although the story of YHWH creating the universe and humans (by very different means than Marduk) is not mentioned in the Moses story, it forms the backdrop to the story. YHWH, like Marduk, is a creator-god. Marduk appears to be more a warrior-god of the storm than YHWH, yet there are hints in the Torah that YHWH is also a warrior- and storm-god, originally perhaps, a local deity of the Midianites associated primarily with Mt. Sinai. Marduk's temple in Babylon was constructed like a mountain and is referred to in Genesis as the Tower of Babel. The story of Moses is, like the story of Marduk, a story of a local deity assuming a more universal role and extending his influence from Sinai to Egypt and, eventually, to the land of Canaan and well beyond.

In both stories humans are viewed as servants of the divine. In the *Enuma elish* they are explicitly created to fulfill that role. In the Moses story it is clear that the Hebrews are expected to become YHWH's servants out of gratitude for what he has done for them—delivered them from slavery, given them the law, and promised them a land in which to live. Here we see one of the oldest laws of human relationships: a gift requires a gift in return.

Humans, in the Genesis story, are created out of the dust of the ground and in the "image of God." In the Babylonian account they are created out of the blood of a demon. They do have a superhuman origin, but it is not a flattering family tree. These are very different conceptions of human origin, even if they agree that humans are created to serve the divine.

It is clear that the Hebrews are not very good at serving YHWH. They start running after other gods like the golden calf. Fidelity is not their strong suit, even though they are not demon bred. Both stories are strongly henotheistic. There may be many gods, but service ought to be focused on one; Marduk in the case of the Babylonians and YHWH in the case of the Hebrews. Just as ancient law codes commanded people to be loyal to their own king and not the king of others, so too they demanded loyalty to their own god and not the god of others.

Conflict and death play a significant role in both stories. Marduk's main conflict is with Tiamat and her "new brood" of monsters and demons. Moses' conflict is first with the Egyptian who beats a slave, then with Pharaoh, and later, when the Hebrews turn to the worship of the golden calf, with the Hebrews themselves. Out of the death of Tiamat comes life. Out of the death of the firstborn of Egypt and the Passover lamb comes life for the Hebrews. A nearly universal teaching of all religions, which we will encounter again and again, is illustrated by this motif: out of death comes life. Death, seen in a religious context, is a sacrificial act. Something old is sacrificed so something new can begin.

When Marduk realizes that he must create humans as servants for the gods, implicit in the text is the assumption that something must die. This becomes clear when Ea, his father and god of wisdom, advises Marduk: "Let one of the kindred be taken; only one need die for the new creation. Bring the gods together in the Great Assembly, there let the guilty die, so the rest may live." In the Moses story it is clear that the killing of the Passover lamb is a sacrificial act. "It is the sacrifice of the Lord's passover, for he passed over the houses of the people of Israel in Egypt, when he slew the Egyptians but spared our houses. And the people bowed their heads and worshiped" (Exodus 12:27).

## 5.3 TYPES AND FUNCTIONS

Recall from Chapter 2 that typologies are systems of classification. They organize different things into groups, classes, or types based on some feature or function they have in common. There are numerous typologies of myths because stories have so many different features. Also the line between myths, legends, and folklore is not always clear. Myths can be grouped in many of different ways. Here is one typology:

1. **Cosmogonic** and **cosmological** myths about the origin and order of the universe.
2. Myths of lesser beginnings, often called **etiological** because they explain why some rite, law, custom, feature of the landscape, and so on, came to be.
3. **Eschatological myths** about the end of the world.
4. Myths of lesser endings, such as the fall of a city or empire.
5. Myths about death and the life after death.
6. Myths about divine, semidivine, and demonic beings.
7. Myths about heroes and saviors.
8. Myths about transformations and incarnations, such as movement from animal to human, human to animal, human to divine, and divine to human.

9. Myths about kings, wise men and women, ascetics, martyrs, and saints. (Some might classify such stories as legends rather than myths.)

I think it is clear that this typology is organized according to subject matter. One limitation of this sort of typology is that there always seems to be something left out. You might already be thinking of stories you would call myths that do not fit any of these types. All typologies seem to require the category "other."

The fact that quite often stories do not fit neatly into one type or another reveals another limitation. For example, should the *Enuma elish* be classified as a cosmogonic/cosmological myth (1), or as a myth about the gods (6), or as a hero myth (7)? It appears to fit all three types.

A third limitation relates to the level of generalization. Each of the types mentioned above could be broken down into subtypes. For example, there are many different types of myths about the beginnings of the universe (1). Some of these talk about the emergence from a primal substance or being, such as the Egyptian story found in the Pyramid Texts (*c.* 2400 B.C.E.) in which Re-Atum, the creator-god, emerges from a watery abyss (Nun) and begins to order the universe. There are also stories of a sexual union between a primal male and female, such as the Japanese myth about feminine and masculine primordial principles forming a great cosmic egg (see Chapter 12, Section 12.10). Creation by a divine craftsman (Demiurge) is also a popular subtype (see Plato's *Timaeus*), as are stories like the *Enuma elish* in which creation takes place by conflict and the ordering of a primal chaos. A subtype that is probably most familiar to you is creation by decree. According to Genesis, YHWH (in some versions, Elohim) creates and orders the universe by speech or his divine word. Creation is achieved by divine command much like a king bringing something about by royal decree.

## Types of Myth

1. Cosmogonic and cosmological
2. Etiological
3. Eschatological
4. Lesser endings
5. Death and the afterlife
6. Divine, semidivine, and demonic beings
7. Heroes and saviors
8. Transformations and incarnations
9. Kings, wise people, ascetics, martyrs, and saints

How do myths function? What do they do for people? Before looking at some specific functions, we need to distinguish between manifest and latent functions. **Manifest functions** are consciously intended and obvious, for example, to tell a story about something or someone. **Latent functions** are hidden and most likely unintended. For example, a myth may function to reinforce the power of a priestly elite. An important clue to the meaning of a myth can often be found by asking and answering the question, what are the main functions (manifest and latent) of this myth? Asking who benefits from this tale can often reveal latent functions.

It is appropriate to begin with some religious functions before discussing social, psychological, and expressive functions. Four important religious functions are (1) **hierophanic** (to reveal something holy or sacred); (2) **numinous** (to elicit and reinforce a sense of awe and finitude with respect to the divine); (3) ritualistic (to give a narrative explaining and justifying ritual actions); and (4) cosmological (to render a picture of the order of the universe). If you think again about the *Enuma elish* and the story of Moses, I think you can readily see how these two myths function religiously in all of these ways. The ritualistic function may not be obvious to you now, but in the next chapter we shall examine two rituals, the Akitu festival and Passover, that are closely linked to these stories.

Three important social functions also stand out in the two myths examined here: (1) integration of individuals into a group (that is, establishing a group identity and social solidarity), (2) supporting and reinforcing a current social order, and (3) criticism of a current social order by presenting a new one or recommending an old one. I think it is rather obvious how the Moses story establishes the identity of a people (1). The Jews are reminded by this story that they are those people freed from slavery, given a divine law, and expected to serve God. Marduk creates the city of Babylon, builds its temples, sets up its laws, and establishes its religious and political life. The Babylonian empire is given divine sanction by this story (2). However, these are not just conservative tales. They are also revolutionary. Marduk overthrows a previous organization of the gods and goddesses and the social organization that accompanied it. Moses and the Hebrews challenge the established social order of Egypt and its gods. To establish a new order requires the destruction of an old order.

Myths fulfill numerous psychological functions, but I will describe two: (1) the establishment of ego identity and (2), on the deep psychological level, the establishment of a self. If we call our sense of personal and individual identity the ego (I), then both the *Enuma elish* and the Moses story invite us to think of ourselves as servants of the divine. If, in addition to our ego identity, we suppose that we are, as we live, creating a wider, more inclusive identity called the self, then *Enuma elish* invites us to create peaceful order out of the chaos and conflicts of our lives. The Moses story urges us to reject all forms of bondage in the name of freedom and self-determination in obedience to a divine law.

Most if not all myths that have survived in writing from the past were originally passed on orally from one generation to another before being written down. Sometimes certain people or clans were responsible for a set of stories. They were the official storytellers. Oral storytelling is a dramatic and often entertaining event. The goal of the telling is in the telling. This is the expressive function of myth. It is fun to tell and hear stories. The very expression of them is fascinating and satisfying.

Some scholars have argued that stories told for the sake of entertainment should not be classified as myths because they lack the serious intent of myth. Even if myths have more serious intent than entertainment, I think we cannot ignore the expressive function. Myths are often good stories, and we all enjoy a good story.

How do myths accomplish these various functions? The answer is complex, but three ways stand out. Myths are *paradigmatic* stories: They provide models for all significant human behavior. They tell us how to live and how to die. They are also *justificatory*, providing a rationale for some ritual, law, social class, or war. And they are *mitigative*, harmonizing oppositions within individuals and groups. Providing paradigms, justifications, and mitigation allows myths to perform their religious, social, psychological, and expressive functions.

The paradigmatic and justificatory practices are important for establishing an **ideology**. An ideology is a set of doctrines or beliefs that form the basis of a political, economic, or religious system. Religious ideologies are particularly powerful because they convince people that the gods create a particular social order when in fact humans create such order.

---

### Functions of Myth

| The primary functions of myth are | Myths accomplish these functions by |
|---|---|
| 1. Religious | 1. Providing paradigms |
| 2. Social | 2. Providing justifications |
| 3. Psychological | 3. Providing ways to overcome conflict |
| 4. Expressive | |

---

## 5.4 THEORIES OF MYTH

The purpose of theory is to provide a general framework that aids in interpreting and explaining. There are a variety of theories available to the student of mythology. I will discuss five such theories here. A sixth theory, called the myth and ritual theory, will be discussed in the next chapter after we have had an opportunity to examine religious rituals.

The first type of theory is sometimes called the **rationalistic theory** and sometimes the intellectualist theory. Its basic premise is that myths are attempts to explain things. Myths are similar to scientific theories that explain, for example, the origin of human life or the cosmos. The difference is that myths are false explanations.

According to this theory, the purpose of the *Enuma elish* is to explain the origin and structure of the universe, human life, and the Babylonian empire. Likewise the purpose of the Moses story is to explain how the Jews escaped from slavery and received the law of YHWH. However, these explanations are false from both a historical and scientific view. History and science offer different explanations that, if not completely true (scientific and historical explanations are constantly being revised and updated based on new evidence), are closer to the truth than myths.

This theory makes it difficult to explain why people, indeed whole societies, often persist in believing what is false. Many Jews (not to mention Christians and Muslims) believe that the Moses story is true, and many believe the account of creation given in Genesis is true. There are no Babylonians left, but if there were, they too might persist in their beliefs about Marduk and the origin of Babylon. Presumably, evolution would weed out false beliefs because they don't work and are not conducive to survival. We have discarded the belief that the world is flat or the earth is the center of the universe. So why have we not discarded myths that, based on present-day scientific and historical evidence, we know are literally false?

**Functionalist theories** of myth are common in the social scientific study of religion (anthropology, sociology, and psychology). According to this type of theory, the meaning of myth is to be found in what a myth does—that is, in its functions. Myths function to satisfy the needs of societies and individuals, such as the need for meaning, identity, and social solidarity. These functions explain why belief in myths persists, even though the stories are literally false. Although there is little agreement on exactly what the basic needs are that myths satisfy, they are often identified as biological (indirectly contributing to survival), psychological (providing meaning and purpose), sociological (creating a sense of belonging), or some combination of these three kinds of needs.

Critics have pointed out several problems with functionalist theories. They question whether the meaning of a myth is totally exhausted by its functions, and whether it is even correct to identify meaning with use or function. Also, as pointed out above, there is lack of agreement about what precisely are the needs that myths supposedly satisfy.

**Symbolic theories** of myth are often closely tied to functional theories and stand opposed to rationalistic theories. Myths, according to symbolic theories, do not explain anything. Rather, they contain symbolic representations; what they contain symbolic representations of, depends on the symbolist. Here is a partial list of the sorts of things different symbolists say that myths represent: repressed material from the individual unconscious, universal archetypes or patterns from the collective unconscious, social organization and structure, transcendent sacred realities. For example, if I think that there are universal archetypes that exist in an unconscious, then one of these might be the Hero archetype. In that case, both Moses and Marduk would be different expressions of a psychological reality buried deep in humanity's shared unconscious. (See the discussion of Carl Jung in Chapter 8.) This would explain why certain stories are universal and why some stories seem ageless—told and retold with countless permutations, from Marduk to Superman.

The basic assumption of symbolic theories is that myths have hidden meanings that must be decoded. The task of the student of mythology is to disclose this hidden meaning. So, for example, the escape of the Jews from Egypt symbolizes the desire to be free that is found in all of us.

This theory does not explain why people continue speaking in a coded language, that is, continue to tell symbolic sacred stories or myths. Add to this the fact that the people who speak this coded language are unaware of the real, hidden meaning of the myths they tell; indeed, many of these believers think the language they speak is literally true. Presumably only the scholar of mythology is in a position to know what myth-tellers and believers are "really" talking about. They are not really talking about the commandments given by YHWH when they tell the story of Moses at Mt. Sinai. They are instead talking about the deep-seated human need to think that the laws humans create are more than conventional, that they are somehow rooted in the eternal or the way things were meant to be. Some argue that symbolic theories are the expression of scholarly arrogance and superiority.

Phenomenological theory claims myths are manifestations of the sacred and opposes all reductionistic interpretations such as the rationalistic and functional approaches discussed above. Myths must be interpreted by careful and nearly exhaustive comparative methods. According to phenomenologists, myths will interpret themselves once you have enough examples to reveal a common pattern. For example, Mircea Eliade (1907–1986) claims that after you study enough myths comparatively you will discover that

> Myth narrates a sacred history; it relates an event that took place in primordial Time, the fabled time of the 'beginnings." In other words, myth tells how, through the deeds of Supernatural Beings, a reality came into existence, be it the whole of reality, the Cosmos, or only a fragment of reality—an island, a species of plant, a particular kind of human behavior, an institution. Myth, then, is always an account of a "creation"; it relates how something was produced, began to be . . . Because myth relates the [deed] of Supernatural Beings and the

manifestations of their sacred powers, it becomes the exemplary model for all significant human activities.[4]

Eliade's view of myth is insightful and clearly applies to the *Enuma elish* and the Moses story, but it does not apply to all myths. Not all myths are about creations, large or small. Another problem with the phenomenological theory has to do with the claim that myths are manifestations of the sacred and provide exemplary models. While this may be true, does it reveal anything of great value about myths? Does it help us discover the meaning of myth, or just restate the obvious in scholarly language?

The final theory we will examine here is the **structuralist theory.** According to this theory, myths are cognitive structures by which people think. Just as language has a syntax that allows people to form meaningful sentences, so myths have a basic logical structure that allows people to organize their experiences and their world into a meaningful whole. This logical structure is most often described as a system of relations that form binary oppositions like "off/on" or "up/down." Sometimes this system is simply a way of classifying things and ordering experience. Other times the oppositions are mitigated or reconciled, thereby relaxing social tensions in the group. For example, the primary binary opposition in the *Enuma elish* is between chaos and cosmos, disorder and order. Babylonian society depended upon the waters of the Tigris and Euphrates rivers. Each year they would flood, causing widespread damage and destruction. Yet the crops depended on the water. One of the first things Marduk does in establishing Babylonian society is to build a system of canals that control this yearly flooding. Thus the order he established did, in a very real sense, overcome the chaotic waters unleashed in floods.

I think you can easily see that one of the difficulties with this theory is very much like the difficulties of the symbolic theory. Myths have hidden structures, a logical base akin to the syntax of grammar that only the scholar can uncover. The speakers of the mythic language remain, for the most part, ignorant of this hidden structure. However, is this a powerful objection? After all, most of us learn how to speak a language before we learn the grammatical rules that govern our speech. Just because we don't know the rules or cannot detect them without some education does not mean they don't exist.

A more serious problem has to do with what appears to be a confusion of syntax (the structural grammar of a language) with semantics (the meaning of a language). Syntax is one of the bases of meaning, but it is not equivalent to meaning. For example, we can form syntactically correct sentences that are meaningless, such as "Sleeping erasers find timely green." It would appear that discovering the structure or syntax of myths is not equivalent to discovering the meaning of myths. What is needed is a "semantics of myth" in addition to a "syntax of myth." Also needed is a more precise "pragmatics of myth" that explores the way myths are used by people.

> *Semiotics*, the study of signs, is divided into three parts:
>
> 1. *Pragmatics*—the study of the way people, animals, or machines use signs
> 2. *Semantics*—the study of the meaning of signs
> 3. *Syntax*—the study of the relations among signs

In spite of the problems, each of these theories of myth (rationalistic, functional, symbolic, phenomenological, and structural) provides different, yet important, insights into the function (pragmatics), meaning (semantics), and structure (syntax) of myth. Indeed, many scholars of myth are eclectic, drawing on elements in different theories when they find them useful to illuminate the myths with which they are dealing. These theories form part of the toolbox of the student of religions.

> ## Theories of Myth
>
> 1. Rationalistic
> 2. Functional
> 3. Symbolic
> 4. Phenomenological
> 5. Structural

## 5.5 MYTH AND SCIENCE

According to the Bible, the Israelites, under the leadership of Moses, spent forty years in the Sinai wilderness. Finally, under the leadership of Joshua, they began the conquest of Canaan, the Promised Land, with the aid of YHWH. The Book of Joshua tells us of the bloody sacking of Jericho after YHWH made its walls fall down. The Canaanite city of Ai fell next. According to the Book of Joshua, YHWH threw the Canaanites into a panic as the Israelite army advanced. Indeed, he even "threw down great stones from heaven . . . and they died." (Joshua 10:11). Not only did YHWH personally kill with the hailstones more men than Israel "killed with the sword," he also made the sun stand still so Joshua and his army could continue the slaughter for almost a day.

> Sun, stand thou still at Gibeon,
> And thou Moon in the valley of Ai'jalon.
> And the sun stood still, and the moon stayed,

Until the nation took vengeance on
their enemies.
Is this not written in the Book of Jashar? The sun stayed in the midst of heaven,
and did not hasten to go down for about a whole day. (Joshua 10:13)

Obviously, the authors of the Book of Joshua believed that the sun moved around the earth. But we now know that it does not.

In 1543, the year Nicholas Copernicus (b. 1473) died, his book on astronomy was published. This book—dedicated to Pope Paul III—revolutionized astronomy because it showed that the earth revolves around the sun. The sun stands still and the earth moves. When Galileo Galilei (1564–1642) confirmed by observation Copernicus's conclusions, and published the results, the Roman Catholic Church vigorously opposed the heliocentric (sun-centered) view. Galileo was brought to trial by the Inquisition in 1633 and forced to deny his heliocentric views. Heliocentrism contradicted not only what was said about the sun in the Book of Joshua, but also the widely accepted geocentric (earth-centered) view inherited from Greek philosophy. It was not until the late twentieth century that the Roman Catholic Church officially apologized for its condemnation of Galileo. In the long run, the heliocentric view prevailed.

In the nineteenth century another conflict between the Christian religion and science broke out. Charles Darwin (1809–1882) published *The Origin of Species* in 1859, and biology has not been the same since. His theory of evolution along with his views on the origin of human beings met with vigorous opposition, and today some conservative Protestant Christians still wage a bitter battle, arguing that the Genesis account of God creating the universe in six days is literally true and contradicts the view that life evolved slowly over millions of years.

When the sacred myths of religion conflict with the established views of science, what should we think? None of us thinks that the world came to be as the *Enuma elish* says, and no one would oppose the Big Bang theory of the origin of the universe on the grounds that there was no Big Bang, but rather a Big Cut, severing in two the Mother of All. So why do some people persist in believing in a literal interpretation of the Genesis myth and use it to oppose evolution?

The answer is complex, but part of it is to be found in the rationalistic theory discussed earlier. If people take myths as explanations of the way things came to be and if those explanations contradict the conclusions of science, then only two choices seem possible: either cling to the truth of the myth and reject scientific accounts as "only theories" or accept the scientific account and reject the mythic explanations as false.

There are other alternatives, however. The symbolic theory (also discussed earlier) is attractive to many people because it allows them to take myths seriously (in a metaphorical sense, although not a literal sense) and to accept as literally true the conclusions of modern science. This is an old strategy. Averroes (Abu-al-Walid Muhammad Ibn Ahmad Ibn Rushd, b. 1126 in Cordova, Spain), an Islamic philosopher and theologian, argued that Islamic faith in the truth of the Quran was in harmony with the scientific and philosophical knowledge of his day. Although his position is somewhat complex, in essence he argued that when the Quran appears to contradict science, the Quran must be interpreted allegorically unless there are compelling reasons to take it literally. Similar arguments have been made by Christians and Jews with respect to the Bible, both before Averroes wrote and since.

This move from a literal to a symbolic or allegorical reading, however, seems to confirm that myths have hidden meanings that many believers do not grasp and only those properly trained in the art of symbolic interpretation can grasp. As Averroes says, "The double meaning [literal and allegorical] has been given to suit people's diverse intelligence. The apparent contradictions are meant to stimulate the learned to deeper study."[5] There is an elitist attitude in the presumption that only learned scholars are capable of understanding the symbolic or allegorical dimensions of myth.

This sort of objection to symbolic theories is, it seems to me, not fatal. Many believers not trained as scholars understand their myths allegorically. Guided evolution (the theory that God uses evolution as the means to create life in the universe) has long been popular with many Jews and Christians. Religions are constantly reinterpreting their sacred stories. If they did not, history would leave them so isolated in the past that they would eventually die. If we studied the history of Jewish, Christian, and Islamic interpretations of the Bible, we would be amazed at the variety and richness among the various readings. One aspect of this variety and richness stems from the many possible ways people have thought about the relationship between religion and science in general. Michael Ruse, who wrote the introduction to Bertrand Russell's *Science and Religion* (1997), thinks there are at least four distinct ways.[6]

The first relationship, and one that most people think of because it gets so much attention, is *uncompromising opposition.* A wall divides two worldviews: the worldview of science and the worldview of religion. From the science side of this wall, those who oppose science on religious grounds appear hopelessly ignorant, confused, and misguided. When a preacher rejects any science that contradicts what the Bible seems to say on the grounds that it is godless "secular humanism" and when a scientist rejects any literal interpretation of the Bible, there seems little room for compromise. For example, if someone argues that the world was created in six days because that is what Genesis says, and rejects all scientific evidence concerning the age and evolution of the universe, he or she draws clear battle lines between science and religion.

Second, some think that science and religion *exist separately.* Science deals with the "how" questions and religion with the "why" questions. Science shows us how things work on the physical level, but religion explains why things are the way they are on the spiritual level. Science, in this view, can never tell us why there is something rather than nothing, but religion can. Science can tell us what that something is and how it works, but it cannot tell us why it is there in the first place. Religion can tell us that the universe exists to fulfill some divine purpose. Science can tell us how the existing universe works. There is no conflict here, only separate tasks and different questions.

Third, some go beyond separatism and argue that science and religion can learn from one another. They exist, or at least ought to exist, *in dialogue.* Scientists and theologians should talk with one another in mutual respect, thereby entering into a conversation from which each can learn because each has something important to contribute from their different perspectives. From the dialogic point of view, uncompromising opposition will get us nowhere, and predetermined separatism creates artificial boundaries. Both science and religion are here to stay, so why not talk, share, and try to understand their different points of view? Perhaps we can rediscover what great theologians of the past knew, that there is a branch of theology, called "natural theology," which depends on human reason to discover important things about God and the world. If both theology and science are based on human reason, then religion and science need to remain in touch. Anselm (see Chapter 4), for one, would support this position.

The fourth position moves beyond dialogue and boldly asserts that science and religion are *integrated.* They are necessarily connected and mutually supporting. Pierre Teilhard de Chardin (1881–1955), a Jesuit priest and scientist, argued that the evolutionary change from simple life-forms to more complex forms such as humans mirrors the spiritual evolution of humans toward a more Christ-like and spiritual existence. Ghose Aurobindo (1872–1950), a leading Indian nationalist and spiritual leader, relied heavily on both the ideas of evolutionary biology and Hindu **mysticism** to craft a comprehensive philosophy that integrated science and religion. Much like de Chardin's notion that we are evolving both spiritually and physically toward becoming more Christ-like, Aurobindo argued that the whole universe was geared toward development in ways that would lead to what he called, "the life-divine."

## Relationships between Science and Religion

1. Opposition
2. Separation
3. Dialogue
4. Integration

The problem of the relationship between myth and science is part of a larger debate about the relationship of religion and science. It is an ongoing debate in scholarly circles. I have recounted a very brief part of the story, but I hope enough to stimulate you to further thought.

## 5.6 SUMMARY

We began by distinguishing between a popular use of the word *myth* (false story) and a technical use (sacred story). Perspective counts: the sacred stories of other people often seem obviously false (mere myths), while our own sacred stories seem obviously true. Two case studies, of the *Enuma elish* and the Moses story, are presented. These stories provide two examples of different sorts of heroes: the divine hero Marduk and the human hero Moses. The *Enuma elish* is also a creation myth, telling us how order (cosmos) is established by conflict with and ultimately the defeat of chaos (Tiamat, the Mother of All). A comparison showed that while there are many differences between these stories, both are about significant beginnings and the ordering of society. Both establish an ideal role for humans as servants of a higher and more powerful divine order. They link the earthly social order with the heavenly divine order, thereby legitimating the former.

A typology of different myths (according to subject matter) with some remarks on both the usefulness and inadequacies of typologies was presented next. Typologies are useful ways to organize vast amounts of material, but we should never forget that they are the creation of scholars and reflect their special interests and concerns.

After distinguishing between manifest and latent functions, we surveyed some of the primary functions of myth—religious, social, psychological, and expressive. Myths often accomplish these functions by providing a model for all significant human action, justifying a social order, and mitigating or reconciling oppositions within individuals or groups.

Our attention turned to different theories of myth (rationalistic, functional, symbolic, phenomenological) along with their advantages and disadvantages. We concluded that no single theory is completely adequate, and we might be well advised to use an eclectic, toolbox approach in which we draw on different theories as needed.

A look at the relationship between myth and science indicated various options. If we take science as the standard of truth and if we adopt a rationalistic approach, there seems no easy way to avoid the conclusion that either science or religion is true, but not both. A discussion of the symbolic approach showed one way out of this dilemma. If we read myths symbolically (as metaphors or allegories, for example), their nonliteral truth is preserved and the well-established conclusions of science can be accepted.

Thinking about the relationship of myth and science is closely tied to thinking about the relationship of religion and science in general. We surveyed four relationships (opposition, separation, dialogue, and integration), presenting the options available to both sides of the debate.

Peter Berger writes, "Religion is the human enterprise by which a sacred cosmos is established." There can be little doubt that myth plays a vital, even essential role in that enterprise.[7]

## 5.7 RESEARCH CASE—THE PRIMAL MAN

A number of Indo-European myths recount the story of creation in a similar pattern. There is a death, usually by violent means (sacrifice, murder, battle) and dismemberment of a primordial, or first, being. The physical and social universe is formed from the pieces of the victim's body.

An example of this story can be found in Rig-Veda 10.90, composed about 900 B.C.E. The Rig-Veda (a collection of poems and hymns from various time periods) constitutes some of the oldest scripture of Hinduism. In this "Hymn of Man," we hear about a cosmic giant called Purusha (person or human being) who is the first male and a victim of a Vedic sacrifice.

> When they divided the Man [Purusha], into how many parts did they apportion him? What do they call his mouth, his two arms and thighs and feet?
>
> His mouth became the Brahmin [priests]; his arms were made into the Warrior, his thighs the People, and from his feet the Servants were born.
>
> The moon was born from his mind; from his eye the sun was born. Indra [a warrior and storm god] and Agni [god of the sacrificial fire] came from his mouth, and from his vital breath the Wind was born.
>
> From his navel the middle realm of space arose; from his head the sky evolved. From his two feet came the earth and the quarters of the sky from his ear. Thus they [the gods] set the world in order. (RV 10.90, 11–14)[8]

Ancient Indian society was divided into four hierarchically ordered classes: the priestly class, the warrior class, the commoner class, and the servant class. The *Laws of Manu* (*Manu* means "the wise one" and is a mythological king described as the ancestor of the human race), another ancient Indian text, details the status, duties, and responsibilities of these classes. Here we are told that Purusha, "the radiant one," appointed teaching, study, sacrifice, generosity, and the acceptance of gifts for the priestly class. The warrior class is assigned the duties of protection of the people, generosity, the patronage of sacrifice, and study. Commerce and agriculture are the proscribed duties of the commoners, and "the Lord assigned only one activity to a servant: serving these (other) classes without resentment" (1:91).[9]

Although Manu is said to be a king and hence a member of the warrior class, *The Laws of Manu* portrays the priestly class as the superior class. Hence it seems safe to conclude that these laws were written by priests and for priests. They instructed priests on the details of law and morality, details that they should teach to all the people. It should also be noted that males who were concerned with controlling the conduct of females wrote them. Hence it is not surprising to find the rules for females to be much more restrictive than the rules for males. For example, Manu counsels that "Men must make their women dependent day and night. . . . A woman is not fit for independence." [10]

I have referred to these social groups as classes (*varnas*) rather than castes (*jatis*) because over time, hundreds, perhaps thousands, of distinct castes evolved. *Jatis* means "birth" and refers to the group into which someone is born. The four classes, or *varnas*, of priests, warriors, merchant-farmers, and servants were and are a convenient and more general way to group all the many different castes. So some castes are assigned to one class and some to another. Theoretically, all the castes, except the outcastes, could be reduced to one of these four classes.

It is important to know something about the social context in which stories like the "Hymn of Man" were created. The links between myths and societies must be understood in order to make sense of myths. Bruce Lincoln writes that Indo-European creation myths like the one about Purusha present

> More a picture of how things ought to be than how things were, describing the social order in the best light. But an ideology—any ideology—is not just an ideal against which social reality is measured. . . . It is also, and this is more important, a screen that strategically veils, mystifies, or distorts important aspects of real social processes. Like any other ideology, myth largely serves to create false consciousness in many members of society, persuading them of the rightness of their lot in life, whatever that may be, and of the total social order. [11]

## QUESTIONS ON THE CASE OF THE PRIMAL MAN

1. Draw a picture of the primal man and indicate which of his parts gives rise to which cosmological and social features. What does this visual image help you to see? What is the significance of the fact that he is a male? What is the significance of the fact that the servant class comes from his feet?
2. Discuss some possible functions of this myth. Be specific and cite evidence.
3. How do Bruce Lincoln's comments about myth and ideology apply to the Purusha myth?
4. Compare the Purusha myth to the *Enuma elish*. How are they the same and how different? Pay particular attention to gender issues and the roles males and females play in these myths.

## SUGGESTIONS FOR FURTHER READING

In addition to the material found in the notes, the reader may wish to consult the following for more information.

Campbell, Joseph. *The Hero with a Thousand Faces*. Reprint, Princeton: Princeton University Press, 1972. This is a popular but much criticized account of what Campbell takes to be the "monomyth" of the hero.

Dundes, Alan, ed. *Sacred Narrative: Readings in the Theory of Myth*. Berkeley: University of California Press, 1984. This collection of essays by leading scholars deals with the problems and issues associated with the interpretation of myth.

Eliade, Mircea. *Patterns in Comparative Religion*. Translated by Willard R. Trask. New York: New American Library, 1963. This volume contains a massive amount of interesting information by one of the greatest scholars of religion in the last century.

Freud, Sigmund. *Moses and Monotheism*. Edited by Katherine Jones. New York: Random House, 1987. This controversial psychoanalytic account of the Moses story is by the master analyst himself.

Griffin, David Ray. *Religion and Scientific Naturalism: Overcoming the Conflict*. Albany, NY: State University of New York Press, 2000. Griffin argues for the harmony of science and religion, criticizing traditional religion for a misguided concept of supernaturalism and traditional science for a misguided understanding of naturalism.

Kirsch, Jonathan. *Moses: A Life*. New York: Ballantine, 1998. The life of Moses is clearly retold and analyzed based on the Bible, Jewish commentary, and recent scholarship.

McCutcheon, Russell T. "Myth." In *Guide to the Study of Religion*, edited by Willi Braun and Russell T. McCutcheon, 190–207. London: Cassell, 2000. After a brief survey of different ways of interpreting myth, the author concludes that myths need to be demystified to be understood. There is also a helpful list of suggested readings.

Polkinghorne, John. *Belief in God in an Age of Science*. New Haven, CT: Yale University Press, 1998. Both a physicist and theologian, Polkinghorne presents in these Terry Lectures an "aesthetic argument" for God's existence in the tradition of natural theology.

Rosenberg, Donna. *World Mythology: An Anthology of the Great Myths and Epics*. 2nd ed. Lincolnwood, IL: NTC Publishing, 1994. Rosenberg provides a useful collection of myths from around the world.

## INTERNET RESOURCES

www.csun.edu~/hcf/11004/enuma.html   This site provides the full text of the *Enuma elish*.

www.encarta.msn.com/   Here you will find the *Encarta Reference Encyclopedia*. Try the *mythology* entry.

www.pantheon.org/   This site takes you to *The Encyclopedia Mythica*, a treasure chest full of myths, folklore, and legends.

# CHAPTER 6

# Sacred Action

Xunzi (HSÜN TZU, pronounced "Shyun'-dz"), a Confucian scholar of the third century B.C.E. wrote:

> The meaning of ritual is deep indeed
> He who tries to enter it with the kind of perception that
> distinguishes hard and white, same and different will
> drown there.
> The meaning of ritual is great indeed.
> He who tries to enter it with the uncouth and inane
> Theories of the system-makers will perish there.[1]

Xunzi warns us not to reduce ritual to simple categories and not to get caught up in theories about ritual, for fear we will lose sight of the ritual process itself. While heeding his advice, it is necessary on an introductory level to simplify somewhat and acknowledge that theories can be helpful as well as misleading. I shall take Xunzi's warning to apply not only to ritual studies but also to the study of religion in general. It is a warning that all our conclusions must be tentative. They are fallible and subject to correction.

This tentativeness is evident right at the beginning because scholars do not agree on how best to define ritual. Some favor a broad definition that would include secular activities (such as sports events) as well as sacred activities (such as worship). Others prefer a narrower definition, using ritual in the sense of a sacred action that usually involves some superhuman reference. The title of this chapter indicates that I will, for the most part, be using the word *ritual* to pick out actions regarded by some people as sacred. I do not intend to exclude a broader understanding and argue that we must always regard actions as sacred if they are to count as examples of rituals. My more narrow focus is purely pragmatic. It is more useful for my purposes.

Ritual, as I am using the term here, involves stylized, symbolic bodily gestures and actions (including verbal actions) usually repeated in specified ways on occasions of significance and in special contexts frequently involving what the participants take to be sacred presences.[2] As this chapter unfolds, we will examine several examples, look at some varieties and some functions of ritual, and explore the myth and ritual theory.

In many respects, the study of ritual is fundamental to understanding religion. Religion lives and breathes through ritual. People are socialized as children into religion by ritual (learning to pray, for example), and people's religious lives center to a great extent on activities in temples, shrines, churches, mosques, and synagogues. Most people learn their religion by doing it, and as long as they do it, they remain committed to it. The proverbial person on the street may know little of the doctrine, history, or theological controversies of their religion, but they know its rites, holy days, festivals, pilgrimage sites, and rituals.

## 6.1 TWO CASE STUDIES

### 6.1.1 Akitu Festival

The first case study is taken, once again, from the ancient religion of Babylon. (See the *Enuma elish* discussed in Chapter 5.) We will examine a scholarly reconstruction of the Babylonian New Year (Akitu) festival involving a ritual dramatization of the creation story and Marduk's victory over Tiamat.

The Babylonian Akitu festival occurred during the first twelve days of the month of Nisan (March–April). It is a seasonal ritual intended to secure both the continuance of the seasonal cycle (summer, fall, winter, spring) and well-being of the community. According to Theodore Gaster (1906–1992), seasonal rituals follow a fairly uniform pattern:

> First come rites of MORTIFICATION, symbolizing the state of suspended animation which ensues at the end of the year, when one lease on life has drawn to a close but the next is not yet assured.
>
> Second comes rites of PURGATION, whereby the community seeks to rid itself of all noxiousness and contagion, both physical and moral, and of all evil influences which might impair the prosperity of the coming year and thereby threaten the desired renewal and vitality.
>
> Third comes rites of INVIGORATION, whereby the community attempts by its own concerted and regimented effort, to galvanize its moribund condition and to procure that new lease of life. . . .

> Last comes rites of JUBILATION, which bespeak men's sense of relief when the new year has indeed begun and the continuance of their own lives . . . is thereby assured.[3]

Assuming Gaster is right about these aspects of seasonal rituals, try to identify each phase as we examine the Akitu festival of Babylon.

The first four days of the ritual were somber, expressing the powerlessness of the king and the desolation of the winter season. Marduk was asked by the priests to have pity on the city. These prayers were offered at a temple called Esagila. The king may have been symbolically slain, and Marduk was regarded as "bound." On the fourth day, the *Enuma elish* was chanted, signifying the passage from winter to spring and from chaos and death to order and new life.

On the fifth day of Nisan the priests enacted rites of atonement. The temple was sprinkled with water, fumigated with incense, and in other ways purified. They beheaded a sheep and rubbed its body against the walls of the temple, thereby absorbing any remaining pollution. This **scapegoat** was thrown into the river. The king was slapped twice by a priest and ordered to kneel in an act of penitence. He was divested of his right to rule, and his crown, scepter, and ring were removed.

During his divestiture, a carnival atmosphere prevailed in the streets. The normal social order was overturned; slaves became masters and masters slaves. A criminal was symbolically enthroned as king, along with stylized combats representing the cosmic battle between Marduk and Tiamat. When Marduk's son Nabu ritually released him from bondage and the king was reinvested with power and authority, the next phase of the ritual began.

From the sixth to the eighth day, the priests and people symbolically acted out the victory of Marduk over Tiamat. And on the ninth day a triumphant procession of the king from Esagila to the House of the New Year's Feast (the Akitu House built outside the city) took place. On the tenth day a feast was held for the king, gods, and priests. That night the return of fertility to the land is signaled by the return of the king to Esagila, where a sacred marriage is consummated between a female temple slave and the king. This elaborate ritual culminates with the couple emerging from "the chamber of the bed" to great jubilation and another feast.

> Around the shoulders of his beloved bride he has laid his arms . . .
> The king, like unto a sun, sits beside her,
> A sumptuous meal is placed before her . . .
> The king is glad,
> The people are passing the day in abundance.[4]

This ritual operates on two levels: a cosmic and a political level. Cosmically, the fertility of the new year is ensured, and politically, the king's authority is renewed. Gaster remarks that for this ancient community, life is not a progression from cradle to grave but a series of leases periodically renewed.

We can clearly see the pattern of mortification, purgation, invigoration, and jubilation to which Gaster refers. For Gaster, the details of the festival "made real" in concrete time and space this enduring, transcendent, and ahistorical pattern. This festival renews the city, the king, and the people, or so Gaster claims. But is Gaster right?

Little is known about the ancient Babylonian Akitu except that it celebrated the agricultural cycle of sowing and harvesting, and during the era of Ur III (2100–1900 B.C.E.), there was a procession to the "Akitu House" built outside the city. Most of the detailed textual information comes from a much later date (perhaps from around 709 B.C.E. when Babylon was under Persian control. Gaster assumes that later versions were nearly the same as earlier ones and creates his "seasonal pattern" based on a synthesis of rituals from diverse cultures and times. Because he was a member of the myth and ritual school (see Section 6.5), Gaster argued, on almost purely theoretical grounds, that the key to the Akitu is to be found in the *Enuma elish* since, according to the theories of that school, myths and rituals are *always* connected.

Jonathan Z. Smith argues that the ritual texts describing the rite do not reflect the ancient Akitu as Gaster thought, but a much more recent version of the ritual that took place during a time when a foreign king sat on the throne of Babylon. It is this historical context that is decisive for interpreting a very puzzling feature of the ritual, the humiliation of the king. The text reads as follows:

> (415) When he [the king] reaches [the presence of the god], the *urigallu*-priest shall leave [the sanctuary] and take away the scepter, the circle and the sword [from the king]. He shall bring them [before the god Bel] and place them [on] a chair. He shall leave [the sanctuary] and strike the king's cheek. (420) He shall place the . . . behind him. He shall accompany him [the king] into the presence of the god Bel . . . He shall drag (him by) the ears and make him bow down to the ground . . . The king shall speak the following words (only once): "I did [not] sin, lord of the countries. I was not neglectful (of the requirements) of your godship. [I did not] destroy Babylon. I did not command its overthrow. (425) [I did not] . . . the temple Esagila. I did not forget its rites. I did not rain blows on the cheeks of a subordinate [some translate 'protected citizen'] . . . I did not smash its walls."
>     (Response of the *urigallu*-priest)
> "Have no fear . . . (435) The god Bel [will listen to] your prayer . . . [The god Bel] whose city is Babylon . . . whose temple is Esagila . . . whose dependents are the people of Babylon . . . (445) The god Bel will bless you . . . forever. He will destroy your enemy, fell your adversary." After (the *urigallu*-priest) says (this), the scepter, circle and sword [shall be restored] to the king. He (the priest) shall strike the king's cheek, (450) if the tears flow, (it means that) the god Bel is friendly; if no tears appear, the god Bel is angry: the enemy will rise up and bring about his downfall.[5]

According to Gaster, this humiliation and restoration of the king is a symbolic death and resurrection motif associated with the agricultural cycle. Smith argues, however, that the historical context cannot be ignored. In the context of foreign rule, a number of important questions probably arose. If the king is the divine center of the human community, just as the king-god is the center of the whole universe, then what is going to happen if the king is the wrong king, a foreign king? What does this imply about the gods? Do rituals of renewal really work any more?

Interpreted in that context, Smith asserts that the ritual was not a historical repetition of some ahistorical cosmogonic pattern, as Gaster thought, but a ritual that tried to make sense of foreign rule and send a distinct political message. Smith interprets the slapping of the king differently from Gaster. "If the king does not comport himself as a proper, native Babylonian king (first slapping), the gods will be angry and 'the enemy will rise up and bring about his downfall' (second slapping)."[6] The Akitu festival becomes, given Smith's reading, "a piece of nationalistic propaganda." It is a ritualized way of sending a strong message to a foreign king: either rule kindly, or the gods will punish you. If you rule well, the gods will bless you and protect you along with Babylon.

Does the Akitu have to do with a dying and resurrected god of vegetation and with an act of atonement involving a scapegoat? It is tempting to think so because this helps to make sense of later rituals described in a variety of texts from the Hebrew Bible to the Roman Catholic Mass (especially the pre-Vatican II liturgy). The Jews celebrated a Day of Atonement involving the use of a scapegoat, and the liturgy of the Mass begins with *mortification* (confession of sins and entreaties for forgiveness). The Mass progresses to *purgation*, which starts with a reading from the Bible. (Recall that this phase of the Akitu may have begun with a recitation of the *Enuma elish.*) Rites of *invigoration* follow as the priest consecrates the bread and the wine, transforming them into the body and blood of Christ, and worshipers join in a sacred meal. One of a number of prayers offered by the priest during this phase reads

> Most humbly we implore Thee, Almighty God . . . that those of us who, from sharing in the heavenly sacrifice, shall receive the most sacred Body and Blood of Thy Son, may be filled with every grace and heavenly blessing.[7]

The Mass ends with rites of *jubilation*, such as prayers, hymns of thanksgiving, and a blessing (benediction) conferring grace. And finally, the central divine figure thought to be present in the Mass is a "dying and rising god" who bestows immortality instead of fertility.

The power of Gaster's theory to explain a wide range of rituals makes it attractive. But we cannot ignore Smith's political interpretation. Smith's theory has the advantage of taking the immediate historical context seriously. Only a detailed and careful reexamination of the evidence for the Akitu festival can help us solve the controversy. Perhaps both interpretations shed light on this ancient Babylonian ritual because the symbolic nature of ritual allows it to send multiple messages simultaneously.

A word should be said about the significance of the carnival phase in which normal social roles are inverted. These are widespread ritual events. (Think of Mardi Gras, which is still celebrated today right before Lent.) Scholars interpret them as socially useful rituals because they relieve tensions that inevitably build up in hierarchical societies in which classes with power and wealth oppress classes with little power or wealth. It is probable that this is a latent function of carnival rites. Even an outlaw can be "king for a day"! However, there is a more sinister side to carnival. Using Karl Marx's notion of religion as an opiate, we could argue that this temporary relief only serves to make the poor more willing to live in their poverty. It is a small price for the powerful to pay in order to repay the lower classes for accepting their normal state of powerlessness.

### 6.1.2 Her Alone They Sing Over (Ishna Ta Awi Cha Lowan)

The second case study comes from Native American religion; specifically, it is one of the seven main rites of the Oglala Sioux. Its name is *Ishna Ta Awi Cha Lowan*, which can be translated as in the title of this section or, literally, as "they sing over her menses." I will refer to it as *Ishna*, for short. It is a ritual intended to prepare young girls for womanhood.

The primary sacred power for the Sioux is Wakan Tanka (Great Mysteriousness), sometimes wrongly translated as Great Spirit. Christian missionaries associated Wakan Tanka with the Christian Creator God, which led to the claim that a "primitive monotheism" characterizes Native American religion. More accurately, Wakan Tanka refers to what is most sacred and designates the totality of spirit beings (see J. R. Walker's comments in Section 4.3.2, Chapter 4). Wakan Tanka is identified as the source of the vision that inspired the initiation rite we will be studying.

Native American religion and culture were nearly wiped out by the European invaders of the Americas. However, they have survived against overwhelming odds, and today are in a period of rebirth. Native American religion shows a vitality and ability to adapt to changing circumstances, even in the face of intensive missionary efforts. Out of the bewildering variety of past forms, Native Americans are now developing a Pan-Indian culture and religion that unites the nations and people in new and creative ways.

In 1932, John G. Neihardt published *Black Elk Speaks*, a book that reinvigorated Native American religion and radically changed perceptions about that religion by nonnatives. The book gives an account of Neihardt's interviews with Black Elk (Hehaka Sapa), who was born in 1863 and died in 1950.[8]

Black Elk lived in two worlds. One world, the world of traditional Native American culture and spirituality, he saw destroyed by the European invaders. The other world, the world of the invaders, he entered as part of the cast of the Buffalo Bill Wild West Show and as a convert to Roman Catholicism. His Christian name was Nicholas, and he learned from the missionaries that the "old ways" in which he had been born and bred were "the work of Satan." However, the old Lakota spirituality lived on in him, and eventually he came to see that his purpose in life was to transmit the old ways to a new generation.

Black Elk was an Oglala Sioux. In 1947, Joseph Epes Brown interviewed Black Elk and the result was a book, *The Sacred Pipe,* in which Black Elk describes the seven major rituals of the Oglala. In the foreword, Black Elk draws an analogy between God sending his son to earth to "restore order and bring peace" and Wakan Tanka turning an animal into a "two-legged person in order to bring the most holy pipe."[9] This animal/person's name was White Buffalo Cow Woman, and, according to Black Elk, she will appear again at the end of this world.

Black Elk introduces his account of this initiation rite as follows:

> These rites are performed after the first menstrual period . . . [and] are important because it is at this time that a young girl must understand the meaning of this change and must be instructed in the duties, which she is now to fulfill. She should realize that the change which has taken place in her is a sacred thing, for now she will be as Mother Earth and will be able to bear children, which should also be brought up in a sacred manner. She should know, further, that each month when her period arrives she bears an influence with which she must be careful, for the presence of a woman in this condition may take away the power of a holy man. Thus, she should observe carefully the rites of purification which we shall describe here, for these rites were given to us by *Wakan-Tanka* through a vision (116).

Black Elk then recounts how Slow Buffalo had a vision of a buffalo cow cleaning her calf and interpreted this as a sign to introduce new rites to prepare young girls for womanhood. A few moons after this vision, Feather on Head brought his fourteen-year-old daughter, White Buffalo Cow Woman Appears, who had had her first period, to Slow Buffalo to undergo the new rites he had received in his vision.

Feather on Head was instructed by Slow Buffalo to make the necessary preparations by building a tipi "just outside the camping circle" with a sheltered way leading to it, and by gathering and placing objects to be used in this purification/initiation rite in the tipi. The people gathered around, and Slow Buffalo entered the tipi with the young girl and her close relatives. Slow Buffalo, seated on the west side of the tipi, burned sweet grass and addressed a prayer to Grandfather and Father Wakan Tanka and to Grandmother and Mother, the Earth. The sacred pipe and other ritual objects, along with the people present, were purified in the smoke of the sweet grass.

Slow Buffalo announced, "all that will be done today . . . will be accomplished with the aid of the Powers of the universe. May they help us to purify and to make sacred this girl who is about to become a woman. I now fill this sacred pipe, and in doing this I am placing within it all the Powers, who are helping us here today!" (119).

Slow Buffalo, after purifying himself with the smoke of the sweet grass, took a pinch of tobacco and offered it to Wakan Tanka, and the four cardinal directions. With each offering he called on these powers to bless, aid, and protect the young girl and all the generations that will come from her.

Tobacco was once again offered to Wakan Tanka and then to the "four-legged buffalo people" (symbolized by a buffalo skull) and the "winged Powers of the Universe." This phase of the ritual concluded with the declaration by Slow Buffalo that the pipe now contained the "whole universe."

The next phase was done in secret, with only the close relatives of the girl, the girl herself, and Slow Buffalo in attendance, because it was "too sacred to be seen by all." Again Slow Buffalo purified himself and then "demonstrates" that he has truly received the power to do this rite from the buffalo by singing a song they had taught him:

> This they are coming to see!
> I am going to make a place which is sacred.
> That they are coming to see.
> White Buffalo Cow Woman Appears
> Is sitting in a wakan [sacred] manner.
> They are all coming to see her!

Then, as Slow Buffalo bellowed like a buffalo six times, red dust came out of his mouth, "just as a buffalo cow is able to do when she has a calf." He then dug out a hollow in the shape of a buffalo wallow near the center of the tipi and piled the dirt in a mound slightly to the east of the hollow. He placed tobacco in the center of the mound, and made a line with tobacco from west to east and from north to south. Black Elk comments, "The whole universe was now within this holy place."

Slow Buffalo painted blue lines on top of this tobacco cross, and again Black Elk interprets, "Blue is the color of the heavens, by placing the blue upon the tobacco, which represents the earth, we have united heaven and earth, and all has been made one."

Slow Buffalo next placed the buffalo skull on the mound facing east (where the sun rises) and painted a red line around its head, between its horns, and down its forehead. He put balls of sage in the eye sockets and he placed in front of its mouth a wooden bowl of water with cherries, which "represent the fruits of the earth."

Slow Buffalo instructed White Buffalo Cow Woman Appears to stand, and he held a bundle of sacred objects (sweet grass, bark of the cherry tree, and hair of a live buffalo) over her head. Slow Buffalo now declared:

> You are the tree of life. You will now be pure and holy, and may your generations to come be fruitful! Wherever your feet touch will be a sacred place, for now you will always carry with you a very great influence. May the four Powers of the universe help to purify you, for, as I mention the name of each power, I shall rub this bundle down that side of you. (123–124)

After the girl sat down, Slow Buffalo recounted his vision from which this rite derives, mentioning how he saw people who turned into buffalo and purified a child/calf. The story ended with the declaration that White Buffalo Cow Woman Appears "is that little calf." After another holy song, Slow Buffalo picked up the buffalo skull and, acting like a buffalo, pushed the young girl with the skull (out of whose nose red smoke came) toward the bowl of water from which she is instructed to drink. Slow Buffalo placed a piece of buffalo meat in her mouth and told her:

> You will cherish those things which are most sacred in the universe; you will be as Mother Earth—humble and fruitful. May your steps, and those of your children, be firm and sacred! As *Wakan-Tanka* has been merciful to you, so you, too, must be merciful to others, especially to those children who are without parents. If such a child should ever come to your lodge, and if you should have but one piece of meat which you have already placed in your mouth, you should take it out and give it to her. You should be as generous as this! (125–126).

The bowl of water was then passed around for all to take a sip. After a closing prayer, White Buffalo Cow Woman Appears was brought out of the tipi and presented to the people as a woman. The people rushed forward to touch her because she was full of sacred power. Then a great feast was held, along with a "give away" during which "all the poor received much." Black Elk comments once more, "It was in this manner that the rites for preparing a young girl for womanhood were first begun, and they have been the source of much holiness, not only for our women, but for the whole nation."

It is important to note that the *Ishna* is both a purification ritual and a rite of passage marking the transition from girl to woman. Arnold van Gennep, in his classic study of many different types of these sorts of rites, found that they exhibit three phases: separation, transition, and incorporation. Victor Turner used the word *liminal* to characterize the phase of transition and argued it is characterized by "**communitas**." (See "Suggestions for Further Reading" for information on van Gennep and Turner.) In a state of liminality people are "betwixt and between" their normal social roles. They exist outside the bounds of ordinary social rules and, socially speaking, are neither fish nor fowl. During this period they experience solidarity with others undergoing the rite or who have undergone it before. A state of egalitarian comradeship exists because all prescribed social roles are momentarily suspended. People feel free and able to truly be themselves in this state of communitas—rather than a child, or an adult, or married, or a student, or any of the other many social roles their cultures expect them to play.

Bruce Lincoln argues (based on a limited number of cases) that van Gennep's phases, while fitting boys' initiation rites into manhood, do not fit girls' initiation rites into womanhood. In the cases Lincoln studied, there was no separation, but there was an enclosing. Since girls had little if any social status in these societies, Lincoln argues that there is no liminal state for women, but what he calls a metamorphosis or magnification in which they are often identified with a goddess, endowed with sacred power, and placed, metaphorically, on a pedestal. Emergence replaces van Gennep's final stage of incorporation, and Lincoln uses the image of insect metamorphosis (caterpillar to butterfly) to indicate that after the rite, the female initiate emerges from seclusion to be presented to the community as a woman.

In the case of the Sioux rite, the first stage is a stage of separation (the girl is taken outside the camping circle), although it is not complete separation because a covered path connects the village to the initiation tipi, much like an umbilical cord. However, there is also an enclosure, since once separated, the girl is enclosed in a tipi, which comes to symbolize, as the rite proceeds, the whole universe.

Since the account I have described is the first time this rite was conducted, it is hard to imagine White Buffalo Cow Woman Appears experiencing communitas with all the other women, because none of them had gone through an initiation exactly like this one. There is, however, clearly a metamorphosis and magnification. She is given new duties and responsibilities. Demands are placed on her that would never be placed on a child. She is, in addition to acting in a holy manner, to be generous, humble, and bear children. She is identified with Mother Earth, the tree of life, repeatedly called holy, and her name itself indicates identity with White Buffalo Cow Woman, the revealer of sacred rites. When she emerges, she is no longer a young girl, but a woman ready for adult roles—marriage and motherhood. While she does emerge from an enclosure, as Lincoln's structure indicates, she is also incorporated into the people by feasting and a "give away" on the part of her family. She is now ready to play new and different roles.

There is clearly a cosmic dimension to the *Ishna*. All the powers of the universe end up in that tipi, the cross connecting the four directions brings order to chaos, and the union of heaven and earth foreshadows the union of male and female from which all good "fruits" will come. The young girl becomes, if only briefly, the very creativity of the universe.

It is of great importance to note that this ritual derives from the vision of a male, is conducted by a male, and that the female plays an almost completely passive role. Women play no significant part in the ritual except to prepare the food for the feast and, if a close relative, to witness it. The father initiates the process, not the mother. Men control this rite throughout. It is conducted by men and ultimately for men, since the roles the initiated woman will eventually play are wife, mother, and domestic servant to her husband. Indeed, the very account we have of the rite is told by a man to a man. Karl Marx would see it as a prime example of a religious opiate, compensating an oppressed class for their sociopolitical deprivation. As Bruce Lincoln puts it, "The strategy is that of placing woman on a pedestal . . . speak of her as a goddess to make her a drudge." [10]

In Sioux society, as in many others, women are considered dangerous during menstruation. Note Black Elk's opening reference to this danger. The ritual that this rite replaces called for separating a woman from the tribe each month during her period and subjecting her to purification rites. Menstrual blood pollutes, or so it was thought. (Blood symbolizes the power of life, and the loss of blood the potential destruction of life.) This reinforces the idea that rituals such as these were self-consciously conducted to control perceived female danger to the community.

While this may be the "dark side" of women's rites of passage, there is also a "bright side"—specifically, the instructions to be kind to the poor and the "give away" by the family in celebration of this happy event, which benefited the poor. These initiation rituals have been and are quite often the means whereby the lives of women take on meaning and purpose. And, as Lincoln also remarks, "This is ultimately the most profound claim that any ritual or any religious system can make: that through their thoughts and actions, people can fill their existence with meaning." [11]

## 6.2 COMPARISON

From a comparative perspective, major differences between the Akitu and the *Ishna* appear. One is a seasonal ritual celebrated once a year, the purpose of which, among other things, is to continue the seasonal cycle. The other is a periodic ritual; celebrated whenever a girl reaches the age of her first menstruation and her family can afford to sponsor the rite of passage into womanhood. Its purpose, among other things, is to continue the community by sanctifying the passage from infertile girl to fertile woman. The Akitu celebrates the beginning of the cosmos and the coming new year, the *Ishna*, the beginning of womanhood and the coming generations.

The specific activities and events of both rituals also differ. A creation myth and hero myth is told (according to Gaster) at an important juncture of the Akitu, while a report of Slow Buffalo's vision is told in the *Ishna*. There is no sacred marriage in the *Ishna* (although the union of heaven and earth is mentioned), nor is a king involved in any way, because the Sioux had no kings. The atonement and scapegoat theme found in the Akitu is absent in the *Ishna*.

The political and social context, not to mention the historical context, were completely different. Babylon was an ancient urban society dependent on agriculture with a well-defined hierarchy of social classes. The Oglala Sioux were a tribal, nomadic hunting and gathering society with less well-defined social classes. The bison was central to the survival of the people as well as to their religion and culture. I hardly need point out, Babylonian religion and culture did not center on the bison.

In spite of these differences, there are some interesting similarities on a more abstract level. Both rituals involve a cosmic dimension and are concerned with purification and fertility. Both end in jubilation, and both have a death/resurrection motif, although it is prominent in the Akitu (if you accept Gaster's reconstruction) and more muted in the *Ishna* ("death" of the girl, "birth" of a woman). The people, in both instances, believe that the Akitu and the *Ishna* contribute to the well-being of the whole society.

The communitas of the liminal phase of the *Ishna*, if there is one at all, is less apparent than it is in the Akitu. The festive carnival on the fifth day of the Akitu exhibits a sense of communitas as social boundaries are temporarily suspended. Also note that just as an outlaw is made king for a day, so White Buffalo Cow Woman Appears is made a kind of "queen for a day." Indeed, she is made more than a queen, for she becomes Mother Earth and the "tree of life" connecting heaven and earth.

## 6.3 TYPES AND FUNCTIONS

There are a number of different ways to classify rituals. Typologies are not true or false, they are more or less useful. The typology I provide here derives from Anthony Wallace, an anthropologist, who argues that ritual behavior is the primary and most fundamental aspect of religion, and it can usefully be understood as purposeful or goal-directed behavior. (See "Suggestions for Further Reading.") Religious rituals aim to bring about or to prevent changes and therefore can be classified in terms of the kinds of changes or transformations they are thought to cause or prevent. As I describe Wallace's categories and give examples, see if you can extend the list of examples based on your own knowledge and experience.

1. **Technological rituals** seek to produce or prevent a change of state in nature so that humans benefit in some way. Examples include rain dances, fertility rites, hunting rituals, prayers for good weather, rituals for insuring a good harvest, and the like.
2. **Therapeutic** and **antitherapeutic rituals** seek to produce a change in the state of human health, either to heal the sick or bring sickness to the

healthy. Examples include laying on of hands, anointing, witchcraft and so-called voodoo rites, prayers for health, and a vast variety of healing rituals using eggs, herbs, special ointments, dancing, singing, and sweating.

3. **Ideological rituals** seek social control by changing the mood, behavior, sentiments, motivations, and values of people, usually for the sake of the community as a whole. Examples include rites of passage, taboos that are ritually transmitted, teaching, preaching, studying sacred scriptures, and even "rituals of rebellion," such as carnival, Mardi Gras, and days of the dead (Halloween).

4. **Salvation rituals** seek to change a person's identity from a spiritually corrupt, polluted, sinful, or lost state to a spiritually saved state that provides freedom from sin, corruption, ignorance, and the like. Examples include baptism, communion, spirit possession, meditation, conversion, and altar calls.

5. **Revitalization rituals** seek to revitalize a culture or a religion seen as dying or in the process of being lost. They try to do for the community as a whole what salvation rituals do for the individual. These are not simple rituals, but what might be called ritual movements involving a number of complex actions. Examples include messianic movements like early Christianity, nativistic movements such as the Indian Ghost Dance, and early Mormon attempts to revitalize Christianity. New religious movements (what some people call "cults"), such as the Unification Church, also fall into this category. Political and religious movements such as the Moral Majority find their home here as well.

I think it is clear that the categories of this typology are not mutually exclusive. A single ritual might fall into one or more categories depending upon its complexity and the presence of multiple goals. For example, the Akitu festival is a technological and ideological ritual complex, while *Isbna* is primarily ideological.

Rituals, like myths, have important social functions. The two rituals we have examined in this chapter function to integrate individuals into a group and to reinforce a current social order. Note, however, that if we follow Smith's interpretation of the slapping of the king in the Akitu, we might want to add that the Akitu also contains a threat to overturn the current social order if the foreign king fails to do his duty for the Babylonians. Rituals can be both reactionary and revolutionary.

In addition to providing religious, social, and psychological meaning, rituals serve an expressive function, allowing people and societies to "act out" some of their deepest fears and hopes. In fact rituals are probably more effective than myths in producing a sense of the sacred. Rituals involve bodily movements and gestures, including vocalization through telling, singing, and chanting; whereas myths primarily recount or tell a story. Bodily memory is often deeper and longer lasting than verbal memory. Ritual is religion dancing, and the feel of the dance lasts far longer than the memory of what was said at the dance.

> ## Typology of Rituals
>
> 1. Technological rituals
> 2. Therapeutic and antitherapeutic rituals
> 3. Ideological rituals
> 4. Salvation rituals
> 5. Revitalization rituals

## 6.4 SACRIFICE

Sacrifice plays such a central role in so many different rituals and as a theme that permeates so much of religious teaching that some scholars argue that to understand sacrifice is to understand religion. The word itself comes from the Latin *sacrificare*, which means "to make sacred." And that is what many have claimed religion is all about—making something sacred.

There are many different kinds of sacrifice. Sacrifices may involve the spilling of blood (for example, the ritual slaying of an animal), or they may be bloodless when vegetable or cultural products are used. Whether bloody or bloodless, every sacrifice has at least four elements: (1) the people who perform the sacrifice, (2) what is sacrificed, (3) the mode of sacrifice, and (4) those who receive the sacrifice.

There are numerous theories of sacrifice, and scholars often appeal to one or more of them to explain ritual sacrifice. Any useful theory must explain why humans are willing to sacrifice things of value, such as crops, cattle, oxen, sheep, and even each other, to invisible powers (not to mention the time, expense, and energy that sacrifices often consume). One theory of sacrifice centers on the principle of "give in order to get (*do ut des*)," which explains why humans are willing to give up things of value in sacrificial rituals. Sacrifices are gifts, given with the hope of a good return on the investment. Giving and getting are basic to human relationships. Exchange establishes a situation of reciprocity. If it works between humans, then it should work to establish reciprocity between humans and gods. Humans offer food, and the gods give prosperity, or peace, or even immortality.

This same principle of giving in order to get also explains why so many sacrifices center on offering thanks. We should always say thank you when we receive a gift. It is not only polite, it may help to get more gifts in the future if we are appropriately appreciative. I do not intend to be cynical here. Undoubtedly, people feel genuine gratitude and wish to express it in some ritual fashion. People may not even be aware that they have mixed motivations when offering sacrifices of thanksgiving. However, if we are to use the theory of *do ut des* (I give in order to get) as a general theory of sacrifice, then it must also explain why people give thanks.

Other theories view the idea of substitution as the key to explaining sacrifice. The most valuable sacrifice is oneself. But mass suicide usually does not contribute to the survival of the species. If a reasonable substitute can be found, then a basic rule of survival, "better him or her than me," requires that the substitute be sacrificially destroyed. Hence the widespread use of the scapegoat in many religious rituals. The scapegoat is the substitute that allows the rest of the members of a society to keep what is most valuable to them: their own lives.

Frequently the sins, pollution, corruption, shame, and guilt of the group are transferred to the scapegoat before it is sacrificed. The substitution thereby becomes an act of atonement. This allows the substitution system to work. If I am the one who deserves to die because of my sins and corruption, then the substitute is only acceptable to the offended gods or goddesses if it carries my sins and guilt.

It could be the case, however, that my relationship to the scapegoat is not one of identification, but of difference. René Girard (b. 1923) has suggested that the scapegoat is made an outsider, an "other," to the members of a group precisely in order for the group to become aware of its own identity in contrast to the otherness of the scapegoat. (See "Suggestions for Further Reading.") The victim is not like me, but different. It is "not-me" or "not-we," and therefore enacting violence upon it is acceptable.

Girard thinks that the human animal has a desire for violence, and it is this desire that stands at the root of sacrifice, ritual, religion, and even society and culture. This desire for violence threatens all members of the group, so society must find a way to control and channel this desire in order to avoid as much as possible indiscriminate violence. Society must also find a way of repressing this desire because consciously admitting it would threaten our sense of superiority to other animals. For Girard, the act of scapegoating is a universal and continually repeated event that occurs in a wide variety of forms and circumstances. It not only controls and legitimates violence, but also renders violence deceptively invisible. Ritualization not only contributes to human survival by controlling our natural desire for violence, but also to our flourishing, by giving a purpose to our existence. We are here to serve superhuman powers, and what better way of serving them than by sacrificing to them?

Still other theories claim that sacrifices are reenactments of primal events, such as the symbolic slaying of Tiamat or the king during the Akitu festival, or the sacrifice of the Primal Man (see Chapter 4). Some theories stress that sacrifices should be understood as a means of communication between the gods and humans. As the smoke rises to the heavens, so too do our prayers.

Sacrifices often occur in situations of danger or the threat of danger. This has biological roots. Animals sacrifice feathers and even body parts to escape danger. Humans throw people off ships into the sea (witness Jonah and whale), cut off fingers, offer enemies goods of great value in order to be spared, and sacrifice slaves, prisoners, and princesses to appease the gods and avert danger.

E. E. Evans-Pritchard (1902–1973) wrote a definitive work on the religion of the Nuer, an East African group whose life centers on raising cattle. (See "Suggestions for Further Reading.") According to Evans-Pritchard, sacrifices among the Nuer can be roughly divided into two main types: personal (sacrifices offered on behalf of individuals) and collective (sacrifices offered on behalf of the group). Evans-Pritchard believes the intention behind the first type is "piacular" (expiatory), and the intention behind the second, confirmatory. In other words, personal sacrifices are intended to get rid of some wrongdoing, illness, or danger, and collective rituals are intended to make some social event (marriage, for example) sacred and blessed.

Which of these many explanations of sacrifice should be taken as basic (if any) is difficult to say. All of them contribute something of value to our understanding of sacrifice and its importance to humans. Perhaps humans sacrifice for many reasons, some obvious and some not so obvious. In any case, sacrifice is a complex act that defies simple explanations; but given its universality and persistence, it seems to be of major significance to human survival and well-being.

## Explanations of Sacrifice

1. Exchanges and thanksgiving
2. Substitutions
3. Ways to channel and disguise violence
4. Reenactments of primal events
5. Communication between humans and superhumans

## 6.5 MYTH AND RITUAL

All of the theories of myth discussed in the previous chapter (rationalistic, functionalist, symbolic, phenomenological, and structuralist) can be and have been applied to the interpretation and explanation of ritual. In Chapter 5 we postponed the discussion of theories associated with the myth and ritual school in order to focus on them here after our discussion of ritual. However, before we turn our attention to the relationship between myth and ritual, let's explore how a rationalistic theory might approach ritual. This is particularly important because it raises the question of the relationship between ritual activity and magic.

As you may recall, the rationalistic theory of myth claims that the intention behind myths is to give explanations of events. This is the same intention behind scientific theories. The basic difference between myth and science is that mythic explanations are false, while scientific explanations are true. You can already guess that when this theory is applied to rituals, rituals turn out to be ineffective "technologies" of a magical nature, in contrast to effective scientific technologies. Rituals do not really usher in the new year, nor do they make a girl a woman. Sacrifices do not really influence the gods or protect people from harm. People might think they do, but they are mistaken.

If you recall the discussion of magic in Chapter 3, you will remember that magic is characterized as a style rather than a distinct category with clear and sharp boundaries separating it from religion. It might even be called a ritual style. The more a ritual is thought to operate automatically, the more it is aimed toward specific practical ends, and the more independent of the need for superhuman powers to work through it, the more a ritual tends toward the magical end of the scale. As these ritual elements diminish, rituals move toward the religious end of the scale. The tendency of rationalistic theory to create a category called magic and to place nearly all rituals in it really explains nothing about rituals. It simply indicates the biases of rationalistic theory.

Can the rationalist's charge of ineffectiveness be refuted? Surely rituals do not really work. Instead of denying the effectiveness of rituals, it might be more fruitful to assume that they do work and ask how they work. The answer resides in the notion of performatives.

There is a certain class of speech or utterance that philosophers have identified as *performatives*. By their very verbalization, performatives create a new state of affairs, a state that did not previously exist. Examples are "You are not guilty," uttered by a judge after a trial, and "I now pronounce you husband and wife," spoken by a minister or priest at the appropriate moment in a marriage ceremony. The first utterance creates a state of freedom for the person formerly held in prison, and the second creates a state of matrimony for people who were formerly unwed.

Rituals teem with performatives. "You are the tree of life," Slow Buffalo says to White Buffalo Cow Woman Appears. "You will now be pure and holy," he says. Not only are the words performatives, the ritual action itself is performative—it accomplishes its intention by its very action. Women's initiation rites intend to transform a girl into a woman, and they clearly accomplish that in a social sense. The group will no longer treat White Buffalo Cow Woman Appears as a girl, but as a woman. This is not a biological transformation (that is already happening) but a social transformation. The terms *girl* and *woman* have more than a biological meaning. They have a social meaning that determines how the individual is to act, how she is to be treated, and the appropriate social roles to be played. The *Ishna* rite of passage addresses social meaning, not biological meaning. And it works on the social level.

Rites of passage claim to renew society, and they accomplish this by providing society with a new, productive member and by bringing the people together for a celebration of life. This social renewal has real physical effects as new children are born and the life of the tribe continues from generation to generation. If girls do not become women in a social sense, the very life of the tribe is in doubt.

The intent of the Akitu to renew the cosmos is more difficult to understand as an effective performative because it involves the claim that the physical, not just the social world of meaning, is renewed. At least this much can be said: this seasonal ritual helps the participants believe it is so and act as if it were so. They prepare to plant and sow, anticipating a good harvest. This activity produces food—a physical necessity for the survival of the people. Words and actions can and do create meaning. They change people and society. In this way rituals are "magical." They make things happen, if not on a cosmic scale, at least on a social scale.

It is now time to turn to the myth and ritual theory, which derives its name from one of its major claims—that myth and ritual *must* go together. They are necessarily connected as "the thing said" and "the thing done." It follows that one cannot be understood without the other. They go together like a script of a play (the myth) and the play performed (the ritual action).

Not all of the members of this widely influential school agree on all particulars. Some claim that, originally, myth and ritual were combined. Ritual action requires a recited story as an essential part. Others claim that rituals came first and myths are derivative, arising as a way of explaining why certain things were done and to establish their verbal meaning.

Theodore Gaster's theory of the seasonal pattern, which we examined in conjunction with the Akitu, is an example of the myth and ritual theory. The seasonal pattern is a ritual pattern intended to renew and revitalize the social, political, and cosmic order. It involves death (mortification and purgation) followed by resurrection (invigoration and jubilation). The *Enuma elish* is not, for Gaster, a mere spoken correlate of what is being done, but a way of translating the ritual, which happens periodically in real time, into an idealized and timeless model that can be told and retold, even when the rites are not being performed. Myth is the idealization of ritual.

As I mentioned, the various theories associated with the myth and ritual school have enjoyed enormous popularity. They have been applied by classicists to Greek myths and rituals, by literary and drama critics to both literature and drama, and by music theorists to the American blues. Their popularity has not, however, stopped criticism. While it is true that some myths are clearly related to rituals, it is just plain "silly," as one critic put it, to claim that *all* are. Further, the claim that the relationship is one of necessity can never be empirically established. The actual evidence from a wide variety of cultures indicates that there is not one kind of relationship between myths and rituals, but a variety of complex relationships that vary with time and place.

## 6.6 SUMMARY

We began with a definition of ritual emphasizing the characteristics of repetition, stylization, symbolic bodily actions, and belief in some sort of sacred presence. Our first case study came from the ancient Babylonian new year Akitu festival intended, according to Theodore Gaster, to revitalize social, political, and cosmic order. The seasonal pattern of death and resurrection echoes the *Enuma elish* creation/hero myth and symbolically reenacts the agriculture cycle of winter and spring. Jonathan Z. Smith adds a political interpretation to the Akitu: it is a reminder to a foreign king to behave properly.

Our second case came from Black Elk's account of the inaugural celebration of a female initiation rite called the *Ishna Ta Awi Cha Lowan*. This rite of passage prepares a girl to assume the duties and responsibilities of an adult female.

Both rituals have a "dark side" insofar as they reinforce blind social conformity and hide the human origin of these rituals by attributing them to a superhuman source. They also have a "bright side" in that they provide meaning and purpose for people. They help people rise above the drudgery, hard work, and injustices of human existence by placing their lives in a larger, sacred context. Though the Akitu and the *Ishna* are vastly different in their context and in their details, they do share some similarities, such as their concern to purge pollution and increase fertility.

Next, a discussion of types and functions centered on Wallace's fivefold typology of technological, therapeutic, ideological, salvation, and revitalization rituals. Each of these types serves different functions, seeking to change nature, restore health, reinforce social order, free people from sin and pollution, and renew the group or society. Integrating the individual into a group and reinforcing a social/religious order emerged as two of the most important functions of rituals.

An examination of sacrifice (what some consider the most important type of ritual that is fundamental to the whole of religion) led to a survey of some theories of sacrifice. Sacrifices have been interpreted as exchanges, as substitutions, as ways to channel and disguise our violent natures, as reenactments of primal events, and as a means of communication with the divine. We paid special attention to the role sacrifice plays in situations of danger, a role that may indicate a biological basis for sacrificial acts. How many of us have tried to strike a deal with God in threatening situations by promising to give up (sacrifice) something of value to us? The greater the danger, the greater the sacrifice.

Rationalistic theories dismiss ritual as ineffective magical acts. This explains nothing, however, and certainly cannot explain why people persist in doing things that don't literally work. A better approach is to examine the performative nature of rituals. Rituals are often effective means for creating new meanings and new social conditions.

An exploration of some of the ideas associated with the myth and ritual school showed that it is often illuminating to interpret a ritual in light of its associated myth, and vice versa, but that there is no necessary link between the two. We have examples of myths that are not connected to any rituals we know about and examples of rituals that are not connected to any myths, so far as we can tell.

## 6.7 RESEARCH CASE—SEDER

The *seder* (literally, "order" of service) is a Jewish ritual meal held in the home on the first night of the seven-day holiday of Passover. It is both a seasonal ritual celebrated once a year and a commemorative ritual recalling the exodus from slavery in Egypt. (See the Moses story in Chapter 5).

The modern-day seder has a long and complex history. It is a combination of what were two separate holidays. One was a pastoral festival of *pesah* (passed over) associated with the new year in the southern tribes of Judah. Central to *pesah* was the sacrifice of a firstborn lamb. Eventually this came to commemorate the exodus from Egypt. The second ancient holiday was a seven-day agricultural festival of *matzah* (unleavened bread) celebrated in the spring in the more northern areas of Israel.

In 620 B.C.E. King Josiah instituted certain reforms in Jewish practice. One of these was the requirement that every male head of a household bring an animal offering to be sacrificed at the Temple in Jerusalem during Passover. This transformed the domestic Passover supper into a pilgrimage to Solomon's Temple, making it a public, cultic act supporting political centralization. After the return from exile and the rebuilding of the Temple, the Passover festival continued to be celebrated at home and at the Temple. It may well be this Passover meal (although the evidence is uncertain) that Jesus was celebrating with his disciples in Jerusalem just before his crucifixion. Christians call it the Last Supper and it forms the basis of the Christian communion ritual (also known as the Eucharist, or the Lord's Supper).

After the destruction of the Second Temple by the Romans in 70, and the forced exile of the Jews, Passover was gradually reinterpreted as a ritual focused on the home and the newly organized synagogues. The sacrifice of an animal was no longer central, and the eating of unleavened bread (*matzah*) became a more dominant symbol.

Today, the *Haggadah* (telling), which recounts the events of the exodus, is recited during the family seder. The story begins with the "humiliation" of the

Israelites and ends with their "glory" as they regain the land of Israel and build the Temple. It is both interesting and unexpected that as the story is told in the seder ritual there is no mention of Moses. The story is told as a story of the people—it is "our story"—and Adonai (the Lord) is given all the credit for the exodus events.

The manual for the seder (also called *Haggadah*) is available in a small booklet and contains a collection of stories, songs, and prayers used at the seder. It prescribes that the oldest male be the "master of the seder." He opens the ritual meal by offering the first cup of wine for "the sanctification of the day," which is followed by reciting the *kiddush*. The *kiddush* tells of God's creation of the world and his selecting the Jews "from every people" and sanctifying them by giving them his commandments.

After the master of the seder removes a shank bone and egg from a platter, he says:

> This is the bread of poverty, which our forefathers ate in the land of Egypt. Let all who are hungry enter and eat; let all who are needy come to our Passover feast. This year we are here; next year may we be in the Land of Israel. This year we are slaves; next year may we be free men.[12]

The seder is an occasion to learn about the history of the Jews, to identify with those who have gone before, and to learn the meaning of certain ritual foods and actions. This process is started by the youngest male asking four questions:

> Why does this night differ from all other nights? For on all other nights we eat either leavened or unleavened bread; why on this night only unleavened bread?
> On all other nights we eat all kinds of herbs; why on this night only bitter herbs?
> On all other nights we need not dip our herbs even once; why on this night must we dip them twice?
> On all other nights we eat either sitting up or reclining; why on this night do we all recline?

Those present take turns recounting the story of the exodus and explaining each symbol present at the table. In the course of doing so, each of the four initial questions is answered.

> The Passover Sacrifice which our fathers used to eat at the time when the Holy Temple still stood—what was the reason for it? Because the Holy One, blessed be he, passed over the houses of our fathers in Egypt. . . .
> This *matzah* which we eat, what is the reason for it? Because the dough of our fathers had not yet leavened when the King over all kings, the Holy One, blessed be he, revealed himself to them and redeemed them . . .
> These bitter herbs we eat, what is the reason for them? Because the Egyptians made the lives of our forefathers bitter in Egypt . . .

In every generation let each man look on himself as if *he* came forth out of Egypt.

In due course the symbolic meaning of other foods is explained. The *haroset* (a paste made of nuts, fruit, and wine) represents the mortar made into bricks by the Jews while in bondage. A bowl of vinegared or salted water represents the tears of suffering. A roasted shank bone and hard-boiled egg symbolize the paschal lamb. At specific places in the ritual four cups of wine are drunk in celebration of God's deliverance. After a closing set of prayers, the seder ends with hymns, the last verse of which reads:

> Compassionate is he, forceful is he, strong is he, he will build his Temple soon.
> Speedily, speedily, in our days and soon.
> God build, God build, build your Temple soon.

You may have noticed that males do the main ritual action, and only males are mentioned in recounting the events of the exodus. Recently, as feminists have confronted the male dominance found in most religions, there have been rewrites of older patriarchal rituals. E. M. Broner and Naomi Nimrod have created a women's seder. In this seder the traditional questions asked by the youngest male child are changed:

> "Why is this Haggadah different from traditional Haggadoth?"
> "Because this Haggadah deals with the exodus of women."
> "Why have our mothers on this night been bitter?"
> "Because they did the preparation but not the ritual. They did the serving but not the conducting. They read of their fathers but not of their mothers."
> "Why on this night do we recline?"
> "We recline on this night for the unhurried telling of the legacy of Miriam."[13]

This, like other feminist rituals, focuses on the themes of bonding among women and personal empowerment. It replaces language that is today considered sexist if for no other reason than its exclusion of women. Reading the traditional *Haggadah* leaves you with the impression that only men were slaves and only men were delivered. The feminist version exposes that as an illusion.

### QUESTIONS ON THE CASE OF THE SEDER

1. How does the seder link the present to the past?
2. Using Wallace's fivefold classification system, how would you classify the seder? Why?
3. How would the theories of the myth and ritual school approach the interpretation of this ritual meal?
4. Do you think the revised feminist version of the seder promotes solidarity among women and is empowering? If yes, how does it accomplish this?

## SUGGESTIONS FOR FURTHER READING

In addition to the material found in the notes, the reader may wish to consult the following for more information.

Bell, Catherine. *Ritual Theory, Ritual Practice.* Oxford: Oxford University Press, 1992. This important work is packed full of useful information and examples.

Burkert, Walter. *The Creation of the Sacred: Tracks of Biology in Early Religions.* Cambridge: Harvard University Press, 1996. See in particular chapters two and six for a provocative and fascinating discussion of the biological foundations of sacrifice.

Evans-Pritchard, E. E. *Nuer Religion.* Oxford: Clarendon Press, 1956. Read the author's careful description and analysis of Nuer sacrifice.

Girard, René. *Violence and the Sacred.* Translated by Patrick Gregory. Baltimore: Johns Hopkins University Press, 1972. Here Girard explains his controversial and provocative theory of the role that violence plays in religion.

Holm, Jean, and John Bowker, eds. *Rites of Passage.* London: Pinter, 1994. This collection of essays by various authors describes the rites of passage commonly found in Buddhism, Christianity, Hinduism, Islam, Judaism, and Sikhism and Chinese and Japanese religions.

Neihardt, John G. *Black Elk Speaks.* New York: Pocket Books, 1971. Black Elk tells his life story to Neihardt. Neihardt made some important changes to Black Elk's account. For an edited version of the original field notes, see *The Sixth Grandfather,* edited by Raymond J. DeMallie (Lincoln: University of Nebraska Press, 1984).

Rappaport, Roy A. *Ritual and Religion in the Making of Humanity.* Cambridge: Cambridge University Press, 1999. This challenging but rewarding study of ritual combines insights from ethnography, ecology, cybernetics, semiotics, and comparative religion. See in particular chapter four, "Enactments of Meaning," for a penetrating discussion of performatives and the ways in which religions create meaning.

Turner, Victor. *The Ritual Process: Structure and Anti-Structure.* Ithaca, NY: Cornell University Press, 1969. Here Turner develops the important concepts of liminality and communitas.

van Gennep, Arnold. *The Rites of Passage.* Translated by Monika B. Vizedom and Gabrielle L. Caffee. London: Routledge & Kegan Paul, 1960. Van Gennep explains the structure and function of rites of passage in this groundbreaking study.

Wallace, Anthony. *Religion: An Anthropological View.* New York: Random House, 1966. Read chapter three for Wallace's discussion of his fivefold typology of myths and their functions.

## INTERNET RESOURCES

http://anthro.palomar.edu/social/soc_4.htm    At this Web site you will find more information on rites of passage from the anthropology department at Palomar College.

www.gatewaystobabylon.com/religion/sumerianakitu.htm   This site provides an account of the Sumerian Akitu festival, which centered on the moon-god Nanna.

www.rigal.freeserve.co.uk/jewish/seder/seder.htm   This site will provide you with much information about the seder, from its history to some of the more unusual seder customs.

www-personal.umich.edu/~bparnes/HAGGADAH/seder.htm   Go to this site for an adaptation of the text of the *Haggadah*. Also type in "Haggadah" in a search engine like GoTo, and carefully check the results for more information.

# CHAPTER 7

# Sacred Space and Time

ONE FUNCTION OF myths and rituals is to establish sacred spaces and times. Every myth of origin, such as the *Enuma elish*, constructs both a place and a time filled with unusual and extraordinary events of power. Every ritual, such as Passover, creates a holy place where the ritual happens and a holy time when the mundane concerns of daily routines are set aside in order to enter a special time of power.

Phenomenologists argue that sacred space and sacred time are fundamental comparative categories. They highlight universal features of all religions because all religions create and express some form of sacred space and sacred time. Myths tell us about the primordial times of the beginning of the universe. Humans renew themselves by making contact with the pristine and holy times in which everything started. Rituals establish a sacred space—a place that is holy and unique. In our ritual behavior we enter this sacred space and thereby come in touch with the power of the sacred. By ritually entering sacred space, we also enter sacred time. In ritual action we temporarily suspend ordinary, profane time and leave behind profane space.

Some scholars of religion, using the comparative method, search for common features in the hope of discovering the basic characteristics of sacred space and time. Fascinated with similarities and often ignoring important differences, they attempt to articulate the essence of sacred space and time. Many claim that sacred space essentially differs from profane space insofar as sacred space is the place where we can make contact with the power of superhuman beings. It is an **axis mundi** or "axis of the world," connecting heaven, earth, and the underworld. It is a place where a road to the divine can be found.

Some scholars also claim that the essential difference between sacred and profane time consists in the direction in which time flows. Profane time is linear, moving from one age to another in succession. The past is left behind as the present arrives, and the future will eventually make the present past. The profane past inevitably disappears, leaving only ripple effects like a rock thrown into water. Sacred time is cyclical and moves in a circle. It always returns to primordial times when everything began. The past, or at least the sacred past in which superhuman power was manifested, is available in any given present.

The linear feature of profane time is not totally absent from sacred time. Indeed many religions teach that time starts with the creation and is moving toward a conclusion, often involving divine judgment. Yet this linear time is different because through myths and rituals we can connect to the power of the beginning at any point along the time line, especially at the beginning of a new year. A new year replicates the beginning of a new universe. Perhaps the image of a spiral better captures the distinctive feature of sacred time. A spiral returns to the beginning but on a different level. There is progression and return.

It is unclear whether there really is an essence to sacred space and time that decisively distinguishes it from profane space and time. We will need to keep that claim in mind as we look at examples and test it against the evidence. Like so many hypotheses based on comparative studies, the hypothesis we formulate will depend on whether we pay more attention to differences than similarities or vice versa.

The first case study in this chapter focuses on sacred mountains. There are sacred mountains all over the world. Mount Sinai, where Moses received the Torah from YHWH, comes immediately to mind. Others include Mount Everest, the five imperial peaks of D'ai Shan in China, Mount Fuji in Japan, Mount Olympus in Greece, Mount Shasta in California, Harney Peak in the Black Hills, and the Andes in South America. Sacred space is always attached to a sacred place. Since prehistoric times, mountains have quite naturally suggested a link between earth and sky—they visually connect humans with their gods. Some of the earliest temples were shaped like mountains, and the grand cathedrals of Europe soar into the sky like mountain peaks. The pyramids of ancient Egypt and of the Mayans are also examples of sacred mountains artificially re-created as sacred sites of connection between heaven and earth.

The second case study has to do with sacred time as well as sacred space, although our emphasis will be on time. We look at the notion of the **Dreamtime** found among Australian Aborigines. This is a time of beginnings in which great power was present on earth. This great power not only created sacred places but also sacred ceremonies and rituals that, when celebrated today, return the Aborigines to this time of power.

After comparing these two cases, we will examine some general features of sacred space and time, looking at the forms they take, the ways in which they are established, and the human needs they fulfill. Separating a time and a place for special purposes not only establishes order and hence meaning in the universe, but also makes sacred power once again available to those who are afraid it will fade.

Following the case studies is a discussion of religion and art. In many ways this deserves at least a chapter to itself, but space limitations do not permit it. There is evidence that art arose out of religion, and many people who have seen religious paintings or heard sacred music have felt the power of art carry them to other places and times. Visions of hells can make us feel afraid, and visions of heavens can make us feel secure. Architecture creates sacred spaces in which we can worship and celebrate a sacred past in the present, thereby making the past real once more.

The research case at the end of the chapter provides an opportunity to practice your evolving skills as students of religion. You will be invited to interpret the case of the Cathedral of St. Andrew from an outsider's viewpoint, applying methods, theories, and ideas developed in your reading so far. Remember that the outsider's viewpoint sympathetically imagines the insider's experience. This is especially important when dealing with sacred space, time, and art because so much of what the experience means is in how it feels.

## 7.1 TWO CASE STUDIES

### 7.1.1 Mount Kilimanjaro

Mountain symbolism is diverse and complex. The mountain as center of the universe, as touching the heavens, as the abode of gods and demons, as the place where the dead go, and as the link between hell, earth, and heaven—all these themes surround and penetrate mountain symbolism. The mountain is awe inspiring, fascinating, and strange. What is up there? Who lives there? Have people climbed it? Majestic mountain peaks like Mount Kilimanjaro prompt us to ask questions that reflect the awe we feel when we gaze on their heights.

Mount Kilimanjaro is located in northern Tanzania on the east coast of Africa. This majestic peak rises more than nineteen thousand feet above the surrounding flat plain and is visible more than a hundred miles in every direction. The contrast between this isolated, towering mountain standing in what appears to be the middle of nowhere and the flat plain below carries your eyes from an endless flat horizon to a vertical shaft thrust into the heavens. You

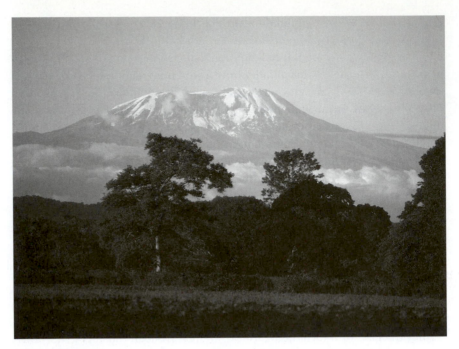

**Mount Kilimanjaro**

know immediately that this is something special. You can actually see the earth touch the sky as the top of the mountain disappears into the clouds. If you saw it, you would certainly understand why the Masai call it "house of God."

Mount Kilimanjaro is not one peak but three widely separated volcanic peaks linked by an elevated plateau. The highest is Peak Kibo, the one most people identify as Mount Kilimanjaro. Mawenzi is the second highest peak, and the oldest and lowest peak is called Shira. The mountain rises through diverse climate zones ranging from dry scrubland, damp jungles, and alpine meadows to arctic glaciers.

To the Chagga people who inhabit the slopes of Mount Kilimanjaro, the mountain is sacred. They tell a story that explains why one of the peaks, Mawenzi, appears disfigured and rough. Very, very long ago, the story goes, when the peaks were still active volcanoes, Kibo and Mawenzi were the wives of Ruwa, the creator. One day Mawenzi arrived at Kibo's home just before mealtime. According to Chagga custom, Kibo had to offer her food. When she finished eating, Mawenzi said she had come to get embers to light her own cooking fire. As she walked home, Mawenzi thought that the food Kibo cooked was very good and, being lazy, she herself did not want to cook. So she returned again just before dinner, saying that while crossing a stream she had tripped and the embers got wet. So Kibo had to feed her again. Mawenzi, realizing that she had a good thing going, came back for a third meal. However, Kibo had prepared just enough food for her husband Ruwa, and she flew into a rage. She began to beat Mawenzi with a wooden paddle, giving her the battered look she has today. People say that Mawenzi is now so ashamed of her battered and ugly face that she hides herself in clouds. Kibo faces away from Mawenzi out of disgust.

This is more than just a charming etiological tale. It identifies two of the most important peaks of Kilimanjaro with the wives of the creator god. It also reflects the domestic conflicts that must have arisen in Chagga society between wives of a chief or a wealthy man.

Living on the mountain is also a sign of superiority. The Chagga call Kilimanjaro "God's backyard" and regard others who live in the grasslands as inferior to them because they live closer to heaven. As one Chagga said, "You are not a full human being if you don't come from Kilimanjaro. In fact, the higher up the mountain you live, the more fully human and blessed you are."[1] Only men who have received the proper initiation can go to the most sacred region above the inhabited zone, which ends at about seven thousand feet.

Before European missionaries converted them to Christianity, the Chagga thought of the mountain as the embodiment of all that was divine, exalted, nourishing, and eternal. Their chiefs were given the title of Kibo, and they used the name in expressions of good luck and long life, such as "May you endure like Kibo." They regarded the side of a village oriented toward Kibo as one of honor, holding their feasts and councils there. If they met someone of higher rank on the road, they would show respect by allowing that person to pass on the side of the road closest to Kibo. They buried their dead with their heads toward Kibo, and in a year or two, they removed the skulls and reburied them in an ancestral grove facing Kibo. There, it is said, they can commune with the ancestors who dwell on Kibo. The Chagga today, even though Christianized, follow nearly the same burial customs. Most of their Christian churches have their altars on the side closest to Kibo.

Most of the time, in the Chagga language, special words are put before place names to indicate what kinds of places they are, such as "flat area so-and-so" or "point of land so-and-so." Usually the word meaning *mountain* is put before different names of mountains, but in the case of Kibo it is not. They simply say, "I go to Kibo," not "I go to Mount Kibo." Two other places are treated linguistically in the same way—home and heaven. This way of talking replicates in language an important difference between profane and sacred places. Sacred places are like the home we spend our earthly lives in and the heaven where we live eternally.

I think this case of a sacred mountain indicates some of the rich and complex symbolism associated with sacred places and hence sacred space. While the theme of connecting earth and heaven is less prominent than other themes, there can be little doubt that Kilimanjaro is holy ground. It is where the ancestors live, a home of the gods, and where full humanity can flower. Mount Kilimanjaro both centers and orients the space of the Chagga. It is where they live and work (hence their home), where the very peaks are divine beings, where sacred events once took place, and where they face to show honor and respect. The mountain draws a boundary between profane grasslands and sacred heights as well as a boundary between different kinds of people. It helps anchor and order the Chagga world, giving life meaning, establishing Chagga identity, and bestowing on the people a sense of belonging to a place. It simultaneously serves religious, cultural, and social functions. And its slopes provide food for the people. It is literally the source of their life.

## 7.1.2 The Dreamtime

The first human inhabitants arrived in Australia about fifty thousand years ago. They developed without much contact with other cultural groups until Captain James Cook landed in 1788 and claimed Australia for Great Britain. The subsequent European invasion killed some 95 percent of the Aboriginal population through massacres, disease, starvation, and forced resettlement. As you might imagine, many social problems of today are the result of this cultural, religious, and human devastation. Imagine 95 percent of the people you identify with dying traumatically over a short period of time.

We must be cautious when generalizing about religious practices and beliefs among Australian Aborigines. Much information has been lost over time, tribes are quite diverse, and all the variations have not been completely mapped. Many changes have occurred over a fifty thousand year history, even though early anthropologists believed these people and their religion were a pure, living example of "primitive" society.

The religion of the Australian Aborigines is usually classified as totemic. Early anthropologists, under the influence of evolutionary models, believed that totemism was one of the earliest forms of religion because it seemed only logical to them that early forms of society would manifest early forms of religion. Today we know that the religion of the Australian Aborigines is far more complex than the simple classification of totemism indicates. The word *totemism* itself comes from anthropologists and does not always accurately reflect what the Aborigines believe and do.

An illuminating example of sacred time can be found in the Australian Aboriginal conception of the Dreamtime or simply, The Dreaming. Aborigines adopted this terminology in order to refer to a primordial epoch, which begins when extraordinary, creative powers rose from the ground, descended from the sky, or appeared from over the horizon. The creative beings of this Dreamtime are called Dreamings and are the ultimate explanation for all things. Anthropologists called these Dreamings totems, but, as we shall soon see, they are far more than totemic ancestral beings from which a tribe or clan descended.

The English word *dream* often connotes something unreal, but this is not at all what the Aborigines mean by it. The Dream beings are not illusions, although they do often reveal themselves in dreams and trance states. For many they are more real than what we hear and see everyday in a waking state. These beings are something quite special and unique.

The Dreamtime is an age of unprecedented creative power when everything we know today originated. However, it is not some Golden Age, after which there is decay over time that will result in some inevitable final destruction. The universe has no end as far as the Aborigines are concerned. If it ever had any evolutionary development, that phase ended with the completion of the creation and the withdrawal of the spirit beings.

According to some Aboriginal myths, the physical world existed as a featureless, formless plain in which spirit beings or Dreamings slept. During the Dreamtime these beings awoke and decreed the laws that govern all aspects of life as well as the penalties for breaking the laws. They established the relationship of each member of the community to the other members and created the ceremonies that must be performed if the created order is to continue. They created animals, plants, humans, natural features of the landscape, tools, rituals—in short, everything of importance that exists today—as they traveled across the land.

After the Dreamings finished their work, they withdrew. The stories of how they left vary from group to group. One example comes from the Achilpa. They tell the story of Numbakulla, who arose "out of nothing" or "out of his own eternity." He traveled about making mountains, rivers, and all kinds of animals and plants. He taught the Achilpa many powerful ceremonies and when finished planted a pole in the middle of a sacred place. After anointing it with blood, he began to climb and told the first Achilpa Ancestor to follow him. However, the Ancestor slid down the pole because of the slippery blood and could not go with Numbakulla into the sky. So Numbakulla went on alone, drew up the pole after him, and no one has ever seen him again. This sacred pole of Numbakulla is today represented by the gum tree erected on the ceremonial ground during a long series of initiation rites.

Though the creative beings of the Dreamtime left the earth, they left behind some of their creative power at sacred sites, called Dreaming-places, and along sacred paths where they once traveled, called Dreaming-tracks. Aborigines can point out places and trails in their land where events took place in the Dreamtime and tell endless stories about this sacred past. However, they will not reveal too much because much of this special knowledge is secret and can only be revealed to those properly initiated.

In one sense this sacred time of great creativity ended when the Dreamings withdrew and finished their work. But in another sense it has not ended. The creative power they left behind is still effective. This is one reason why the Aborigines say the Dreamtime is eternal, even though they tell stories about when it ended. In some regions they hold that Dreamings reincarnate themselves as humans. Women become pregnant not from sexual activity, but from having a "spirit child" enter their womb when, for example, they pass some place of particular power. Mircea Eliade cites an early anthropological source:

> The tribes of central Australia have . . . a huge rock known as Erathipa which has an opening in one side from which the souls of the children imprisoned in it watch for a woman to pass by so that they may be reborn in her. When women who do not want children go near the rock, they pretend to be old, and walk as if leaning on a stick, crying: "Don't come to me, I am an old woman!"

Eliade comments, "The idea implicit in . . . these rites is that certain stones have the power to make sterile women fruitful, . . . because of the spirits of the ancestors that dwell in them. . . ."[2]

Even the present social order is explained by the Dreamtime. While women play major roles in many Dreamtime stories, today males dominate Aboriginal society. According to one story, this came about when two female creators momentarily left their powerful creative objects unprotected and men stole them, thus appropriating their power. As this story indicates, the power of males is derivative from females and achieved by theft. This simple story speaks volumes about gender relationships.

The rituals and ceremonies of the Aborigines recall and "re-present" today the power of the past. Participants wear designs that symbolize Dreamings, and they mime their actions. Each new generation is introduced to Dreamings in their initiation rites. For instance, the Wulamba, a group from the northern tip of Australia, hold an annual ceremony in which the women and children of the tribe wriggle under a mat while the men dance around, poking it with sacred poles. If asked why they do this, they will tell a story about a Dreamtime event in which the Djanggawul beings (a brother and two sisters) created the first humans. The brother pulled children out of the womb of his sisters, and when a girl baby came out it was placed under a mat to protect it from the sun. The mat now symbolizes the womb of the Djanggawul sisters, and the poles represent sacred objects used in the creation.

Though the sacred past is over, it is also not over. The Aborigines have a sacred obligation to make sure it is relived, reenacted, and re-presented so the cosmic order created during Dreamtime will endure. This cosmic order is cyclical and is manifested in the successive round of the seasons that bring rebirth to the earth after the plants and animals have died, left, or temporarily gone "to sleep." If that cycle stops, the lives of the Aborigines stop.

The basic assumption of Aborigine religion is that deities, spirits, humans, animals, and plants form a dynamic, interactive, and interdependent matrix. The present only exists because of the Dreamtime. The present and the future are dependent in a crucial way upon the past. If the past is forgotten—if the Dreamtime ceases to be celebrated in song, art, dance, ritual, and myth—the present and future will die. The power of creativity will cease. Hence the Aborigines are religiously and morally obligated to keep the cosmos in good working order now that the Dream beings have left.

## 7.2 COMPARISON

At first sight it appears that any comparison between Mount Kilimanjaro and Dreamtime must concentrate more on differences than similarities. We also need to ask whether comparison is even fruitful. What can we learn from a comparative approach that we have not already learned?

I think comparing these cases can highlight certain features that might be useful in cross-cultural analysis. It can also bring the concepts of sacred space and time into sharper focus. Certainly one thing comparison can do is remind us how social values get reflected in religious stories and how religious stories serve to legitimate social values by obscuring their human source.

One similarity is that in both of these cases the subordinate status of women is given religious legitimation. Notice that Kibo does the cooking for her husband and for any guests that might show up. Notice the supreme god Ruwa has more than one wife. There is no tale I know of told by the Chagga that speaks of a woman having more than one husband. In Australia men dominate the ritual and ceremonial affairs and hence inherit from the Dreamings the primary responsibility for keeping the universe running and preventing it from returning to formlessness. A story is even told about how they got this power from a primal theft of creative objects originally belonging to females. Males may dominate now, but only because of a past, primordial deceit.

Gender roles are not the only social arrangements reflected in these stories. The Chagga actually use the location where people live on Mount Kilimanjaro as a way of distinguishing between different grades of people. The higher on the mountain people live, the higher their social status, indeed, their human status. The Australian Aborigines use the stories about the ancestors created in Dreamtime to distinguish different groups and their status. These stories of descent not only identify tribes, but also establish their social power.

In both cases space and time become sacred because the stories link them to superhuman beings and their activities. Two important peaks of Kilimanjaro are related to the supreme god by marriage. Kilimanjaro is "God's backyard," and during the Dreamtime the superhuman and creative Dreamings are active on earth. They left tracks that are visible today, and the creative power of the Dreamings can become available today by repeating the rites and singing the songs they created.

People ascribe eternity to both Kilimanjaro and the Dreamtime and yet also talk about them as if they are not eternal. The Dreamtime comes to an end when the Dreamings leave, and clearly the Chagga believe that Mount Kilimanjaro was not always as it is now. What probably motivates this sort of talk is the need of both groups to explain how things came to be and also to make the power of their sacred origins available now. Causes precede effects, so the causes of the present must be in the past. And if the causes cannot be seen now, that past must, in some sense, be over. However, if something is also eternal, people can tap into its power any place they may be or at any time. Kilimanjaro and the Dreamtime are always with the Chagga and the Aborigines no matter how far from the sacred mountain they travel or how far in the past the Dreaming (for example) took place.

A comparison of these cases shows that both sacred time and sacred place establish order and hence meaning, but in different ways. In the Dreamtime the superhuman powers create sacred places throughout Australia, but these sacred places do not cause the Dreamtime. If the creative powers had continued to sleep, or never arrived in the first place, there would be no sacred space, only, according to one of the stories, a featureless surface. Likewise, for the Chagga, the peaks of Kilimanjaro would not exist if certain events had not taken place in the sacred time of the past. If the wives of Ruwa had not quarreled, things would look very different. Things that exist today need an explanation, but the time in which they came to be just happens. It is without precedent. The Dreamtime needs no explanation because nothing of any significance happened before its creative explosion.

Humans order things by establishing connections and by orientation. Both Dreamtime and Kilimanjaro order in the same way. Kilimanjaro connects the earth with the sky and orients the living and the dead, the sides of villages, and different structures. The Dreamtime connects the present with the past and orients life around the ceremonies and rituals given in the past that sustain the tribes in the present. People can find the answers to questions about who they are and where they came from in sacred time and space. Answers to these questions not only establish identity, but also promote a sense of belonging. All of us feel more secure when we know our past and the place from where we come.

## 7.3 FEATURES OF SACRED SPACE AND TIME

Sacred space and time take many different forms. Some of the most obvious sacred places that embody sacred spaces are temples, shrines, churches, mosques, synagogues, altars, cemeteries, arks, reliquaries (structures containing relics), convents, and monasteries. Humans create these sorts of sacred places for a variety of purposes such as to pray, conduct rituals, bury the dead, house the gods, store sacred objects, and much more. Within these spaces sacred time is celebrated—the creation; the hoped for time of salvation; the birth or life of a prophet, savior, or holy person; significant past events crucial to a religion's history; and special present events of marriage, baptism, initiations, and deaths.

Some sacred places are natural, such as Mount Kilimanjaro and the features of the Australian landscape. They may be rocks, mountains, lakes, springs, rivers, and valleys. These sacred locations may be places of great beauty and majesty, but they do not have to be physically impressive. Ordinary looking places that only the members of a particular religion find special can also be sacred. Entering these sacred places carries people into both sacred time and space. Frequently, people conduct ceremonies and rites in such natural settings. These places are often associated with some action of superhuman powers, such as conflicts with demons, or special events, such as the Buddha's enlightenment under the bodhi tree.

Sometimes natural settings are combined with constructed spaces. For instance, one of the most famous places of divination in the ancient world was located at Delphi. The site is awe inspiring. Located on a sacred mountain overlooking a vast valley with a grand view of the ocean, one glance tells you that this is indeed a special place. It is also special because of the stories associated with the site. According to one story, Zeus, wishing to find the center of the earth, let two eagles loose from two ends of the earth. The sacred birds met at Delphi; hence Zeus designated it the "navel" of the earth. Like human navels, which mark the center of human beings and the place where they were once attached to their mothers, Delphi marks the center of the earth around which everything is oriented and a place where earth and heaven were once connected. But in the realm of sacred time, once connected means always connected. So a temple compound was built at the site, and from time to time a medium, called the Pythia, went into a trance, was possessed by the god Apollo, and uttered oracles in answer to the questions posed by pilgrims.

Delphi was a gate, or opening, to superhuman power and knowledge. So too are many other sacred spaces. People may enter a mosque, church, or synagogue to talk with the divine through prayer. They may go to a shrine honoring a saint or spiritual hero to ask for healing, a long life, or some special blessing. Native Americans enter a sacred circle to dance, drum, sing, and pray because there they can communicate with the holy. Christians enter special places at special times to become possessed by the Holy Spirit, to offer praise, and to hear the great stories of creation, life, death, and salvation.

In addition to functioning as openings to superhuman power, sacred spaces and sacred times draw a boundary between the pure and the impure. People "enter" and "exit" these places and times. Such places are marked off, distinguished, separated from profane places and times. Those that enter must cleanse themselves with water to wash off the pollution and impurities of daily life. So Muslims symbolically bathe before entering a mosque, the devotees at Delphi washed in a sacred spring before entering the sacred compound, and Roman Catholic Christians cross themselves with holy water.

Besides the boundaries between those within and those without, sacred places draw boundaries among those who are within—between priest and laity, men and women, children and adults, preachers and hearers, healers and the healed, sinners and saints. Sacred places and sacred times can create distinctions as well as erase distinctions. Those who arrive at Mecca for pilgrimage cover themselves with white robes. This act not only symbolizes purity, but also obliterates all distinction of social class and monetary status. Everyone is dressed the same. Paradoxically, what is worn in sacred places and times can both establish social and gender differences and conceal them.

Sacred space and time provide opportunities that are uniquely open to superhuman power and mark all kinds of social and religious boundaries. In addition, they provide a stable center of orientation. For example, Delphi is the center of the earth. The spatial and temporal orientation is both vertical and horizontal. Cathedral towers rise from earth to heaven, and under the cathedral the holy are buried. In Europe, cathedrals were often built in the center of town on a high hill. All roads, as they say, lead to the holy city of Rome. From Chaco Canyon, an ancient Native American holy site in New Mexico, roads radiate in all directions.

The sacred history narrated in the Bible orients us in time. Calendars mark time from events that are sacred to different religions, such as the birth of Jesus. Seasonal celebrations like the Akitu, Passover, Ramadan, and Christmas periodically reclaim the past for the present, and the sacred liminal periods of rites of passage mark human development. Religions locate us in time and space, thereby ordering our lives, making time meaningful, and pointing out the way. They provide maps and time lines that help us negotiate life.

## Functions of Sacred Time and Space

1. Provide spatial and temporal openings to superhuman power
2. Establish spatial and temporal boundaries
3. Orient people in time and space

Sacred space and time are paradoxical. They are times and places that are here and yet not here. The Dreamtime is not now; yet it is now as the songs are sung, the rituals performed, and the tracks followed. The Dreamings are gone, but what they made remains. The superhuman wives of Ruwa are no longer wandering the high plateau of Kilimanjaro arguing and fighting, yet they are still there as Kibo and Mawenzi for all to see.

Similarly, sacred times and sacred spaces make what is strange familiar and what is familiar strange. The world of superhuman power and the feats of superhuman beings are different and strange to creatures who are limited, conditioned, and powerless in all kinds of important ways, and yet this strangeness becomes familiar and comfortable as we tell about it, sing about it, and celebrate it. And the places and times we know so well—that familiar mountain over there, that date on the calendar, this returning fall or spring—become tinged with the unfamiliar and strange power of the gods when they become holy sites and holy times.

So far I have been giving a phenomenological description of sacred space and time. To change theoretical focus for a moment, let me speculate on the possible biological origins of the human need to create special times and places. We can observe similar behavior in nonhuman animals. Animals have seasonal times for mating, ritualized mating behaviors, and special places they travel for food, shelter, and protection during the year. Elephants have burial grounds, birds annually migrate, salmon return to the stream of their birth to spawn, bears often return to the same dens to hibernate and, in the spring, to their favorite hunting and fishing grounds. The evolutionary value of such behavior is evident.

I am not suggesting that the special times and places that other animals utilize are sacred to them in the same sense as they are for humans. However, they are certainly special. They may well be regularly marked with scent, and protected, sometimes by violent fights often involving injury or death. Humans will also mark their sacred places with emblems, symbols, walls, temples, and frequently fight over them. Think of the battles waged over holy sites in Jerusalem, India, and many other places around the world. The fact that people will lay down their lives for a place or for the freedom to celebrate a holy day indicates that establishing special places and times is as important for the survival of human animals as it is for the nonhuman animals with which we share the earth.

## 7.4 RELIGION AND ART

Religion and art are two of the most important forms of cultural creativity. Think of different kinds of art like architecture, painting, dance, sculpture, music, poetry, literature, and drama. Like religion, these arts concern themselves with space, time, order, meaning, and appearance. Also like religion, they use symbols, signs, emblems, and codes to convey meaning and elicit emotional responses. It is impossible to do an analysis of sacred space and time without talking about the sorts of art that symbolize, structure, and order time and space and mark them as sacred.

Traditionally, religions have assumed an instrumental view of art: art does not exist for the sake of art, but to serve other purposes. For example, icons (images) such as paintings of saints can serve a devotional function. The consecrated statue of a god makes the god present in space and time. The worshiper who offers sacrifices and prayers to the image is not offering devotion to the actual image or idol, but to the divine *in* the image. The divine inhabits the image or statue, either temporarily or permanently. The image is the instrument or means of the divine presence and not the object of devotion.

The paradox of sacred space and time is repeated on the artistic level. The god is there in the idol and not there. The spirit of the divine dwells in a sanctuary and does not dwell there. This paradoxical and ambiguous relation between what we can call the materiality of art and the superhuman power it symbolizes accounts for the tension often found in religions between creating sacred art and destroying it.

From time to time, **iconoclastic** controversies erupt, and "purification" movements arise. The Protestant "plain style" churches of New England, with few or no images, are a reaction to the elaborately decorated cathedrals and churches of medieval Europe, with their ornate stained-glass windows and profusion of images and statues of saints, angels, Christ, and sacred scenes from the Bible filling almost every available space. The Roman Catholic and Orthodox traditions of Christianity have emphasized what Paul Tillich called the **sacramental principle**—the drive to make the material sacred, stemming from the belief in the incarnation of the divine in human form. The Protestant tradition, in contrast, has emphasized what Tillich called the **prophetic principle**—the drive to distance the divine from the material in order to avoid idolatry and allow the world to come under the critical judgment of the transcendent divine. Thus in a traditional Catholic church the altar provides a sacred space to house the consecrated bread and wine, the very body and blood of the crucified Christ; while the pulpit dominates the Protestant church, the place from which the word of the Lord can be proclaimed, condemning human efforts to save themselves and offering hope of divine forgiveness to those who surrender their lives to God.

Some religions remain permanently iconoclastic, forbidding any and all images of either humans or the divine. Judaism and Islam come immediately to mind. Synagogues and mosques are empty of statues and sacred images. Devotion and prayer is directed to a spiritual reality, not a material representation of it. However, even in iconoclastic religions, all art does not disappear. Islamic mosques contain beautiful and intricate geometric designs and calligraphy of the highest quality. Line, shape, and artistic renderings of the Arabic language of Allah found in the Quran remind the worshiper of the revelation of Allah's will. Likewise, Hebrew letters adorn synagogues, and wonderful calligraphy highlights the sacredness of the Torah, as the scrolls containing scripture are exhibited for the devout to kiss.

The Taliban, when they were in control of Afghanistan, destroyed the statues of buddhas carved centuries ago. These were invaluable world art treasures. World culture and history is diminished by their destruction. But the Taliban believed they were on a holy crusade to wipe out idolatry by destroying these precious, priceless statues. Most iconoclastic movements destroy other people's art, just as many believers declare the sacred stories of others to be "mere myths."

Religious art, in addition to serving a devotional function, also serves a teaching function. The great Buddhist **stupa** at Borobudur, Java, visually displays the Buddhist view of reality. It represents all the levels of the Buddhist picture of the cosmos, from bottom to top. The path from the prison of ignorance to the freedom of enlightenment circles its sides. In churches, stained-glass windows tell stories from the Christian Gospels. Even the way images or icons are painted can convey information. Many Greek Orthodox icons have elongated and nearly transparent features. The golden light comes from behind the image, telling the faithful in graphic form how they should understand the material world. The material is a veil for the spiritual light that shines through it. In some paintings of Jesus and Mary, the tension between the material and the spiritual is almost totally resolved in favor of the spiritual. The golden halo of light immediately signals that these are no ordinary people.

### 7.4.1 Architecture

Sacred buildings are one of the most visible symbols of a religion's teachings, wealth, and power. Architecture is the most complex of the fine arts, and is used effectively by many religions to express their vision of the spiritual. Geometry, building materials, verticality, orientation, enclosure, and ornamentation come together in architecture to create sacred space and time, to teach about superhuman realities, and to inspire devotion. Of the many different kinds of religious architecture, we will focus on three of the most common types—the shrine, the temple, and congregational structures.

Shrines are structures, some simple and some complex, that mark a burial place of importance, house revered relics of founders and saints, or commemorate the site of some sacred, miraculous event. Shrines need not be buildings intended to house people, but may be simple memorials such as the cross with flowers often seen by a road. Many shrines mark places of pilgrimage, so they are often circular or square structures with external space that allows pilgrims to pray or circle them (circumambulate). A stupa is a memorial structure inspired by Gautama Buddha's burial mound. Stupas have characteristic shapes, like the one pictured in Figure 7.1. Some look like a bell planted on the ground with its handle pointing toward the sky. Relics are enclosed in the domes, and parasols, a sign of royalty, float above them. In Japan and China the stupa form has evolved into a many-storied pagoda tower. Pagodas and stupas are emblems of the cosmic order in miniature as well as homes for sacred relics.

A temple is a building that houses images and statues of gods and goddesses. The temple and shrine are among the oldest types of religious structures. Just as humans require houses, so too do the gods. Temples are homes of the gods, and the priests attend the sacred images housed there as they would royalty in a palace. Wealth, available materials, cultural tastes, local

FIGURE 7.1 Example of a Stupa

circumstances, as well as religious practices account for the variety of temple architecture. Hindu temples have a square shape because Hindus believe that the square is the perfect form. They are elaborately decorated with figures of all sorts, including animals and humans along with demons, gods, and goddesses. Altars are usually outside, in front of the temples, where offerings to the divine within can be given. Usually, the area where the gods and goddesses dwell is a darkened sanctuary suggesting mystery and holiness. On certain occasions however, the images are revealed. Diane Eck writes:

> A common sight in India is a crowd of people gathered in the courtyard of a temple . . . for the *darśan* of the deity. *Darśan* means "seeing." In the Hindu ritual tradition it refers especially to religious seeing, or the visual perception of the sacred. When Hindus go to a temple, they do not commonly say, "I am going to worship," but rather, "I am going for *darśan*." They go to "see" the image of the deity . . . present in the sanctum of the temple, and they go especially at those times of day when the image is most beautifully adorned with fresh flowers and when the curtain is drawn back so the image is fully visible.[3]

Temples are often located in temple compounds surrounded by a wall. Within the temple precinct are other buildings such as dining halls, schools, and residences for priests, nuns, or monks. Gates leading into the compound, usually at the cardinal points of the compass, mark the separation of sacred from profane space. There are gates within the compound itself, marking off different areas, and frequently, in the more elaborate temples in China, India, and Japan, there will be refreshing gardens, ponds, meandering streams, and piles of rocks reminiscent of mountains. Often the chanting of monks can be heard, or sacred music will be playing, and it, along with the strong smell of incense, will gently and gradually separate the devotee or the visitor from the profane time of the hustle and bustle of the outside streets into the calm, sacred time of the temple compound. Walking from a busy street in a Chinese city into a Daoist temple compound is like walking into another world.

Congregational structures require a different sort of architecture. Sacred spaces to house worshipers rather than gods and goddesses need to be created so people can congregate with other believers to pray, sing, hear sermons, and read scripture. Typically, these buildings have one roof with a large space inside to hold people together in one place. Jewish synagogues, Islamic mosques, and Christian churches are typical examples of congregational structures. The architecture of these buildings creates spaces for people to congregate and engage in corporate worship.

A Jewish *synagogue* (Greek, meaning "assembly") is not a temple where priests offer sacrifices to the gods that dwell therein, but an unconsecrated house of worship and study created for and run by the laity. Jewish law requires no particular architectural design, and any place with ten males over the age of thirteen and a Torah scroll can serve as a synagogue. However, synagogues do have some features reminiscent of temple worship, as we shall see shortly. This should be no surprise since the temple at Jerusalem located on Mount Zion was the primary place of Jewish worship before the Romans destroyed it in 70 C.E.

Many synagogues are rectangular, with a large room where people can gather. The visual center of the room is the holy ark (*aron kodesh*) that houses the Torah scrolls and is in the wall facing east, toward the holy city of Jerusalem. The ark represents the Ark of the Covenant that, according to tradition, contained the tablets given to Moses on Mount Sinai and on which YHWH had inscribed the Ten Commandments. The ark is covered by a curtain (*parokhet*) symbolizing the curtain that covered the holy of holies in the Jerusalem Temple. Over the ark hangs the "eternal light" reminding the faithful of the seven-branched menorah that burned in the Temple. Near the ark is a pulpit or lectern that may be fixed or mobile.

Another focal point, in addition to the ark, is a raised platform called the *binah* from which the Torah scroll is read and singing is led. This platform is often in the center of a synagogue, but may be located on the west wall, where the people enter, or integrated into the front, eastern area, where the ark is located. In Orthodox synagogues, the men usually pray on the main floor, and the women are situated in a gallery above. This separation by gender reinforces traditional patriarchal views with respect to gender. In Reform and Conservative congregations, the genders mix and have no assigned spaces.

The church, like the synagogue, is a congregational structure built so people can gather for worship. However, it does retain some features of temple worship, such as an altar (although the altar is inside the building, not outside).

FIGURE 7.2  Cruciform Ground Plan

The altar is located in either the center of the church or at the end facing east, toward the holy city of Jerusalem. Early churches borrowed their architecture from Roman public houses called *basilicas*. They have three aisles, walls with high windows, a wide nave where people sit or stand, and an altar area. The high windows cause the light to filter in from above, giving the impression of a divine light penetrating the darkness of this material and sinful world.

Christians and, later, Muslims also borrowed the dome from the Romans. The dome symbolizes the vault of heaven, reminding the faithful that the church or mosque is a microcosm of the macrocosmic universe created by divine power. Christian domes are often richly decorated with angels, saints, and even the starry heavens. Sometimes they have a transparent hole in the center of the dome, as a reminder that the *axis mundi* runs through this place. Vaulted ceilings and huge columns give a vertical feeling to churches and mosques, drawing attention to the heavens above and suggesting a connection between what is below and what is above.

A popular floor plan is the Latin cross (see Figure 7.2). The congregants enter at the foot of the cross (typically the west end) and occupy the nave, which is oriented to the east, where the altar is often located. There may be chapels in the cross arms of the church. Often the baptismal font is located near the west entrance. Other churches have a simple rectangular floor plan, often with a steeple area whose base serves as the entrance. A pulpit is usually located near the front. Modern church architecture takes many forms, with different kinds of floor plans, but, whatever the architecture, there must always be some sort of space in which people can gather to worship.

The architectural features of Islamic mosques vary according to time and location. Generally, they reflect local architectural designs. Once again, a space must be provided for worshipers to gather and pray, and features must provide for the ritual demands of worship. Before entering a mosque, worshipers must wash, often at a fountain in the courtyard, and take off their shoes, which are placed on racks near the entrance. The prayer hall proper, unlike synagogues and churches, has no benches or chairs because Islamic prayer requires room for prostration. The floor is usually covered by carpets, and like the synagogue but unlike the church, there are no images of any kind on the walls, ceilings, windows, or floors.

The central focal point is an arch (*mihrab*) orienting the congregation toward the holy city of Mecca. To the right of the arch is a raised platform (*minbar*) that serves as a pulpit from which prayers are led by the prayer leader, called an **imam**. On Fridays, sermons are given. Women enter through a different door than the men and stay in a segregated area of the mosque hidden from the view of males. Some mosques have a tower (*minaret*) from which the haunting and beautiful call to prayer is given. The main function of a mosque is to provide a sanctified place for fulfilling the Islamic obligations to say prayers five times a day at fixed times. Many mosques not only serve as places of prayer, but also as places that provide child care, health services, and food and shelter for the hungry and homeless.

### Major Types of Sacred Architecture

1. Shrines memorializing sacred tombs, relics, and places
2. Temples housing gods and serving as a place of sacrifice
3. Congregational structures providing assembly places

My classification of religious architecture in terms of shrines, temples, and assembly places for congregations, like all classification schemes, is too simplified. Some mosques, for example, serve as shrines, and some assembly halls serve as temples, providing places for the divine presence on the altar. Buddhist temples can be places for housing venerated images of the Buddha as well as places for assembly. Remember that the same building can serve different functions, and there are other types of structures such as monasteries and convents that we have not discussed. Whatever the type, all embody the idea of a sacred space in which people can become close to superhuman reality, and the architectural splendor or simplicity reinforces the sacredness of the place.

## 7.4.2 Music

An art form closely related to religion and even more universal than architecture is music. Myths abound about music coming from other realms or from superhuman beings. These stories indicate that many religious traditions find in music a revelation of something special and otherworldly.

Music, like religion, has the power to transform human lives and to transport us into another time and place. The tension between the here and the not-here is repeated in music. We know that music is made of patterned sound waves that can be mathematically represented. Yet it is so much more than its analyzable structure, precisely because through the music we hear a "beyond," an "other," that is in the sound but not reducible to the sound. Myths, before they became written literature, were sung, chanted, or in other ways musically performed, thereby bridging the gap between myth (what is said or sung) and ritual (what is done or performed).

Ceremonial space, whether it is in a building or in the open, is pervaded by sounds that fill the area with tangible energy and power. The music signals that something special is happening here. It frames ritual activity, often starting it and ending it. It is synchronized with ritual time by techniques such as repetition, contrast, development, and variation. Music can also serve as an *axis mundi*, channeling communication with the spirits.

The Australian Aborigines believe the Dreamings gave their songs to them, and when they sing them now they ritually become their own ancestors. These sacred songs from the Dreamtime are not just sung, they are danced. As the singing and dancing return the participants to that creative time when the ancestors brought all things into existence, the modern-day Aborigines can participate in those creative acts, thereby ensuring health, food, and the perpetuation of the social and cosmic order.

The peoples of sub-Saharan Africa use music and dancing to get into and out of trance states. Changes in intensity and pitch affect the mood of worship. Much of the singing and dancing is repetitive. Repetition is probably the most widespread and basic way to structure time through music. Hindus chant **mantras** like *Om*, which they believe to be sacred sounds that capture the echoes of creation. The chanting of mantras often induces trance states because of the repetition, and it facilitates meditation and prayer by focusing the mind on a sound that reverberates throughout the body. *Om* sounds like "aum" when chanted. The *a* starts with an open mouth and symbolizes ordinary waking consciousness. The *u* occurs as the mouth begins to close and symbolizes dreaming consciousness. The *m* occurs with the mouth shut, is prolonged, and gradually fades into nothingness. It symbolizes sleeping consciousness, and the silence that follows as the sound fades away symbolizes the mystical consciousness where union with absolute reality occurs. *Oṃ* is not merely the leftover echoes of creation; it is a channel, a means, for taking individual consciousness back to its origin and on to its fulfillment.

Music enhances devotion. Bach's magnificent religious chorales carry our emotions away to other times and places, even if we do not believe. Music makes present what is absent and creates moods of exaltation. The start of music marks the beginning of sacred time, and its ending marks the close of sacred time. Without the arts, our sense of the sacred would be greatly diminished.

## 7.5 SUMMARY

Myths and rituals create sacred time and space. Every religion manipulates space and time in its attempt to express the otherworld in terms of this world. Both sacred space and time provide channels of communication between here and there, then and now. Sacred space creates an *axis mundi*, and sacred time recycles the power of the past into the present. The first case study, of Kilimanjaro, described how mountains are sacred spaces in part because they visually connect the earth with the sky. They are homes for the gods and for the ancestors, and they draw boundaries between what is sacred and what is profane.

The Dreamtime, our second case study, illustrated how a powerful and sacred past can be made present once more. The massive outpouring of creative energy in the past is over and yet is not over. The power can be recovered through story, song, and dance. For the Australian Aborigines, all aspects of the universe—spirits, ancestors, animals, plants, humans—are interactive and interdependent, thanks to the work of the Dreamings.

Our comparison of the sacred mountain Kilimanjaro and the sacred time called the Dreamtime showed how stories about these times and places serve to legitimate the customs of a society by saying, in effect, "we do things this way in our society because the gods did things this way in that sacred time and space long, long ago." The tension between being eternal and being over allows the Aborigines to tap into the power of the Dreamtime and make it available today.

What is created in sacred space is dependent upon some sacred time when it first happened. The notion of sacred time can be used to explain what goes on today, and the notion of sacred space creates an enduring geography. Both sacred time and space function to connect the human and the superhuman, thereby orienting humans. When a friend asks who you are, you might reply by telling stories about what happened in your past and the place you come from. Thus we establish identity and a sense of belonging within history and this world. So too religions establish identity and a sense of belonging within the universe as a whole by expressing and establishing sacred space and time through their myths and rituals.

When we discussed some general features of sacred space and time, we used the example of Delphi to illustrate how certain places can function as the center, or navel, of the world. Sacred places are the places where all things above and below meet. As we enter and exit sacred places and times, boundaries are drawn, not only between what is sacred and what is profane, but also between and among people. Social status can be created and erased in sacred places at sacred times.

Thus the functions of opening to the superhuman, establishing boundaries, and creating orientation contribute to making sacred space and time something greater than our ordinary times and places. In addition, sacred space and time have a paradoxical aspect. They set up a tension between what is here and what is not here, between what is familiar and what is strange.

Humans mark the places and times that are special to them, and so do nonhuman animals. There may be a biological foundation to the human desire to establish sacred time and space. Establishing such places contributes to our survival, and, paradoxically, some of us are willing to die to preserve them. Perhaps the loss of some life is necessary for the survival of life as a whole. Sacred space and sacred time may demand human sacrifices, but they contribute to the ongoing story of life.

Art is the perfect instrument for creating and maintaining sacred space and time. The sacred idol or holy icon reflects the tension between the here and the not-here. The worshiper is devoted to the god or goddess within, who is there in the consecrated idol, yet not there. However, iconoclastic movements within religions reveal the tension and ambiguity of the divine presence and absence. According to Tillich's sacramental principle, some religions tend to make the material spiritual, while the prophetic principle drives the faithful to separate the material from the spiritual as far as possible. Judaism and Islam are examples of religions that are permanently iconoclastic, yet even they have sacred art, which appears in the form of geometric ornamentation and calligraphy.

Art serves religious devotion and instructs the faithful. It inspires and teaches in dance, painting, sculpture, architecture, music, and more. Architecture in particular has been used to create sacred spaces within which sacred time can be experienced. Shrines, temples, and congregational structures represent just three of the most common types of religious architecture. Shrines, such as stupas built to hold the Buddha's relics, or wayside crosses, clearly indicate their memorial function. Temples shelter the gods and goddesses as well as provide places to offer prayers and sacrifices. Synagogues, churches, and mosques provide spaces for people to congregate as a community in prayer.

Music is perhaps the most universal of all the religious arts. According to some, it is a blessing given by the gods. Music can serve as a vital and inspiring communication link between the human and the superhuman. It uses repetition to create trances in which the sacred appears and mantras to focus our wandering minds in meditation. Music ushers people into another time and place and creates boundaries between the sacred and profane by marking the beginnings and endings of ritual performances. Religious art makes the divine absence present and the distant divine closer. It is difficult if not impossible to imagine sacred space and time without some kind of art.

## 7.6 RESEARCH CASE—THE CATHEDRAL OF ST. ANDREW

The Cathedral of St. Andrew is located at Wells, England. Its architectural style is Gothic. Among other things, Gothic designates an architectural style developed in Western Europe between the twelfth and sixteenth centuries. It is characterized by the use of ribbed vaulting, pointed arches, and steep roofs. Cathedrals are Christian churches that contain the *cathedra*, or "throne," of a bishop.

Wells is located west of Oxford in a lush countryside with deep springs or "wells." The abundant water supports rich and luxurious vegetation. The location is peaceful and quiet, adding to the grandeur of the church. It may well have been a Celtic sacred site prior to the Christianizing of England. The construction started before the end of the twelfth century, and, while additions and restorations have taken place since, much of the original structure survives today. It is no longer a Roman Catholic church, however, but an Anglican church. During the sixteenth century, Protestant iconoclasts plundered and desecrated the church. In 1685 it was used by Protestant troops as a stable.

The ground plan is in the form of a cross, or *cruciform* (see Figure 7.2). The main body of the church is divided into three main sections—the sanctuary, the choir, and the nave. As you approach the main entrance, which is located at the foot of the cross facing west, you see two massive towers in which there are niches containing various sculptures representing saints, angels, and biblical scenes, one of which shows the dead rising naked from their tombs. There are about three hundred figures, some as tall as eight feet and many smaller ones. At one time the west front was covered with a variety of stunning colors—silver, gold, scarlet, purple, and blue. At sunset, just looking at the front must have transported people, however briefly, into heaven. There are also floral and fruit designs along with geometric patterns. The whole cathedral, but especially the front, is a virtual "sermon in stone."

As you enter through large and impressive doors, you find yourself in a porch area called the *narthex*. There is a small fountain containing holy water, which has been blessed for the special purpose of defeating the devil. Worshipers dip their fingers into this water and make the sign of the cross on themselves, thereby symbolizing the baptism that first made them members of the church or "Body of Christ."

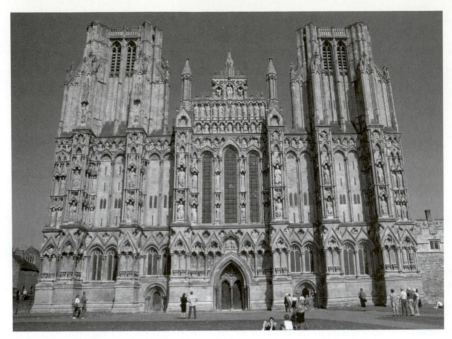

The Cathedral of St. Andrew at Wells, England

Beyond the narthex is the nave, where the lay worshipers stand facing east toward the choir and sanctuary, which contains the high altar. The baptismal font is on the extreme west wall of the nave, just beyond the narthex. Baptism is the first of seven sacraments practiced in the Roman Catholic Church. (Protestant Christians usually recognize only two of the seven, baptism and Holy Communion, as genuine sacraments.) The faithful believe that baptism washes their sins away and inducts them into the Body of Christ. The other six sacraments are holy chrism or confirmation, the mass that celebrates the Eucharist, penance or absolution, holy matrimony, holy orders (ordination), and extreme unction (preparation for death).

The pulpit is located before the sanctuary and choir at the front of the nave. Near there, you find what is called the *crossing*. It is the place where the arms of the cross intersect with the main part of the church. The two arms are usually referred to as the north transept and the south transept. In the Cathedral of St. Andrew, chapels dedicated to St. Calixtus and to St. Martin occupy the transepts. One of the rare works of Christian art showing God the Father is found on a tomb in the chapel of St. Calixtus. God the Father is shown seated in majesty upon a throne, and between his knees is a cross bearing the crucified body of Christ, the Son of God.

The nave, flanked with magnificent pillars, seems to stretch up to heaven. There are scenes from the Old Testament on the south wall, and opposite, on the north wall of the nave, are scenes from the New Testament. Traditional Christian theology taught that the Old Testament contains "types" that prefigure the realities of the New Testament. So, for example, the tree of life in the Garden of Eden might be paired with, on the opposite wall, the cross of Christ. Or Moses leading the people of Israel across the Red Sea might be paired with a scene of Jesus' baptism by John the Baptist.

The stained glass windows of St. Andrew present abstract arrangements of different colored glass. They are constructed from pieces of glass taken from the windows destroyed by reforming Protestants. The present abstract forms are nonrepresentational and give an almost modern feel to this ancient cathedral.

The tombs of bishops and nobles on the sides of the nave are elaborately decorated. One on the south wall has a panel portraying the annunciation to Mary that she would be the mother of the Messiah. Mourners are also depicted along with the Holy Trinity. Wells was not a major pilgrimage site because it had no saint of its own, but one bishop who had good teeth was venerated by the laity as a saint in the late thirteenth century because people believed that a visit to his grave can cure dental troubles.

Footfalls of nearly seven centuries have worn down the eighteen-step stairway linking the north transept with the Chapter House, where the clergy of Wells deliberated. From earliest times it is said that visitors called these steps "the heavenly stairs." Inside the Chapter House, at the head of the stairs, are fifty-one stalls raised above a bench. A window ledge bears the painted arms of King James I with a Latin inscription declaring the king to be the "nurturer" of the church.

Inside the north transept stands the oldest clock in England. It dates from the fourteenth century. Every hour on the hour horsemen engage in a tournament. Also, Christ rises and ascends to heaven. Symbols of the four evangelists (Matthew, Mark, Luke, and John) adorn the four corners. The clock displays the twenty-four hours of the day along with the month and phases of the moon. The Greek goddess of the moon, Phoebe, is painted on the central disk of the circular moon window. A Latin inscription proudly declares, "This spherical globe shows the world in microcosm, its archetype."

Within this fantastic space, the main Christian rites of passage, called sacraments (baptism, confirmation, ordination, and marriage) were celebrated. In addition, the mass was celebrated every day. Catholics believe that in the mass the bread and wine become the body and blood of Christ. Participation unites worshipers with the death and resurrection of Christ and bestows the grace of God's forgiveness and assurances of eternal life. Also within this space each year the sacred seasons of the Christian calendar were and are celebrated.

The Christian year starts with the season of Advent (four weeks) when the announcement and preparation for the birth of the savior are celebrated. It is followed by Christ Mass (Christmas), or the celebration of the birth of Jesus the Christ, lasting twelve days. The season of Epiphany, celebrating the appearance of Jesus as the Christ, is celebrated for one to six weeks.

The season of Lent (forty days) follows Epiphany, during which the faithful seek forgiveness of their sins and perform penance. Lent culminates in the Easter, or Paschal, season, which celebrates the resurrection and ascension into heaven of Jesus the Christ. The Day of Pentecost, also known as Whitsunday, ushers in the long Trinity season. Pentecost celebrates the founding of the Christian church when the Holy Spirit inspired the first apostles to spread the gospel, or good news, that Christ has overcome death. Trinity ends with All Saints Day (popularly known as Halloween), and then the cycle begins again with Advent. Interwoven within this cycle are Old Testament events that serve as prophecies intended to validate the ritual events and the Christian story. Alan Watts writes:

> From this point of view, history begins with Adam and begins again with Christ, so much so that what happens in between occurs within a epoch of darkness wherein God is known only through "types and shadows." That is to say, the *Old Testament*—the Law of Moses, the Prophets, and the history of Israel—is significant to the Catholic mind only because it is a symbolical foreshadowing of Christ. Thus the *Old Testament* stories enter into the Christian story in so far as they seem appropriate "types" of the various "mysteries" of the life of Christ which are celebrated throughout the course of the Christian year.[4]

At the Cathedral of St. Andrew in Wells, sacred space, sacred time, sacred history, sacred art, and sacred ritual all blend in a complex aesthetic experience of the sacred. The mysteries of the faith are revealed, yet concealed enough to elicit that sense of awe and mystery so essential to religion. Now you see it and now you don't. The sacred presence is felt in, around, and under the stone, the statues, the incense, the chanting, the stained glass, and the architecture, but it is never quite captured by it. In the end, the spirit blows where it will, no matter how inspired and brilliant humans are at bringing it into time and space.

## QUESTIONS ON THE CASE OF THE CATHEDRAL OF ST. ANDREW

1. In what ways do the architecture and decoration of the Cathedral of St. Andrews at Wells announce that this is sacred space?
2. Why do you think the cathedral is oriented toward the east? What is the significance of entering the church from the west?
3. What is the significance of the cruciform ground plan? Why do you think important people like bishops and nobles are buried in the church?

4. What connections do you see between this case and the first two cases that opened this chapter? Be specific.

## SUGGESTIONS FOR FURTHER READING

In addition to the material found in the notes, the reader may wish to consult the following for more information.

Andronicos, Manolis. *Delphi*. Athens: Ekdotike Athenon S.A., 1976. This book contains a description with pictures of the history and archeology of Delphi.

"Architecture and Religion." In *The HarperCollins Dictionary of Religion*, edited by Jonathan Z. Smith, 67–71. San Francisco: HarperCollins, 1995. I am indebted to this article for basic information about temples, shrines, and congregational structures.

Bernbaum, Edwin. *Sacred Mountains of the World*. Berkeley: University of California Press, 1997. This book is filled with beautiful pictures of sacred mountains from around the world, along with insightful commentary.

Eliade, Mircea. *Australian Religions: An Introduction*. Ithaca, NY: Cornell University Press, 1971. One of the foremost religion scholars of the last century provides a phenomenological description.

———. *The Sacred and the Profane: The Nature of Religion*. Trans. Willard R. Trask. New York: Harper & Row, 1961. The first two chapters contain a classic and widely influential study of sacred space and time.

Holm, Jean, and John Bowker, eds. *Sacred Place*. London: Pinter, 1994. This collection of essays by various authors describes sacred place in different religions.

Kessel, Dmitri. *Splendors of Christendom*. Lausanne, Switzerland: Edita Lausanne, 1964. This is a truly marvelous photographic collection, with commentary, of different kinds of churches ranging from Byzantine to modern. The chapter on Wells is particularly helpful.

van der Leeuw, Gerardus. *Sacred and Profane Beauty: The Holy in Art*. Trans. David E. Green. New York: Holt, Rinehart and Winston, 1963. The author provides a classic phenomenological study of the differences between sacred and profane art.

Weitzmann, Kurt. *The Icon*. New York: George Braziller, 1978. This is a photographic study, with commentary, of Christian holy images from the sixth to the fourteenth century.

## INTERNET RESOURCES

http://www.ewpret.com/kilimanjaro.htm   This Web site provides pictures and information on Mount Kilimanjaro.

http://www.aboutkilimanjaro.com/lettersphotos/news/chagga.htm Here you will find some basic information on the Chagga.

http://www.britannia.com/history/somerset/churches/wellscath.html This informative site gives you a brief history, some wonderful quotes, and a description with pictures of St. Andrew at Wells.

http://www.newyorkcarver.com/cathedrallinks.htm   This site gives a virtual tour of great Gothic cathedrals.

http://members.tripod.com/siekman/religion.html   At this site you will find basic information about the Australian Aboriginal religion.

http://www.navajo.org/nnhistory/mtns.html   This site provides information about and pictures of the four sacred mountains of the Navajo.

# CHAPTER 8

# Religious Experience

IN 593 B.C.E. A JEWISH PRIEST named Ezekiel had a vision of a heavenly throne with fire shining bright around it. Ezekiel took this vision as the appearance of the "likeness of the glory of the Lord." With the vision came a voice calling Ezekiel to undertake a prophetic ministry to the "rebellious people of Israel" who were in exile in Babylon (Ezekiel 1 & 2).

Somewhere around 531 B.C.E. a man named Siddhartha Gautama sat down under a tree in India to meditate. While meditating he achieved enlightenment. Wisdom, serenity, and release from suffering came with this enlightenment. The gods rejoiced and the demons ran in fear. This man arose from his meditation as a buddha, a perfectly and completely enlightened being.

Around 35 B.C.E. a Jew named Saul set out on the road to Damascus to investigate the Jews in the synagogues there to see if they were members of a new Jewish movement called the Way. The Jewish sect to which Saul belonged regarded the Way as a heresy because it taught that a man named Jesus was the Messiah ("Christ" in Greek) sent by YHWH to redeem the Jews. On the road to Damascus Saul was temporarily blinded by a bright light from heaven and heard a voice saying, "Saul, Saul, why do you persecute me?" Saul asked, "Who are you?" The voice replied, "I am Jesus, whom you are persecuting . . ." This experience converted Saul to the new movement, and he became Paul, the apostle (messenger) for the Way. He helped to convert others and to turn this Jewish movement into a new religion that today we call Christianity.

One night in 610 a forty-year-old Arab named Muhammad ibn Abdullah was meditating in a cave on a mountain named Hira, near a city called Mecca.

Suddenly he heard a voice saying, "Recite!" This voice so frightened Muhammad that he thought he was going mad. Later he came to believe the voice was that of the angel Gabriel, a messenger sent by Allah (God). More revelations followed, and eventually a new religion called Islam was born.

I am not concerned with the historical accuracy of these accounts. Rather, I wish to pose a question. If you had to classify all of these different experiences under a single title, what would you call them? Most likely you would call them all, no matter how different they are, "religious experiences." But why would you call them that? What is it about them that makes them religious?

Scholars coined the term *religious experience* some three hundred years ago as a convenient way to refer to a wide variety of different experiences. It is a collective term that gathers together many different kinds of experiences— enlightenment, prophetic calls, visions, voices, conversions, revelations, and many more. What could all of these different experiences have in common that would allow us to refer to all of them by the same term?

Ever since the term was first coined, scholars have been debating that question. Some maintain, as we shall see below, that there is a common core to these experiences; others maintain there is not. While controversies rage about exactly what is meant by religious experience, one thing is clear—we have to pay close attention to what the person having the experience says about it. Two people can experience an inexplicable bright light. One may exclaim it is the light of the Lord, and the other finds it a curious, abnormal event of no great moment. A **religious experience** can be any kind of experience, from visions and voices to intense feelings of love and devotion, that the person having the experience believes to be religiously significant.

Much of this chapter will be devoted to discussing what might make an experience religiously significant for someone. First, however, that ambiguous word *experience* needs to be clarified. This word can refer to sensations, emotions, conceptual thought, intuitions, hallucinations, dreams, ecstatic states of great joy, and moments of serene calm. Besides having a variety of meanings, there is another ambiguity that is significant in our study of religious experience. It amounts to the difference between "I *seem* to see a book" and "I *see* a book." The first refers to what immediately appears to someone's consciousness. If the person is telling the truth, then we cannot doubt that he or she "seems" to be seeing a book. But seeming to see a book and actually seeing a book are two different things. The second statement, "I see a book," can be doubted because there may in fact be no book present to be seen. The person could be dreaming or imagining. That people seem to see books is quite true, but it is not the same as actually seeing real books.

We must keep that distinction in mind when we study religious experiences. Undoubtedly, Ezekiel, Paul, and Muhammad *seemed* to hear a voice. But that is not the same as hearing a voice. A question about the reality of the object of an experience is different from a question about what someone's immediate experience was like. What it was like is what they reported it to be like. However, critical questions can still be raised. Muhammad himself had doubts at first, and most religions admonish their followers to "test the spirits." There can be religious deception.

After examining two classic cases of religious experiences, one from Islam and the other from Buddhism, we will examine some attempts to organize these experiences into types. Two particular types will receive more detailed study: shamanic ecstasy and mysticism. While there are many different theories about religious experience, we will focus on the psychoanalytic theories of Sigmund Freud and Carl Jung. Your research case will return to an examination of mystical experience by looking at one of the great mystics of the Christian tradition, St. Teresa of Avila.

## 8.1 TWO CASE STUDIES

### 8.1.1 Muhammad

One night in 610 a forty-year-old Arab named Muhammad ibn Abdullah (*ca.* 570–632) was in a cave on Mount Hira near a city in Arabia called Mecca. Suddenly he heard a voice, a voice like reverberating bells. The voice said, "Recite!" Startled and frightened, Muhammad stammered that he did not know what to say. Once again the voice commanded him to recite, and once again Muhammad replied that he did not know what to recite. Finally, words came to him: "Recite in the name of your Lord who has created, Created man out of a germ-cell. Recite for your Lord is the Most Generous One Who has taught by the pen, Taught humans what they did not know" (Quran 96:1–5).

Muhammad did not know what to make of this experience, just as he did not know what to make of previous experiences that occurred when he was sleeping in the cave and dreaming. On one of these previous occasions a mysterious, personal presence had come to him and announced, "Muhammad, you are the Messenger of Allah." He was so struck by terror that he feared he might be going mad or some *jinn* (desert spirit) was playing tricks on him. Where was the voice coming from? What did these experiences mean?

Islamic tradition tells us that Muhammad consulted his wife, Khadija, who assured him he was not mad. She suggested they speak with her cousin Waraqa ibn Qusayy, who was a Christian. Khadija thought that she might know about such things because Christians had prophets to whom Allah spoke. Waraqa told Muhammad that the voice had been "sent down" by Allah through the angel Gabriel and that Muhammad had been called to be a prophet to his people.

The night when the recitations started is called, in later Islamic tradition, "The Night of Power and Excellence," because it was the beginning of a series of revelations to Muhammad lasting about twenty-two years. At first, when Muhammad shared these recitations, proclaiming them to be revelations from Allah, many of his people did not believe him. However, he was eventually accepted as a prophet and became known as the "Messenger (*Rasul*) of God."

Eventually Muhammad's revelations were written down in a book called the Quran (The Recitation). This book became the basis for a new religion called Islam (submission) whose followers are called Muslims (those who submit). In addition to the Quran, Muslims recognize both the Hebrew Bible (Old Testament) and the New Testament as containing revelations to prophets who preceded Muhammad. However, Muslims believe that the prophetic era, which started with the Jews, came to an end with Muhammad and that the Quran is the definitive and final revelation from God.

The first converts came from Arabia, where Muhammad lived and preached, but eventually Islam became a worldwide religion. Today it numbers about 1.2 billion members and is the second largest religion in the world. It is also the fastest growing religion in the United States.

The central core of Islamic teaching and practice is to be found in the **"Five Pillars of Islam."** *

1. Witness that there is no God but Allah and that Muhammad is his Prophet.
2. Perform mandatory prayers five times a day.
3. Give alms to the poor.
4. Fast from sunrise to sunset during the month of Ramadan.
5. At least once during life make a pilgrimage to Mecca.

While Muhammad came to believe that the voice he heard involved a movement from heaven to earth, another experience, known as the "Night Journey," involved a movement from earth to heaven. The story of this journey occurs in the Hadith (report), which is a collection of narratives about the actions and sayings of Muhammad. It is second only to the Quran as an authoritative source for Muslims.

The Kaaba, a Meccan shrine once central to pre-Islamic Arab polytheism, continued to be a sacred shrine and holy site for Islam once it was purged of its many idols. One night when Muhammad was sleeping near the Kaaba, a remarkable event took place. It is uncertain whether it was originally considered to be a dreamlike, spiritual experience or an actual physical event, but the angel Gabriel came to the sleeping Prophet and, after splitting open his chest and belly, drew out Muhammad's heart and bowels. Gabriel washed these in a

---

*Different groups of Muslims have different lists of pillars but these five make up the most common list.

golden basin "filled with faith" (another version has Zamzam water from the spring beneath the Kaaba) and replaced them in the Messenger's body, which was then closed up.

After this, a small horse, whose name was Buraq and is often depicted with the head of a woman, was brought to Muhammad and he mounted. Gabriel then led Muhammad through the sky to Jerusalem, where Muhammad prayed at the holy temple, referred to by Muslims as the "farthest mosque."[1] Gabriel then led Muhammad in an ascent through the seven heavens. At the first heaven the gatekeeper asked, "Who is it?"

> Gabriel answered, "Gabriel." It was asked, "Who was accompanying you?" Gabriel replied, "Muhammad." It was asked, "Has Muhammad been called?" Gabriel replied in the affirmative. Then it was said, "He is welcomed. What an excellent visit his is!" The gate was opened, and when I went over the first heaven, I saw Adam there. Gabriel said (to me), "This is your father, Adam; pay him your greetings." So I greeted him and he returned the greeting to me and said, "You are welcomed, O pious son and pious Prophet."[2]

In the second heaven Muhammad saw Yahya (John) and his cousin Isa (Jesus). He saw Joseph in the third heaven, and eventually he met Moses in the sixth heaven. Moses wept because the followers of the Prophet Muhammad "will reach Paradise in greater numbers" than the Jews. In the seventh heaven Muhammad meets Abraham and ascends to the "farthest limit" of the heavens:

> Then Al-Bait-ul-Ma'mur (i.e., the Sacred House) was shown to me and a container full of wine and another full of milk, and a third full of honey were brought to me. I took the milk. Gabriel remarked, "This is the Islamic religion which you and your followers are following." Then the prayers were enjoined on me: They were fifty prayers a day (147).

On the descent Muhammad passed Moses, who asked what he had been ordered to do. Muhammad replied that he had been commanded to enjoin on the faithful fifty prayers a day. Moses said that people cannot bear that many prayers and told Muhammad to go back to Allah and ask for a reduction. Allah reduces them to forty, but again Moses advises that this is too much and instructs Muhammad to go back to Allah for more reductions. After repeated trips between Moses and Allah, bargaining over the number of prayers Muslims must say a day, the number five was finally reached.

> When I came back to Moses, he said . . . go back to your Lord and ask for reducing your followers' burden." I said, "I have requested so much of my Lord that I feel ashamed, but I am satisfied now and surrender to Allah's Order." When I left, I heard a voice saying, "I have passed My Order and have reduced the burden of My Worshippers" (148).

Later, when an Islamic mystical movement called **Sufism** developed, the mystic Sufis placed great importance on the Night Journey and traced their authority back through a long line of *shaykhs*, or masters, to Muhammad, who "had been with God." For them, this Night Journey into the heavens showed that Muhammad himself was not only a prophet, but a mystic as well.

It is clear that the main focus of these stories is not on giving precise and detailed information about the psychological features of Muhammad's experiences. They probably were embellished as they were orally passed on in the Muslim community, and when they were written down, it is clear that the editors' purpose was, in part, to establish Muhammad's authority as the Messenger of Allah. Nevertheless, they provide us with enough information to discern the kinds of experiences that stand behind the stories.

The first collection of experiences is revelational.[3] These sorts of experiences involve a human becoming an agent or spokesperson of the divine. Revelations can be personal or communal. In the personal type, the message relates primarily to the life of the individual who receives the revelation. In the communal type, the revelation relates to a wider group of people. These experiences can also be specific or general. Specific types of revelational experiences come in extraordinary and unusual forms, such as hearing voices from an unseen presence, or having a vision of some spiritual being. General revelations come in and through ordinary forms such as watching a sunset, watching the moon reflected on ocean water, or experiencing grand vistas from the tops of high mountains.

Muhammad's first experiences of the angel Gabriel commanding him to recite are not only communal, but also specific. Revelations of this sort continued for some years until the entire Quran was completed. Hence Muslims believe that the Quran contains the very words of Allah transmitted by Gabriel to Muhammad in Arabic.

According to the influential German sociologist Max Weber (1864–1920), we can distinguish between emissary prophets and exemplary prophets. **Emissary prophets** believe that the divine has commissioned them to convince others to believe the messages revealed to them concerning a wide variety of topics such as how to worship, how people should conduct their lives, and what is proper to believe. **Exemplary prophets** see their task as helping others have their spiritual experiences rather than convincing others to believe what they have to say. It seems clear that Muhammad understood his experiences with Gabriel as commissions to be an emissary of Allah.

If we understand **ecstatic** experiences to involve intimate contact with gods, goddesses, spirits, or God, with the primary psychological feature of losing control of one's self, then Muhammad's Night Journey is more ecstatic than revelational (although it does include a revelation concerning how many times a day Muslims should pray). The English word *ecstasy* comes from a Greek word, which literally means "to stand outside of one's self." Two widespread and common forms of ecstatic experiences are possession by some spiritual force, which temporarily replaces the normal personality, and extraordinary out-of-body journeys to spiritual realms. The Night Journey to Jerusalem and the ascent through the seven heavens is an extraordinary, ecstatic journey.

Muhammad's hearing of voices and his ecstatic journey may be associated with dreaming, as some of the traditions indicate. This might cause the modern reader to doubt the authenticity of Muhammad's experiences. However, we must remember that one of the first theories of dreaming in the ancient world was the theory that spiritual powers communicated to humans through dreams. The fact that you dreamt something was not a strike against the authenticity or truth of what you dreamt at that time, but a strike in favor of authenticity, particularly if the dream involved revelations from spiritual agents.

These stories functioned among Muslims to confirm Muhammad's status as a prophet and the divine authority of the Quran. They also functioned, as the Night Journey clearly indicates, to affirm the superiority of Islam over both Judaism and Christianity, its monotheistic rivals. Jesus is only in the second heaven, and while the Jewish prophets Moses and Abraham are encountered in the higher heavens, none gets as far as Muhammad does. The message is clear: the Prophet Muhammad supercedes all previous prophets.

It is interesting that, at first, Muhammad himself doubts the authenticity of his experiences. He was well aware that the insane hear voices and that demons can be the source of misleading revelations. His doubts are an important clue to how people come to ascribe religious significance to their experiences. The characteristics of these experiences (hearing voices, ecstatic travel to the heavens) may be uncommon, but there is nothing about them that compels people to conclude they come from a divine source. It is the judgment that they are authentically divine that gives them their religious significance. A different judgment would result in a different conclusion, such as "it may have been just a weird dream."

This is an important point to keep in mind because, as we shall see, scholars have spent much time and energy looking for some distinctive characteristic of experiences that makes them religious. It may well be that the religious quality of certain experiences has less to do with emotional features and more to do with judgments made about them, judgments that enter into the experience itself, or are made after the fact. Once Muhammad was convinced that it was indeed an angel sent by Allah who was speaking to him, the subsequent revelations not only increased, but also were identified immediately as revelations from Allah.

**Types of Religious Experiences**

1. Revelational
   a. Individual or communal
   b. General or specific
   c. Exemplary or emissary prophets
2. Ecstatic
   a. Possession
   b. Out of body

## 8.1.2 Buddha

A son of a king living in northern India, named Siddhartha Gautama (566–486 B.C.E. or 448–368 B.C.E.), became enlightened and thereby joined an illustrious host of enlightened beings called buddhas. However, this particular buddha, often called Shakyamuni ("shak-yu-moo'ne"), meaning "sage of the Shakya clan," became the founder of what is today the fifth largest world religion with some 370 million adherents.

The dominant religion of his own day was ancient Hinduism, sometimes called Vedic Hinduism. It contained polytheistic, henotheistic, and monotheistic elements. However, in Siddhartha's eyes, questions concerning the gods and offering sacrifices to them seemed unimportant compared to the great human task of becoming enlightened.

After his enlightenment experience, Buddha[†] preached what has become known as the core of Buddhism, the "**Four Noble Truths**":

1. There is suffering.
2. The cause of suffering is desire.
3. There is a way to overcome desire and become free from suffering.
4. The **eightfold path** leads to freedom from suffering.

This eightfold path leads to **nirvana**, or release from suffering and from the nearly endless cycle of rebirths that keep people attached to lives of suffering. The path is known as the "**Middle Way**" because it avoids the extremes of living a life of severe austerity and living a life of self-indulgent pleasure seeking. It consists of

1. right understanding,
2. right thoughts,
3. right speech,
4. right action,

---

[†]I will capitalize Buddha whenever I am referring to the historical Buddha (also called Shakyamuni and Siddhartha Gautama).

5. right livelihood,
6. right effort,
7. right mindfulness, and
8. right concentration.

Following the first two disciplines (right understanding and thoughts) leads to wisdom about the nature of reality and about the nature of one's own self. Cultivating the morality associated with right speech, action, and livelihood leads to living an appropriately ethical life of compassion toward all living beings. The practices associated with the last three (right effort, mindfulness, and concentration) lead to developing the appropriate mental discipline for expanding awareness and stilling the mind.

According to tradition, his father secluded Prince Siddhartha in the palace to protect him from the outside world. He married, had a son, and lived a life of luxury in the palace. Then one day he ventured forth, curious about the outside world. He was immediately horrified by the misery and suffering he found among those less fortunate than himself. He vowed to find the solution to suffering and, leaving the palace and his family, ventured forth seeking a teacher who could show him how suffering can be overcome.

He began to practice extreme austerities, eating barely enough to keep alive, drinking little, and living under harsh conditions. His teachers claimed that by engaging in ever more severe ascetic practices he could learn to gain complete control of his body and detach himself from pain. Prince Siddhartha practically starved himself to death, but he found that he did not overcome suffering by this means. Remembering a meditative trance state he had entered when a boy, he thought that meditation, not ascetic austerities, might be the path to overcoming suffering.

> I thought of a time when my Sákyan father was working and I was sitting in the cool shade of a rose-apple tree: quite secluded from sensual desires, secluded from unprofitable things I had entered upon and abode in the first meditation, which is accompanied by thinking and exploring with happiness and pleasure born of seclusion. I thought: Might that be the way to enlightenment? Then following up that memory there came the recognition that this was the way to enlightenment.[4]

So Shakyamuni determined to meditate until he reached enlightenment. He sat cross-legged under a *pipal* tree, a variety of fig tree considered sacred in India. This tree would later become known as the *bodhi* tree or tree of enlightenment. What happened next varies in the different accounts that exist. No firsthand account from Buddha himself exists, and later accounts embellish the story with miracles and tempters.

I will follow the account found in *The Deeds of the Buddha (Buddhacarita)*, which dates from the first or second century. This account has become widely popular among Buddhists. The author (perhaps the poet Ashvaghosha) is less interested in the psychological features of the experience than in the moral and spiritual teachings of Buddha.

According to *Buddhacarita*, when Shakyamuni began to meditate, Mara, the evil god of passion and ruler of the realm of desire, tempted him with his daughters—Discontent, Delight, and Thirst. Shakyamuni, now known as a **bodhisattva,** or buddha-to-be, resisted the temptations of desire. Mara then attacked him with his sons—Fury, Gaiety, and Sullen Pride. Eventually Mara assailed the bodhisattva with his whole army of tempters because he knew that if this bodhisattva succeeded in gaining enlightenment, he would lose control of his kingdom where people were kept in bondage to desire. Shakyamuni defeated this attack, and Mara, along with his army, ran away in defeat.

> The great seer, free from the dust of passion, victorious over darkness' gloom, had vanquished him. And the moon, like a maiden's gentle smile, lit up the heavens, while a rain of sweet-scented flowers, filled with moisture, fell down on the earth from above.[5]

Now the Bodhisattva Shakyamuni put himself into a meditative trance and eventually gained complete mastery over "all the degrees and kinds of trance." During the first watch of the night, he remembered all of his past lives—thousands of births and thousands of deaths. This turned his mind toward compassion for all the people trapped in the world of suffering and rebirth, called **samsara.** The Bodhisattva Shakyamuni came to see that samsara was without real substance, which was contrary to what most people thought.

In the second watch of the night, he obtained the "supreme heavenly eye" with which he looked upon the entire world, "which appeared to him as though reflected in a spotless mirror." He came to understand the law of **karma,** which controls the endless samsaric round of rebirths and deaths. That whole process depends on what sort of deeds people do. Bad deeds lead to a bad rebirth, and good deeds lead to a good rebirth. Karma is an ironclad law of cause and effect. What we sow is what we shall reap. However, once again he found nothing substantial in this samsaric world of constant change.

In the third watch of the night, entering even deeper into meditative trance, the Bodhisattva saw that karma was linked to ignorance. This great "mass of ill" involving birth, old age, death, and rebirth was fueled by ignorance.

> When the great seer had comprehended that where there is no ignorance whatever, there also the karma-formations are stopped—then he had achieved a correct knowledge of all there is to be known, and he stood out in the world as a Buddha. He passed through the eight stages of Transic insight, and quickly reached their highest point. From the summit of the world downward he could detect no self anywhere. Like the fire when its fuel is burnt up, he became tranquil. He had reached perfection, and he thought to himself: 'This is the authentic Way on which in the past so many great seers, who also knew all higher

and lower things, have traveled on to ultimate and real truth. And now I obtained it!"⁶

At that moment dawn broke, and when he understood that he had "reached the state of all-knowledge" the earth swayed "like a woman drunken with wine," crowds of seers gathered, rain fell from a cloudless sky, fruits fell from trees out of season—"in an effort, as it were, to show reverence for him." At that moment all the anger, ill, sadness, and evil in the world temporarily disappeared. The world "became quite quiet, as though it had reached full perfection." The gods and all living things rejoiced. Only Mara felt deep displeasure.

Even though Buddha had pledged to enlighten all beings, he now began to wonder whether that was possible. People, he saw, were so confused by their ignorance, and what he had learned was so contrary to what most thought about the world and self, that he thought no one would understand him. As a bodhisattva, however, he had made a vow to teach the path of enlightenment to all who would listen, and so he began to think about a teaching career. When Indra and Brahma, two of the chief gods of heaven, saw this, they came to the Buddha to encourage him to teach the path to enlightenment, saying:

> "As a generous lord shares his wealth, so may also you bestow your own virtues on others!" . . . And the sage pondered over their words. In consequence he was confirmed in his decision to set the world free.⁷

The core of this experience appears to be the understanding gained by Siddhartha Gautama during the night. This is confirmed by accounts much earlier than this one. Earlier accounts contain no temptation by Mara and no embellishments of the miraculous. There is, however, a description of the knowledge gained by Gautama. During the first watch he remembers all his past lives. During the second he attains knowledge of how karma works, and during the third watch he comes to understand the Four Noble Truths and how they can help to destroy the things that hinder deliverance from suffering, sensual desires, desire for existence, ignorance, and false views with respect to the true nature of things.

The English word *enlightenment* is a translation of the Sanskrit word *bodhi*, which means "awakening," or "understanding." The opposite of being awake is being asleep, and the opposite of understanding is ignorance. Enlightenment involves coming to know something you did not know before. It comes, according to Buddhism, in degrees—first learning about past lives, then understanding how karma works, and finally, understanding the link between ignorance and suffering along with what can be done about it. While those on the path experience various degrees of enlightenment, only a buddha experiences complete understanding of all things.

Using Weber's distinction between an emissary prophet and an exemplary prophet, it seems clear that Buddha falls into the latter category. He has something to teach, but most importantly, he has a kind of experience, insight, and freedom from suffering that he wants others to share. Is this experience revelational? It seems to be, insofar as Buddha comes to learn things he did not know before. But these "revelations" do not come from any god. They are more like discoveries than revelations that descend from above. In fact, images of descent are not as prevalent as images of ascent. Not only does Shakyamuni's knowledge expand in the course of the night, but also there is a brief reference to ascending the eight stages of trance until he reaches the "highest point."

The fact that Shakyamuni's enlightenment occurred while he was meditating and entering into trance states has led most scholars to classify this as a mystical experience. Mystical experiences will be discussed in more detail later in the chapter. For now I wish to focus on meditation.

In Buddhism, the word *meditation* is a general label for a wide range of consciousness-altering practices. One such practice is called the "cultivation of tranquility" and is referred to as right concentration in the eightfold path. Tranquility is cultivated by concentrating the mind in ways that reduce the range and intensity of emotions along with the uncontrolled wanderings of the mind.

Buddhism often represents progress toward tranquility by describing a series of altered states of consciousness called **dhyanas** (a word that can also mean meditation). As the meditator progresses through the stages in the series (usually represented as ascending to higher and higher states of consciousness), both emotional and cognitive states are gradually reduced. For example, when the first *dhyana* is obtained, the meditator can still feel joy and happiness, but negative emotions such as suffering and grief do not occur. By the time the fourth *dhyana* is reached no emotional states, either positive or negative, remain. There is only an emotionally neutral condition called equanimity.

There are four more *dhyanas* (for a total of eight) beyond equanimity culminating in a state called cessation because all cognitive and emotional states have ceased to influence the meditator. Our account of Shakyamuni's enlightenment says that he quickly ascended these eight states, thereby achieving total tranquility and peace.

Another meditation practice found in Buddhism is called the "cultivation of insight" and is referred to as right mindfulness in the eightfold path. To achieve insight the mediator must expand consciousness by the practice of mindfulness, which involves a close, careful, emotionally detached observation of every process that makes up the individual's psychological and physical life. For example, I might apply mindfulness to my breathing or to feelings of fear and anger. The idea is to pay careful attention to the causally connected chain of events that make up such physical activities as breathing or various emotional states like fear. By carefully noting how they arise and pass away, the meditator comes to understand, according to Buddhist thought, the insubstantiality and impermanence of all things.

Many of us assume that there is some sort of permanent, substantial self or soul that persists through change and is the seat of our emotions and thoughts. Some believe that this self or soul can survive even such a radical change as death. Becoming mindful of our bodily states and of our mental states teaches us that such states come and go. They do not last. They are impermanent and insubstantial. It is a short step from there to the conclusion that there is no self or soul that persists through change.

When the Buddha realized this during the third watch, he realized how ignorance keeps us bound to samsara. The second Noble Truth tells us that desire is the cause of suffering. More specifically, it teaches us that selfish desire is the cause of suffering because through it we become attached to things. Once attached to the things we like, we do not want them to change. We want them to remain permanent so that our permanent self can enjoy them. But nothing remains the same, and when things change we are sorrowful. In a word, we suffer. But if there is no self to begin with, if what we call a permanent self or soul is an illusion, then selfish desire and attachment make no sense. It is simply impossible to continue to enjoy pleasant things forever. It is ignorance of our true nature and the true nature of everything else that leads to the illusion of a substantial, unchanging self. Suffering is the inevitable result of this ignorance.

In the first watch, Buddha saw that samsara, the world of rebirth and suffering, is insubstantial. It is changing and will not last. In the second watch he understood that karma, whether it is good or bad, is also insubstantial and changing. In the third watch he achieved "a correct knowledge of all there is to be known," and as he surveyed the world from the highest point of "Transic insight," he could "detect no self anywhere."

In order to help you understand Shakyamuni's enlightenment experience, I have had to explain some Buddhist philosophy and meditation practices. This indicates that descriptions of his enlightenment experience serve more as teaching devices than as careful descriptions of the psychological features of the experience. Just as the story of Muhammad's ascent to the highest heaven helps to establish his authority as the last prophet with a fuller revelation than the Jewish and Christian prophets that precede him, so this story of Shakyamuni becoming a Buddha establishes his authority to teach the knowledge of the true nature of things.

## Two Types of Buddhist Meditation

1. Cultivation of tranquility (right concentration)
2. Cultivation of insight (right mindfulness)

## 8.2 COMPARISON

We begin our comparison by noting the vast difference in time, in place, and in culture that separates Muhammad from Buddha. Over a thousand years of history and thousands of miles of geography separate them. The culture of Arabia, with its tribal society of nomads and warriors, is far removed from that of North India, an urban society dependent on agriculture. Muhammad, living where and when he did, was most interested in questions of polytheism versus monotheism, disobedience, and finding a way to learn to submit to Allah's will now in preparation for a life in paradise to come.

Given Buddha's historical and cultural context, it is not surprising that his spiritual concerns should be very different. The problem was human suffering, not disobedience, and while most people went to temples and offered sacrifices to the many gods, it was clear to the young "Prince of the Shakya clan" that worshiping gods and offering sacrifices was not very effective. If it were, why did so many people still suffer? There must be another path, a path Gautama determined to discover.

Muhammad's first experiences of revelations from the angel Gabriel appear far removed from the enlightenment experience of Shakyamuni. Buddha hears no voices and receives no divine command to write down the final and most perfect revelation from the divine. He does discover truths—truths important for overcoming suffering—but no god reveals them. Muhammad realizes that his prophetic task is to get others to believe that the revelations he has received are true. "Believe my message from Allah," he cries to his fellow Arabs. Buddha realizes that his "prophetic" (that word somehow does not even seem to fit the situation) task is to get others to follow a path that will lead them to enlightenment. Suffering is an intensely personal experience, and so too is the way to overcome it.

Comparing the Night Journey of Muhammad with the enlightenment experience of Buddha may produce greater similarities than we have so far found. Both experiences are ecstatic, and ascent images prevail. Muhammad rides a horse up through seven heavens led by an angel, and Buddha passes through various states of consciousness produced by meditation. However, in those heavens Muhammad encounters past prophets and gets a command from Allah about praying, while Buddha encounters no other beings, except for the initial encounter before his enlightenment with the god of evil desire, Mara, nor does he get commands. Instead, he gets insights into the "true nature" of things.

It should be noted, although it is not surprising, that the insights into the "true nature" of things that Buddha discovers are precisely the teachings of Buddhism. An interesting question is which came first, the insights or the teachings? Likewise the revelations that Muhammad receives correspond precisely to the teachings of Islam. Again, which came first, the experience or the teachings? Because these seem to be foundational experiences, we are tempted to say that in these cases experience precedes teachings. Experiences reported by the followers of Buddha and Muhammad may be shaped by the teachings of the tradition they inherit, but surely the first experiences of the founders of these religions are not?

I think it is quite difficult to say for sure one way or another. Perhaps this should be dismissed as one of those impossible-to-answer, chicken-and-egg-type questions. More likely, the interplay between doctrines and experiences is complex and ongoing, even for foundational experiences. One thing is clear: these experiences attributed to the revered religious founders become models for subsequent experiences and the authoritative standard by which both teachings and experiences are to be judged. Perhaps it is best to think of them not so much as foundational experiences, but as standards of true teachings and practices presented *as if* they were foundational experiences.

One final point of comparison is worth bringing up. Within the Islamic religion there has been a fierce resistance to the tendency of many religions to deify their founders. Muhammad, no matter how favored by Allah or how pious he was, is a human being. There is only one God and hence only one source of ultimate truth. Muhammad remains the human agent of the divine. However, we could read the Night Journey as an expression of the tendency to make founders gods. In the Night Journey, Muhammad communes with Allah, indeed bargains with Allah, in a most intimate way. Normally humans are not allowed such access; only gods or other divine beings can enter the realm of the divine.

Various schools of Buddhism have reacted in different ways to the question of Buddha's possible divinity. The oldest traditions retain the notion that he is a human being who became enlightened. Other human beings can become enlightened too. Shakyamuni has no monopoly on buddhahood. Other schools of Buddhism have deified Buddha. He is worshiped, prayed to, and otherwise treated as divine. Indeed, according to one tradition he was, is, and always will be divine. His appearance as the human named Siddhartha Gautama of the Shakya clan is just that, only an appearance. He was not really human; he only seemed to be. Perfect beings cannot be human.

Perhaps an experience of getting a revelation from above works against any tendencies to make a human divine in a way that getting insights through meditation does not. Few humans are capable of discovering the "true nature" of things and learning the "final and complete truth." If that is what Buddha discovered, he may well have been divine or very close to it because such truth is normally reserved for the gods alone. It would be very difficult for his followers to resist this kind of reasoning given the pious descriptions of his enlightenment that they heard.

## 8.3 DEBATES ABOUT THE NATURE OF RELIGIOUS EXPERIENCES

The modern scholarly interest in the topic of religious experience begins with a Christian theologian named Friedrich Ernst Daniel Schleiermacher (1768–1834). Schleiermacher was dismayed that many of his well-educated, urbane, and cultured friends had come to despise religion. Among intellectuals in general he discovered an antireligious attitude. He believed that they could only adopt such an attitude because they misunderstood what religion is really about. They confused it with dogmas, rituals, repressive moral codes, and conservative institutions. However, the heart of religion is to be found, according to Schleiermacher, in experience, not in dogmas, rituals, or organizations.

Schleiermacher thought he knew the answer to the question posed above about which came first, the experience or the teachings. Experience came first for Schleiermacher, and this is what his cultured friends did not understand. Dogmas, doctrines, teachings—the sorts of things some people think of when they think of religion miss the mark. Experience is primary, all else secondary and dependent.

Not only did Schleiermacher think experience was the most important part of religion, he also thought that all the different types of religious experience could be reduced to a common core. This common core, he argued, is absolutely unique and irreducible to anything else. There is, in other words, a distinct religious feeling. What is this unique and distinctive feeling at the core of all religious experience?

Schleiermacher characterized it in different ways, but in a book titled *The Christian Faith* he identified the unique and irreducible feeling at the heart of all religious experience as "the feeling of absolute dependence." It is a moment in consciousness when we become aware of our finitude. We lead lives that are conditioned and limited by all kinds of factors. We do not have complete control of our lives or our environment. We shall die. We are dependent on an "other"—a power much greater than ourselves—and when we face the limiting situations of life (such as serious illness or death), this dependency on a greater power becomes clear to our consciousness.

While Schleiermacher believed that he had identified a universal core of all religious experience, it is quite clear that what he means by a feeling of absolute dependence is absolute dependence *on God*. He writes:

> The common element in all howsoever diverse expressions of piety, by which these are conjointly distinguished from all other feelings, or, in other words, the self-identical essence of piety, is this: the conscious of being absolutely dependent, or which is the same thing, of being in relation with God.[8]

This formulation of the core of religious experience (what Schleiermacher here calls "piety") has proved remarkably influential. It is often stated as a sense of finitude that pervades all human life. We may not always be conscious of this feeling, but in crisis situations it emerges. We often pray out of fear for our lives. So-called foxhole conversions are common. This feeling at the heart of all religion is always "waiting in the wings" of human consciousness, ready to take center stage when conditions are right and erupt into religious experiences of one kind or another.

However insightful Schleiermacher's analysis is, there is a major problem. It is impossible to identify a feeling of absolute dependence without the concept of God. But there is no hint in many religious experiences of any feeling of absolute dependence on a divine power. Such a feeling is present in Muhammad's experience, for example, but it is not present in Buddha's enlightenment experience. Schleiermacher's understanding of religious experience betrays a theistic bias.

In his book *The Idea of the Holy*, Rudolf Otto (1896–1937) continued the examination of religious experience begun by Schleiermacher. Like Schleiermacher, he thought there was a distinctive religious feeling. However, while he thought that Schleiermacher had identified an important feature of religious experience, he had erred by making it too subjective. Schleiermacher's description made religious experience merely an awareness of a state of consciousness. Given this account, Otto thought, the divine could only be *inferred* as the cause of the feeling of absolute dependence.[9]

However, like Schleiermacher, Otto had theological motives. He wanted to show that there is an element in religious experience that cannot be explained away. To Otto, religious experience was not reducible to mere wish fulfillment, delusion, or chemical reactions in the brain. He called religious experiences numinous experiences, and he characterized them as an experience of the Holy. He further described them as *mysterium tremendum et fascinans*.

The word *numinous* is derived from the Latin word *numen*, which means "a spirit." By the term "Holy" Otto means a pre-ethical, indeed prerational object of the numinous experience that can only be characterized as a mysterious "Wholly Other." That is, it is something utterly different from anything else we might encounter and beyond all normal moral and rational categories that we frequently use to help us understand the world.

*Tremendum* literally means "to be trembled at," and this trembling Otto characterizes as an experience of dread, awe, urgency, and majesty. Some have compared it to the experience we have when, in the grip of fear, the hairs on the back of our necks stand up, or the experience we might have in the presence of a great king or an important and powerful person.

This encounter with a mysterious and awe-inspiring Wholly Other also leaves us fascinated. Fear is involved, but fascination is involved as well, and this fascination draws us toward the mysterious, holy object. It is something like looking over a cliff. We are fearful of the great height and danger, yet drawn toward the precipice, sometimes so strongly that we must make an effort to pull back.

Otto provides a variety of examples, including Moses' encounter with the burning bush (see Chapter 6) and the revelation of the divine name YHWH. Muhammad's first encounter with the mysterious voice of an unseen presence clearly has numinous qualities. While there are numinous aspects to his Night Journey experience of marvelous travel and ascent into the heavens, they are less pronounced. Numinous qualities are even less pronounced in the Shakyamuni's enlightenment experience. In fact, there is no sense of the presence of the Wholly Other, let alone fear, dread, awe, or wonder.

Experiences like Shakyamuni's enlightenment have led some scholars to conclude that however valuable and insightful Otto's characterization of the numinous element in religious experiences may be, it is not the whole story. Ninian Smart, in his book *Worldviews* (1995), argues that at least one additional type of experience must be added to Otto's numinous type. This additional type Smart calls the "mystical experience" and explicitly cites Buddha's experience as an example.

In mystical experience, unity, not duality, is the central theme. Otto emphasizes difference and a sharp duality between the subject of the numinous experience and its holy object, but descriptions of mystical experiences are very different. Where numinous experiences are dualistic (a subject encounters an object), mystical experiences are often nondual (subject and object become intimately related, in some cases united). Where numinous experiences are often turbulent, mystical experiences are quiet. Where numinous experiences often involve hearing voices and experiencing images, mystical experiences (at least in their more developed state) are often empty of any auditory or visual events.

We will learn more about mystical experiences later in the chapter, but for now we can conclude that there are at least two major types of extreme religious experiences: the numinous and the mystical. I use the word *extreme* because for most people religious experiences are not nearly so dramatic. Most experiences that people identify as religious are of the *confirming* type.[10] They involve a feeling or kind of intuition that the religious beliefs we hold are true. These experiences can range from a generalized sense of sacredness associated with natural settings, such as the awe and wonder inspired by majestic mountains or immense oceans, to specific awareness of some kind of divine presence while in church or synagogue, perhaps when singing hymns, or praying.

More intense than the rather common experiences that confirm what we already believe are the *responsive* types of experiences in which there is a sense that the divine is aware of us.[11] These are experiences of being saved from sin, of miraculous interventions (often associated with apparently inexplicable healings), sanctioning experiences in which an event is seen as the divine punishment for some kind of wrongdoing, and experiences of sanctification in which an individual experiences divine aid in living a better life.

> **Additional Types of Religious Experiences**
>
> 1. Feelings of absolute dependence (finitude)
> 2. Feelings of awe or wonder (numinous)
> 3. Feelings of unity (mystical)
> 4. Feelings of confirmation
> 5. Feelings of divine presence (responsive)
>    a. Miracles
>    b. Salvation
>    c. Sanctification

## 8.4 SHAMANIC ECSTASY

The shaman ("shah'men" or "shay'men") is a religious functionary found in tribal societies, who engages, with the aid of spirit guides and helpers, in healings, divining, and other activities important to the community. Shamans embody the local interests of the community they serve by addressing such everyday concerns as illness, finding game for the hunters, making rain, and guiding people through critical life transitions such as birth and death. We have already encountered a type of shaman, Slow Buffalo (see Chapter 6), who received a vision detailing a new rite of passage to guide young girls into womanhood.

The individual who becomes a shaman often inherits the job or has an experience of being called by a spirit. Sometimes an initiation ritual conducted by other shamans confirms the shamanic calling. Sometimes a person's first cure or successful entry into trance or possession states may validate shamanic powers. Frequently the ecstatic states involve journeys to the underworld or to the heavens in search of a lost soul (soul-loss is often considered the primary cause of illness), game animals, or spirits to aid the tribe in some way.

A typical account relates how an Eskimo shaman descends to the bottom of the sea in order to get the sea goddess to release seals. He makes this ecstatic journey on behalf of the whole community, which is experiencing famine because of the lack of game. He enters a trance and, with the aid of his spirits, travels to the bottom of the sea. He must successfully pass all kinds of obstacles, each putting him in grave danger. During this journey the people sing songs and hear strange voices, including breathing that sounds as if it comes from "under water." Sometimes they witness the shaman's clothes flying about the house where this séance is taking place.

At the bottom of the sea he meets the sea goddess, whose hair is tangled because the people have broken taboos (forbidden acts). She is angry and tells the shaman in "spirit language" what sins have been committed. He calms her by combing her hair (the sea goddess has no fingers), and the sea goddess releases the seals. Then the shaman returns from trance, gasping for air as if he were emerging from under water. For a long time there is silence. At last the shaman speaks, "I have something to say." The people respond, "Let us hear, let us hear." The shaman then demands a confession of sins, and one after another the people confess breaches of taboos and repent.

Shamanistic ecstasy is the most ancient extraordinary type of religious experience known, and it continues to the present day. Shamanism is still practiced in traditional cultures, and you can learn how to be a shaman in workshops run by New Age gurus. There are elements of shamanistic experience in many other types of religious experiences as well. The Night Journey of Muhammad is a good example. The ascent into heaven has definite shamanistic elements, although the only "spirit guides" are the angel and the spirits of previous prophets. Shakyamuni's enlightenment experience involves discovering supernormal truths and gaining supernormal powers, even though it does not involve contact with spirits. Buddha, like many shamans, utilizes trance techniques as well, although the method for entering trance and the trance states themselves appear to be quite different from shamanic trances.

## 8.5 MYSTICAL TECHNIQUES AND STATES

### 8.5.1 Typologies of Mystical Experiences

Scholars have offered a variety of typologies of mystical experiences. One influential typology derives from Walter T. Stace's book, *Mysticism and Philosophy* (1961). According to Stace, there are two types of mystical experiences. One he calls *extrovertive* and characterizes as a "unifying vision" in which the unity of all things is apprehended behind the multiplicity of the world. It is as if the many things that normally appear to us have a unitary or inner core that is often described in terms of Life or Consciousness. The second type he calls *introvertive* and characterizes as "the unitary consciousness" in which all sensate and conceptual content disappears, and the mystic experiences a state of pure consciousness. All sense of space and time disappear.

Both of these experiences, Stace believes, are also marked by a sense of having experienced the final truth about things, and by feelings of sacredness, joy, paradoxicality, and ineffability (cannot be fully expressed in words). Stace goes beyond description, however, by asserting that the introvertive experience is "superior" to the extrovertive because the subject/object dualism and the sense of space/time are transcended in the introvertive, but not in extrovertive experience.

This value judgment caused R. C. Zaehner to revise Stace's typology in his book, *Mysticism: Sacred and Profane* (1961). According to Zaehner, Stace does not give adequate attention to theistic mysticism. Zaehner argues that we must

## Stace's Typology of Mysticism

1. Introvertive
2. Extrovertive

distinguish among nature mysticism, soul or monistic mysticism, and theistic mysticism. Zaehner describes nature mysticism as the experience of the mystic's ego or self expanding to include the whole universe or dissolving into nature so that "without and within are one." It is closest to Stace's extrovertive type. Soul or monistic mysticism is, Zaehner believes, the same as what Stace calls the introvertive type. The monistic mystic experiences a total transcendence of the subject/object distinction and identifies with what she or he takes to be ultimate reality. Theistic mysticism involves an ecstasy of union, but not identity, with the divine. Theistic mystics believe their experiences are due to the grace of God, and they are overcome by intense feelings of bliss and love.

Zaehner, like Stace, makes his own value judgment about which is superior. Theistic mysticism is superior as far as Zaehner is concerned because it involves a strong moral sense, whereas nature mysticism is premoral and monistic mysticism is amoral. It should come as no surprise that Stace is attracted to the philosophy of Shankara, the Hindu mystic philosopher who taught that the true self is identical with ultimate reality (see Chapter 4), and Zaehner is a Roman Catholic Christian with a strong attraction to Christian theistic mystics.

## Zaehner's Typology of Mysticism

1. Nature mysticism
2. Soul or monistic mysticism
3. Theistic mysticism

No typology is perfect because there are always excluded cases, borderline cases, and hybrid cases that do not fit neatly into the categories. Hence other attempts have been made to create more complex and less biased categories. Shakyamuni's enlightenment experience is mystical but does not quite fit any of Stace's or Zaehner's categories. It does not qualify as nature mysticism because it does not involve experiencing oneness with nature. Nor is it a type of theistic mysticism because there is no union with God. The last type, soul or monistic mysticism, seems just the opposite of what Buddha experiences.

He comes to see that there is no substantial soul or self and that believing there is constitutes the ignorance that keeps people attached to things, thereby prolonging their suffering. However, there do seem to be monistic implications associated with his experience insofar as the "soul" dissolves into the impermanence that characterizes the nature of all things.

## 8.5.2 Mystical Experience: Pure or Culturally Conditioned?

A debate rages today about whether mystical experiences are conditioned, shaped, and informed by the cultural, historical, and religious context of the mystic or transcend such contextual conditioning. Those who argue that the context is decisive point to the fact that Christians, Muslims, Jews, and members of theistic religions in general have, by and large, theistic mystical experiences; while Buddhists have experiences of the insubstantiality of the soul, monists experience identity with an impersonal ultimate reality, and Daoists find unity with the Dao. Those who argue that mystical experiences transcend culture, history, and the different religious traditions treat the differences among mystics as matters of how they interpret their experiences and not descriptions of the experience. We must, they argue, take seriously the mystic's claims to have had pure experiences, untainted by contextual factors.

This debate is important because if it could be proved that mystics from different times, different places, and different religions all have the same or nearly the same experiences, the case for religious truth would be strengthened. One reason we trust our sense experiences is because, by and large, people agree about them. If I seem to see a tree and nobody else does, that is cause for concern. If I seem to see a tree and everybody else does as well, I can have greater confidence in the trustworthiness of my senses. Likewise if mystics from around the world, from different historical periods, and from different religions all have the same or nearly the same experiences, that is cause for some confidence that their experiences may provide genuine knowledge of ultimate reality. If they all have different experiences that reflect their religious traditions, that is cause for doubting whether they are in touch with any reality outside of the workings of their own minds.

One reason this debate is so difficult to resolve is because we lack clear guidelines concerning how interpretation can be distinguished from raw experience. This is not a simple matter of "looking and seeing." Careful examination of a number of different mystical experiences will not yield convincing evidence concerning where in the mystics' reports experience ends and interpretation begins. The reason why this is not a simple empirical matter is because so much of the argument rests on theories about the nature of experience. Some theories of experience reject the possibility of raw experience of any sort, mystical or not. Other theories of experience accept that possibility.

Another reason why it is so hard to resolve this debate centers on the role that judgment plays in determining the value and nature of experience. When describing and classifying experiences, judgments about their significance by those who have religious experiences in general and mystical experiences in particular are decisive. But they are not decisive when it comes to explanation (although some scholars have maintained that they are decisive for both description and explanation). Others might develop different explanations that are more compelling. Scholars of religion cannot ignore what people say about their religious experiences, but they can offer different explanations. A theistic mystic might claim that God is the cause of his or her experience, but social psychologists might argue that such talk reflects the socialization process of theistic mystics: they are taught by their environment to talk about God as the explanation of their experiences. However, the social psychologist must begin with what mystics say because it is undoubtedly true that theistic mystics *seem* to experience God.

These problems take a further twist when we note that the explanations given by the mystic and by the social psychologist might be compatible. It is true that we all learned from our linguistic and cultural environments to talk about seeing trees. We have been socialized to talk like that. This does not mean, however, that when I *seem* to see a tree, I really don't see a tree. Of course the theistic mystic has been socialized to speak about "union with God," but it does not follow that such a thing could never actually happen.

### 8.5.3 Mystical Techniques

Debates about mystical experiences become more complex when we look at the techniques employed by mystics. We can borrow the Sanskrit word **yoga** from Hinduism and use it as a general term for any discipline or path designed to promote religious experiences, many of the mystical type. There are many different types of yoga, but several have been particularly influential and widespread.

*Raja,* or royal, yoga was first described in detail by the Indian sage Patanjali ("*puh-tuhn'juh-lih*") sometime in the third century. He defined yoga as the "cessation of the mental whirlwind." Patanjali asserts that through the practice of raja yoga one can isolate the individual eternal spirit from matter and unite it with the supreme spirit. His yogic path consists of eight hierarchical stages; hence it is sometimes called "Eight-Limbed Yoga."

The first two limbs, or stages, involve purification and preparation for advanced stages. The first stage, called restraint, consists of ethical prohibitions against injury and dishonesty, and the second includes the practice of such virtues as cleanliness, studiousness, and serenity. The next three stages teach how to develop correct posture for prolonged meditation, breath control, and detachment from the senses. Mastering these physical techniques (often called Hatha yoga) prepares one for the mental discipline of the last three stages. These are called concentration, meditation, and absorption or *samadhi.* Mastering these three stages results in obtaining superhuman powers called *siddhis* as well as absorption into the supreme spirit. According to Patanjali, a god may aid yogins in achieving *samadhi*.

Buddhism adapted the techniques of concentration in order to cultivate tranquility and made them part of the eightfold path. In addition to techniques of concentration, Buddhism added insight meditation, or mindfulness, which we discussed in conjunction with Shakyamuni's enlightenment experience.

Various meditation and concentration techniques have been developed and practiced by mystics around the world in order to promote altered states of consciousness. These states, usually called trance states, do not automatically result in mystical experiences, but sometimes they do promote intense experiences of oneness.

Another type of yoga is called *bhakti* yoga, or discipline of devotion to the divine. It promotes devotion as a way to experience a loving union with the divine. According to one version there are several stages: hearing the Lord, glorifying him in song, remembering him, attendance at his feet, worship, adoration, servanthood, friendship, and offering oneself to him. By these methods one attains love for the Lord, which intensifies into passionate attachment and even obsession. When one arrives at total love one sees the divine in everyone and everything.

You may have seen members of the Hare (Lord) Krishna sect dancing and singing in public. They are lovers of Krishna as the supreme Name and Form of the divine. Their goal is to overcome selfishness in complete devotion to Krishna. Devotion to the divine or an incarnation of the divine occurs all over the world and in most religions. Sikhism, which we will discuss in more detail in Chapter 10, characterizes its path to salvation as the practice of bhakti yoga. From a Hindu viewpoint, Christianity, with its worship of and devotion to Jesus the Christ, is another form of bhakti yoga.

Still another type of yoga is called *karma* yoga, or the discipline of action. This discipline has taken many forms throughout history. In the early period of religious history in India, it was interpreted primarily as the performance of ritual actions associated with sacrifices. Today it promotes liberation from selfishness through self-sacrifice and doing one's duty. Liberation from self-interest can be gained, according to this yoga, by learning how to act without attachment to the fruits of one's action. Mohandas Gandhi (1869–1948) interpreted his nonviolent resistance to the British as a type of karma yoga. If we can characterize the goal of bhakti yoga as a loving union with the divine, then we can think of the goal of karma yoga as a union of human and divine wills. If one is successful at following this yoga, one's own selfish will disappears and one's will and the will of the divine become united. From this point of view, the practices of Muslims that promote submission to the will of Allah are one kind of karma yoga.

*Jnana* yoga, or the discipline of knowledge, is intended to overcome ignorance and the false views that keep us bound to a world of many things.

Through the disciplined study of scripture and philosophy, the devotee eventually learns that behind the experiences of the many things that make up the world lies an ultimate oneness. In other words, the devotee comes to know that nondualism, or monism, is true. This is not just an intellectual understanding, but an intense personal experience of identity with ultimate reality.

There are other yogas besides raja, bhakti, karma, and jnana, but we can see two important ideas in these four types. First, all of these disciplines are intended to overcome selfishness, and second, the type of mystical experience that these paths promote varies according to the techniques employed. Raja yoga promotes a mysticism of absorption, bhakti yoga encourages a mystical loving union with the divine, karma yoga teaches how to realize a union of wills between the self and the divine, and jnana yoga leads to a mystical identity with and knowledge of the oneness that lies at the foundation of reality.

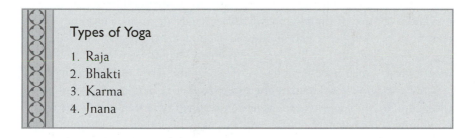

**Types of Yoga**

1. Raja
2. Bhakti
3. Karma
4. Jnana

## 8.6 PSYCHOANALYTIC THEORIES

It is obvious that religious insiders have their own explanations for their experiences. Indeed, it is their religious explanations that indicate to the scholar of religion that such experiences should be classified as religious experiences in the first place. However, the outside scholar has an obligation at least to suggest explanations other than the religious.

One form of the symbolic theory of religion (see Chapter 5) that used to be quite popular (although its influence is waning) relies on psychoanalytic theory. There are a variety of such theories, but we shall concentrate on two versions here—the theories of Sigmund Freud (1856–1939) and Carl Jung (1875–1961).

According to Freud, religion in general and religious experience in particular is a projection of unconscious wishes and desires. Religion is just one of the ways humans sublimate or redirect psychic energy into socially acceptable forms. Our deepest psychological motivations reflect emotional relationships of childhood dependency on parents. Our adult relations with our gods symbolize childhood relations with our parents. So gods and our imagined relationships of love, guilt, security, and sacrifice with them symbolically reflect actual childhood relationships.

Freud thought that mystical experiences of oneness with the divine reflect very early feelings of security experienced as small infants. Freud characterized mystical experiences as "oceanic feelings" and thought they reflected long-repressed experiences in the womb. He explained ecstatic experiences of rapture, trance, and intense love as self-produced substitutes for unconscious and repressed sexual desires.

He also found the repetitive and obsessive nature of religious rites reminiscent of neurotic behavior. Just as neurotics may compulsively wash their hands to get rid of unconscious feelings of guilt, so those who practice religious rituals and seek religious experiences are motivated by unconscious feelings of guilt that first arose in relationship to parents. The practice of asceticism and self-mortification is a way of acting out in a socially acceptable way repression of illicit sexual desire and its accompanying guilt.

Religious doctrines like eternal life and its rewards are, according to Freud, illusions stemming from our desires to have our wishes and needs for security and approval fulfilled. In religion, we unconsciously picture reality the way we want it to be. This is, of course, unrealistic and at base irrational. Therefore, Freud concluded, the true liberation of humanity could only happen when humans outgrew their need for religious illusions and faced reality squarely.

If we imagine how Freud might apply his theory of unconscious symbolic projection to Muhammad's experiences, we would have to probe Muhammad's childhood and particularly his attempts to obey his father and the guilt he felt when he failed. By learning to submit to the will of Allah, who is a projected father figure, Muhammad relieved his unconscious guilt feelings and finally got approval for his obedience, an approval he never felt from his own father.

It is more difficult to apply Freud's theory to Shakyamuni's enlightenment experience because there is no obvious symbolic substitute father figure. The initial struggle with evil personified as Mara could be explained as Shakyamuni's struggle with his own desires to do "bad" things. Freud might say that the insight into the nature of suffering and how to overcome it is symbolic of the deep unconscious relief Buddha felt when he finally overcame what he considered to be his "evil" tendencies.

As you can imagine, Freud's view of religion has been criticized from many different angles. One of his early critics was a former student and heir apparent to Freud himself named Carl Gustav Jung. Jung thought that Freud's view of the unconscious as filled with repressed childhood experiences of parental relationships was far too narrow. Jung saw the unconscious not just as a garbage dump, but as a collective unconscious of the human race containing far more material than Freud thought.

Jung believed that the unconscious is filled with creative energy. Among other things, it contains **archetypes,** which are recurring patterns in which the human ego (individual self) finds itself in relation to the collective unconscious. Archetypes can be thought of as the psychological version of instincts.

One of these psychological instincts is the realization of what Jung called the archetype of the "self."

As the individual ego develops from child to adult it passes through (if its development is normal) three main stages: (1) dependency, (2) autonomy (freedom), and (3) integration. Each of these stages corresponds to levels of religious experience and the mythological expression of religious ideas.

The first stage (dependency) is the stage of infancy and childhood in which the unformed ego finds itself in complete dependency on its environment, in particular, the mother. This appears in religious mythology and experience as a projected trouble-free state of bliss typically symbolized in stories about some "paradise of innocence" like the Garden of Eden or some past Golden Age. In religions that emphasize goddess worship, the mother-goddess who supplies all that is necessary and nourishes her children also symbolizes this stage.

The second stage (autonomy) corresponds to adolescence and young adulthood in which the dependent ego must now assert its independence and difference from parental power that, from this perspective, now appears to have been dominating and restrictive. This struggle for independence is expressed in religious myths of heroes who, through conflict, suffering, struggle, and sacrifice, gain a reward or treasure (see the Marduk and Moses myths discussed in Chapter 5).

Obtaining the treasure signals the transition to the third stage (integration) in which the psyche must come to terms with its weakness, in particular, its own lack of wholeness. The creation of a balanced, integrated, and whole self is the challenge of "the second half of life." Here religious symbols dominate. Spiritual paths to inner peace and harmony emerge on center stage. Religious experiences of the harmony of all opposites, mystical unions, and mystical marriages, speak with ever greater intensity and appeal as we grow older and enter our final years.

If the ego is the center of consciousness, the self-archetype is the center of an integrated consciousness and unconsciousness. It has a more holistic and unselfish outlook than the ego and is the transformative and creative power that draws people toward the final stage of integration. Jung believes that this self-archetype is frequently symbolized by the "god-image." The gods, goddesses, saviors, spiritual teachers, and other spiritual beings are projections of the self-archetype. They are idealized "others" that, once projected, can now offer advice and guidance to us as we work through our anxieties about the end of our lives. This projection is necessary because many egos are in danger of being overwhelmed by the self-archetype. Gods are easier to deal with "out there" than "in here." Nevertheless, in some cases divinity is understood as a higher spiritual self within everyone.

While both Freud and Jung talk about projection, the projections are very different in each. For Freud, the father figure is projected as divine in order to relive the secure dependency experienced in childhood. For Jung, what is projected is the self-archetype that plays a positive role in helping the ego to integrate conflicting desires and finally gain a peaceful wisdom as a realized self. The gods, for Jung, help us to become better people.

Jung would analyze the experiences of Muhammad and Buddha differently from Freud. If we apply his theories to these cases, a Jungian analysis might go something like the following. Allah is the self-archetype communicating wisdom and guidance to Muhammad. He is not the domineering projected father figure that Freud finds. The prophets encountered in the Night Journey are wise old men who are offering advice and guidance to a Muhammad who is struggling to overcome his selfishness in order to reach successfully the stage of integration. His ascent into the heavens is symbolic for a descent into the collective unconscious. Muhammad, in turn, becomes an idealized self for Muslims who seek to model their lives after him in their own journeys toward integration.

Buddha finds wisdom within himself in his enlightenment experience. Rather than relating to a projected self-archetype, he connects with the self-archetype within. His trance states are, once again, symbolic for the journey within the collective unconscious to recover a wisdom that has always been there but, before this experience, was blocked from conscious awareness.

Buddha's awakened knowledge of past lives symbolizes a total integration of all aspects of his personality, and his discovery that ignorance is the cause of karma allows him to gain freedom from its ironclad laws. Paradoxically, the discovery that the individual self is without substance allows him to discover the larger, more inclusive self within. The discovery of the insubstantial nature of what most of us take to be real allows Buddha to discover the truth about an ever changing world. His discovery of insubstantiality paves the way for recovering the psychological reality that is at the base of religious experiences and ideas.

Jung was much taken with number symbolism. The seven heavens correspond to the seven planets (the moon and the sun were thought to be planets) that were recognized in the ancient world. But since the planets were thought to control events on earth, their mystical correspondence to the seven-day week, the seven phases of the moon, the seven metals, the seven colors of the rainbow, the pilgrimage ritual of going seven times around the Kaaba, and so on, is psychologically significant. It was widely believed that the number seven is the number of perfection and completeness. It has also been associated with mystics and philosophers. Seven is the perfect number to symbolize the completeness of Muhammad's Night Journey, and the attainment of a fully integrated self.

Likewise the number eight has mystical significance. The eight trances of Buddhist meditation are reflected in the eightfold path as well as Eight-Limbed Yoga. It is generally held to be the number of new beginnings as well as infinity. In some cases it symbolizes the achievement of higher consciousness. Jung would probably find this a most appropriate number for Shakyamuni's enlightenment.

It is no accident, Jung would say, that the symbolism of seven and of eight should appear in these experiences. These numbers derive from the collective unconscious and serve to underscore the significance of the foundational experiences of Muhammad and Buddha.

I do not know if Freud or Jung would approve of the above application of their psychoanalytic theories. They would probably have much more to say with far greater profundity. However, this application of their ideas gives us some idea of how we might proceed with our own psychoanalytic explanation. Whatever metaphysical realities may stand behind these experiences, psychoanalytic theories remind us of their symbolic character and the psychological realities on which they are based.


## 8.7 SUMMARY

We started by observing that a religious experience is any experience that the experiencer believes is religious. We then distinguished between "seeming to see x" and "actually seeing x." We noted that the one word *experience* could include both of these meanings. We must listen carefully to the reports of what *seems* to be happening, but we can still draw different conclusions about what is *actually* happening.

We examined two cases, one from Islam and the other from Buddhism. A context for understanding these experiences was briefly sketched, including a description of the Five Pillars of Islam and the Four Noble Truths of Buddhism.

We thought it appropriate to classify Muhammad's call as a specific, communal revelational experience that established him as an emissary prophet. His Night Journey through the seven heavens was more ecstatic and mystical in nature, involving an intimate relationship with Allah.

Buddha decided to fulfill his vow of teaching others, even though he realized it would be quite difficult to make others understand his enlightenment. What he taught was how to become enlightened, and following Weber's categories, this makes him more of an exemplary prophet than an emissary prophet. His enlightenment experience is more mystical than revelational. We developed in more detail the last two steps of the eightfold path when we examined Buddhism's teachings concerning the two primary types of meditative practices (cultivation of tranquility and cultivation of insight). The heart of Buddha's enlightenment seems to be a knowledge or wisdom that will, he is convinced, release people from the bonds of suffering and the grip of karma.

A comparison of these experiences showed greater similarities between Muhammad's Night Journey and Shakyamuni's enlightenment than between

Muhammad's call to recite and Shakyamuni's experience. Even so, we found the differences, not the similarities, more pronounced.

Although the experiences we looked at are foundational to the religions of Islam and Buddhism, it is probably a mistake to think that experience comes first and doctrines later. There appears to be a complex interaction between the two. There is a tendency for religions to deify their founders, a tendency that Islam fights because of its unwavering commitment to monotheism. In the case of Buddhism, some schools retained the idea that Shakyamuni was just a very special human being who became a buddha, while others made him into a god.

In our survey of scholarly debates about religious experience, we described the views of Schleiermacher and his attempt to identify the core of religious experience as the "feeling of absolute dependence." We noted that Schleiermacher's definition of religious experience is not inclusive enough because of his theistic bias.

Rudolph Otto, like Schleiermacher, did think there was a unique, irreducible essence to all religious experiences, an essence he identified as numinous. His definition appeared to be too narrow because of his theistic bias, so, following Ninian Smart, we added another main type, the mystical. Usually religious experiences are not nearly so intense as the examples we reviewed. Confirming and responsive types of experiences are more common than either numinous revelations or mystical ecstasies.

Turning our attention to shamanism, we discussed typical shamanic experiences. The shaman is of great importance to tribal societies because she or he aids the people in times of crisis. We noted that there were even shamanic elements in Muhammad's Night Journey and Shakyamuni's utilization of trance.

After the discussion of shamanic experiences, we turned to an analysis of mysticism, noting, in particular, the different typologies of Stace (introvertive and extrovertive) and Zaehner (nature, soul, and theistic). There is an ongoing debate between those who claim mystical experiences reflect the religious culture of the mystic and those who claim they are pure experiences. One reason why this debate is difficult to resolve has to do with the problem of distinguishing what part of a mystic's report is pure description and what part is interpretation.

An examination of mystical paths and disciplines (yogas) showed that different kinds of disciplines (raja, bhakti, karma and jnana) apparently lead to different kinds of mystical experiences. Technique and experience are very closely connected.

We turned to the psychoanalytic theories of Freud and Jung to see how they might analyze religious experiences. Freud saw religious experiences as the resurfacing in ego consciousness (although in symbolic form) of repressed childhood experiences. He argued that the liberation taught by religion is only a partial liberation because repressed material is still in symbolic form. There needs to be a "second liberation" that can be attained by a proper psychoanalytic understanding of religious symbols.

Jung saw the unconscious in a more positive light than Freud did. Even so, like Freud, he thought the unconscious was the key to understanding religious experiences. He saw the unconscious as a collective unconscious containing the wisdom of the human race encoded in archetypes. The archetype of the self is particularly important because it acts like a magnet, drawing humans through the various stages of life to the final stage of wholeness and integration.

## 8.8 RESEARCH CASE—ST. TERESA OF AVILA

One of ten children, Teresa of Avila (1515–1582) was a Spanish Roman Catholic Christian. Her strength of character (some used the word "uppity") is partly revealed in the fact that as a child of seven she, along with her brother of eleven, ran away from home in order to journey to the "country of the Moors" (Muslims) so they could be "martyrs for Christ." An uncle encountered them outside the walls of Avila and promptly escorted them home. While this incident reveals her determination, it also reveals a pious resolve and a desire to suffer for Christ. She retained that desire throughout her life.

Teresa entered a Carmelite convent at the age of nineteen in order to become a nun. To do this she had to defy the will of her father. This experience was so traumatic that she later recalled that "it felt like every bone in her body was being sundered."[12]

She became seriously ill in 1538, lapsed into a three-day coma, and was taken for dead. Teresa managed to revive, but she was left so paralyzed that it was three years before she could walk.

At the age of thirty-nine Teresa underwent a spiritual transformation and began to have visions and raptures that carried her away in ecstatic love and joy. After a terrifying vision of hell, she vowed to reform her Carmelite order. In 1560, she founded a strict order of Carmelites called the Reformed or Discalced (sandal-less) Carmelites, and in 1568 she convinced her friend and fellow mystic, John of the Cross, to found a reformed house for men.

Her teachings were based primarily on her interpretation of her mystical experiences, not on the technical theology of her day. In one memorable vision, an angel pierced her heart with a flaming arrow, which left her burning with love for God. Her spiritual directors were suspicious of her many visions and raptures, fearing she might be mentally unbalanced or, worse yet, seduced by Satan.

Her life coincided with the time when Spain was the greatest power on earth, controlling the seas and establishing colonies in the New World. It also coincided with the Spanish Inquisition, which critically reviewed her writings for "erroneous" teachings. She was under great suspicion, in part, because she did what women were not supposed to do. She wrote books and founded convents.

One Alonso de la Puente, an energetic prosecutor for the Inquisition, found her works definitely heretical. After her death he sought to have her writings destroyed. His prosecution reflects the attitude that many in positions of power had when she was alive. His sexism and fear shows through in this statement:

> That learned men should come to learn from a woman and recognize her as a leader in matters of prayer and spiritual doctrine . . . is an argument for the novelty [heresy] of this doctrine, in which this woman was wise, and the men who subjected themselves to her were foolish; for in the ancient doctrine of the Church educated and learned men knew more than women.[13]

Alonso, amazed that a woman could even write heretical things, speculated that the writings were so diabolical she was probably not the true author because "they exceed the capacity of woman." Oddly enough, this sexism cut both ways, because on the occasion of her beatification in 1614, the Jesuit Cipriano de Aguayo argued that since no "ignorant woman" could write what she did, it must have been written by "divine inspiration."[14]

News of the conflicts among Christians spawned by the Protestant Reformation in Northern Europe, the corrupt lifestyles of many priests in Rome, and the many souls yet to be saved in the New Indies (the Americas) made Teresa's heart burn even more intensely with a desire to serve God perfectly. Teresa thought that if Christ has so few friends, these few must serve "His Majesty" (Teresa's way of referring to Jesus the Christ) more passionately.

In *The Interior Castle,* which she wrote in 1577, Teresa used the metaphor of seven series of mansions containing many different rooms to represent various stages of spiritual development. The castle is the soul, which the Christian enters through prayer. In the fifth mansion, God through the "Prayer of Union" possesses the soul. Progressing through the sixth and seventh mansions, the soul experiences a spiritual betrothal and finally a spiritual marriage—the most intimate of unions with the divine.

In 1556, Teresa first experienced rapture. She heard Christ speaking to her not, as she put it, through her bodily ears but in her soul. About two years later she experienced "intellectual visions" that convinced her Jesus was at her side. These visions, which were without images, did not pass but became a part of her everyday life. She said of it, "In the prayer of union or quiet some impressions of the Divinity are bestowed; in the vision, along with the impressions, you see that also the most sacred humanity accompanies us and desires to grant us favors."[15] She did have visions of Christ involving images of him, but she regarded them as inferior in quality because they were transitory.

The last stage in her mystical journey centered on the "mystery of the Holy Trinity." In 1571 she "entered" a part of her soul in which the three persons (Father, Son, and Holy Spirit) of the Trinity dwell. Shortly afterward she experienced herself dwelling in God. She wrote that "It seemed to me there came the thought of how a sponge absorbs and is saturated with water; so, I thought, was my soul, which was overflowing with that divinity and in a certain way rejoicing with itself and possessing the three Persons. I also heard the words: "Don't try to hold Me within yourself, but try to hold yourself within Me." [16]

On November 18, 1572, Teresa received the "grace of the spiritual marriage." Christ told her, or so she believed, that from then on she should consider as her own all that belonged to Him. She was then given the strength to engage in service to others, which constitutes the "fruits of the spiritual marriage."

Teresa used metaphors to explain the difference between the "prayer of union" and the "spiritual marriage" that takes place in the very center of the soul.

> Let us say that the union is like the joining of two wax candles to such an extent that the flame coming from them is but one, or that the wick, the flame, and the wax are all one. But afterward one candle can be easily separated from the other and there are two candles; the same holds for the wick. In the spiritual marriage the union is like what we have when rain falls from the sky into a river or fount; all is water, for the rain that fell from heaven cannot be divided or separated from the water of the river. Or it is like what we have when a little stream enters the ocean, there is no means of separating the two. Or, like the bright light entering a room through two different windows; although the streams of light are separate when entering the room, they become one." (*The Interior Castle*, 7.2.4)

Later, in the following chapter of *The Interior Castle*, she spoke of the spiritual marriage like this:

> There are almost never any experiences of dryness or interior disturbance of the kind that was present at times in the other dwelling places, but the soul is almost always in quiet. There is no fear that this sublime favor can be counterfeited by the devil, but the soul is wholly sure that the favor comes from God; for . . . the faculties and senses have nothing to do with what goes on in this dwelling place [the center of the soul]. . . . Nor does the Lord in all the favors He grants the soul here, . . . receive any assistance from the soul itself, except what it has already done in surrendering itself totally to God. . . . So in this temple of God, in this His dwelling place, He alone and the soul rejoice together in the deepest silence. There is no reason for the intellect to stir or seek anything, for the Lord who created it wishes to give it repose here . . . At times . . . sight is lost and the other faculties do not allow the intellect to look, but this happens for only a very short time. In my opinion, the faculties are not lost here, they do not work, but remain as though in amazement.

Alison Weber, in her study of St. Teresa of Avila, is less interested in the psychology of Teresa's mystical experiences than in the rhetoric Teresa employs. She was struck by the profusion of self-depreciatory remarks, confessions of incompetence and of wretchedness. Looking at rhetoric like "[I am] the most wretched person on earth" forced Weber to wonder whether Teresa was really sincere in these sorts of statements, or, given the times, Weber asks, was "self-depreciation the only self-referential language available for women?"

Weber became convinced after a careful study of the rhetoric Teresa employs that

> Self-depreciation was rhetorical but that it had a very non-traditional function. It seemed possible that Teresa's "rhetoric for women" was a "rhetoric of femininity." that is, a strategy that exploited certain stereotypes about women's character and language. Rather than "writing like a woman," perhaps Teresa wrote as she believed women were perceived to speak.[17]

In a sermon given in 1627, on the occasion of Teresa's nomination as copatron saint of Spain (the other was Santiago de Compostela, the Moor Slayer), Jesuit Rodrigo Niño found in Teresa's life a true miracle. He argued that "Sanctity in women usually consists in being quiet, obeying, staying in a corner and forgetting about oneself." But Teresa's case was different. It was "a new miracle and rare prodigy" because she obtained sanctity "not by keeping quiet, but by speaking, teaching and writing; not only by obeying, but by ordering, commanding, governing; not by observing enclosure but by traveling, disputing."[18]

Alison Weber comments:

> The only way to comprehend such virtue in a woman was to reassign her gender, to transform her into a "virile woman." Teresa was a prodigy because of her sex and a saint in spite of it. Her rhetoric of femininity, which served her own needs of self-assertion so successfully, also paradoxically sanctioned the paternalistic authority of the Church over its daughters and reinforced the ideology of women's intellectual and spiritual subordination. With her golden pen she won a public voice for herself, if not for other women.[19]

## QUESTIONS ON THE CASE OF ST. TERESA OF AVILA

1. How literally do you think we should take the metaphors of water and light that Teresa uses to characterize the spiritual marriage? Why?
2. Do you think Teresa has had some sort of universal mystical experience that transcends religions, cultures, and historical contexts? Why or why not?
3. Using either the theory of Freud or of Jung, write a psychoanalytic commentary on Teresa and her experiences.
4. Compare Teresa's experience of the spiritual marriage with both Muhammad's Night Journey and Buddha's enlightenment.

5. How do you react to Alison Weber's rhetorical analysis of Teresa's writings? What do you think accounts for your reaction?


## SUGGESTIONS FOR FURTHER READING

In addition to the material found in the notes, the reader may wish to consult the following for more information.

Eliade, Mircea. *Shamanism: Archaic Techniques of Ecstasy*. Princeton, NJ: Princeton University Press, 1964. This is a famous and influential comparative study of shamanism packed full of many interesting examples.

Freud, Sigmund. *The Future of an Illusion*. Translated by James Strachey. New York: W. W. Norton & Company, 1961. Freud's writings on religion are scattered among several books and articles. In this book he articulates his view that religious beliefs, while not delusions, are illusions.

Glock, Charles Y., and Rodney Stark. "A Taxonomy of Religious Experience." In *Religion and Society in Tension*. Chicago: Rand McNally & Company, 1965. This taxonomy arranges types of religious experience according to intensity. The types are confirming, responsive, ecstatic, and revelational. Glock and Stark classify mystical experience as one kind of ecstatic experience.

Goleman, Daniel. *The Varieties of the Meditative Experience*. New York: E. P. Dutton, 1977. A sympathetic account of meditation from someone who practices it. Part Two contains a useful survey of meditation in various religious traditions.

Jung, C. G. *Psychology & Religion*. New Haven, CT: Yale University Press, 1938. This book contains Jung's Terry Lectures at Yale, in which he presents a condensed account of his views of religion.

Kessler, Gary E. "Religious Experience: What Is It and What Does It Prove?" In *Philosophy of Religion: Toward a Global Perspective*, 150–209. Belmont, CA: Wadsworth Publishing, 1999. A collection of writings that present different views concerning religious experiences and mysticism.

Otto, Rudolf. *The Idea of the Holy*. Translated by J. W. Harvey. New York: Oxford University Press, 1958. Here you will find Otto's classic account of the numinous experience.

Paloutzian, Raymond F. "Religious Conversion" and "Religion and Experience." In *Invitation to the Psychology of Religion*, 2nd ed. Boston: Allyn and Bacon, 1996. Paloutzian presents a summary of some of the latest psychological research on religious experiences.

Proudfoot, Wayne. *Religious Experience*. Berkeley: University of California Press, 1985. This book contains an insightful analysis of Schleiermacher's and others' views. Proudfoot argues that the cognitive dimension of religious experiences is vital for understanding them.

Rahula, Walpola. *What the Buddha Taught*, 2nd ed. New York: Grove Press, 1974. While dated in some ways, this is still one of the best introductions to early Buddhism.

Schleiermacher, Friedrich Daniel Ernst. *On Religion: Speeches to Its Cultured Despisers*. Translated by J. Oman. New York: Harper and Row, 1958. Schleiermacher argues that the essence of religion is in experience and is an expression of our "sense and taste for the infinite."

Stace, W. T. *Mysticism and Philosophy.* Los Angeles: Jeremy P. Tarcher, 1960. Stace discusses his famous distinction between introvertive and extrovertive mysticism.

Teresa of Avila. *The Interior Castle.* Translated by Kieran Kavanaugh and Otilio Rodríquez. New York: Paulist Press, 1979. In this book you can accompany Teresa as she travels to the center of her soul to meet the "God within."

Teresa of Avila. *The Life of Saint Teresa of Avila by Herself.* Translated by J. M. Cohen. London: Penguin Books, 1957. This is Teresa's famous and influential spiritual autobiography written for the discerning eyes of those who would judge her mystical authenticity.

James, William. *The Varieties of Religious Experience: A Study in Human Nature.* New York: Simon & Schuster, 1997. These Gifford lectures by James are full of wonderful quotations that illustrate a wide variety of religious experiences. Few commentators notice the subtitle of this influential and much analyzed work.

Zaehner, R. C. *Mysticism: Sacred and Profane.* London: Oxford University Press, 1961. Zaehner objects to Stace's typology and adds the category theistic mysticism.

## INTERNET RESOURCES

http://deoxy.org/shaman.htm   There are more than thirty-six thousand Web sites on shamanism. Approach them with caution because most are trying to sell you something, and many are geared to the wanna-be shaman.

http://dir.lycos.com/Society/Religion_and_Spirituality/Mysticism/   Here you will find links to many Web sites relating to mysticism. Be sure to use your critical judgment to evaluate these sites. Some are scholarly and some are not.

www.mala.bc.ca/~mcneil/teresa.htm   The site contains a bibliography on St. Teresa of Avila and links to one thousand other sites.

http://www.psywww.com/psyrelig/fonda/jamvre1.htm   Here you will find Marc Fonda's notes on William James's *Varieties of Religious Experience* along with a good outline of this important book. But don't rely on what others tell you. Read the book for yourself.

# CHAPTER 9

# Evil

E LIE WIESEL WAS BORN IN Romania in 1928, and just shy of his fifteenth
birthday, he and his family were rounded up by the Nazis because they
were Jewish. His family was murdered, but he survived to write about his experiences and to bear witness to the evil of the Holocaust.

In one of his books, simply called *Night,* he tells of his journey into a night
of incomprehensible fear, pain, suffering, and death. Shortly after arriving at
Auschwitz, men and women were separated. He watched his mother and sisters disappear into the crowd of other female prisoners. Little did he know that
he would never see them again.

As he walked in a line with his father, he saw flames. Another prisoner
said:

> Do you see that chimney over there? See it? Do you see those flames? . . . Over
> there—that's where you are going to be taken. That's your grave, over there.
> Haven't you realized it yet? You dumb bastards, don't you understand anything?
> You're going to be burned. Frizzled away. Turned into ashes.
>
> He was growing hysterical in his fury. We stayed motionless, petrified.
> Surely it was all a nightmare? An unimaginable nightmare?[1]

Wiesel could not believe that they would burn people in his day and age.
Europeans are modern, civilized people, he thought. Besides, humanity would
never tolerate it. People would not stand by and let such a horrible thing happen. He voiced these thoughts to his father, who told him, "Humanity is not
concerned with us," and began to weep.

His body was shaking convulsively. Around us, everyone was weeping. Someone began to recite the Kaddish, the Prayer for the dead. I do not know if it has ever happened before, in the long history of the Jews, that people have ever recited the prayer for the dead for themselves.[2]

There is so much pain and suffering in the world, and so much of it seems pointless. Why is a baby tortured and murdered? Why did the horrible events of September eleventh occur? What brings someone to blow up a building, killing many innocent people? Nearly every day newspapers describe cases of what we can call *moral evil*, that is, suffering and pain inflicted on others by human beings. Much of it seems so senseless.

Watch television and you will see graphic accounts of natural disasters like floods, earthquakes, and tornadoes. Just one example is a report of an earthquake in western India that killed thousands of people. Many were buried alive and died slow, agonizing deaths. These are cases of *natural evil*. As if it were not enough to live in a world of appalling moral evil, we live in a world filled with natural evil as well. Why? What is the point of all this human suffering and pain? If we add to this the pain inflicted on other-than-human animals, it truly seems that we live in a senselessly painful universe.

There are magnitudes of pain and suffering. A toothache is one thing, the Holocaust is another. We can understand toothaches. And we can understand the causes of many natural disasters. But as it becomes harder and harder to understand pain and suffering, and as it seems so much of it is without good purpose, the problem of evil emerges. If I asked you to define evil, many of you would probably respond by saying that it is intense, pointless suffering.

Humans want explanations; we want to know why things happen. Knowing why reassures us that we live in a **nomos**, that is, an orderly world operating according to understandable laws. Such a world has meaning and purpose because we can understand why things happen by understanding the laws according to which they operate. However, many things that happen are **anomic**. They seem random, without explanation, and they threaten the meaning a *nomos* provides. Unexplainable evil, or at least what seems to be unexplainable, is anomic. It threatens the very *nomos* by which we make sense of things. It has cosmic implications, because the orderly universe in which we think we live may dissolve into chaotic meaninglessness, unless we can find a satisfactory theodicy.

In its narrow and theological sense, a **theodicy** is any proposed solution to the problem of evil that reconciles the existence of an all-good and all-powerful God with the evil that exists in the world. In its broad sense, a sense in which social scientists often use it, it refers to any ideological (religious or secular) explanation of anomic events. Here I will use the word mostly in its broad sense to refer to any attempt to make sense of evil. However, near the close of the chapter we will turn our attention to theological theodicies characteristic of monotheism.

A theodicy can overcome anomie because it seeks to answer what we can call the existential *why* rather than the scientific *why*. There are many scientific explanations for events that produce great pain and suffering. We know what causes earthquakes and floods. We even know why some people commit vicious crimes. However, the *why* that evil makes us ask is not the scientific *why*, it is the existential *why*. Why did this evil thing happen to me, to my friends, to my family, to my society? Why did the World Trade Center collapse when all those innocent people were inside?

The Azande, an African tribe, build large granaries high off the ground so mice and other animals cannot get to the grain. Sometimes people sit under these granaries to get some shade. Occasionally these granaries collapse, killing and injuring the people under them. If you ask the Azande why this happens, they will say it is witchcraft. A witch did it! The Azande know perfectly well that these granaries collapse because termites weaken the structures. They know the answer to the scientific *why*. What is puzzling to them is the existential *why*. Why did it collapse just now, killing my father or sister? Given their worldview, which includes belief in witches, witchcraft makes a good theodicy for them. It explains why some particular person suffered or died, and it reinforces the plausibility of their worldview.[3] It restores *nomos*.

Religions play a central role in resolving the problems that arise from evil. Anomie in general and evil in particular are two of the greatest challenges religions must face. If a religion is to maintain its plausibility and continue to provide meaning and purpose to human life, it must face the problem of explaining evil. It must find ways to reassure people that in spite of anomic events, there still exists an overarching *nomos*. If a religion cannot reassure people that life makes sense, even in the face of horrible evil and death, it cannot survive. In this chapter we will look at the different kinds of theodicies constructed by religions to reassure people that their lives have meaning and serve a purpose, even in the face of the anomic threat that evil poses.

We begin with two case studies; the first looks at the Hindu notion of karma and the second at the development of messianic movements among Muslims. After comparing these cases, we turn to the task of constructing a typology of theodicies relying heavily on the work of two important sociologists of religion: Max Weber and Peter Berger. From types, we turn to functions and explore how theodicies aid us in maintaining a meaningful existence. A section is devoted to the traditional theological problem of evil and some of the philosophical problems it raises. After a summary, you will find your own research case. I think you will find it particularly interesting because it deals with one of the oldest and most obvious kinds of theodicy called dualism (see Chapter 4). According to dualism, a perfectly good god is not responsible for the evil in the world; an evil god is responsible. Life is given meaning and purpose as we are enlisted in the fight against evil on behalf of good. This is an ancient story about the conflict between the good guys and the bad guys that is still played out in secular forms. It can be found in novels, television, and movies as well as religions.

## 9.1 TWO CASE STUDIES

### 9.1.1 Karma

We covered Hinduism in Chapter 4 when discussing the various ideas of ultimate reality. As you may recall, your research case was on Ganesha, an important Hindu deity. Here we will concentrate on the karma theodicy as found in classical Hinduism. However, let me warn you once again that Hinduism as such does not exist except as a collective concept used to designate a number of different ideas and sects found in or originating in India. Particular Hindu groups differ in a variety of ways, even in terms of the deities they worship. Some scholars claim that all these groups have little, if anything, in common. Others maintain that if they do have anything in common, it is the belief in karma and reincarnation.

Karma can mean, among other things, the law of cause and effect governing our lives. It states, as does the Bible, "as a man [person] sows, so shall he [or she] reap." The doctrine of karma is coupled with the idea of samsara, the wheel of rebirth. How we behave in our previous lives determines what we reap in this present life. Likewise, what we do in this life will determine our next reincarnation. The wrong we do will return to haunt us, and the good we do will return to make our next life better. Our only hope of escaping our karma is to somehow break out of samsara and stop the endless rounds of death an rebirth. Each of the various yogas we discussed in Chapter 8 constitutes, in the Hindu context, ways to be liberated from samsara.

In classical Hinduism the ideas of karma and samsara were linked to both the caste system and the idea of **dharma,** or the duty appropriate to one's caste. Progress between this life and the next largely depends upon fulfilling one's caste obligations in this life. Good karma results from following one's *dharma,* and bad karma results from failing to fulfill one's *dharma.* The *Chandogya Upanishad* illustrates the idea of karma in relation to caste when a sage says:

> Now, people here whose behavior is pleasant can expect to enter a pleasant womb, like that of a woman of the Brahmin [priests], the Ksatriya [warrior] or the Vaisya [merchant/farmer] class. But people of foul behavior can expect to enter a foul womb, like that of a dog, a pig, or an outcaste woman. (5.10.7)[4]

In India, there are different theories about how karma works. One important variety is the naturalistic or nontheistic view. The law of karma, according to this view, operates blindly, impersonally, and automatically. It is like a natural law of physics. If we jump off a cliff, we will fall because of the physical force of gravity. Physical laws do not really care what we do. Whether we jump or not, the power of physical laws is still effective. Indeed they are not even aware of us or who we are. They could care less. Nevertheless if we jump, we will fall. We can bank on it. So too with the law of karma; but instead of being a physical law, it is a moral law. Our moral actions will automatically lead to the corresponding consequences. If we steal in this life, someone will steal from us in our next reincarnation.

In addition to naturalistic views, there are also theistic ones. According to the theistic theory, some superhuman divine agent oversees the law of karma by linking the actions in one life with those in another. Since there are different varieties of theism within Hinduism, exactly how this is done depends on how people think of the divine in relation to the law of karma. If they think that the law of karma depends upon the divine will, then it is a law that a divine being might break if deemed necessary. If they think that even the divine is subordinate to the law of karma, then the deity cannot intervene in its operation. In this view, God is the implementer of a law that cannot be changed, even by God.

To simplify our discussion, we will focus on the naturalistic or nontheistic interpretation of karma. I think the implications for a theodicy in the broad sense are clear. There is no reason to blame someone else for our misfortunes. If we now lead a life of suffering and pain, it is our own doing. We got ourselves into this mess, and only we can get ourselves out of it. We have no excuses, no deity to blame. However, the law of karma does reassure us that it is a just world after all. Sooner or later in this life or the next, we all get what we deserve.

Recall the creation myth of the primal man we studied in Chapter 5. By deriving the various castes in hierarchical order from the primal man, this sacred story reinforced the divisions and the norms of classical Indian society. The doctrine of karma does the same. It is a powerful appeal to our own self-interest that reinforces fulfilling our social obligations to those above and those below us on the social ladder. It is in our best interests to meet our social and ethical obligations as defined by the priests (Brahmin) for our caste. Disobedience of *dharma* (duty) is the basic offense against our own clear interests in improving our lot in this life and the next. If we are ultimately successful in moving up the caste ladder, we will finally have an opportunity to escape this samsaric world with all its pain and suffering.

## 9.1.2 The Mahdi

**Eschatology** refers to ideas about the last things. These "last things" may refer to the end of this world and human history as we know it or may refer to the end of an era or period of history that will be followed by a "heaven on earth." Typically, religions associate eschatology with a time of judgment, when good people will be rewarded and evil people punished. Hence eschatological movements can function as theodicies, reassuring the faithful that however unjust and evil things appear now, in the end, justice and goodness will reign supreme.

One type of eschatology is associated with **millenarianism.** This idea appears in the New Testament Book of Revelation in reference to the final struggle between God and Satan and the coming of the Messiah to reign for one thousand years. Scholars of religion often use the term to describe a variety of non-Christian and Christian **apocalyptic** movements that expect some kind of redeemer or messiah shortly, who will defeat Satan in battle and begin a utopian age of peace, joy, and harmony.

In Chapter 8 we looked at some of the basic beliefs found in Islam. However, we did not distinguish between the two main branches of Islam: *Sunni* Islam and *Shia* Islam. Most Muslims belong to the Sunni branch, but a significant minority belongs to the Shia branch. While both of these groups share much in common, they part company when it comes to ideas about who should be the religious and political ruler on behalf of Allah here on earth.

The story of how the Shia movement started is complex, but at its heart is the Shia claim that only members of Muhammad's family should be considered his legitimate successors. The Sunni reject this claim and argue that any descendent of the tribe to which Muhammad belonged can rule. Ali, the fourth caliph (ruler) after Muhammad, was assassinated along with his two sons Hasan and Husain. The Shia consider them martyrs to the holy cause of Islam.

The word *Shia* does not designate one group, but several. The largest Shia sect is called Twelver Shia because it traces the religious and political leaders (called imams by the Shia) to the twelfth in succession, whose name was Muhammad al-Mahdi. He vanished in 874, and thereafter the Twelvers believe that he went into a type of supernatural hiding called *occultation.* They also believe that he, along with Jesus, will return as the messiah of the last days.

Twelver Shia has a complex theory of the Imam. In every age there is a human who represents Allah on earth and who designates a successor. All Twelvers are required to acknowledge the Imam of their age because they believe that the institution of the Imam is a covenant between Allah and humans. Twelvers regard imams as free of sin. They are doorways to Allah and convey what Allah wills directly to the faithful. Unlike some other schools of Islam, the Twelvers believe that Allah is essentially good and cannot will evil and that humans have freedom to obey or disobey Allah's will. They deny, in other words, a widely held Islamic belief that Allah predestines (determines) all things. It is not surprising, given these ideas, that from time to time people arose claiming to be the Mahdi ("meh-dee," meaning "rightly guided one"), the messiah of the end times.

As you may recall, Sufism refers to Muslim groups that practice a mystical version of Islam. There have been and are many such groups providing teachings and practices that promote the possibility of attaining a mystical union with Allah. Although the traditional goal of Sufism is to promote spirituality by withdrawing from society, some Sufi groups become reform movements seeking to purify Islam of what they see as corrupting elements. Often these reform movements take on a political character.

In the Sudan, in North Africa, a millenarian Mahdist movement arose, led by Muhammad Ahmad ibn 'Abd Allah (1834–1885). He was a member of one of the Sufi orders in the Sudan and used his association with Sufi organizations to build a political and military movement. He proclaimed himself to be the long-awaited Mahdi of the last days. Popular lore in the Sudan included stories about a mahdi or messianic figure who would be sent by Allah to rescue the community from oppression and restore Islamic justice. The Sudan had been under colonial rule for some time, and the people, longing for freedom from outside rulers, readily joined a Mahdist movement that offered them hope.

Muhammad Ahmad proclaimed that the *jihad*, or "struggle by the sword" (see Chapter 11), against the enemies of Islam was second only to the rule concerning the recitation of prayers five times a day. He also added to the traditional Five Pillars of Islam (see Chapter 8) the requirement that his followers profess faith in him as the Mahdi. As his Mahdist movement became more powerful, Ahmad declared a holy war against the Egyptians and Turks who ruled the Sudan at the time. His eschatological vision included, after securing the independence of the Sudan, the conquest of Egypt, Arabia, Syria, and Turkey. He preached that a time of justice, well-being, and the glorious triumph of "true Islam" under his leadership lay just around the corner of history.

Many of the upper classes of the Sudan were offended by Muhammad Ahmad's claims to be the Mahdi, but the peasants flocked to his support. They found his egalitarian policies that allowed slaves to fight alongside their masters attractive. More attractive still was the promise that he would defeat the foreign forces ruling the Sudan, thereby lifting the powerless and suffering peasant class to a position of power.

This Sudanese Mahdist uprising, which started in 1881, attracted the attention of the whole world when, in 1885, a garrison controlled by the British defender of Khartoum, General Charles George "Chinese" Gordon, was overrun after a long siege. The Mahdists killed Gordon, and the prophecies of Muhammad Ahmad seemed about to be fulfilled. An independent Sudanese state was established, and the Mahdists came into power.

In the summer of 1885 Muhammad Ahmad died. His followers were undaunted and erected a shrine over his grave, declaring him to be a saint worthy of veneration. His shrine became a pilgrimage site, even though Ahmad himself had outlawed saint veneration and visits to shrines as part of his crackdown on the Sufi movement after he gained power. In spite of the fact that his own beginnings were in Sufism, he saw more clearly than most that other Sufi orders could successfully challenge his claim to be the Mahdi.

The Mahdists continued in power until 1898, when the British sent an expedition to avenge the death of Gordon. The British campaign was a success, and the Mahdist movement in the Sudan collapsed. Like so many other eschatological and millenarian movements, the promised end of evil and suffering was not realized. Yet the Mahdist movement left an important political legacy because the notion of the Mahdi now became a symbol that could be used to mobilize the masses against foreign oppression and encourage them to fight for national liberation. We still feel the echoes of this nineteent-century movement in the beginning of the twenty-first century as militant Islamists seek to restore political power.

## 9.2 COMPARISON

The karma theodicy and the eschatological theodicy of the Mahdi are different in important respects. The karma theodicy assumes reincarnation, and the eschatological theodicy does not. The karma theodicy places the responsibility for evil squarely on the shoulders of human beings. We suffer because we deserve to suffer. Likewise only we can make things better by learning from our karma and doing better this time around. The eschatological theodicy of Madhism attributes evil to Satan and helps us live with present suffering by offering a promise that in the end Allah will reward the faithful and punish the wicked. But this coming time of compensation is not so much due to human effort as is the case with the karma theory, but due to a messianic figure who will come to save us. We must, however, be willing to follow him even unto death.

Both theodicies have a vision of a just world, but it is a very different vision. According to the karma account, the world is just because justice is a by-product, so to speak, of the law of karma. This law is simply the law of cause and effect with a moral twist. Such a law creates justice by making evil actions reap evil effects and good actions reap good effects, at least eventually. According to the eschatological account, the world is just because there is a divine being who will someday make it just by rewarding those who deserve rewards and by punishing those who deserve punishments.

Both these theodicies explain why bad things happen to good people, although in very different ways. The karma theory says that bad things happen to good people because of their karma. The eschatological theory says that bad things happen to good people because trial and suffering brought about by Satan are the lot of the faithful as they await the time of deliverance.

These theodicies also tell people that they should not despair. Despair is only appropriate if there is no hope. The karma theodicy holds out hope for improvement for those willing to do their duties, and the eschatological theory holds out hope for the eventual redemption of those who are faithful. Both serve to reinforce the morality taught by the respective religions that espouse them.

The karma theodicy is, however, more conservative than the eschatological theodicy. The duties we should fulfill, on the karma account, are the conventional duties of our society that are appropriate to our class and traditionally taught by religion and culture. The morality reinforced by eschatological theodicies is usually counter to the conventional morality of the corrupt and evil world in which we now live. It may be proclaimed as the original morality taught by the founding prophets and corrupted over the centuries, or it may be an entirely new morality, appropriate to the end times. In the case of the Sudanese Mahdist movement, it was both. Muhammad Ahmad called on his followers to return to the pure Islam originally proclaimed by the Prophet Muhammad and to follow a revised set of pillars based on his present divine inspiration. He went so far as to drop the pilgrimage to Mecca from the traditional list of five to make room for jihad, understood as holy war.

Both of these theodicies deal with the anomic nature of evil by reminding us of a *nomos*, or purposeful order, that makes life meaningful and worthwhile. Because the karma theodicy does not require a god to make it work, it never has to face the question of why a perfectly good divine being who cares for creation permits evil to occur. The eschatological theodicy of the Mahdi must face this challenge. But however it answers that question, it assures us that there is ultimately a divine purpose to what goes on in this sinful and wicked age.

## 9.3 TYPES OF THEODICIES

There are many different types of theodicies, and like any typology, the number of types increases as the distinctions become more refined. Here I wish to examine four broad types. These types are not unrelated, and many of them appear, in one form or another, in the same religious tradition. Even so, one or another of them tends to dominate particular traditions. Also, these theodicies are not exclusively religious. Frequently they have their secular counterparts.

### 9.3.1 Karma Theodicies

In our first case study, we have already looked at one form of karma theodicy. The case we analyzed presupposed the existence of a soul that transmigrates from body to body. This soul carries with it the karma of previous lives so that when bad or good things happen to someone in this life, they are happening to the person who deserves them. However, not all karma theodicies assume there is a soul. Indeed one form, found in Theravada (Way of the

Elders) Buddhism, denies there is a soul (the so-called no-self doctrine) and still supports a theory of karma. How can this be?

As we saw in Chapter 8, part of Buddha's enlightenment experience was the realization that there is no soul substance underlying what we call a person. This realization, if true, means that clinging to the objects of our desires makes no sense. If selfish clinging is the cause of suffering, as the second Noble Truth proclaims, then suffering can be eliminated once we realize that acting selfishly gains us nothing in the absence of a real, substantive self or soul.

Even though Theravada Buddhism denies the existence of a soul substance, it still supports a theory of karma. Thus Nagasena, a Buddhist monk, explains to a king how the apparent inequalities of life can exist:

> "Venerable Nagasena," asked the King, "why are men not all alike, but some short-lived and some long, some sickly and some healthy, some ugly and some handsome, some weak and some strong, some poor and some rich?"
>
> "Why, your majesty," replied the Elder, "are not all plants alike, but some astringent, some salty, some pungent, some sour, and some sweet?"
>
> "I suppose, your Reverence, because they come from different seeds."
>
> "And so it is with men! They are not alike because of different karmas."
> (Milindapanha)[5]

While both Hindus and Buddhists appeal to the law of karma to make sense of the good and evil that humans experience, this appeal appears much harder to make for a Buddhist who denies the existence of the soul. If the soul is not reborn in a new body to reap the consequence of past actions, how can the new person be significantly related to the previous person?

Different schools of Buddhism give different answers to this problem, but one common answer is found in the claim that karma itself is reborn. Thus Nagasena quotes the Buddha to the effect that

> "Beings each have their own karma. They are . . . born through karma, they become members of tribes and families through karma, each is ruled by karma, it is karma that divides them into high and low."[6]

A favorite Buddhist analogy uses a lamp and a flame to illustrate this idea. If the flame from one lamp is used to light another, and another, and another, though each lamp and flame is different (like each of our bodies and personalities are different in different lives), the flame (karma) provides a causal connection.

For Buddhism, reality does not consist of static and unchanging substances, but it consists of events. Events do not come into existence without previous causes. Events are the effects of previous actions (remember the word *karma* means action) and, in turn, are causes of subsequent events. So there is a network of cause and effect between all events, and it is no different with those events we call persons.

This may not solve all the problems that arise when Buddhists try to combine the no-soul teaching with a theory of karma, but it does remind us that it is not necessary to believe in transmigrating souls in order to believe that karma explains why inequalities and apparent pointless suffering exist. According to this theodicy, we have nowhere to hide. There is no God or Satan we can blame. We cannot escape our responsibilities for the mixture of good and evil that makes up our world.

## 9.3.2 Eschatological Theodicies

Eschatological theodicies attempt to make our experiences of what seem to be pointless pain and suffering meaningful by promising that someday things will be made right and justice will triumph. There are two types of eschatological theodicies: this-worldly and otherworldly. As the names indicate, a this-worldly eschatological theodicy claims that things will be made right in this world, and an otherworldly eschatological theodicy claims that things will be made right in some other world such as heaven.

The case of the Mahdist movement in the Sudan is one example of a this-worldly eschatological theodicy. Another example comes from what anthropologists call *cargo cults*. This term refers to religious and sometimes political movements that seek to bring about a time of wealth, cooperative living, and all that is imagined to be good. Melanesia is particularly noted for its cargo cults, but there are similar movements in Africa and the Americas.

These cults usually arise in times of rapid socioeconomic and religious change associated with colonialism. Under colonial rule, people often experience poverty and other sorts of deprivation. Exchange, the normal means for acquiring wealth, does not work because colonial rulers and missionaries show little interest in native goods. A way of obtaining the kinds of goods that Europeans want has to be found. Otherwise there can be no exchange. Hence these cults search for the "road to cargo," and look forward to a time when the ancestors will return, the colonial masters will depart or share their wealth, and equality will be restored. Typically a prophet or messiah figure emerges in these movements. He or she claims to have a message from the ancestors or from God about the road to cargo, and this stimulates cargo-cult development.

In the New Hebrides (now Vanuatu), for example, a movement began in 1940 and was led, in turn, by three prophets, each named Jon Frum. People thought these prophets to be manifestations of the indigenous spirit Karaperamun. These prophets encouraged cooperative work and revived practices outlawed by the Presbyterian missionaries. Positive experiences with American troops during World War II led some members of the Jon Frum cargo cult to build model airfields so the planes filled with cargo could land. They spoke of Jon Frum as "king of America" and believed he would soon return to displace the British. Cataclysmic events such as the leveling of mountains would accompany his return, and he would establish a reign of bliss in which there would be no need for work, no sickness, and the natives would get back their youth.

The primary weakness of this-worldly eschatological claims is that they can be disconfirmed when the hoped-for time of a paradise on earth does not arrive. When the prophecies of a better time to come do not come true, these movements often dissolve, reset the dates for it to happen, claim it is really here but hidden, or that the time of bliss is really otherworldly, not this-worldly. Otherworldly theodicies have the advantage of making disconfirmation virtually impossible because the long-awaited rectification of injustice and evil happens after death.

Otherworldly eschatological theodicies abound in the three missionary religions of Christianity, Islam, and some schools of Mahayana (Greater Vehicle) Buddhism. Typically these theodicies teach that there will be a reward for the faithful after death in a blessed paradise and a punishment for the unfaithful in hell. As the Christian hymn says, "we are but strangers here, heaven is our home." We might add, "and we hope hell is not."

Both the Bible and the Quran refer to a day of judgment when all people will be judged for their beliefs and actions in this life. This judgment day signals the end of human history and the restoration of justice. The living and the resurrected dead will appear before God for consignment to damnation in the never ending fires of hell or to an eternal paradise with God. In Christianity, the day of judgment marks the second coming of Christ who will punish evil and redeem the righteous.

Hell is the final abode of the wicked and place of everlasting torment. On a popular level, hell is often pictured as a place under the earth where graphic tortures take place. However, among some theologians, there is a tendency to see hell not so much as a place, but as a state of endless separation from God, the only true Good. Hence it symbolizes the frustration of the goal of human life, which is to achieve happiness and meaning. It is, if you will, a truly pointless evil because there is no hope that the suffering might one day stop. It is a condition of permanent anomie.

Some have found this severe doctrine of an eternal hell too difficult to accept. Surely if evil is pointless suffering, then God must not be responsible for the worst example of it, namely, hell! Modifications have tried to take the sting out of this teaching by making hell a temporary state. This is done when hell is reconceived as a kind of purgatory where sinful souls atone for their evil deeds and, once cleansed, move on to a happier state. In some Mahayana Buddhist schools, there are no eternal hells, but different levels and kinds of purgatories into which those with bad karma may be reborn. Sooner or later they will be purified and move on to different kinds of heavens until permanent release from all suffering is achieved. Only liberation can be permanent, not suffering.

Other religions, like Roman Catholic Christianity, combine a doctrine of hell with a doctrine of purgatory. For most people, especially those who have not committed the unforgivable sin against the Holy Spirit, forgiveness and hence salvation is always possible once they pay the price for sin. Here there is hope, even beyond the grave in that part of hell where purgation takes place.

Heaven or paradise is the postdeath abode of the blessed. In Christianity it is pictured, on a popular level, as a celestial city with streets paved with gold where those who are saved offer eternal praises to the Trinity. In Islam paradise is usually referred to as "the garden," which is both the first home of Adam and Eve before their sin and the last home after the death of the faithful. This garden is supposed to have four or seven levels and to contain rivers, shade trees, fruits, jeweled couches, flowing fountains, and all things necessary for the bliss and peace of those who dwell there.

Opinions vary among both Muslim and Christian theologians about how literally to take all this detail. Many argue that such descriptions are symbolic of all things beautiful, pleasing, and good. The true joy of paradise is living in the eternal presence of God. It marks the fulfillment of human existence, which is worth all the temporary sufferings we may endure in our earthly lives.

### 9.3.3 Theodicies of Participation

A theodicy of participation deals with evil, suffering, and misfortune by relativizing such events. It reassures us that in the grand scheme of things our individual suffering is of little significance. Our lives as individuals have less value than some greater reality in which we participate. If we keep that in mind, we will be able to bear evil and suffering.

There are many different versions of this kind of theodicy depending on how people think of the "greater reality" and how they understand the process of participation. What is perhaps its oldest form encourages people to transfer their sense of identity to the family, clan, or larger social unit, including the ancestors. For example, in traditional Chinese religions identity formation involves coming to understand oneself as part of a larger family unit that includes both the living and the dead. Undergoing this sort of socialization process leads people to subordinate their own self-interests to the more enduring interests of the ongoing family. We are, this theodicy teaches, only one very small part of a much larger process of life stretching back and forward into endless time. Fidelity to the family, especially the revered ancestors and living elders, is the overriding value. All else, including our own identity and suffering, becomes insignificant in comparison.

This sort of theodicy operates in many religions, including the religion of the Australian Aborigines discussed in Chapter 7. What is of paramount importance to the living is to keep the memory of the ancestors alive, to perform the rituals they taught in the Dreamtime, and to carry out family, clan, and tribal obligations. In a very real sense a person becomes the group. We are, this theodicy teaches, small pulses of a life process that encompasses all of space and all of time.

A similar kind of theodicy operates among mystics. Here the social unit is replaced by nature, the One, the divine, or the "suchness" of the process we call reality. We might dip into almost any of the mystical literature in the world and find passages that speak of a mystical, self-transcending participation in an ultimate reality that is far more important than the momentary evils that may afflict us. Indeed, from this more inclusive viewpoint, not only do such evils seem less important, but they do not seem to be evils at all. In the grand scheme of reality, they are unreal nothings.

Rabia (d. 801) was a slave-woman who became a Sufi mystic. To her the love of Allah was all that really mattered. She declared herself ready to suffer the pangs of hell if it would glorify her one true love, Allah. And Rumi (d. 1273), another influential Sufi mystic, so lost his own sense of individual identity that he could declare

What to do, O Muslims? For I do not recognize myself;
Not a Christian I nor Jew, Zoroastrian nor Muslim.
Not of the East am I nor West, nor land nor sea;
. . . . . .
Not of this world am I nor the next, not of heaven nor hell;
. . . . . .
My place is no place, my trace has no trace;
Not body nor soul, for I belong to the soul of Love.
One I seek, One I know, One I see, One I call.
*He is the first, He the last; He the outward, He the inward.*[7]

The theodicy of participation can also take secular forms. Soldiers are trained to identify with their nations to the point of suffering death so the nation lives on. Some people identify so deeply with the value of humanity and its greater good that, paradoxical as it seems, they are ready to risk their own lives to save the lives of others.

The sort of self-transcendence discussed here can be evaluated both negatively and positively. Negatively perceived, it may seem little more than masochism. Some people denigrate and devalue their individual identity to the point that they willingly invite pain, suffering, and even death for the sake of that "greater reality" with which they identify. When the individual becomes nothing, when family, nature, or God become everything, and when the individual finds ultimate happiness in what is other than him- or herself, this is, or at least is very close to, the heart of the masochistic attitude.

Viewed from a positive perspective, self-transcendence for the sake of a greater good appears altruistic. It may even be the pinnacle of unselfishness. People often think of heroic self-sacrifice as the noblest of acts. We frequently praise those who put the happiness of others before their own pleasure. Most of us are taught from a very early age that selfishness is bad and unselfishness is good. We think a community of purely selfish people to be no true community at all.

However we may evaluate theodicies of participation, the point is that self-transcendent participation can aid people in making sense of anomie. The theodicy of participation, like the other kinds, can legitimate experiences of anomie by helping us believe they have meaning and purpose. An added benefit is the assurance that we are not alone in our suffering.

### 9.3.4 Dualistic Theodicies

Dualistic theodicies face the problem of explaining evil head-on by claiming that some sort of superhuman force is responsible for evil. This kind of theodicy comes in various shades ranging from limited dualism to absolute dualism. In its limited form, some superhuman evil force has less power than some superhuman good force. Both Christianity and Islam, for example, assure us that Satan is both a force responsible for evil and a force that God has already defeated, although the final battle is yet to be fought. In its absolute form, the two superhuman forces of good and evil have equal power, and the victory, if there is to be a victory, is not certain.

Dualistic theodicies are often combined with apocalyptic themes proclaiming a final conflict at the end of history between good and evil. Often this conflict is symbolized as a horrible war or battle between the power of light (good) and the power of darkness (evil).

In Chapter 4 we looked briefly at the religion of Zoroastrianism and its dualistic view of the world. Your research case in this chapter will focus on yet another example called Manichaeism. There have, however, been many different dualistic religions in the history of both the West and the East. Their attraction is obvious from the viewpoint of the human need to explain what appears to be pointless suffering. What better way to explain all of the vast turmoil, pain, inhumane acts, and suffering we encounter in this world than by attributing anomie to a superhuman force of great evil?

### 9.4 THE THEOLOGICAL PROBLEM OF EVIL

At the outset of this chapter we distinguished between two different kinds of problems associated with our experience of evil. The first we referred to as the broad problem of making sense of evil, and the second as the narrow or theological problem of evil. It is now time to turn our attention to the theological problem and some of its possible solutions.

The theological problem of evil appears in a monotheistic context. It arises from the apparent incompatibility of the existence of one divine creator of this world who is all-good (omnibenevolent), all-powerful (omnipotent), and all-knowing (omniscient) with the existence of evil. As the Scottish philosopher David Hume (1711–1776) put it, "Is he [God] willing to prevent evil, but not able? Then he is impotent. Is he able, but not willing? Then he is malevolent. Is he both able and willing? Whence then evil?"[8] Thomas Aquinas (1225–1274), a brilliant Roman Catholic theologian, said that the existence of evil is the *best* argument against the existence of God.

Philosophers and theologians distinguish between two different kinds of arguments about God and evil. The first is called the deductive or logical argument, and the second is named the inductive or evidential argument. J. L. Mackie (1917–1981), an English philosopher, put the deductive argument like this:

> In its simplest form the problem is this: God is omnipotent; God is wholly good; and yet evil exists. There seems to be some contradiction between these three propositions, so that if any two of them were true the third would be false. . . . However, the contradiction does not arise immediately; to show it we need some additional premises, or perhaps some quasi-logical rules connecting the terms "good," "evil," and "omnipotent." These additional principles are that good is opposed to evil, in such a way that a good thing always eliminates evil as far as it can, and that there are no limits to what an omnipotent thing can do. From this it follows that a good omnipotent thing eliminates evil completely, and then the propositions that a good omnipotent thing exists, and evil exists, are incompatible.[9]

This deductive or logical problem of evil is a problem only for people who believe that there is a God as defined by Mackie. This is neither a scientific problem that might be solved by some sort of experiment nor a practical problem that might be solved by some sort of action. It is a logical problem involving the clarification and reconciliation of a number of different beliefs.

The inductive or evidential problem of evil does not rely on the mere existence of evil to try to prove God does not exist. It does not argue that evil per se is logically incompatible with God's existence. Rather it points to the degree, variety, or amount of evil that does exist and argues that this kind of evil makes it highly improbable that God exists. If a wholly good, all-powerful, and all-knowing creator God exists, we would expect much less suffering, or less variety of suffering, or less intense types of suffering in the world than is the case.

William Rowe, a contemporary American philosopher, states the inductive or evidential problem like this:

1. There exist instances of intense suffering which an omnipotent, omniscient being could have prevented without thereby losing some greater good or permitting some evil equally bad or worse.

2. An omniscient, wholly good being would prevent the occurrence of any intense suffering it could, unless it could not do so without thereby losing some greater good or permitting some evil equally bad or worse.
3. There does not exist an omnipotent, omniscient, wholly good being.[10]

Notice that this inductive argument is not purely logical, but relies on empirical evidence. If there were no instances of intense suffering that could not be justified on the grounds that they lead to a greater good or prevent a greater wrong, then this argument would lose its force. This is not to say that instances of intense human or animal suffering are good. In themselves they are evil, even if they are instrumentally good because they lead to a greater good or prevent a greater evil.

What might a greater good be that justifies God's permitting intense suffering to exist? One kind of answer that people give to this question is punishment for sin. God would not be an all-good God if he did not punish sin. So evil is justified on the grounds that it is good to punish sin. The Christian theologian St. Augustine (354–430) suggested this answer when he said that "evil is either sin or the punishment for sin."

Many people have found this answer rather harsh. It smacks of a "blame the victim" mentality. Its plausibility becomes even more questionable when we think of instances in which innocent babies burn to death. Then there are cases of apparently really good people suffering intense pain and horrible deaths, not to mention innocent animals who can hardly be guilty of sin. Here something like reincarnation can help, because it would claim that the innocent in this life were not so innocent in previous lives. This would turn this sort of theodicy into a karma theodicy, only with God as the adjudicator of karmic effects. Augustine, however, could not adopt this idea because he did not believe in reincarnation.

If this kind of theodicy (let us call it the recompense theodicy) is to work, then sooner or later people must bring in the issue of free will. If my sin is not freely done, then I am guilty of nothing and deserve no punishment. So perhaps free will is the greater good that explains why God permits instances of evil? This is sometimes called the Free Will Defense. This kind of theodicy says, in effect, a world in which human beings have freedom of choice, even if it sometimes leads to sin and evil, is better than a world in which there is no free choice.

If this is true, then it might well explain the existence of moral evils caused by humans, but it does not seem to explain natural evils like the intense suffering caused by hurricanes, floods, earthquakes, and the like. How could our sins cause such things? We might also wonder, if God is all-powerful, why God cannot create free human beings who do not sin? Is it not the case that we seem to be both free to make choices, yet genetically and environmentally limited in important ways? Perhaps an omnipotent God has the power to create humans who can make genuinely free choices, yet are limited in what they can do. One of those limits is that they cannot inflict intense and senseless pain and suffering on themselves or others. It appears that the free will theodicy is, at best, quite limited in its ability to justify the existence of evil.

Some have claimed that the greater good that God brings about by permitting evil is better human beings. John Hick (see "Suggestions for Further Reading") has called this a "soul-making" theodicy because it holds that any world leading to personal moral development must include the experiences of pain and loss. God's purpose in creating this world is to aid us on our road to spiritual and moral growth, not to give us a paradise of constant pleasure in which we will be as comfortable as possible. Evil is for our own good.

While this soul-making theodicy, like the theodicies of recompense and free will, has some initial plausibility, it becomes more difficult to maintain the more specific we become about the sorts of evils we are talking about. If we grant that some experiences of pain and suffering help build our character for the better, how much pain and suffering is necessary? This world in which we live contains a large amount of intense pain and suffering, much of which appears pointless. Think of the last century alone: two world wars, Hitler, the Holocaust, the gulags of Stalin, the massacres by Pol Pot, Milosevic's ethnic cleansing, AIDS, terrorism, starvation, and on and on it goes. Would not a world with either less suffering or less intense suffering do as well when it comes to building character?

All of these monotheistic theodicies (recompense, free will, soul-making), if persuasive, would be satisfactory answers to both the logical and evidential problems of evil. If we can show that there is a good reason for evil of whatever type to exist, then we can show that there is neither a logical contradiction between the existence of God and the existence of evil, nor is there decisive evidence against God's existence.

The theological theodicies we have been considering attempt to hold God's qualities of omniscience, omnipotence, and omnibenevolence constant and still defuse various versions of the problem of evil. However, another move in this debate is possible. We might, for example, modify our understanding of omnipotence in such a way that the problem of evil in both its deductive and inductive forms disappears. This is exactly what process theodicy tries to do.

According to process theologians and some process philosophers, change or process constitutes all reality, including God. (You may wish to compare this to the Buddhist doctrine of impermanence.) However, not any old sort of process is the order of the day; rather, this process is social. The world consists of actual entities, ranging from the smallest forms of energy to God, that freely respond to the activity of other actual entities that in turn respond. Reality is a marvelous dance of mutually responsive energy, and no other actual entity, including God, can wholly determine the dance ahead of time.[11] Of course partial determination takes place as in any society of interacting beings, but in this vision of reality, total determination is simply not possible. The dance is too complex.

This theory implies that even omnipotent power or the greatest possible power of which we can conceive is not total. God cannot create a stone that God cannot lift because it is simply not logically possible to do so. It would be a contradiction to say God has the power to create an unliftable stone or the power to do other contradictory things like creating square circles. Likewise, according to process theology, it is not possible for God to totally control every event that happens in a world of free relationships among entities. As one contemporary process theologian named Schubert Odgen puts it, God does not have all the power that there is "but only all the power that any one individual could conceivably have consistent with there being other individuals who . . . must themselves also have some power, however minimal."[12]

If this process view of omnipotence is correct, then God cannot eliminate all degrees and types of evil, let alone all evil. God can only minimize evil while creating as many possibilities for good as possible. This picture of God, some argue, is much closer to the biblical picture of God freely interacting with his free creatures with love, forgiveness, and mutual respect than to the picture of a God with infinite power, which some philosophers and theologians paint.

While this picture of a God limited in power is attractive to some, others find it unacceptable. A limited or finite God who is not in full control of his creation and whose will can not only be frustrated but also be defeated by evil may not be a God worthy of worship. In the end, does such a God have enough power to secure our salvation? Could we ever be sure of that?

If one way to try to solve the monotheistic problem of evil is to modify the definition of God, another way is to deny the existence of evil. If evil does not exist, the problem of evil and the need for any kind of theodicy evaporates. But how can someone deny what seems so obvious to all of us—that there is evil?

We learned of the Hindu theologian Shankara and his school named Advaita Vedanta in Chapter 4. As you may recall, Shankara taught a radical nondualism. Only Atman/Brahman exists; all else either does not exist or only appears to exist. Among the "all else" is evil. Since we do experience what we take to be pointless suffering, evil's existence is apparent, but it is not real. It seems to exist, but does not really exist. It is *maya*, a trick or illusion that arises out of ignorance concerning our true self.

We find very similar ideas in the West, as the teachings of Mary Baker Eddy (1821–1910), the founder of Christian Science, indicate. According to her book, *Science and Health with Key to the Scriptures*, God is Mind or Spirit and is the only true reality because God is Truth. If this is so, she reasons, then illness, disease, pain, suffering, and even death only *seem* real, as the contents of a dream might seem to be real as long as the dream lasts. Evil is an illusion, a bad dream, something that, in the last analysis, does not really exist. She writes in *Science and Health*:

> the only reality of sin, sickness, or death is the awful fact that unrealities seem real to humans . . . until God strips off their disguise. They are not true, because they are not of God. We learn in Christian Science that all inharmony of mortal mind or body is illusion, possessing neither reality nor identity though seeming to be real and identical.
>     The Science of Mind disposes of all evil.[13]

If, as some argue, limiting God's power results in a divine force not worthy of worship, then denying evil may result in a religion that we need not take seriously. If there is no real evil, then there is no real salvation. The solution to a problem takes on seriousness to the extent that we believe the problem is real. If there is really no problem to be solved, then why should we worry about how to live, what to believe, and whether anything is sacred?

The keys to this debate are the words *real* and *evil*. What is it for evil to be real? Neither Shankara nor Mrs. Eddy deny that evil is "real" to our minds. They only deny that it has a reality independent of what we think and imagine. We might imagine this metaphysical evil as some kind of horrible, if not fatal, flaw in the structure of the universe. The denial of the existence of metaphysical evil amounts to the denial of dualism as a satisfactory answer to the problem of evil. However, to deny that dualism is the solution does not make the problem of evil go away. It just limits the options we have when trying to solve it.

If we mean by evil something like pointless suffering, then suffering requires a sufferer. As a variation on the old metaphysical chestnut, "If a tree falls in the forest, does it make a noise if no one is present to hear it?" we might ask, "Can there be suffering if there is no one there to suffer?" If the answer is no, then claiming that evil does not exist outside human experience but only in human experience does not get us very far along the road to a satisfactory theodicy because evil still exists at least as a psychological reality if not a metaphysical one.

## 9.5 HOW THEODICIES WORK

Our discussion in this chapter has centered around the idea that a theodicy can overcome anomie because it seeks to answer the existential *why*. But why do humans need an answer to the existential *why*? Why is the scientific answer insufficient?

There are many things we fear, but some of our most basic fears are of being alone and of living a pointless life. We also fear intense pain and suffering, but we know that some of us may have to endure pain at some point in our lives. Believing that we are not alone and that suffering makes sense or has a point makes dealing with suffering easier than trying to cope totally alone and in despair. Theodicies assure us that we are not alone and that there is a point to suffering. They provide comfort in difficult circumstances.

On a more cosmic scale, theodicies provide us with assurances that the universe in which we live makes sense. Anomic events like evil threaten the meaningful order (*nomos*) we so desperately want. Theodicies tell us that in spite of anomic threats, the *nomos* continues. Theodicies help maintain macrocosmic as well as microcosmic meaning.

What is necessary for a theodicy to give comfort and maintain a sense of cosmic meaning? Not all theodicies work all the time for all people. Perhaps the idea of karma does not work for you because you have difficulty believing in rebirth. Perhaps we live in such a fragmented and individualistic world that theodicies of communal and family participation seem rather old-fashioned. Perhaps theodicies of mystical participation or punishment for sin seem odd in our scientific age. Perhaps we have seen too many bad things happen to too many good people, and so most theodicies have a hollow sound. They seem like the ideas of people scrambling to patch leaks in the cosmic boat while it is sinking.

If theodicies are going to work, they must seem plausible and they must legitimate by explaining and justifying the way things are in the world. Their power to legitimate is directly connected to their plausibility. Religions need plausible theodicies to legitimate their worldviews. The plausibility required is both intellectual and emotional. Theodicies must make sense to our minds and to our hearts.

From a sociological point of view, theodicies become plausible to us through a process of socialization. We are taught in thousands of ways as we grow up in a religion and in a society that its theodicies answer the problem of evil. Socialization processes are never perfect, so doubts may remain. But when we need explanations, when we or a loved one suffers intense and apparently pointless pain, we often fall back on the answers we have been taught in spite of our doubts. We do, after all, need some kind of comfort.

The need for comfort is illustrated by two kinds of responses to evil that we have not yet discussed. The first has been called a "theodicy of submission," but it is not really a theodicy because it gives up trying to make intellectual sense of evil and recommends that we simply submit to the mystery of divine rule. It is a kind of antitheodicy because it denies there is an adequate rational explanation for evil. This is equivalent to claiming that a theodicy is not possible. There is no rational explanation, at least none we can now grasp.

The Book of Job in the Hebrew Bible provides a good example of this sort of response to evil. Job is visited with unspeakable horrors because Satan bets God that if Job suffers enough he will stop believing in God. Job's friends employ the theodicy of recompense to help Job see that his apparently undeserved suffering is really punishment for sin. However, Job protests that he is righteous, not sinful. His suffering is undeserved.

The recompense theodicy is no longer plausible to Job, yet he continues to seek an answer. Finally God tells Job to stop whining and realize that God is God, the Sovereign Ruler of the whole universe. God challenges Job by saying, "Dare you deny that I am just or put me in the wrong that you may be right?" (Job 40:8). Job finally submits to God's power and majesty. He admits his ignorance of God's purposes, he admits his self-centered absorption in his own suffering, and he repents in "dust and ashes" for ever daring to question God's justice.

Submission to divine mystery may be one way to bring the hunt for theodicy to a close after all the rational answers have proved implausible. However, for some, submission will not work, only protest will do.

Elie Wiesel, whose dramatic account of his Holocaust experiences begins the chapter, does not, in spite of all the evil he and other Jews have experienced, want to give up belief in God. For Jews to stop believing in God means that Hitler wins in the end. True, Hitler did not succeed in destroying the Jewish people, but if Jews lose their faith, he will have succeeded in destroying the Jewish faith, the heart and soul of a Jew. Wiesel wants to believe, but he does not want to buy into hollow theodicies that are offensive to those who suffered and he does not want to simply submit to the mystery of divine power. He wants to protest God's actions; he wants to put God on trial and question God about God's guilt and responsibility.

In his play *The Trial of God*, Wiesel tells a tale about the aftermath of one of many *pogroms* (organized and deliberate massacres of Jews), which took place in Russia in 1649. God is put on trial for permitting the massacre, and Berish, one of two survivors, acts as prosecuting attorney. Sam, the defense attorney, lists all the usual reasons God has for permitting evil, including the assertion that the ways of God are simply beyond human understanding. Berish will buy none of it and says, "I lived as a Jew and it is as a Jew that I shall die—and it is as a Jew that, with my last breath, I shall shout my protest to God." [14]

You may recall the irony of Wiesel's account of Jews saying the kaddish (prayer for the dead) as they were about to be killed. Why pray to a God who will not save you from intense and apparently pointless suffering? Though the kaddish is a prayer of faith, it is also, in this instance, a prayer of protest. Wiesel recalls that he learned from his teachers that a good Jew may oppose God as long as he does so in order to defend God's creation. In our language we can say, "in order to defend God's *nomos*."

This "theodicy" of protest is, paradoxically, an antitheodicy. When all the usual theodicies no longer seem plausible, when they fail to offer comfort, when submission to mystery seems a cop-out, and when atheism appears to offer only despair, perhaps protest is all the believer has left to prevent the floodgates of anomie from opening.

## Types of Theodicies

1. Karma theodicies
2. Eschatological theodicies
   a. This-worldly
   b. Otherworldly
3. Theodicies of participation
4. Dualistic theodicies
5. Monotheistic or theological theodicies
   a. Recompense
   b. Free will
c. Soul-making
d. Restricting God's power
e. Denying the existence of evil
6. Antitheodicies
   a. Submission
   b. Protest

## 9.6 SUMMARY

We began with Elie Wiesel's account of his journey into the Holocaust night. Intense pain and seemingly pointless suffering occur every day throughout the world in large amounts and in a profusion of kinds. Some of it is natural evil, such as the suffering caused by floods and earthquakes, and some of it is moral evil, the terrible pain we often inflict on our fellow creatures.

Evil is an example of an anomic event. It threatens the stability of our orderly world (*nomos*) with disorder and meaninglessness, unless we can find a satisfactory explanation. Theodicies, in the broad sense, provide such explanations, thereby restoring order and meaning to a troubled world. Theodicies in the narrow, theological sense seek to reconcile the existence of evil with the existence of a perfectly good and all-powerful deity.

Events that result in pain and suffering can be scientifically explained. The Azande know that a granary falls because of termites. But why did it fall just then, crushing their family and friends as they sat in its shade? Theodicies offer answers to this existential *why*. They explain, like witchcraft does for the Azande, why this terrible event happens when their family and friends happen to be enjoying the shade the granary affords.

With our opening case we ventured into some Indian ideas about karma and samsara. Failure to fulfill the duties (*dharmas*) of one's caste can result in a bad rebirth. Evil is our own doing, and the universe in which we live is so ordered that the results of what we do, be they good or bad, will sooner of later, in this life or the next, come back to haunt us. In the long run the universe, in spite of its apparent injustices, is a just *nomos* because the scales of good and evil are eternally being balanced.

Eschatology refers to the last things—events at the close of history. Among some Shia and Sunni Muslims, one of these last events will be the return of a messianic figure called the Mahdi. An examination of a Mahdist movement in the Sudan showed its millenarian, messianic, and apocalyptic features. Muhammad Ahmad proclaimed himself the Mahdi of the last days in 1881 and led a revolt against colonial rulers that resulted, albeit briefly, in a period of self-government. Eschatological theodicies that encourage us to follow a messianic leader to help usher in the hoped-for utopia have been and remain potent sources of revolutionary liberation movements.

Both types of theodicy, the karmic and the eschatological, reassure us that, in spite of evil, the world is good and just. However, the karma theory builds justice into the very fabric of the universe by making it a natural, moral law, while the eschatological theory promises justice as the result of some divine intervention. The karma solution is conservative because it promises a better life if we obey the rules. The eschatological solution is radical and revolutionary because it promises a better life only if the old, corrupt order is replaced by the new.

A survey of four general types of theodicy (karma, eschatological, participation, and dualistic) showed something of the variety of answers religions have given to the problem of evil. Early Buddhism illustrates how a karma theory might work, even while denying the existence of a reincarnating soul. We found that Melanesian cargo cults illustrate this-worldly eschatologies, while Islamic and Christian ideas of heaven and hell exemplify otherworldly eschatologies. Participation in the life of the ancestors along with mystical identification with ultimate reality provide examples of the theodicy of participation. Dualistic theodicies constitute a fourth type. They attribute the responsibility for evil to the actions of an evil cosmic power in conflict with a good cosmic force.

The theological problem of evil emerges when we try to reconcile the existence of one, perfectly good and all-powerful creator God with the existence of evil. In its deductive or logical form, the argument about God and evil asserts there is a logical contradiction between the existence of God (defined in a certain way) and the existence of evil. In its inductive or evidential form, the argument asserts that the existence of a perfectly good and omnipotent God is unlikely given the amount and variety of evils that exist in our world.

Both versions of the monotheistic problem of evil provide powerful arguments for atheism unless they can be defused by showing that God has good reasons for permitting evil. Of the many attempts to solve the theological problem of evil, we initially examined five: the recompense theodicy, the free will theodicy, the soul-making theodicy, the process theories, and attempts to deny the reality of evil. The last two are the most radical because they require us either to modify the traditional philosophical understanding of God as infinite or to deny the existence of evil. Each of these theodicies, whatever their many advantages may be, face significant and, some would claim, fatal objections.

Theodicies work to maintain a *nomos* in the face of anomic events by providing meaning and comfort to us as we live lives that often involve intense suffering and always end in death. However, theodicies are only as good as their power to legitimate meaning. This power depends, to a large extent, on their intellectual and emotional plausibility. While the processes of socialization go far in teaching us to view our religious theodicies as plausible, not everyone can be perfectly socialized. Those who find serious problems of plausibility with theodices, yet wish to maintain their faith in a divinely created order, often resort to admonishing us to submit to God in the face of a mystery we will never, this side of heaven, understand. Others develop antitheodicies of protest. They believe in God and yet protest God's actions. As Elie Wiesel dramatically says, we must put God on trial.

## 9.7 RESEARCH CASE—MANICHAEISM

All religions are **syncretistic** to one degree or another. They combine and blend elements from different sources as they move from one location to another and survive historical changes. Manichaeism ("man-i-kee'iz-uhm") is a blend of many different elements.

Manichaeism is a religion based on the teachings of Mani (The Living), who was born in Babylonia in 216 of Iranian parents. He probably grew up in a Christian community that practiced adult baptism. In 228 Mani received his first revelation by an angel who was his "heavenly twin" and who came to release Mani from the "error of the sectarians." A second revelation in 240 caused him to publicly break from the baptist community, and he began to preach that purity comes through knowledge, not through bathing.

Mani was the author of at least seven scriptural documents preserved now only in fragments. In these texts his heavenly twin angel teaches through him that there exist two opposing principles, light and darkness. Light symbolizes good and is associated with the Father of Greatness, and darkness symbolizes evil and is associated with the Prince of Darkness. There are three stages to the conflict between light and darkness: a preliminary stage in which both powers are separate, a stage in which both become mixed and engage in a battle for the control of the universe, and a final stage in which light and darkness will return to their separate abodes. Humans now live in the second stage, and they are particles of divine light trapped in material bodies. Eternal rounds of reincarnation in the prison house of our corrupt and polluted bodies are our lot until we come to know our true light-selves. This knowledge releases us from the bonds of matter and the snares of the Prince of Darkness.

The story of how the second stage came to be is a sordid story of violence, cannibalism, and sex. The world in which we live was created as a result of the first clashes of the Father of Light and the Prince of Darkness. This account includes a story of how the Primal Man and his sons (five elements of light) were devoured by demons. These battles resulted in a division of the universe into a *lower reign*, including the earth and under the control of Prince of Darkness, and an *upper reign* controlled by the Father of Light. These cosmic battles also generated monsters. Primordial matter caused the demons Ashaglun and Namrel to eat the monsters and then to mate, bringing Adam and Eve into existence. The Prince of Darkness wants Adam and Eve along with their offspring to mate as much as possible, thereby producing as many bodies as possible to trap the light. But a Savior named Jesus the Splendor is sent from above, arouses Adam from his ignorant slumber, and reveals to him the divine origins of the light within (the soul).

Mani was commissioned by his twin angel to undertake a worldwide mission. He proclaimed the religion he founded to be a universal religion containing a message for all people. He also claimed to be the final prophet in a line of prophets that included the Buddha, Zarathustra, and Christ. He traveled in the Middle East, perhaps as far as India. His religion, spread by a traveling merchant class, achieved success throughout much of the Roman Empire. It traveled along the Silk Road as far as China, where it survived until the thirteenth or fourteenth century.

The Manichaean church was made up of two classes: Elect and Auditors (Hearers). Auditors belonged to the church only by serving the Elect, who made up the true church. Manichaean pictures, found in central Asia, show Auditors kneeling in front of male and female Elects. The Elect wore white robes, observed ascetic rules, and lived in monasteries like Buddhist and Christian monks. Some had no fixed dwelling. They wandered around like foreigners in a strange and alien land. The Auditors were obligated to offer them alms and hospitality.

Manichaeans practiced an ethic of nonviolence, and the Elect were expected to lead chaste lives, while the Auditors were to practice strict monogamy. People were instructed to pray four times a day, fast on Sundays, and give a tenth or a seventh of their earnings to the church. They were to confess their sins weekly and annually at a collective ceremony called the Bema that was celebrated in the memory of Mani's suffering and his struggle to bring liberating knowledge to the world.

Agriculture was thought to harm the divine light by trapping it in matter. Because preparing bread and vegetables polluted those who did it, the Auditors prepared the food for the Elect, and when the Elect ate it, they released the "captive light," thereby becoming "saviors of God."

Mani died in prison during the reign of the Sassaniam emperor Bahram I (274–277). The "Manichee," as they were called, suffered persecution by the Roman emperor Diocletian in 297 and later by Christian as well as Islamic rulers. Although Manichaeism no longer survives (there are, however, attempts to revive it), its ideas are still influential in many different forms, ranging from the religious to the secular. The dramatic story of the battle between the forces of darkness and the forces of light still attracts audiences.

## QUESTIONS ON THE CASE OF MANICHAEISM

1. How did Manichaeism "solve" the problem of evil? Besides dualism, what aspects of other kinds of theodicies appear in its teachings?
2. What sort of social conditions would need to be present for Manichaeism to have such wide appeal in the ancient world? Have you ever felt like you did not belong here, that you were an alien in a strange world, a world to which you did not really belong? Why?
3. Why do you think the symbolism of light and dark was used to represent good and evil, spirit and matter, and why do you think the same kind of symbolism persists to this day?
4. How does Manichaeism legitimate an ascetic and celibate lifestyle?
5. Do you find the Manichaean theodicy plausible? Why or why not? How would you modify it, if you could, to make it more plausible?

## SUGGESTIONS FOR FURTHER READING

In addition to the material found in the notes, the reader may wish to consult the following for more information.

Berger, Peter L. "The Problem of Theodicy." In *The Sacred Canopy: Elements of a Sociological Theory of Religion*. Garden City, NY: Doubleday & Anchor, 1967. Berger presents a sociological analysis of various types of theodicies. Much of my discussion is based on Berger's ideas.

Griffin, David. *God, Power, and Evil: A Process Theodicy*. Philadelphia: Westminster Press, 1976. As the subtitle implies, Griffin explains and defends a process theodicy.

Herman, Arthur L. *The Problem of Evil and Indian Thought*. Delhi: Motilal Banarsidass, 1976. Herman offers a careful discussion of the history of the problem, the Indian doctrines of rebirth, including the "karma thesis," along with a philosophical critique.

Hick, John H. *Evil and the God of Love*. London: Macmillan, 1966. Hick provides a clear and spirited defense of the soul-making theodicy.

Holt, Peter M. *The Mahdist State in the Sudan 1881–1898: A Study in its Origins, Development and Overthrow*. 2nd ed. Oxford: The Clarendon Press, 1970. Holt provides a detailed historical study. For a brief overview of the Mahdist movement and Shia Islam intended for the beginning student, see *An Introduction to Islam*, 2nd ed., by Frederick Mathewson Denny (New York: Macmillan, 1994).

Humphreys, Christmas. *Karma and Rebirth*. London: Curzon Press, 1983. Humphreys, a British convert to Buddhism, provides a vigorous defense of karma as the best answer to the problem of evil.

Jung, C. G. "Answer to Job." In *Collected Works*, vol. II. 1938. Translated by R. F. G. Hull. Princeton, NJ: Princeton University Press, 1958/1969. Here you will find Jung's classic psychoanalytic study of Job and the problem of evil.

Livingston, James C. "Theodicy: Encountering Evil." In *The Anatomy of the Sacred*. 3rd ed. Upper Saddle River, NJ: Prentice-Hall, 1998. Livingston provides a well-organized and clear discussion, which has strongly influenced my own.

Ormsby, Eric L. *Theodicy in Islamic Thought*. Princeton, NJ: Princeton University Press, 1984. Ormsby describes and explains Islamic thinking about the problem of evil.

Plantinga, Alvin. *God, Freedom, and Evil*. Grand Rapids, MI: Wm. B. Eerdmans Publishing, 1977. The philosopher Alvin Plantinga provides a logical and lucid modern defense of the free will position.

Reichenbach, Bruce R. *The Law of Karma: A Philosophical Study*. Honolulu: University of Hawaii Press, 1990. Reichenbach provides a careful study of karma in both the Indian and Buddhist contexts.

Rubenstein, Richard. *The Cunning of History*. New York: Harper and Row, 1978. Rubenstein discusses the meaning of theodicy in the context of modern genocide.

Weber, Max. "Theodicy, Salvation, Rebirth." In *Sociology of Religion*. Boston: Beacon Press, 1964. Weber first used the term theodicy in the broad sense and developed a useful typology that Peter Berger (see above) elaborated in *The Sacred Canopy*.

Wessinger, Catherine. *How the Millennium Comes Violently: From Jonestown to Heaven's Gate*. New York: Seven Bridges Press, 2000. The author begins with the notion that religion involves people's ultimate concern. She then argues that when this concern centers on the imminent end of the world, and when authorities of "this world" frustrate this concern, violence often is the result.

Widengren, Geo. *Mani and Manichaeism*. Translated by Charles Kessler. New York: Holt, Reinhardt and Winston, 1965. Widengren has packed this book with information about Manichaeism. Some of it is dated, as recent scholarship has shown, but it still provides an excellent foundation.

Worsley, Peter. *The Trumpet Shall Sound: A Study of "Cargo" Cults in Melanesia*. New York: Schocken, 1968. Worsley provides more information about the Jon Frum movement and others like it.

## INTERNET RESOURCES

http://www.philosophers.co.uk/portal_article.php?id=35   The philosopher Roy A. Jackson explores some of the arguments and issues relating to the theological problem of evil.

http://www.i-cias.com/e.o/mahdi_el.htm   This site will lead you to some basic information found in the *Encyclopaedia of the Orient* concerning "El Mahdi" and his role in the Sudan.

http://www.fordham.edu/halsall/islam/1885khartoum1.html   Here you will find information about the death of General Gordon along with an account of attempts to save him and his troops after Gordon's December 14, letter saying, "Farewell. You will never hear from me again. I fear that there will be treachery in the garrison, and all will be over by Christmas."

http://essenes.crosswinds.net/bnei3.htm   In 1981 the "Manichaean Orthodox Church" was "restored," and here is the Web site. You will find information from the perspectives of insiders who are trying to restore their version of an ancient religion in the modern world. A translation of an eighth century Syriac version of the Manichaean creation myth can be found here along with other texts. The information about ancient Manichaeism found on this site should, from a scholarly viewpoint, be used with caution.

# CHAPTER 10

# Human Existence and Destiny

THE AMERICAN psychologist and philosopher William James (1842–1910), in his book *The Varieties of Religious Experience*, claimed that there was no unique or special religious feeling. However, he did think there were common features of what he called the "intellectual content" of religious experiences:

> there is a certain uniform deliverance in which religions all appear to meet. It consists of two parts:
>
> 1. An uneasiness; and
> 2. Its solution.
>
> 1. The uneasiness, reduced to it simple terms is a sense that there is *something wrong about us* as we naturally stand.
> 2. The solution is a sense that *we are saved from the wrongness* by making proper connection with the higher powers.[1]

Although James seems to think these two parts characterize all religions, they do not. They do, however, characterize **religions of salvation**, which teach that things are not as they should be and need to be transcended or changed. We can contrast salvation religions with **religions of sanctification**, which teach that things are as they should be, and the religious task is to maintain this situation. Christianity is a clear example of a religion of salvation, and the religion of the Australian Aborigines is a good example of the sanctification type.

This distinction between religions of salvation and religions of sanctification is not absolute. These are ideal types, because in the muddy waters of the real world, religions often combine elements of both salvation and sanctification. Many religions offer descriptions of what is wrong and how it can be put right as well as descriptions of what is right and how it can be maintained. In this chapter, however, our main concern will be with religions of salvation.

It is not surprising that many religions find things wrong with the way things are. In the previous chapter, Elie Wiesel and others vividly reminded us of some of the things that are wrong. Our own experiences of life and the societies in which we live often convince us that things are not right. The fact that we are all headed toward death is enough to make many of us dissatisfied and uneasy with the human condition. If we add this uneasiness about death to experiences of physical and mental illness, moral failure, anxiety, frustration, loss, and alienation, we can easily understand the human desire for salvation—for healing, for making whole, for restoring health, for overcoming death, for, in short, making things right.

The very structure of human consciousness invites dissatisfaction. We are self-conscious creatures. We are aware, and we are aware that we are aware. Lurking behind our experiences of the world, there is always an I—the ego, or self—that remains, or at least appears to remain, the subject of our experiences. Consider the simple experience of seeing this book and then becoming aware that you are seeing this book. Even when we make that subject who is aware of this book an object of our thoughts, a "new" I, or subject, pops up. We might now say, "I am aware that I am aware of seeing this book." If there were enough time, this process might go on forever. I am aware that I am aware that I am aware that I am aware that I am seeing this book. That last sentence is potentially endless.

Why should this invite dissatisfaction? It invites dissatisfaction because it separates us from the things we wish to know. Objects, such as books, are "out there," and we are "in here." What we can know about the "out there" is limited by our consciousness. A division between subject and object plagues us. We can never know the book as it is in itself. We can only know it as it appears to us.

The division between subject and object also pertains to our selves. Division, and hence alienation, is built into the structure of consciousness because we can never turn around fast enough to catch our selves being ourselves. We forever elude ourselves. We cannot gaze on ourselves in leisure. At best, we can catch a glimpse of our selves receding to become a subject of yet another level of awareness. So there is alienation from the living and nonliving things that we believe exist outside of us, and there is an internal alienation buried deep within the very structure of self-consciousness.

According to some religious, psychological, and philosophical perspectives, this inner and outer alienation breeds anxiety and uneasiness—a sense that there is something wrong about our lives. If we assume that humans seek to know themselves, others, and the world in the most intimate way possible, then the subject/object division that is created by self-consciousness can only frustrate that goal. Separation from loved ones leaves us feeling uneasy. Separation from our selves and the world in which we live makes us feel still more uneasy. Some psychologists hold that this is the basis of "free-floating anxiety"—as James would have it, a general sense that there is something wrong.

Self-consciousness also opens up the possibility of transcendence and enjoyment. We come to realize, the more we explore self-consciousness, that we can go beyond our immediate selves. We can take trips into fantasylands, imagine ourselves as different people, think about the past, and contemplate the future. Our contemplation of the future, however, soon brings before us death, the potential loss of self-consciousness. We might, when deeply depressed and alienated, contemplate the loss of self-consciousness as a release from all our cares and anxieties. We find refreshing our momentary loss of self-consciousness in sleep. Then we wake up, and the preciousness of awareness contributes to our fear of a permanent sleep from which we never wake. We can and do both welcome death and fear its arrival because while it provides what may be the ultimate transcendence of self-consciousness, it also threatens the existence of all awareness.

In one sense the experience of self-awareness traps us in a subject/object dualism, and in another sense that experience makes it possible to go beyond our present conscious situations. Perhaps our hopes for something better (for a "solution") can be found in this ability to go beyond. But what is it to "go beyond?" Does transcendence mean a new, purified, and immortal self-consciousness free from alienation; does it mean an end to all consciousness in an eternal nothingness; or does it mean a merging into a greater divine whole? Perhaps it means waking up to a new way of seeing things, a way that sees things as appropriate and right just the way they are.

We will begin with two case studies. One case focuses on Sikhism ("sik'iz-uhm"), a religion that started in India and has now spread throughout the world. The other case focuses on Christianity, a religion that has developed a number of different varieties in its nearly two thousand year history.

These case studies will provide us with an opportunity to analyze more carefully what religions claim is wrong with human existence, the ways they recommend to overcome this wrongness, and their different views of human destiny. A medical analogy may help. Just as a doctor diagnoses a disease and offers a cure, many religions offer a diagnosis of the human condition and offer a cure. The Four Noble Truths of Buddhism, discussed in Chapter 8, provide a good example of this sort of structure. We will close with a research case highlighting a particularly influential form of Japanese Buddhism, called Zen (meditation) Buddhism.

## 10.1 TWO CASE STUDIES

### 10.1.1 Sikhism

Have you ever seen men and perhaps some women wearing turbans and dressed in white? If so, you may have seen some members of a religion called Sikhism. There are some 23 million Sikhs spread throughout the world, many of them living in the United States and Canada.

Sikhism originated in the Punjab region of northwest India. The word *sikh* is derived from a verb meaning "to learn." The first Sikhs were the disciples (learners) of Guru (teacher) Nanak (1469–1539). Eventually these learners of Guru Nanak evolved into members of a distinct religion with its own scriptures, beliefs, and practices.

Nanak was born about forty miles from Lahore, which is located in present-day Pakistan. He was strongly influenced by the bhakti (devotional) tradition as it was found among both Hindus and Muslims, and he traveled about singing hymns in praise of the one God. At twenty-nine, Nanak had a mystical experience in which God told him, "I am with thee. Through thee my name will be magnified." Nanak interpreted this experience as an instruction from God to go into the world to pray and to teach others how to pray. He opened his mission with the pronouncement, "There is no Hindu, there is no Muslim."

The history of Sikhism is complex, and as with all religions, changes were introduced as it evolved. Ram Das (1534–1581), the fourth guru, made the office of guru, or teacher, hereditary and founded the city of Amritsar, now regarded as the sacred center of the faith. The fifth guru, Arjun (1563–1606), compiled the writings and hymns of the first four gurus into a scripture called *Adi Granth*. The sixth guru, Hargobind (1595–1644), created a small army of Sikhs who were sworn to fight for justice and religious liberty. Guru Gobind Singh (1666–1708), the tenth guru, introduced an initiation rite involving nectar (*amrit*) stirred with a double-edged sword and the wearing of five symbols. They are uncut hair, a comb, a sword, a steel bracelet, and short trousers. This rite initiates Sikhs into a core community called the Khalsa. Male members replace their caste names with Singh (lion), and women abandon their caste names for Kaur (princess). One aspect of the symbolism of the dress and the name change is to eliminate class identity by raising everyone to the status of a warrior, the class of Guru Nanak.

The four sons of Guru Gobind Singh were killed in battles with the Moghuls. It is said that he took this as a sign that with him the line of individual gurus had come to an end, and he passed on the guruship to the whole community and to the writings of the *Adi Granth*, which now became known as the *Guru Granth Sahib*.

The Sikhs teach that Akal Purakh (their name for God, meaning "the being that is beyond the limitations of time") is beyond the categories of male and female, although they often use male pronouns when speaking of God. In essence God is not only beyond all gender distinctions, but also beyond all characteristics and hence beyond human understanding. However, God does manifest himself/herself as a personal being who transcends his/her creation and is present in it (immanent). God is the divine Guru, the inner teacher who saves people by grace. The Mool Mantra (basic sacred chant) that prefaces every Sikh prayer goes like this:

> There is One God
> His Name is Truth.
> He is the Creator,
> He is without fear and without hate.
> He is beyond time Immortal.
> His Spirit pervades the universe.
> He is not born,
> Nor does He die to be born again.
> He is self-existent.
> By the guru's grace shalt thou worship Him.[2]

Sikhs affirm the doctrines of rebirth and karma. There is, they teach, an eternal soul (*jiva*) that can inhabit many different kinds of bodies. Its rebirth is decided by its actions. The soul reaps in its next birth what it sowed in its previous births. The bodies the *jiva* can inhabit range from inanimate rocks to human bodies. Guru Arjan in the *Guru Granth Sahib* states:

> In so many incarnations, you were a worm and an insect; in so many incarnations, you were an elephant, a fish, and a deer.
> In so many incarnations, you were a bird and a snake. In so many incarnations, you were yoked as a ox and a horse.
>
> Meet the Lord of the Universe—now is the time to meet him. After so very long, this human body was fashioned for you.
>
> In so many incarnations, you were rocks and mountains; in so many incarnations, you were aborted from the womb . . .[3]

We wander through rounds of rebirths for a variety of reasons, but the fundamental reason is selfishness born from being separated from God, our source and creator. We are self-centered rather than God-centered. We are obsessed with ourselves and thus remain largely unaware of the Truth. Preserving the self at all costs becomes our struggle, and so we become aggressive, proud, and a slave to our desires and impulses. This leads to lust, anger, envy, and attachments to worldly things. In short, our *jivas*, or souls, belong to God and with God, but now live alienated or separated from him because of self-centeredness.

Selfishness and all its spin-off vices can only be overcome by "walking according to *hukam*, the will of God, as preordained." *Hukam* is a complex concept with different but related senses. It means God's order, his commandments, and the rules according to which the created universe runs. It is an expression of God's will, which ultimately underlies all that happens—life and death, joys and sorrows, reincarnations, and our final release or liberation. God is responsible for everything, and the *jiva* must overcome its self-centeredness by learning to submit to *hukam* without complaint. Living in a human body is itself a gift of God because it is only while in this body that we have a chance for release.

How do we learn to move from self-centeredness to God-centeredness? While human effort is partially involved, it is primarily by God's grace. A living spiritual teacher or guru can facilitate this grace, or free gift.

The doctrine of guruship is one of the most distinctive aspects of the Sikh tradition. In ancient Hinduism, gurus, or spiritual teachers, were taught knowledge of the sacred Vedas. Many gurus were from the priestly class. Spiritual power was thus concentrated in the highest Hindu class. However, a parallel tradition in India maintained that the authority of the guru did not lie in class or in knowledge of the Vedas but in personal enlightenment. This "guruship of enlightenment" was combined with a sense of mission, a mission to teach any sincere seeker regardless of gender, rank, class, or caste. Guru Nanak was a teacher in this egalitarian tradition, and he added to it the notion that God is the ultimate Guru or Primal Guru (often called the "Sat Guru," or true teacher).

The ten human gurus of the Sikh tradition all emphasized that only God was the Guru, and they were but faithful messengers through whom the divine Word (*shabad*) was revealed. They believed that this Word appeared as a sound that became articulate in the words they spoke, chanted, and sang. The hymns not only speak about God, they embody divine sounds, which have the power to enlighten and transform.

Once grace awakens and enlightens the soul, making an effort to serve humanity and to live according to God's truth is imperative. This means living a life in service to others and in devotion to God. Devotion to God is manifested both inwardly by praying and meditating on the Name (*Nam*) of God and outwardly in acts of communal worship and charity. Sikhs believe that meditation, communal worship, and concentration on the divine *Nam* are sufficient for attaining the "realm of Truth." Ascetic practices and elaborate rituals led by priests are not necessary. The poet Bhai Burdas sums up the Sikh ideal practice:

At dawn a Sikh wakes up and practices meditation, charity and purity.
A Sikh is soft-spoken, humble, benevolent, and grateful to anyone who asks for help.
A Sikh sleeps little, eats little, and speaks little, and adopts the Guru's teachings.
A Sikh makes a living through honest work, and gives in charity; though respected a Sikh should remain humble.

Joining the congregation morning and evening to participate in singing hymns, the mind should be linked to the gurbani [divine sound] and the Sikh should feel grateful to the Guru.

A Sikh's spontaneous devotion should be self-less for it is inspired by the sheer love of the Guru.[4]

The goal of this kind of life is God-realization, which is often characterized as union with God. This union is sought and hopefully can be achieved in an individual's present life, not in some afterlife. Those who achieve this union or oneness with God still must work out their past karma in this life. So they go on living in a body. However, they will accumulate no additional karma, and thus, after death, their souls will live in the divine presence and they will never again be reborn.

There are many references to heaven and hell in Sikh literature, but these seem to be states, rather than places. More importantly they are part of the ongoing process of reincarnation. If we die with good karma, we merit a certain kind of heaven, and if we die with bad karma, we merit a certain kind of hell. But these states are temporary, not eternal. Only union with God will bring eternal and final bliss. However, the Sikhs' mystical devotionalism is not world rejecting, but world affirming. They do not separate themselves from society, work, and affairs of the world. They do not become monks or nuns, but marry, raise children, and engage in honest work and public affairs.

### 10.1.2 Christianity

The designation "Christian" was first used, as far as we know, in Antioch around 135. It was used to name an emerging religious movement made up of Jews and Gentiles who worshiped a "Christos," named Jesus of Nazareth, who was executed by the Romans as a political criminal in Judea in the first part of the first century of the common era (C.E.).

"Christos" is the Greek translation of the Hebrew title Messiah, which refers to someone anointed by God for a special mission. The kings of ancient Israel were often given this title, and even the Persian King Cyrus, who liberated some of the Jews from exile in Babylon, was called Messiah or Christ. By the first century C.E., some Jews believed that a new messiah would arise to deliver the Jews from the hands of the Romans. The debate about the new messiah spawned various Jewish sects. The first disciples (learners) of the Jewish teacher (rabbi) named Jesus formed one of these Jewish sectarian movements.

When Jesus died and the hoped-for deliverance from Roman rule did not materialize, his first followers were devastated, and some thought that they may have been mistaken about who Jesus was. However, a story soon circulated that Jesus was not dead, but had risen from the dead. Various followers swore they had witnessed this miracle, and some even claimed to have seen the resurrected Jesus rise into heaven after appearing to various followers.

This story explained why the end of the present age and the delivery from Roman rule did not occur before Jesus died or with his death. The time was not right. When it was, Jesus would return in a "Second Coming" with a divine army of angels and defeat not just the Romans, but all the "demons" like them that ruled this sinful world.

This story, or the "Good News" (gospel), about the life, teachings, death, and resurrection of Jesus had appeal beyond the Jewish community. Eventually more Gentile learners joined this Christian movement, as the Romans called it. The Roman name stuck, and the Christian movement eventually became a new religion distinct from its parent religion, Judaism. However, its Jewish roots remained deep—so deep that Christians claimed to be the true fulfillment of Jewish law and prophecy. They even took over from Judaism the designation of the "Chosen People of God."

Crucial to this process was the creation of a scripture, or canon, of official documents. Different groups preferred different writings. Eventually, however, the majority settled on a Greek translation (called the Septuagint) of the Jewish scriptures, which they now called the Old Testament, and a collection of writings called the New Testament (see Chapter 12).

The Old and New Testaments (usually called the Bible) became the scriptural foundation of Christian teachings and eventually assumed the status of divine revelation among the growing congregations. The Bible was designated the word of God because it bore witness to the divine creative Word (Logos), which, according to the Gospel of John, became incarnated in Jesus the Christ (Messiah).

The story of how Christianity spread from Judea to Syria, then into all parts of the Roman Empire and beyond, eventually to become the largest religion in the world, is too complex to recount here. But today, as in the beginning, there is no single entity or group to which the term "Christian" refers. Instead, there are *Christianities* with widely variant organizational and ritual structures, not to mention beliefs and histories. Christianity has proved to be a creative religion, developing new and different forms as it moves through history and cultures. Even though at times it appears rather rigid and unwilling to change, Christianity has proved amazingly flexible.

According to Christianity, what is wrong with human existence as presently lived is that it is lived in sin. Generally, sin is any thought or action that has a negative impact on the spiritual health of persons, or on their ethical interactions with other persons and the environment. In the New Testament, the Greek word used for sin is *hamartia*, which means wandering from the path or missing the mark. It was commonly used for an arrow that has gone astray and missed its target.

*Hamartia* is described in many different ways. Christians often think of it as idolatry. Idolatry is more than the worship of gods other than the one preferred by Christians. It is trusting in something that is less than ultimate. The idolater's loyalty and devotion is completely given to people, things, institutions, or ideologies that are not ultimate (and hence not divine), but are passing fancies of the human imagination.

Christians also describe sin as rebellion against God's will. This view is inspired by the story of the disobedience of Adam and Eve in the Garden of Eden, a disobedience that constitutes the original, or archetypal, sin. Sin is transgression, the failure to follow God's will in thought, word, and deed. This failure to obey God is rooted in selfishness and the elevation of one's own will over the divine will.

Sin is also linked to temptation. In Genesis, the temptation of Adam and Eve by a snake (much later identified as Satan or the Devil) comes from outside human nature. Evil is there, in the environment, waiting to lure people into selfish and disobedient acts. However, temptation also arises within humans themselves. Humans are created, according to Genesis, out of "the dust of the ground." Hence, the "temptations of the flesh" are an ever present cause for concern. Yet, according to the Bible, humans are also created in the image of God.

Christians have disagreed over exactly what this image is, but there seems to be general agreement that humans have a dual origin. They are creatures of God, like all other aspects of creation, but they are closer to God than all other creatures. Under the influence of Greek philosophy, some Christians have talked about this dual origin in terms of body and soul, the material and spiritual components of human nature.

Some Christian theologians also describe sin as alienation or separation from God, symbolized by the expulsion of Adam and Eve from Eden. Some forms of early Christianity adopted the widespread religious symbols of light and dark to paint a picture of sparks of the divine light (souls) separated from God by the material darkness (body) of the world. Theories of sin as bondage or enslavement to both matter and Satan also emerged from this metaphor of separation.

Closely associated with the interpretation of sin as separation is the view that the original sin of Adam and Eve was a "Fall" from divine intimacy and grace in which the "image of God" was damaged. Christians debate precisely how much damage resulted from this first sin of Adam and Eve. Roman Catholic theologians generally argue that the divine image was not lost by the "fall into sin," but it was flawed and damaged in significant ways. Protestant theologians usually argue that original sin affected human nature more severely than Roman Catholics think.

Roman Catholic moral theology distinguishes between different kinds of sin, for example, venial sins and mortal, or deadly, sins. Venial sins are less serious than mortal sins and do not result in eternal unhappiness. Mortal sins turn the soul from God and deprive it of God's forgiving grace and eternal happiness. Thomas Aquinas argued that a sin must cause grave injury to the self, or to the community, or to God and his purposes for creation to qualify as mortal. Such sin must also, according to Aquinas, come from a moral agent who is aware of the wrongness of the sin, but does it anyway.

Protestant theologians reject the distinction between mortal and venial sins. All sins are equally damning, and all sins equally require God's forgiveness. The Protestant reformer John Calvin (1509–1564) captured this idea in a teaching known as "total depravity." Protestants teach that since the original Fall from unity with God, all people live in a state of sin. Sin is not so much those things that people think or do, but a state, a condition, in which they exist.

Sometimes the New Testament characterizes this state as "bondage to sin." We are trapped, enslaved, chained to sin, and without God's forgiving grace, we deserve eternal damnation. "We are slaves to sin," says the Apostle Paul in Romans 6:20, and in another place, he bitterly complains that the good that he wants to do, he cannot do because of the bonds of sin.

The Gospels of the New Testament are filled with stories of demonic possession and exorcisms. Some Christians still maintain a firm belief in demonic possession, an event that graphically reveals how much we are at the mercy of Satan and his forces of evil. We are slaves of Satan, the Prince of Evil and Darkness, who rules this world until Jesus the Christ returns and defeats him and his demonic hordes.

Sin, in Christianity, has also been characterized as ignorance or a lack of true knowledge about God and our sinful state. It is not just faithlessness and disbelief; it is ignorance of our true origins and our true nature as the sons and daughters of God. We are made in God's image, and until we come to know that image within our souls, we are lost in the darkness and not living in the divine light of knowledge and truth.

For many Christians, sin is not just personal or individual; it is also social and communal. It pervades the structures of society, resulting in the triumph, at least temporarily, of injustice over justice. Recent Roman Catholic as well as Protestant theologians have explored the social dimensions of sin as injustice. Liberation theology preaches the need for both spiritual and physical freedom from injustice, class conflict, and economic oppression. People deserve to be treated fairly and equally because they are all God's children.

## Understandings of Sin

1. Idolatry
2. Rebellion
3. Disobedience
4. Transgression
5. Alienation
6. Fall from divine grace
7. Bondage
8. Selfishness
9. Ignorance

### Types of Sin

1. Venial/mortal
2. Personal/communal

When Christian thinkers turn to the topic of salvation, or the cure for sin, their views vary considerably according to how they understand the problem of human existence. In spite of specific differences, there has been general agreement on three main features of salvation.[5] First, Jesus the Christ is necessary for salvation because it is through his work that people are saved. Second, left to their own devices without any divine aid, people are incapable of saving themselves. They need help. They need a savior who gives them grace. Third, while the fruits of salvation can be tasted in this life, its complete enjoyment is in life after death.

When we turn to the specifics, differences of opinion arise almost immediately. What does it mean to say Jesus the Christ is necessary? What sort of work did he do, and how can it save us? Exactly why are people incapable of saving themselves? What sort of help do they need, and what is grace? How should we best characterize the experience of salvation in this life? What precisely is life after death? Christian theologians vigorously debate the answers to these questions.

We cannot examine the many answers to each of the above questions in any detail here. In general, most Christians agree that the work of Christ consists of atonement (at-one-ment), the fruits of which provide salvation for all who have faith in Christ as their Savior and Lord.

There is no official doctrine concerning exactly how this atonement is accomplished, and so creative theological speculation has filled in the gaps. Some of these theories postulate that God offered his Son as a ransom to the Devil for the release of humans from the bondage of sin. Others focus on the idea that Christ's sacrifice on the cross was given in order to satisfy God's righteous wrath over human sin. Still other theories suppose that Christ's sacrifice on the cross provides a moral example of unselfishness for selfish humanity. Whatever the specifics of the theories may be, they all focus on atonement as due to the mercy of a just God. It is an undeserved gift. It is an act of divine grace.

These Christian stories of sin, atonement, and salvation have shaped Western civilization. They have inspired wars and efforts to find peace, acts of injustice as well as justice, feudal and democratic governments, capitalism as well as socialism, dominance as well as submission, quietism as well as activism, asceticism as well as indulgence—the list could go on and on. Much of the great art of Western civilization has been inspired by these stories, and many of the great legal institutions have evolved laws based on the principles of justice and mercy embodied in these stories of sin and salvation. There is much to celebrate, and there is much to criticize.

Critics point out that these stories of sin, atonement, and salvation have inspired patriarchal sexism, justified oppression, and promoted inquisitions. The arrogance and smug superiority encouraged by notions that faith in Jesus is the only way to be saved have inspired wars, conquests, and justified colonial rule. Dividing the whole of humanity into two categories, the saved and the damned, has inspired rejoicing on the part of some and anxiety among those who think they are damned.

In one way or another, for good or bad, these stories in both their sacred and secular versions form the passion play in which billions of people have lived and died. Christian stories of sin, atonement, and salvation, along with similar stories told by many other religions, provide meaning and hope to humans who often despair of finding any great truths by which to live and, unfortunately, sometimes provide justifications for perpetuating unjust power.

### Christian Atonement Theories

1. Ransom
2. Satisfaction
3. Moral example

## 10.2 COMPARISON

Both Sikhism and Christianity describe the human condition in remarkably similar terms. Both agree that the root of our troubles resides in our separation from God. This separation results in selfishness, which in turn leads to all the other sins that keep God and humans apart. However, beyond the obvious similarities, there are important differences.

So far I have been doing the comparisons of the opening cases for you. You have advanced enough in thinking about religion to try your own hand at comparing these opening cases. I will help by providing categories that you can use and offering some suggestions.

*A. Fall and Reincarnation*   There is no doctrine of the Fall in Sikhism, and there is no doctrine of reincarnation in Christianity (although some Christian theologians have suggested this idea from time to time). How is this fact significant for understanding the differences relating to salvation found among Sikhs and Christians?

*B. Devil*   Do you find it significant that there are no teachings about a devil or Satan in Sikhism? Why?

*C. Grace*   While both Sikhs and Christians acknowledge that humans cannot save themselves and thereby affirm the necessity of grace, they disagree about how God's grace is delivered. Describe how they differ on this issue.

**D. Devotion**   Both Christianity and Sikhism think of the way, or road, to salvation primarily in terms of a life of devotion. For both, devotion involves similar activities of worship, hymn singing, praying, meditating, and the like. However, Sikhism has no priesthood and no sacraments in the sense of visible vehicles of grace, such as baptism and a sacred meal. Do you find this fact an indication of a significant difference? Why or why not?

**E. Scripture**   What role does scripture play in both the Sikh and Christian traditions with respect to the issue of salvation?

**F. Gifts**   In both traditions the ancient notion of exchanging gifts is represented, although in different ways. In Christianity what does God give? In Sikhism what does God give? Be specific. What do the devotees in both traditions give in return?

**G. Heaven and Hell**   While both Christians and Sikhs hope for union with God and see this as the final human destiny, their views of heaven and hell differ radically. How do they differ?

It may have occurred to you as you were making these comparisons that from a psychological and sociological viewpoint we might describe both the Sikh and Christian views of human existence and destiny in terms of elaborate schemes of social control. These schemes are designed to reinforce socially acceptable, well-ordered, and conventional moral behavior. Such behavior affects the power structures and distribution of wealth found in the cultures where Christianity and Sikhism had the most success.

Social control, however, is only part of the story. These schemes of control also provide meaning and hope to people. They are not merely the effects of social conditions, but they also create social conditions by their ability to empower and mobilize people in just causes. The step from the desire for spiritual liberation is not that far from the desire for physical liberation. The desire for spiritual health is not that far from the desire for psychological well-being. And the desire for divine justice is not that far from the desire for human justice.

## 10.3 RELIGIONS OF SALVATION AND SOCIETY

The sociologist Max Weber was particularly interested in religions of salvation because of their possible social consequences. The need for salvation arises, Weber thinks, as humans attempt to resolve discrepancies between the actual situation they find themselves in and some imagined ideal situation. Humans wish to live an ideal life, but they find their actual lives less than ideal. What can they do?

Religions of salvation try to resolve this gap between the real and the ideal in many ways. Weber believed that most of these ways would fit into one of two patterns. One strategy is to escape from the awareness of life's imperfections. This Weber called *mysticism*. The other strategy is to gain mastery over the world in order to bring it into conformity with the ideal. This Weber called *asceticism*. Weber is using the words *mysticism* and *asceticism* in a very broad sense to encompass, on the one hand, all religious attempts to escape imperfection and, on the other hand, to designate all religious attempts to transform imperfections into perfections. Because the word *asceticism* is usually used to designate individual practices of self-denial, I will use the term *world-transformation* to designate what Weber calls asceticism.

Although Weber did not relate this insight to the biological phenomenon called "flight or fight," I think we can readily see the parallels. Just as all animals exhibit a flight or fight reaction when faced with situations they consider dangerous, religions of salvation, when faced with the evils of life in this world, either try to escape these evils or fight these evils. Mystical views of salvation represent the flight strategy and world-transforming views represent the fight strategy.

Weber was particularly interested in salvation strategies that try to change the world. If world-transforming strategies did have significant social impact, then Karl Marx's assertion that religious ideologies are largely by-products of economic conditions might well be false or, at least, only half the story. Weber further noted (although critics have questioned whether he was right about this) that the change from medieval feudalism to capitalism accelerated in Europe around the time of the Protestant Reformation in the sixteenth century. According to Weber, capitalism was more likely to gain a firm footing in Protestant countries. This suggested to Weber that Christian Protestantism, or at least some forms of it, may have strongly influenced and reinforced the rise of capitalism.

In a controversial and influential book titled *The Protestant Ethic and the Spirit of Capitalism* (1905), Weber argued that the Protestant movement started by John Calvin did have an important influence on the rise of capitalism. Calvin taught that God created human beings in order that they might glorify him. Everything people do should somehow add and not detract from God's glory. Just as our heavenly life will be one of constantly glorifying God, so too should our earthly life.

Calvin also developed the concept that ordinary work was a divine calling and an appropriate way to glorify God. Prior to Calvin, the Protestant reformer Martin Luther (1483–1546) developed the notion of calling, or vocation, in opposition to Catholic teachings. Luther, a former German monk, accused the Roman Catholic Church of perverting the Christian gospel. One of its many perversions was to draw a sharp distinction between the clergy and the laity in such a way that the life of the clergy, especially the life of monks and nuns, was elevated in spiritual value over the life of the laity, who were largely merchants and peasants. If one truly wished to glorify God, the Roman Church taught, then one should withdraw from the evils and temptations of the world and work for the church full time.

The teaching that religious callings (vocations) have more spiritual value than secular work obviously had its advantages in recruiting the best and the brightest to work for the Roman Church. Luther's assertion that secular work was just as much a calling from God as was religious work unleashed a flood of social energy by destroying one of the keystones of the feudal system and empowering both the merchant and peasant classes with a newfound dignity. Calvin focused that energy by arguing that whatever one's vocation may be, sacred or secular, the work should be well done. Hard, devoted work glorified God, and sloppy, lazy work detracted from God's glory.

In addition to the concept of living for the glory of God and the broadening of the notion of vocation, Calvin added a third idea, the idea of predestination. Christianity had long taught that God chooses in advance those who will be saved. They were called "the elect." Calvin portrayed God as assigning from all eternity, salvation to some (the elect) and, by default, damnation to others.

Calvin's understanding of predestination was motivated in part by his desire to protect the absolute sovereignty of God as well as to reject the whole Roman Catholic apparatus of salvation. No church, no sacraments, no priests would do a person any good when it came to matters of salvation. Nothing will prevail on God to change his mind. God has either elected you or he has not: end of story.

Of course Calvin taught that we should still go to church, worship, listen to sermons, work hard, and lead a moral life because this glorified God, and giving God glory was the sole purpose of living. Combining Calvin's understanding of predestination with the obligation to glorify God resulted in an extreme sort of individualism: You are on your own religiously. No church or pious community can help. Nothing can help you in any way to move from the list of the damned, if you are unfortunate enough to be there, to the list of the elect.

If extreme individualism was one social consequence of this view of salvation, another was anxiety about fate. Granted that this side of death there is no way of knowing for sure whether we are among the elect or not, there might be signs from which we could infer our fate. What might these signs be? This is the question that burned in the back of the good Calvinist's mind.

According to Weber, the signs of election include success in work, accumulation of wealth, and a morally upright life. Surely God could not have abandoned those who work hard, thereby glorifying God by their fine examples? If we do not engage in idle chatter, unproductive recreation, or sleep too much instead of work long and hard and late, surely we must be among the elect?

Calvin, by combining the ideas of predestination, calling, and living a life glorifying God, produced what Weber called "ascetic Protestantism," but what we can call "world-transforming Protestantism." This kind of Protestantism played a role, Weber thought, in the rise of capitalism because it reinforced the sort of work ethic demanded by capitalism and led to the accumulation of surplus wealth that could be invested.

There have been many criticisms of what some call the **Protestant ethic thesis.** Exploring them here, however, would take us too far afield. If we assume that there is at least some truth in what Weber says about the social and economic consequences of world-transforming Protestantism, we can see how religions of salvation, or at least certain versions of them, might have profound effects on social history.

We are also in a better position to understand the economic success that many Sikhs have achieved. In many ways Sikhism is like world-transforming Protestantism. Guru Nanak rejected the caste system of India and the traditional Vedic reliance on a priestly elite. He encouraged his followers to live and work hard in the world, not to abandon it by becoming monks or nuns. He showed how the traditional householder stage of life had spiritual value. People need not leave their family obligations to seek enlightenment. It can be found here and now, in the midst of family and work. As humans, we now have the opportunity to sing the praises of God and to glorify him in all that we do.

There are some important differences between Calvinistic forms of world-transforming Protestantism and what we might call world-transforming Sikhism. Perhaps the most important is the doctrine of reincarnation. Nanak's God, like Calvin's, controls all things and saves us by his grace, but, if we are Sikh, we need not be overly concerned with this because we will get another chance to obtain union with God (although we may not if we squander our opportunity as a reincarnated human being). We do, however, have to be concerned about securing a better rebirth; so hard work, a moral life, and pious practices are very much worthwhile. As we sow, so shall we reap. As we invest, so shall we gain.

## 10.4 WHAT IS WRONG WITH HUMAN EXISTENCE?

James's identification of "uneasiness," or a sense of something "wrong," as the first "deliverance" of salvation religions is deliberately vague. Different religions and even the same religion at different times and in different contexts specify the "wrongness" in different ways. Our brief look at only two cases (Sikhism and Christianity) has taught us that there are a variety of ways to describe the human condition, such as selfishness, separation from God, sin, disobedience, bondage, mortality, immorality, injustice, and ignorance. If we look at other traditions, we could add notions like pollution, powerlessness, imperfection, disharmony, imbalance, loneliness, alienation, depersonalization, hypocrisy, and much more.

Most theistic traditions locate the problem with human existence in the divine-human relationship. That relationship is out of sorts, not right, unhealthy, and disharmonious. It is important to point out that lurking behind the feeling of wrongness in a theistic context is the idea of divine displeasure and offense. When things go wrong for us, we sometimes feel that the "gods are out to get us." It is quite natural to feel, when misfortune strikes, that some greater power may have been offended by our actions. Think of your childhood and how your parents' anger affected you. Think about how you feel when you experience the displeasure of someone you want to please. We become uneasy in such situations and search for ways to relieve the tension or make amends. Sometimes we blame others when things go wrong, and sometimes we blame ourselves. If the "other" is a perfect divine being who can do no wrong, blaming ourselves seems the only alternative. Religious notions of sin, selfishness, disobedience, offense, and the like have their home in feelings and experiences that are natural to human existence.

It should be obvious that nontheistic traditions would not use language like "separation from the divine." It seems pointless to wonder how we might have offended the gods if there are no gods to offend. Perhaps this is why many nontheistic traditions speak of ignorance as the primary problem with humans. We are ignorant. Our ignorance is compounded by the fact that we think we are not ignorant. We think we know. Theistic traditions often use similar language, understanding ignorance to be ignorance of the divine. However, nontheistic traditions would not define ignorance in this manner. Rather, they are more likely to characterize ignorance in terms like "ignorance of our true natures," or "ignorance of the true nature of reality."

Our discussion indicates that we need to be careful about generalizing when describing how religions characterize the defects of mere mortals. The devil, as they say, is in the details. Different traditions can use similar words or words that can be translated in similar ways—sin, ignorance, selfishness—but what these words mean can only be determined by the context in which they are used. A theistic versus a nontheistic context is just the tip of the iceberg. Details about reincarnation or the denial of reincarnation, what ignorance is all about, or how disobedience occurs, lead to uncovering differences, whereas similarity of language obscures differences. Interpretations of exactly what causes the uneasiness of which James speaks and precisely what is the nature of the wrongness vary widely from tradition to tradition.

One thing is clear: when it comes to salvation religions, a necessary first stage is the recognition of something wrong. James's uneasiness marks a structural feature of salvation religions. If there is nothing wrong, then there is nothing to make right. The whole idea of salvation, or putting things right, would become incoherent if we believed there was no serious problem with human existence.

## 10.5 THREE PATHS TO SALVATION

James quite rightly notes that religions of salvation, which identify a problem with human existence, must also identify a solution. He deliberately describes the solution in terms equally as vague as those he uses for the problem. He says that the solution is "a sense that *we are saved from the wrongness* by making proper connection with the higher powers." Exactly what are the "higher powers" and what is the "proper connection" are left unspecified. Likewise, he does not say how the proper connection might be established.

In this section we will look at the *how* question. Religions of salvation offer paths, or ways, to overcome what is wrong. If they did not, they would hardly attract followers. The very idea of a path, or way, is deeply embedded in traditions of salvation. Dao means "Way," and early Christianity referred to itself as the "Way." The yoga paths of knowledge (jnana), devotion (bhakti), action (karma), and meditation (raja) can be found in one form or another not only in Hinduism, but in many other religions as well. Shinto, the indigenous religion of Japan (see Chapter 12), means the "way of the *kami*" (divine presences). In Judaism the Torah is the way to God, and in Islam **Sharia,** which is the religious and moral law, is the Arabic word for "path" (see Chapter 11).

Just as there are many different descriptions of the problem with human existence, there are many different descriptions of what to do about it. Here we will look at three different paths, or ways (merit, faith, and worship), but we need to keep in mind that there are many more.

### 10.5.1 Merit

To merit something is to deserve it. The idea that you deserve something is closely related to the principle *do ut des:* "I give in order that you shall give." We discussed this principle in relationship to theories of sacrifice. Sacrifice can be viewed as a gift given in the expectation that a gift will be received. The more that is given the more that is received. This principle of giving in order to get is based on notions of reciprocity. One good turn deserves another.

*Do ut des* is a very old idea. We can observe its operation among animals engaging in aggressive behavior. Males of many species will fight for control of females. These battles are sometimes fatal, but most often, after a clear dominance has been established, one male will submit to the other and be allowed to leave the field of combat with his life. One gives submission, the other gives life.

Merit is a kind of giving and receiving. It refers to religious and ethical practices that aim at improving the future spiritual well-being of oneself or others. When devotees "make merit" they do something or give something that makes them worthy of a reward. Among Buddhists the practice of making merit has become central to the lives of laity, monks, and nuns.

Stories of the Buddha's previous lives and the merit he acquired because of his good deeds are popular among Buddhists. If Shakyamuni improved his rebirths to the point of eventually achieving enlightenment by meritorious deeds, then careful attention to those deeds and how he did them can benefit all who seek to improve their own lives. When we link the notion of karma to the idea of merit, then good karma becomes synonymous with merit and bad karma with demerit.

In Buddhism, the activity of making merit became so important that catalogs of things to do to get merit developed. One of the more comprehensive lists details "ten meritorious deeds":

1.  Giving
2.  Observing moral precepts
3.  Meditating
4.  Showing respect for superiors
5.  Attending to the needs of superiors
6.  Transferring merit
7.  Rejoicing in the merit of others
8.  Listening to the Buddha's teachings
9.  Preaching what the Buddha taught
10. Having right beliefs[6]

The most meritorious practice on this list is the first one, giving, or *dana*. It is even more meritorious than observing moral precepts. Although it may involve giving gifts to the poor and needy, its most meritorious form for laity consists in giving gifts to the community of monks and nuns. These gifts are usually material, such as food, shelter, and clothing. One of the most meritorious forms of giving is to build a monastery. In return, the monks make merit by giving the teachings of the Buddha to the laity, thus improving their spiritual lot. The ideology of merit binds the religious professionals to the laity in a mutual relationship of giving and getting. The monks and nuns get material support so they can engage in religious practices full time, and the laity get spiritual support so they can improve their karma.

Not all giving, however, gets equal amounts in return. Attention must be paid to what is given (both quantity and quality are important), how it is given (with good or bad intentions), when it is given, and to whom it is given. The rules governing these aspects of giving often become elaborate. Proper respect must be shown according to rank. The abbot requires a kind of respect that the novice does not. Generous funding for a major festival will gain more merit than the gift of one or two new robes.

What is the aim of the merit maker? What does he or she want in return? Usually those who wish to make merit are interested in three things. First, the aim may be, and usually is, to gain rewards in this life and the lifetimes to follow. Typically the merit maker hopes to gain long life, health, wealth, a better rebirth, and above all, she or he hopes not to move down the samsaric scale to worse rebirths in which there is greater suffering. Second, the merit maker may have, as a long-term goal, enlightenment and the liberation from all suffering (nirvana). The oldest parts of official Buddhist literature, or canon, deny that nirvana can be gained by merit alone. However, popular Buddhist literature promotes a different view by claiming that even the smallest acts of merit, if accompanied by the vow to obtain enlightenment in some future life, can contribute to advancing on the path to enlightenment.

A third aim of the merit maker may be to share his or her merit with others. This is called the "transfer of merit," and it rests on the idea that if we clearly indicate who is to benefit from a good deed we intend to do, that other person gets the merit. We do not lose any merit, however, because the intention to transfer merit is itself meritorious. Typically, members of the devotee's family, living or dead, are the objects of the transfer. It is particularly meritorious to transfer merit to dead parents so that they might have a better rebirth.

A Chinese Buddhist text called *The Sutra on the Merit of Bathing the Buddha* portrays the "Pure Wisdom Bodhisattva" asking the Buddha three questions, one of which relates to the kind of merit that will be gained from washing the image of the Buddha. The Buddha responds:

> "Noble son, the consequence of performing this bathing of the Buddha image is that you and the great multitude of men and gods will presently receive wealth, happiness, and long life without sickness; your every wish will be fulfilled. Your relatives, friends, and family will all be at ease. You will bid a long farewell to the eight conditions of trouble and forever escape the fount of suffering. You will never again receive the body of a woman, and will quickly achieve enlightenment."[7]

It is not surprising that this text appeared at a time when Chinese Buddhism was promoting and developing devotional forms. It is also not surprising that it reflects the sexism deeply embedded in a masculine monastic tradition. Although it is reported that Buddha did say that women could attain the fruits of spiritual practices, he initially declined to found an order of nuns when his aunt, Mahapajapati, requested it. When an order of nuns was finally established, nuns were subordinated to monks by requiring them to follow more monastic rules than monks. These "eight weighty rules" made the most senior nun subordinate to the most junior monk and forbade nuns to admonish or teach monks.

Buddhism was not alone among the religions to exhibit sexist attitudes and to develop the path of merit. During the Middle Ages (and today) women were not allowed to become Roman Catholic priests, and Christian systems of merit reached their highpoint. While theological theories of merit all stressed the necessity for divine grace to assist in the creation of merit, human actions in order to be meritorious had to involve in a significant way human free will. Both obligatory acts, such as praying, and nonobligatory acts (called supererogatory), such as praying day and night, could be meritorious. Obligatory acts, however, only earn merit at the discretion of God, while supererogatory acts ensure divine recognition and the bestowal of merit.

While medieval Catholicism had no doctrine of rebirth, as did the Buddhists, it did have religious professionals who needed support from the laity. In return for that support, merit was earned, and that merit could reduce the punishments for sin that a person was likely to receive after death. Supporting monks, nuns, the clergy, doing penance for sins, performing good works, and participating in the sacraments were all ways of obtaining merit that would significantly impact what happened to someone after death. Merit alone could not get people into heaven; only God's grace could do that. But it could reduce their time in purgatory, that intermediate state between heaven and hell where many expected to end up. Time spent in purgatory and the nature of the punishment dispensed there could all be significantly changed by the amount of merit accumulated in the individual's lifetime.

Christian merit, like Buddhist merit, could also be transferred. The Roman Church provided special opportunities for the laity to help lighten the load of their deceased relatives in purgatory. Many thought of this system of transfer as well as the whole system of merit as a transaction: the more I give, the more relief I or my dead parents get. The pope claimed to control a treasury of the merits accumulated by Christ for his sacrifice on the cross and the merits saints got for their supererogatory acts. From this treasury of merit the pope can dispense merit to those he deems worthy.

The potential for abuse in this system should be apparent. When money was needed to build St. Peter's Cathedral in Rome, emissaries of the pope traveled around Europe selling "indulgences" guaranteed by the pope to reduce the burden of purgatory, not to mention the debt of construction. Catholic theologians denounced such practices as abuses of power, but the laity (particularly the peasant class that had a hard enough life in this world) bought into (pun intended) the transactional aspect of the merit system in the hopes of escaping or at least reducing the hardships of purgatory.

A popular nineteenth-century work titled *The Beauties of the Catholic Church* clearly articulated both the notion of transfer and the transactional features of merit. The author, Gregor Rippel, wrote, "She [the church] appears before the tribunal of the judge, not only as a suppliant, but also as the stewardess of the treasure of the merits of Christ and his saints, and from it offers to him the ransom for the souls in purgatory, with full confidence that he will accept her offer and release her children from the tortures of the debtor's prison."[8]

Ideas found among Mormons (members of The Church of Jesus Christ of Latter-day Saints) echo some of these ideas of the transfer of merit. A Mormon can research his or her family history and have dead relatives baptized in the Mormon faith. This will assure that "the family" will be together in paradise.

Who benefits from these merit schemes? Presumably individuals who are unworthy benefit because the accumulation of merit makes them worthy of something desirable that they do not now possess. Transfer strategies theoretically benefit others, especially dead relatives, but they benefit the individual merit maker as well. The problem with transfer strategies is that they appear to contradict the individualism built into the ideas of merit: I gain merit because I do something meritorious. If I can get merit from others without doing anything meritorious, then the notion of merit is severed from the notion of deserving a reward for what I have done. This theoretical objection to transfer schemes is, however, just that—theoretical. In practice merit transfer worked to make people feel that they could help relatives, even after they were dead. It restored some power to effect changes in situations over which people normally have no power. The magical style of religion discussed in Chapter 3 stands behind the religious concern with merit making.

Clearly the class of religious professionals benefits from merit schemes. The monks, nuns, clergy, and other nonproducers of material goods get material goods from the merit-making lay producers. Before we condemn this as an elaborate con job, we must hasten to note that the community at large also benefited. Or at least they believed they benefited spiritually, and in the realm of the spiritual, believing often makes it so.

The potential abuse of merit schemes and the magical nature of merit making have prompted criticism from both within and without religious circles. After Vatican II, few Catholic moral theologians except the most conservative pay much attention to the idea of merit. The Thai Buddhist monk Buddhadasa Bhikku developed a controversial but insightful criticism of merit, as the following quotation from one of his sermons indicates:

> To give with an expectation of a return is like investing with the expectation of a profit. For one to "make merit" in the truest sense, one must give with a pure heart without expectation of a return. . . . What is called merit or merit making is for those caught up in the world because it tempts people to lose their way in the grasping of the senses, to look for pleasure and enjoyment in this or that. Indeed, of all the things that tempt people to be led astray and preoccupied nothing exceeds merit making. Nothing is so destructive of human freedom.[9]

Criticisms of the path of merit are not just of recent origin, as we shall soon see.

## 10.5.2 Grace through Faith

Shinran (1173–1262), a Japanese Buddhist monk, launched an attack on merit making. He was a member of a sect that had first developed in China called "Pure Land Buddhism." He eventually developed his own version of Pure Land

Buddhism called "Pure Land True Sect" (*Jodo Shin-shu*). According to Pure Land teachings, there is a Buddha of Infinite Light named Amida (also called Amitabha), who lives in the Western Paradise called the Pure Land. Amida Buddha is particularly concerned with the plight of humans on earth and has vowed that all who, with sincere trust and devotion, call on his name will be saved. Hence the fervent repetition of his name, called the *nembutsu*, became a popular practice. This practice was thought to invoke Amida's grace and his power to save.

Shinran was convinced that the age in which he lived was a degenerate age of great wickedness. In such an age, no one had the power to save himself or herself by meditating, chanting, praying, or making merit by acts of devotion to images of the Buddha. Humans are too wicked even to muster the sincerity and trust necessary to chant the *nembutsu* correctly. The path of merit will not work. It will not lead to rebirth in the Pure Land of Amida Buddha. All so-called good works, however noble, are always tainted with selfishness. "What's in it for me" motivates people, even in their religious practices. Shinran wrote, "However good a man may be, he is incapable, with all his deeds of goodness, of effecting his rebirth in Amida's Land of Recompense. . . . Good deeds are of no effect . . . as regards to rebirth."[10]

If merit making does not work, what does? Is there any hope of salvation, or are humans forever trapped in the cycle of rebirth (samsara) with no hope of release (nirvana)? Shinran preached that there is hope, but it is not to be found in merit schemes. It is to be found in the great love and compassion of Amida. Amida's grace and Amida's grace alone has the power to save us from ignorance and selfishness. And that grace is offered freely with no strings attached. Believe it! Have faith in Amida, and trust the power of his grace. Even though we are unworthy, even though we are unacceptable and do not deserve rebirth in the Pure Land, Amida's compassion will prevail. His grace will make the unworthy worthy.

The critics of Shinran complained that the way of faith is too easy. This is cheap grace! All you have to do is believe. What could be easier? Surely the path of merit making was much harder. Shinran responded that the path of faith is the most difficult of all the ways to salvation. It is most difficult because pride always tempts us to think we can save ourselves. It is very difficult, if not impossible, to give up our selfish pride and simply trust in the power of Amida.

Critics also argued that this way of grace through faith was not, after all, without its conditions. There was a string attached. The string is, you have to believe. The human effort to believe in the unseen power of Amida is required. Shinran has not totally banished a merit system; he has simply made believing a new act of merit making. Shinran responded by arguing that all "merit" needed for salvation comes from the Buddha; none of it comes from us. Even our faith is itself a gift freely given by Amida Buddha because of his great compassion for suffering human beings. Chanting the *nembutsu*, Shinran claimed, is an act of thanksgiving to Amida for his love and forgiveness, not an act of merit making.

Shinran attracted even more criticism when he broke his vows of celibacy and got married. However, married clergy eventually became the norm in Japanese Buddhism. His daughter took over after Shinran's death and began to build an organization. This was the first time in the history of Japanese Buddhism that the continuity of a school was based on heredity. This too, eventually, became a common practice.

Two hundred and twenty-one years after Shinran's death, Martin Luther was born in Germany. Luther would grow up to become a Roman Catholic monk, much to his father's dismay. Luther was a pious monk. He did all that was required to gain merit in the eyes of God. Nevertheless, he was haunted by a deep sense of sin and guilt. Surely a perfectly righteous God could never find the penance, prayers, devotions, vows, and good works done by an imperfect and sinful human acceptable.

Luther's doubts about his abilities to save himself led him to distinguish between "internal sin" and "external or actual sin" of thought, word, and deed. Pious acts such as prayer, confession, and penance might be sufficient to make people feel good about the actual sins they commit and confess, but they do nothing when it comes to effectively dealing with internal sin. In fact, the making of merit can be spiritually detrimental because it can reinforce the human tendency to ignore internal sin.

> When they are rid of this kind of sin [actual sin] through confession, they go their way, feeling secure, and do not trouble themselves with the thought that, with a single sigh to God, they might cure also that internal sin. . . . A man, therefore, who considers only his actual sin, and is anxious that it should be purged out, soon becomes presumptuous and secure because he knows that he can be cleansed by the sacrament and by confession, and so he walks about without fear and is no longer conscious of any sin.[11]

Luther could not walk about without fear, and he could not shake his continual consciousness of sin. When a representative of the pope came to town selling indulgences in order to finance the construction of St. Peter's in Rome, Luther was outraged. Desperately poor peasants were buying these indulgences in the belief that they would get reduced sentences in purgatory for themselves and their already dead relatives. The more years they wanted cut from their sentence, the more it cost.

Luther began to preach against indulgences, then gradually broadened his attack on the whole elaborate system of making merit taught by the Catholicism of his day. He protested and clearly saw the need to reform Christianity. He eventually became one of the early leaders of what came to be called the Protestant Reformation.

In addition to the theological issues, such as selling indulgences, there were social, political, and economic causes of the Protestant Reformation. If we confine our focus here to the theological issues, I think we can see how a criticism of one part of an interconnected merit system could become a criticism of the institution it supported. The Roman Catholic Church of Luther's day claimed to be God's representative on earth with the right to dispense merit and grace, which was needed to unlock heaven's gate. Grace came through the seven sacraments, and the central sacrament, the Eucharist, could only be validly performed by a duly ordained priest. Only bishops of the Church could ordain priests. There was no chance of salvation outside the institutional structure of the Roman Catholic Church.

Luther believed that this church wrongly emphasized "good works" as a means of salvation. Luther argued that we are not saved by what we do, but by what God does. And what God does is to send his Son, Jesus the Christ, as our only Savior and Lord. Faith in God's saving work in Christ is the only means of salvation. Over and over again, in sermon after sermon, Luther hammered home the message that we are "saved by faith alone" and not by any works. *Sola fide,* "faith alone," became one of the rallying cries of the Reformation. Like Shinran, Luther argued that we do not have the power to save ourselves. We are so lost in sin that outside aid is needed. Shinran preached that this outside aid was available by faith in Amida's compassion. Luther preached that it was available by faith in the forgiveness of sins freely offered by God in Christ.

Also like Shinran, Luther came under fire for promoting an "easy way" to salvation that would lead people to ignore morality. Again like Shinran, Luther responded by pointing out that good works and merit making done in order to get something are not really good works. They are selfish works designed to benefit the one who does them. As long as we remain motivated by our desire to get into heaven and escape hell, we are acting out of self-interest. Only when we desire nothing for ourselves can we truly be morally good. Selfishness can only be overcome when we give up trying to save ourselves and do what is right solely because it is right, not because it will save us or bring us merit.

> So the Christian who is consecrated by his faith does good works, but the works do not make him holier or more Christian, for that is the work of faith alone. And if a man were not first a believer and a Christian, all his works would amount to nothing and would be truly wicked and damnable sins.[12]

Luther, like Shinran, eventually left his monastic life and married, thereby establishing a tradition of married clergy among Protestants.

If the principle behind merit making is *do ut des,* what is the principle behind the path of faith? Is faith a "giving," or is it a "receiving" only? It appears to be a getting without any giving, and this is paradoxical. According to the path of grace through faith, we have nothing worthy to give (no merit). If the principle of *do ut des* (I give in order that you shall give) is valid, then we should get nothing in return. But the claim is that we do get something. We get the greatest gift of all—salvation. What is going on here?

The path of merit and the path of faith seem entirely opposite. One advocates a road to salvation marked by effort and merit making, while the other advocates a path marked by trusting without expecting anything in return. Furthermore, the claim is that if you expect something in return, you will not get it.

These paths may not be as different as they seem. According to Buddhism, one condition of successful merit making is proper motivation. Proper motivation is usually described in terms of proper respect, proper faith, and proper intention. What is proper intention? Recall that Buddhadasa said, "For one to 'make merit' in the truest sense, one must give with a pure heart without expectation of a return." Buddhadasa here denies that the principle of *do ut des* applies to authentic merit making.

If the basic problem with human existence is selfishness, then it is no surprise that selfless service to others (merit making in its "truest sense") and unselfish trust in a gracious power to save us do not seem very far apart. However, they are not identical because the path of faith claims that the only thing we might be said to give is faith, and we really do not give that. It too, is a gift. It is here that the deepest paradox of the way of grace through faith is located.

Of course merit systems can cease to be authentically motivated and become abused. Motivations are notoriously corruptible. However, faith systems can also cease to be authentic and be turned into "cheap grace" by those who believe it is a shortcut to heaven requiring little cost. The danger of slipping into magical thinking about any path is always present.

### 10.5.3 Worship

Jacques Malan observed a company of baboons in South Africa in the 1920s. He was amazed by what he noticed. For most of the day the baboons were busy grooming, getting food, squabbling, "philandering," and participating in other fairly routine activities. However, no matter how they might be occupied, according to Malan, when the sun touched the horizon at the end of the day:

> they left their ground, swarmed over the ridge, and barked themselves into ecstasy at the sinking sun. At such times they seldom busied themselves with anything, but remained in a sort of rapt watching attitude until the sun had gone. Then they returned to their ground . . . In the mornings the rising of the sun was nearly always greeted with the same chorus of barking, and its movement over the rim of the horizon watched with the same peculiar raptness.[13]

Is this worship? As far as we know, one of the earliest objects worshiped by humans was the sun. Could worship have started in *heliotropism*, the reflexive tendency found among many living things to orient themselves toward the sun?

The analogy between human worship and baboon behavior seems a bit stretched. However, honoring the more powerful with reverence, awe, respect, submission, devotion, prayers, chants, songs, dances, and the like is very ancient. Losers must submit to the victors in battle, and veneration of kings and queens has been commonplace for centuries.

There are two aspects to worship: the inner and the outer. Inner worship involves motivations, intentions, attitudes, and feelings of honor, respect, fear, reverence, and submission. Outer worship refers to the countless number of cultic practices devised by religions so people can learn to worship and to express their feelings of worship in an appropriate and ordered manner.

Among Hindus the practice of **puja** ("honor" or "worship") is widespread. Gestures of respect, offerings of foods and service to various deities punctuate each day. Puja can be observed with varying degrees of complexity. Simple offerings to images of gods and goddesses of water, flowers, food, songs, chants, and prayers are the most common forms. There are also extended and complex pujas involving invocations, bathing and dressing the images, offerings of hospitality, and more.

Temple pujas use metaphors and symbols of divine royalty. The deity is the king or the queen of the universe, and the temple is his or her palace. Priests perform the duties of waking, bathing, dressing, feeding, and putting to bed the images. Periodically, temple images are placed on portable thrones and taken in procession around their "kingdoms," just as monarchs of old established their authority by touring their lands. People gather to watch these processions, offering adoration and praise.

An important part of puja is the experience of **darshana**, or "seeing" the image and thereby the divine in the image (see Chapter 7). When a deity is prepared for viewing, people often rush to see it, wishing to catch a glimpse of the divine. The devotees not only "see" the divine, but the divine "sees" them. This seeing creates a personal visual connection between the human world and the divine. The worshiper offers food, which the deity "sees" and makes sacred. This food is then returned to the worshiper as a tangible symbol of divine grace and forgiveness.

Another form of worship, particularly popular among the women of India, is *vrata*, or the taking of vows. Taking a vow is a ritualized act undertaken for a specific period of time and directed toward a specific goal. Various forms of renunciation (such as fasting) accompany the *vrata* to underscore the seriousness with which the vow is taken. Stories of the deity are often told when the vow is taken, and the devotees are instructed to meditate on the image and adopt the proper attitude of reverence. For example, devotees of Sasthi, the goddess who protects children, are urged during the vow ritual to contemplate her image.

She whose golden limbs, draped with jewels, glisten like mountain snow,
whose hands proffer boons and dispel fear,
   whose swollen milk-engorged breasts stain the shimming silk of her blouse,
in whose belly rests the male child, the primordial unborn man—
   this goddess Sasthi, . . . may you fix clearly in your mind.[14]

The goals of *vrata* are immediate and pragmatic: healing, success in marriage, the birth of children (especially sons), harmony in the home, wealth, and the like. An exchange takes place. If the deity delights in the offered vow, she or he will grant the wish in return. The vow creates a relationship of trust between the divine power and humans. It is a solemn promise, a sworn oath, a way of saying, "I will not deceive you, if you do not deceive me."

The German philosopher Friedrich Nietzsche (1844–1900) once remarked that religion is needed to "breed an animal *with the right to make promises.*" Walter Burkert remarks in a similar vein:

> Why must people have religion? In the ancient world, the obvious answer would have been, for the validation of oaths. Without gods there would be no oaths, and hence no basis for trust and cooperation, for legal action, or for business.[15]

Prayer is at the heart of worship because it involves direct address to the divine in the form of praise or petition. The expectation is that the divine will address the worshiper. Prayer, and hence worship, is a two-way street establishing a relationship with the divine. This relationship is often experienced as therapeutic. We can tell our troubles to the Lord, and he will help.

Religions encourage people to pray informally and formally. Formal, fixed prayer is a central feature of most worship services. We have had occasion to mention that formal prayer five times a day (dawn, noon, midafternoon, sunset, evening) is one of the central pillars of Islam (Chapter 8). This kind of prayer is called **salat** in Arabic. Muhammad declared that prayer is the key to paradise. He also said that the key to prayer is purification. Hence, before praying, Muslims ritually wash themselves in preparation.

Prayer is done facing the holy city of Mecca. The basic ritual unit of *salat* consists of standing, bowing, sitting in a semi-kneeling position, and full prostration with the forehead touching a clean floor or ground. This performance usually takes no more than seven to ten minutes. On Fridays congregational *salat* occurs along with a sermon. Prayer is not just something said, it is something done with the whole body. It is a physical act that symbolizes the heart of the Islamic message, submission to the will of Allah.

Before doing *salat*, the faithful need to mentally rehearse what is about to be performed and form a sincere intention. This is indispensable, and without it the performance of *salat* is invalid. As an aid to proper mental preparedness, the *salat* begins with *"Allahu akbar,"* ("God is greater"), a phrase that is repeated at fixed points throughout.

While there are detailed instructions about what to do and what to say while performing *salat*, private prayers can be added.

> You may say in your prostration "Glory be to You, my Lord! I have wronged myself and done wrong. Forgive me!" or something similar. You may utter a private prayer in the prostration if you wish, and there is no set time for this, but at least your members should remain still in a fixed position.[16]

Another form of Islamic prayer is called the *dhikr* ("th'ikr," Arabic for "remembrance"). It centers on the ritualized remembering of the holy names of God. The Sufis developed this form of prayer into a mystical meditation technique. A variation can be found among the Sikhs.

According to Sikh doctrine, before the creation, God lived without form. When he made himself manifest, he first formed himself into *Nam*, or "Divine Name." *Nam* is the key to God-consciousness. To contemplate *Nam* and to remember *Nam* in prayer is to place the presence of God in one's consciousness.

> Through remembrance of the Lord one is freed from rebirth.
> Through remembrance of the Lord death's messenger flees.
> Through remembrance of the Lord death itself succumbs.
> Through remembrance of the Lord all enemies are scattered.
> Through remembrance of the Lord all barriers fall.
> Through remembrance of the Lord one remains alert.
> Through remembrance of the Lord our fears are dispelled.
> Through remembrance of the Lord all pain is relieved.
> Through remembrance of the Lord one is numbered with the devout.
> Steeped in the remembrance of God's divine name,
>     we gather all the treasures which his grace supplies.[17]

"Calling on the Name" is an ancient and widespread practice. Besides the practice of *Nam* and *dhikr*, there is the *nembutsu* of Pure Land Buddhism, the liturgical "Lord Have Mercy" (*Kyrie*) of Christianity, and calling on the name of Osiris by the ancient Egyptians for a better life after death. Many practices in the mystical tradition of Judaism (known as the Kabbalah) focus on the unspoken, holy, and true hidden name of the divine. The name YHWH given to Moses by the voice from the burning bush has inspired much speculation on its true meaning. The letters have been used as talismans (signs to ward off evil). Jesus taught his disciples to pray in the Name of the Father.

There may be several different sources for the prayerful practice of Calling on the Name. Perhaps it derives from invoking the name of a monarch in order to be saved from some punishment, including death. Perhaps it derives from magical beliefs that knowing the "true name" of a superhuman power can transfer that supernormal power to otherwise ordinary people. Whatever its source or sources, it has proved to be a nearly universal form of prayer and meditation. The practices have remained remarkably similar, even as the "Name" has changed.

Religions teach many ways to overcome selfishness and sin. But to make that "proper connection with a higher power" requires some investment. We make merit, trust in unseen grace, worship, honor divine images, make vows, pray, and remember God. I think we can see how each of these ways reorients us away from pure self-interest. Puzzles, however, remain.

The greatest gift given, salvation, is invisible. We can easily understand why people might make an investment in order to get better health (we do it all the time when we give money to our HMOs), but better health is something tangible. It is visible. And these visible gifts are promised by religions. But the greatest gift of all is not tangible, at least not in this life. So why make merit or why pray for the gift of a stronger faith, or why worship when the goal is so elusive, hidden, and often not guaranteed?

**Paths of Salvation**

1. Merit
2. Faith
3. Worship

## 10.6 WHERE ARE WE GOING?

We have seen that different religious traditions interpret the "unease" and "wrongness" of which James spoke in many different ways. Likewise the remedies for overcoming the wrongness, for making what James called the "proper connection," vary and have different social implications. Here we focus specifically on the results of making that proper connection. I will call that result salvation.

The English word *salvation* comes from the Latin *salus*, meaning "whole" or "healthy." Salvation, in a general sense, is connected to a state of being that is safe from destructive forces (anomie or lawlessness). It is a result of being delivered from the wrongness of human existence. The ways in which the wrongness is characterized determine the ways in which salvation is characterized. So salvation may be described as deliverance from pain, suffering, loss, death, sin, punishment, bondage, ignorance, and so on. Gerardus van der Leeuw, an early phenomenologist of religion, described the essence of salvation as power experienced as good. What counts as good, of course, depends on what counts as evil or bad.

By focusing on salvation as the result of overcoming wrongness, I do not want to imply that salvation has only to do with the religious "endgame." Any fully developed religion of salvation must have at least three structural elements: a notion of the human problem, a notion of how to overcome the problem, and a vision of the right goal or outcome. We have discussed the first two elements; here we focus on the third.

Of the many different types of salvation, we will discuss four: limited, unlimited, this-worldly, and otherworldly.[18] Limited salvation refers to the overcoming of specific problems such as illness, danger, and other threats to our well-being. These may be physical or psychological, but most often they are a combination. Limited salvation does not last. Our enemies can attack again, even though we have been delivered before. Illness can return, even though we were healed before. Despair, dread, anxiety, and fear can be temporarily overcome, but that deliverance may not last.

Unlimited or absolute salvation refers to a final and complete overcoming of all unease and wrongness. It is final because, unlike limited salvation, the problems will never return. In the state of absolute salvation, sin and death no longer occur, the rounds of reincarnation (samsara) finally end, and a complete release from all attachments (nirvana) is achieved or graciously granted.

This-worldly salvation refers to saving states that happen this side of death and in the world in which humans live and die. It should not be confused with limited salvation because for some religions there is the possibility of ultimate or final salvation in this world. So, for example, truly liberated persons in Sikhism, Hinduism, and Buddhism no longer accumulate karma. They remain in the world only because it takes time to "burn up" the remaining effects of past karma. Different religions often regard "living saints" as enjoying complete salvation. In some traditions, the only salvation that exists is this-worldly, not otherworldly. In these traditions salvation amounts to getting the "right understanding" of life, the world, and death. Part of that right understanding is the realization that there is no life after death. This is the last attachment humans must give up before their salvation can be complete.

Otherworldly salvation refers to after-death states. Once again, we should not confuse this with absolute salvation. Life immediately after death may be and often is thought of as incomplete. We may have to go through purgatory, pass through purifying hells, or await the final day when our body will be resurrected to join our soul in some heaven. Heavens are often arranged hierarchically from incomplete to complete. Immediately after death we might enter a lower (even the lowest) heaven and work our way up to higher levels.

## Types of Salvation

1. Limited
2. Absolute
3. This-worldly
4. Otherworldly

Frequently, salvation is equated with enjoying some kind of immortality or life after death. We must be careful here and remind ourselves that not all kinds of life after death are necessarily enjoyable. There are hells and purgatories, which, presumably, we want to avoid if possible. But there are also unavoidable states that are not enjoyable. The early Greeks thought of life after death as survival in an underworld that they called Hades. Life in Hades was not particularly enjoyable. It was a "ghostly" survival. Shades of our living selves wandered about in a cold, dark, and largely lifeless world. It was much like living in a cave, with no hope of ever again enjoying the green, living, and sun-drenched earth. An early Hebrew notion of life after death is similar. The ancient Hebrew equivalent to Hades was Sheol. It existed under the earth and was thought of as a kind of cavern or pit. Life there was a sort of twilight existence and without pleasure. It was not desirable in any respect and so unwelcome that Job could say to his friends, "Let me alone, that I may find a little comfort before I go whence I shall not return, to the land of gloom and deep darkness. (Job 10:20b–21).

Do not misunderstand. Hades and Sheol are not places of punishment. They are morally neutral. They are simply places where the dead live. The Egyptians probably introduced the idea of the afterlife as reward or punishment for deeds done in this life. According to the Egyptian *Book of the Dead*, Osiris judges the person that has died, weighing a person's heart on a scale against the "feather" of Maat, the god of truth.

According to the Egyptians, what survived was a person's *ba*, or life force, which existed apart from the body, but nevertheless had needs that must be met while in the body. Accordingly, they buried the mummified corpse with whatever was needed in order to continue living the "good life." The mystery cults of Greece introduced the idea of an immortal *psyche* (Life Force) as the vehicle of survival. The Persians, however, could not imagine some disembodied existence as desirable, so they introduced the notion of resurrection of the body. But what sort of body is resurrected? Is it the physical body? If so, how could that be immortal since it is flesh, and all flesh decays? Perhaps it was a transformed body—a body that was no longer physical but spiritual.

The idea of the resurrection of a spiritual body made its way into the New Testament. St. Paul writes in I Corinthians 15:40–44:

> There are celestial bodies and there are terrestrial bodies; but the glory of the celestial is one, and the glory of the terrestrial is another. . . . So it is with the resurrection of the dead. What is sown is perishable, what is raised is imperishable. It is sown in dishonor, it is raised in glory. It is sown in weakness, it is raised in power. It is sown a physical body, it is raised a spiritual body. If there is a physical body, there is also a spiritual body.

Over time Judaism, Christianity, and Islam put these ideas of judgment, soul-immortality, and resurrection together in different ways. There were controversies over whether judgment took place at the time of death, or later. Whether the dead "sleep" until the resurrection or whether the soul departs for paradise awaiting its spiritual body. Within Christianity, by the medieval period, the prevailing popular view envisioned judgment at the time of death resulting in the soul either going to eternal damnation or eternal paradise. Then, when Christ returns, there will be a general resurrection of the bodies of those who "died in Christ," now transformed from physical to spiritual bodies.

All these ideas of judgment, immortal souls, and resurrected bodies center on the notion of *individual immortality.* We, as individuals, somehow survive death and enjoy, if "saved," life in a paradise of glory and bliss. Similar ideas are found in Pure Land Buddhism, various Hindu sects, and Chinese popular religion. There are also, however, *nonindividualistic* views of life after death. In some Hindu schools, for example, life after death is characterized by metaphors such as salt dissolving in water and rivers flowing into the ocean. At death the individual completely merges with the one true reality, Brahman. In this view, salvation is *moksha*—release or liberation from individuality, not the timeless continuance of individual existence. *Moksha* is, perhaps, the ultimate overcoming of the subject/object dualism that we discussed at the beginning of this chapter. Because individual consciousness is so prized in the West, *moksha* may appear decidedly negative. But according to at least one influential Hindu interpretation, it is not negative at all but the realization of full and complete, absolute consciousness. Shankara calls it being, consciousness, and bliss (*satchitananda*).

Still other nonindividualist views locate immortality in some larger unit like the tribe, community, race, or nation. We spoke of this in Chapter 9 as a theodicy of participation.

In Buddhism, views of what happens after death vary a great deal by school and sect. Presumably Buddha himself refused to speculate because it was beyond the abilities of mere mortals to know or describe.

> When a monk does not look on the soul as [eternal] he refrains from such views and clings to nothing in the world; and not clinging he does not tremble, and not trembling he attains Nirvana. He knows that rebirth is at an end, that his goal is reached, that he has accomplished what he set out to do, and that after this present world there is no other for him. It would be absurd to say of such a monk, with his heart set free, that he believes that the perfected being survives after death—or indeed that he does not survive, or that he does and yet does not, or that he neither does nor does not. Because the monk is free his state transcends all expression, predication, communication, and knowledge. (*Digha Nikaya*, 2.64ff) [19]

Nirvana is the extinction of all attachments, even attachments to ideas like an immortal soul. To posit a future life in some paradise is to invite craving and attachment, which is the cause of suffering. To be free is to cling to no views about a possible afterlife because once we have views we cling, and once we cling we become attached, and once we become attached we are locked into suffering and the samsaric lives of seemingly endless rebirths.

Just as in Christianity, controversies developed as Buddhism expanded. According to some schools, the monk who has realized nirvana ceases to exist when he dies. Nirvana is, in other words, a psychological state of freedom. According to others, the monk who has realized nirvana becomes, after death, one with true reality, which is empty of all substance. And, as we have seen in the case of Pure Land Buddhism, some sects hold that at death the enlightened go to live with Amida Buddha in a perfect paradise.

> This world Sukhavati, [the Pure Land], Ananda, which is the world system of the Lord Amitabha [Amida], is rich and prosperous, comfortable, fertile, delightful and crowded with many Gods and men. And in this world system, Ananda, there are no hells, no animals, no ghosts, . . . and none of the inauspicious places of rebirth. And in this our world no jewels make their appearance like those which exist in the world system Sukhavati.
>
> And that world system Sukhavati, Ananda, emits many fragrant odours, it is rich in a great variety of flowers and fruits, adorned with jewel trees, which are frequented by flocks of various birds with sweet voices . . . And jewel trees have . . . many hundreds of thousands of colours. They are variously composed of . . . gold, silver, beryl, crystal, coral, red pearls or emerald. Such jewel trees, and clusters of banana trees and rows of palm trees, all made of precious things, grow everywhere in this Buddha-field (*Sukhavativyuka*, 15–16).[20]

Compare this description of the Pure Land with Islamic and Christian descriptions of heaven: It is said that gates to Allah's palace in paradise are made of "green emerald," and the soil smells of the finest "musk and saffron." There are jewels everywhere and wonderful fruit trees of which the righteous will eat. In the New Testament book of Revelation (20:15ff), the "New Jerusalem" has gates of pearls, streets of "pure gold," and the foundations of its walls are adorned with every kind of jewel: jasper, sapphire, agate, emerald, onyx, amethyst, beryl, topaz, and more.

While the goal of salvation may be invisible, religions have found ways to make it at least symbolically visible with descriptions of palatial paradises, perfect tranquility, absolute bliss, perfect joy, and more. What humans have considered "living the good life" is reflected in their elaborate visions of life after death.

## 10.7 SUMMARY

We started this chapter with James's description of the two necessary features of religion: a sense of wrongness and its solution. Contrary to what James thinks, these are not features of all religions, but are features of salvation religions, which seek change from some kind of undesirable state to a better state. By way of contrast, religions of sanctification seek to maintain a sacred order that already exists.

A discussion of the nature of human conscious revealed how our experience of self-consciousness uncovers both a problem and the possibility of a solution. The problem is alienation, dissatisfaction, and a sense that we are separated from what is most valuable. The possible solution lies in the experience of self-transcendence that self-consciousness makes possible. We noted that religions describe this self-transcendence in different ways, such as gaining a new immortal self, the extinction of self-awareness, merging with a greater whole, or seeing the life that we lead and the world in which we live in a new way.

In our opening case, we focused on Sikhism and its development. We looked at the Sikh understanding of wrongness as selfishness born of separation from God, the means to overcome it through worship and prayer, and the solution—union with God. The problem of human existence resides in a persistent self-centeredness. God-centeredness is the ideal life, and God's grace can help us attain it. We must learn to walk according to God's will (*hukam*), and we can learn this by living a life of devotion in which we sing God's praises and meditate on the *Nam* (Divine Name).

In our second case, we walked through the origins of Christianity as a Jewish sect. What is wrong with human existence, according to Christianity, is sin. Christians understand sin in many different ways: as missing the mark, idolatry, disobedience, transgression, alienation, selfishness, bondage, injustice, and ignorance. Protestant and Roman Catholic views differ insofar as Catholics believe all sins are not equal (some are mortal and some are venial) and Protestants believe any sin leads to damnation unless forgiven. Although there are many different theories of salvation among Christians, all theories see the work of Jesus Christ and the need for divine grace as central.

We briefly noted different views of the saving work of Christ (atonement): ransom, satisfaction, and moral. Humans participate in Christ's saving work (however it is understood) by a life of devotion to God in Christ. Christians may understand salvation in a this-worldly or otherworldly fashion, although otherworldly salvation has been most common. Whether Christians understand salvation as the arrival of a perfect society on earth or as becoming members of a perfect society in heaven, one thing is clear: hell is to be avoided. All human hope collapses in hell.

We also noted that stories of sin and salvation have shaped Western culture in a deep way, sometimes for good and sometimes for bad. They have inspired wonderful visions of justice as well as dreadful deeds of injustice.

With some guidelines, you took over the task of comparing Sikhism and Christianity. Some points of comparison are that both regard sin as selfishness and separation from God, both see salvation as impossible without divine grace, and devotionalism plays a major role in both. However, there is no doctrine of the fall into sin and no teachings concerning atonement, the incarnation of God, or the role of the devil in Sikhism. Christianity has no doctrine of reincarnation and no theory of guruship in the Sikh sense of the term.

Views on what is wrong with humans and how it might be corrected have social implications. Marx claimed that religious ideologies, like all ideologies, are by-products of economic forces. Social forces change religion, but religion does not change society. Max Weber challenged the Marxist analysis. He believed Marx oversimplified the relationship between economics and religion. Religion may indeed be, in some circumstances, a by-product of economic arrangements. But it can also change economic arrangements, as his distinction between world-transforming ("ascetic") and mystical-type religions tried to show. His famous and much disputed Protestant ethic thesis maintains that Calvinist versions of Protestantism contributed to the rise of capitalism.

The unease and wrongness highlighted by William James as a structural feature of salvation religions is described in a wide variety of ways. If we look at the language religions use, similarities appear to overwhelm differences. Talk about sin, ignorance, bondage, disobedience, vice, transgression, and selfishness appears in a wide variety of religions. But similarity of language can obscure important differences. Ignorance in Christianity is not the same as ignorance in Buddhism or Hinduism. Even the understandings of sin within the Christian tradition can be very different. Context is decisive.

We focused on only three of the many different paths to salvation: the way of merit, the way of faith, and the way of worship. Merit systems are built on the principle of *do ut des*. We give in the hope of a return. Making merit seems far removed from the systems of faith of which Shinran and Luther spoke. Faith systems emphasize that salvation is totally dependent on God's gracious gift of forgiveness. In such systems, we do not give in order to get. Indeed, it is precisely that attitude that must be overcome if the grace of Christ or of Amida is to flow freely. In spite of the apparent differences, many merit systems also emphasize the attitude of faithful giving without the hope of reward as the key to true merit. Proper intention is what counts.

Worship may have its origins in heliotropism, but it may also have its origins in the deference and veneration demanded by chiefs, kings, queens, and other absolute rulers. We examined puja, *darshana*, and *vrata* as examples of worship found in Hinduism. The *salat* and *dhikr* of Islam provide examples of prayer, a vital part of any worship. In prayer, people call on a divine name.

We examined salvation as the end or goal of this process of identifying what is wrong and seeking a solution. Salvation may be limited or unlimited, and it may be this-worldly or otherworldly. It may also be individual and nonindividual. Individual forms usually involve some picture of heaven or paradise where the immortal soul or resurrected spiritual body abides with God in a jeweled city or a beautiful land. Nonindividual forms often involve the idea of merging, becoming one with, or being absorbed in a greater divine reality. Sometimes the focus is on the immortality of the group, in light of which the importance of individual immortality fades. Some views of the afterlife, however, are neither individualistic nor nonindividualistic. Early Buddhists refused to speculate about such matters as an afterlife because they believed it was beyond human knowledge and description. Later schools of Buddhism did, however, elaborate on the nature of nirvana.

## 10.8 RESEARCH CASE—ZEN BUDDHISM

There are three major forms of Buddhism, and within each, there are numerous schools and sects. Out of the many different groups that early Buddhism comprised, only one remains active today. It is called Theravada (Way of the Elders) Buddhism. This form of Buddhism places emphasis on the disciplined life of the monk and generally views the path to enlightenment as a matter of individual effort. Buddhas are ideal examples of humans who have become enlightened. Today Theravada Buddhism is primarily found in such Southeast Asian countries as Sri Lanka, Thailand, Laos, and Cambodia. Mahayana (Great Vehicle) Buddhism predominates in China, Korea, Vietnam, and Japan. It developed out of early Buddhism sometime around 100 B.C.E. and places emphasis on buddhas as savior figures whose aid is necessary for enlightenment. Vajrayana (Diamond or Thunderbolt Vehicle) is a third type of Buddhism found mostly in Tibet, although at one time it was more widespread. It developed in the sixth century and its Tibetan form in the seventh century. Vajrayana emphasizes both individual effort and the aid of various buddhas. It teaches that enlightenment is beyond all oppositions, such as samsara/nirvana, male/female, self/other, effort/grace, sacred/profane.

Zen Buddhism is a Japanese school within the Mahayana tradition that was imported from China, where it is called Chan Buddhism. It is the largest school of Buddhism in Japan. The word *Zen* means "meditation," and it is characteristic of this school to emphasize the life of meditation as an essential feature of the Buddhist path.

There are two main sects of Zen Buddhism—Rinzai Zen, introduced to Japan by the monk Eisai (1141–1213), and Soto Zen, introduced to Japan by Dogen (1200–1253). Rinzai Zen claims enlightenment is a sudden experience that can be induced by the practice of **koan** meditation. A *koan* is a short paradoxical question given by a master to a student designed to shock the student out of dualistic modes of thought. Some famous *koans* are "what is the sound of one hand clapping?" and "does a dog have the Buddha nature?"

Soto Zen emphasizes gradual enlightenment and the practice of **zazen** or "sitting meditation." In *zazen* practice, the meditator assumes the lotus, or cross-legged, position with the buttocks elevated by means of a cushion so that the back is straight and the head is erect. The hands are folded on the lap. The seated meditators empty their minds and go into deep meditative states usually by concentrating on their breathing. According to Dogen, *zazen* should not be thought of as a method for attaining enlightenment but a way of expressing the innate enlightenment (Buddha-nature) we all possess. Dogen claims we are already enlightened, but we don't yet realize it. If we undertake *zazen* with the faith that we are already buddhas, then, as we forget ourselves in meditation, the Buddha-nature will gradually unfold in all aspects of our lives. Our entire life will become one of selfless, compassionate service.

Ritualized chanting and rites paying homage to buddhas also play a role in Zen practice. Typically, each day at a monastic temple begins with ritualized acts of worship followed by periods of meditation and work. At sunset another worship service takes place. Worship itself is an act of meditation and should be done "mindfully," that is, with complete attention. Today, in many Zen centers, *koan* practice, *zazen*, mindful work, and mindful worship may be combined in different ways.

D. T. Suzuki (1870–1966), who aroused much interest in Zen Buddhism in the United States, asserted that **satori** is the essence of Zen. Satori is the Japanese Zen term for enlightenment. Suzuki interpreted it as

> an intuitive looking into the nature of things in contradistinction to the analytical or logical understanding of it. Practically, it means the unfolding of a new world hitherto unperceived in the confusion of a dualistically-trained mind. Or we may say that with *satori* our entire surroundings are viewed from quite an unexpected angle of perception . . . Logically stated, all its [the world's] opposites and contradictions are united and harmonized into a consistent organic whole.[21]

There is and has been much debate over satori with regard to both its nature and its effects. It is apparently a flashing, momentary, and seemingly spontaneous intuition much like a sudden discovery or insight. Suzuki emphasized its transforming effect:

> All your mental activities will now be working in a different key, which will be more satisfying, more peaceful, more full of joy than anything you ever experienced before. The tone of life will be altered.[22]

If the basic problem with human life is suffering because of cravings and attachments, then the effects of satori gradually lead to learning to live a joyous, peaceful life of compassion. Such a life is possible once selfishness is overcome. Craving things for ourselves and becoming attached to things that please us make no sense once we overcome dualistic thinking. Once we have seen reality in its deepest sense, we realize there is no real difference between others and ourselves. We are all interconnected parts of the ongoing flow and dance of what we call the universe.

In 1949 a laywoman named Nakayama Momoyo wrote about her life before and after Zen practice. She told of her struggles as a single mother in prewar and wartime Japan and how she became overwhelmed with grief when her son died. During a Zen retreat of intense *koan* meditation, she underwent an experience she later recounted in the following manner:

> "Gong!" rang the temple bell, and suddenly, I cried out and returned to myself. It was attained! "Heaven and Earth are of one piece. The universe and I are one body. I am the Buddha! We're jointed in one!" . . . Apart from buddha mind, there is nothing. That is joy. This too is joy. My life is full in this vast, delightful and pure world. In one of my teacher's lectures she spoke the lines,
>
> > My clear dew mind
> > Is a ruby
> > When amongst the autumn leaves.
> > It's because my mind is clear or colorless that it can adapt to any and all circumstances.
>
> Because of the kindness of the buddhas and patriarchs [Zen masters who transmitted the enlightenment experience "mind to mind"], a life worth living, a life that requires only the slightest effort, has begun.[23]

## QUESTIONS ON THE CASE OF ZEN BUDDHISM

1. How does Zen Buddhism solve the problem of suffering?
2. How do you think *koan* and *zazen* practices work?
3. Is "salvation" in Zen this-worldly or otherworldly? Support your answer with reasons.
4. Compare and contrast Zen with Sikhism and Christianity. In what ways are they the same and in what ways different?
5. Would you classify Zen as a salvation religion? Why or why not?

## SUGGESTIONS FOR FURTHER READING

In addition to the material found in the notes, the reader may wish to consult the following for more information.

Badham, Paul, and Linda Badham, eds. *Death and Immortality in the Religions of the World.* New York: Paragon House, 1987. This collection of essays examines different religious views of the afterlife along with some philosophical critiques.

Bauman, Zygmunt. *Mortality, Immortality and Other Life Strategies.* Stanford, CA: Stanford University Press, 1992. Bauman argues that humans try to cover up the terrible fact of nonexistence after death, and religions are the primary institutions in most societies that "obliterate what is really known to be true, that humans have no destiny at all."

Cole, W. Owen, and Piara Singh Sambhi. *The Sikhs.* Brighton: Sussex Academic Press, 1995. I recommend this careful discussion of Sikh history and beliefs.

Gier, Nicholas F. *Spiritual Titanism.* Albany, NY: State University of New York Press, 2000. Gier presents an insightful comparative study of Titanism, the religious tendency to attribute to human beings divine characteristics.

Hawkins, Bradley K. *Buddhism.* Upper Saddle River, NJ: Prentice-Hall, 1999. This book provides a clear and concise introduction to Buddhism.

Holm, Jean, ed. *Human Nature and Destiny.* London: Printer Publishers, 1994. This is a collection of essays about how different religions describe human nature and human destiny.

Hoover, Thomas. *Zen Culture.* New York: Random House, 1977. Zen is more than a religion, it is a culture. Hoover explores the cultural expression of Zen in archery, landscape gardening, painting, No theater, the tea ceremony, Haiku, and more.

Johnstone, Ronald L. "Religion and the Economy." In *Religion in Society: A Sociology of Religion.* 6th ed. Upper Saddle River, NJ: Prentice-Hall, 2001. I have relied heavily on Johnstone's discussion of the Protestant ethic thesis because it is clear and insightful.

Kasulis, Thomas P. "Nirvana." In *Buddhism and Asian History,* edited by Joseph M. Kitagawa and Mark D. Cummings. New York: Macmillan, 1987, 1989. Kasulis's article, originally published in *The Encyclopedia of Religion,* provides an overview of the many different meanings of nirvana in Buddhist thought.

Neville, Robert Cummings, ed. *The Human Condition.* Albany: The State University of New York Press, 2001. This volume in the Comparative Religious Ideas Project includes essays by leading scholars on different religious views concerning the human predicament.

Pagels, Elaine. *Adam, Eve, and the Serpent.* New York: Random House, 1988. Pagels shows how certain ideas concerning sexuality, moral freedom, and human value based on the stories of Adam, Eve, and the serpent in Genesis have affected the development of Western culture.

Plaskow, Judith. *Sex, Sin and Grace: Women's Experience and the Theologies of Reinhold Niebuhr and Paul Tillich.* Lanham, MD: University Press of America, 1980. Plaskow argues that traditional Christian views of sex, sin, and grace have been dominated by a male perspective. "Women's sin" is primarily the failure to take responsibility for self-actualization, which is an aspect of sin typically overlooked by male theologians.

Singh, Sher, trans. *Guru Nanak on the Malady of Man.* Delhi: Sterling Publishers, 1968. A collection and translation of selected hymns of Guru Nanak having particular reference to what is wrong with human existence without God.

Singh, Trilochan, et al., trans. *The Sacred Writings of the Sikhs.* New York: Samuel Weiser, 1973. This contains selections from the Sikh scripture, *Adi Granth.*

Underhill, Evelyn. *Worship.* New York: Harper and Row, 1936. A classic study from a primarily Christian point of view. For Underhill, the heart of worship is human response to the "Eternal."

Weber, Max. *The Protestant Ethic and the Spirit of Capitalism.* Translated by Talcott Parsons. New York: Scribner's, 1958. Weber's classic statement, first published in German in 1905, is translated here.

Wilson, Brian. *Christianity.* Upper Saddle River, NJ: Prentice-Hall, 1999. This book, in the *Religions of the World* series, provides a concise introduction to the history of Christianity and some of its main teachings and practices.

## INTERNET RESOURCES

http://www.clas.ufl.edu/users/gthursby/rel/sikhism.htm    At this site you will find online guides to the Sikh tradition.

http://www.clas.ufl.edu/users/gthursby/rel/xianity.htm    Here you will find all kinds of links to Web sites containing information about Christianity.

http://www.clas.ufl.edu/users/gthursby/rel/buddhism.htm    This Web site is overflowing with links to information about Buddhism, including Zen.

# CHAPTER 11

# Religion and Morality

HOW SHOULD ONE LIVE? The Greek philosopher Socrates (470–399 B.C.E.) said that this is the most important question humans can ask of themselves. Should we live according to God's commands, submitting our own will to the divine will? Should we live a virtuous life centered on creating social harmony? Should we follow the Golden Rule, doing unto others as we would have them do unto us? Should we order our lives by some moral natural law that is built into the structure of the universe? Should we live a life dedicated to the well-being of all living things and the world in which they live? There are many different answers to the question about how we should conduct our lives.

Humans, who are controlled less by instincts than other animals, have the freedom to select different lifestyles. This freedom is not absolute. It is limited. But the limits are constantly changing as cultural, social, scientific, and technological changes occur. We cannot just ask and answer the question about how we should live once, but we must keep asking and trying to answer it as we mature and as new moral problems arise.

In an important sense we might view religions as elaborate and complex answers to the question about how we should live. These answers are moral in the very broad sense of providing norms or values for the conduct of life. This moral viewpoint is based on a distinction between what *is* the case and what *ought* to be the case. We often distinguish between what is real and what is ideal. The real is what is the case, and the ideal is what ought to be the case. Religions, as we have seen in Chapter 10, take into account the gap between how we do live and how we ought to live. They try to close this gap as much as possible by creating a vision of the good life and by urging people to make how they do live conform ever more closely with how they ought to live. Religions seek to make the ideal real.

We can think of **morality** as a set of norms designed to regulate and govern the conduct of humans with one another, with other living creatures, and with their environment. Technically *ethics* is the philosophical study of morality, although the word is often used interchangeably with morality. Here we will, for the most part, use the words *ethics* and *morality* interchangeably.

Religions are connected to morality or ethics in many different ways. Religions *identify* moral norms. They tell us what is morally right and what is morally wrong. Religions also *legitimate* moral norms. They justify them by telling us why we should consider them moral and thereby see ourselves under some obligation to follow them. Religions also *motivate* people to shape their lives according to a set of religiously transmitted norms. They do this in a variety of ways, including preaching, telling moral tales, offering saints and moral heroes as examples, instilling guilt when norms are broken, and promising just retribution. Religions also help *renew* moral commitments by instilling a sense of hope and providing opportunities for forgiveness and for membership in groups working to build moral communities.

From what I have said so far, it would appear that religion is primarily a conservative moral force. It endorses and supports the conventional moral norms as they are culturally and religiously transmitted. However, religions also *criticize* moral norms and often endorse radical revisions in conventional morality. This critical function is part of the prophetic principle we discussed in Chapter 9. Religious prophets may condemn conventional morality in the name of a higher morality. For example, Martin Luther King, Jr., a Christian preacher, condemned segregation laws and the conventionally accepted attitudes they embodied in the name of a higher moral standard of human equality. We cannot naively assume that because something is legal, it is also morally good.

I will elaborate on these themes as we discuss the nature of morality, how religions identify and legitimate moral norms, and how they use retribution and guilt to motivate and renew moral commitments. We will start with two cases. The first analyzes the divine command theory of ethics. There are different versions of this theory, but most assert that what is morally good is what the divine commands, and what is morally wrong is what the divine prohibits. Our second case introduces a religious tradition originating in China that we have so far not had an opportunity to discuss. It is called Confucianism and is so permeated with a concern for developing virtue that some have claimed it is not really a religion at all, but a moral philosophy.

The research case at the end of the chapter also introduces a religion that we have not discussed before. It is called Jainism, and it originated in northern India about the same time as Buddhism (sixth century B.C.E.). You may have already heard of one of its central teachings called **ahimsa** ("ah-him'suh"), which is often translated as "nonviolence." Literally, it refers to a state of not desiring any harm toward self or others.

> ## Relations between Religion and Morality
>
> 1. Religion identifies and legitimates moral norms.
> 2. Religion motivates people to follow moral norms and to renew their moral commitments.
> 3. Religion criticizes some moral norms in the name of a higher morality.

## 11.1  TWO CASE STUDIES

### 11.1.1  Divine Command Theory

The divine command theory of ethics is common to many religious traditions, especially the monotheist faiths of Judaism, Christianity, and Islam. We will focus on Islam in our analysis.

We introduced Islam in Chapters 8 and 9, and I refer you to those discussions for background information. Here we will be particularly interested in the Islamic idea of *Sharia* ("sha-ree'ah"), which is often translated as "divine law," but literally means a path to water. It refers to the entire body of moral, ritual, and legal directives that Islam claims is ordained by Allah. The *Sharia* is the answer Islam gives to Socrates' question about how we should live.

Al-Ashari (d. 935), the founder of an Islamic school of theology named after him, argued that Allah is an "Overwhelming Monarch" who is subject to no one or no thing. If this is so, then

> nothing can be wrong on God's part. For a thing is wrong on our part only when we go beyond the limit set for us and do what we have no right to do. But since the Creator is subject to no one, nothing can be wrong on His part.
>
> Question: Then lying is wrong only because God has declared it to be wrong.
>
> Answer: Quite so. And if He declared it good, it would be good; and if he commanded it, there could be no opposition to it.[1]

Al-Ashari was arguing against a position associated with a rival theological school called the Mutazila. These theologians had argued that there was a rational basis for good and evil. If we were to ask both of these theological schools whether something is good only because God commands it, or whether God commands something because it is good, the Asharites would answer that God's commands and prohibitions are the *only thing* that make something right or wrong. The Mutazila theologians would answer that God commands something *because it is good*. In other words, God knows that something is good or bad and commands or prohibits it accordingly. God does not command lying but prohibits it because lying is morally wrong. Its wrongness can be established on rational grounds, or so Mutazila theologians argued.

Al-Ashari opposed the Mutazila view. He boldly declared that even lying would be good if God commanded it. In other words, morality is based on the divine will alone. It makes no difference what human reason and rationality may say about it. The basis of morality is not in human reason, but in Allah's will.

Al-Ashari's position is a good example of a strong form of the divine command theory of ethics, which states that we find the foundation of all morality in God's will. In other words, the meaning of good is equivalent to what God commands, and the meaning of wrong is equivalent to what God prohibits.

This is more than just an arcane theological debate. There are serious and important practical implications. Al-Ashari advocated a divine command theory because he wished to protect God's absolute sovereignty and power. If God commands something because it is good, limits are placed on divine power. There are things God can command and things God cannot. What these things are can be determined by human moral reason. This implies, al-Ashari argued, that human reason determines what God can or cannot do.

The Mutazila school opposed the Asharites on this issue because they believed that such a strong version of the divine command theory reduces morality to a matter of blind obedience. If divine fiat or command determines what is right or wrong, the consequences of what people may do and their intentions for doing it have no moral validity. Surely this is contrary to our rational intuitions. Would we call people morally good if they really wanted to lie, but did not do so only because God prohibited it? Would not people be like children who did what was right only because their parents, who have greater power, required it, not because they really wanted to do it? We might say that what such children do is good, but we would hardly call them morally good because their actions amount to mere conformity with the wishes of a greater power.

The Asharite position, the Mutazila theologians argued, makes the ground of morality arbitrary. If God should command lying instead of honesty, then lying would be good, given the Asharite version of the divine command theory. Let's say God should have a change of heart and decide that honesty should be forbidden and lying commanded. If this is possible, Asharite theory hardly seems like a firm foundation for morality. Of course it could always be argued that God's will is eternally the same, so God's will about honesty and lying would never change. However, if we are to avoid limiting God in any way, we must allow for the logical possibility that God's will might change and turn morality as we now know it on its head.

Identifying the basis of morality with God's commands raises the issue of where these commands can be found. They can be found, according to Islam, in the *Sharia*, or divine law. While we have been using the word *morality* to talk about the divine command theory, we must keep in mind that *Sharia* is a much broader concept. Muslims do not make sharp distinctions among what is legal, what is religious, and what is ethical or moral. The *Sharia*, as the totality of divine law, contains religious duties such as prayer along with moral and legal duties. As the Sunni tradition of Islam developed, it specified four sources of *Sharia*. The first and most obvious source is the Quran, the Holy Scripture containing the infallible revelations of Allah to Muhammad. The second source is the *Sunna*, or "customs," of the Prophet Muhammad derived from his words and actions. Some of this material has been recorded in the Hadith, which Muslims believe contains the authentic accounts of what the Prophet said and did. Muslims consider both the Quran and the *Sunna* of Muhammad as divinely inspired sources.

The Quran and the *Sunna* do not explicitly address every situation that arises. So Muslims often appeal to a third source of *Sharia* called analogical reasoning. Analogies are drawn between new situations and the material found in the Quran and *Sunna*. If the analogy is close, a trained interpreter of the law can deduce what should be done in new situations. A fourth source of divine law is called *ijma*, or consensus of the community. This does not mean that the whole Muslim community votes on what should be done in situations not covered by the other three sources, but that a consensus is reached by those who are learned (*ulama*) and whose views are respected and widely accepted.

These religious authorities both interpret the *Sharia* and administer it. They serve as preachers, teachers, arbiters, judges, notaries, witnesses, prayer leaders, and heads of Sufi mystical orders. The *ulama* have often been necessary for Islamic governments to succeed because their cooperation provides a stamp of approval that legitimizes a ruler's decisions. Their lack of cooperation often spells death to a regime—witness the role of the Ayatollah Khomeini (d. 1989) during the Iranian revolution against the Shah. The *ulama*, however, have also been criticized for being too conservative, too rigid in their interpretations, and out of touch with the needs of Islamic peoples in the modern world.

### Four Sources of Sharia

1. Quran
2. Sunna
3. Analogical reasoning
4. Consensus of the community

Because the *Sharia* is rooted in a divine command theory, we would expect it to be rather static, inflexible, and unable to cope with a new and changing world. However, as our discussion of the four sources of *Sharia* shows, it is a dynamic system that has been changing and evolving since the earliest days. Large numbers of Muslims take it very seriously not only because they consider it one of the most impressive aspects of their religion, but also because it makes Islam a comprehensive religion—that is, one that integrates all aspects of life from diet and dress to business and prayer.

Not every government of Islamic countries has used the *Sharia* to administer the country. So, alongside the *Sharia*, secular laws reflecting different viewpoints have arisen. Nevertheless, the attempts of recent Muslim revolutionaries (often called fundamentalists) to restore *Sharia* as the sole system of law in Islamic countries indicates the importance of *Sharia* to Islamic identity.

Reports on television and in the newspapers often focus on Islamic movements that appear militant and uncompromising. They give the impression of a monolithic and uniform set of laws over which there is little disagreement and about which there is little discussion. But in the history of Islam, different legal schools have developed, and tolerance of the differences among them has been widely practiced.

An examination of the different understandings of the moral and religious duty of jihad (often translated "holy war" but less misleadingly translated as "struggle," or "effort") illustrates the diversity of opinions that have developed among Islamic interpreters of the *Sharia*. This issue is particularly important in light of the horrible terrorist attacks of September 11, 2001. Osama bin Laden and his followers justified such attacks on innocent civilians by invoking the idea of jihad. However, as the following discussion will show, bin Laden's understanding of jihad is very different from the classical Islamic tradition.

In its broadest sense, jihad refers to the duty of every Muslim to make a sincere effort to submit to Allah's law and spread belief in Allah throughout the world. This "sincere effort" does not necessarily imply military warfare, as the notions of the "jihad of the tongue" or "jihad of the pen" indicate. The broader interpretation of jihad rests on *sura* 16:125ff of the Quran, which reads, "Call men to the path of your Lord with wisdom and kindly exhortation. Reason with them in the most courteous manner. Your Lord best knows those who stray from His path, and those who are rightly guided." In other words, faithful Muslims have an obligation to use forms of peaceful persuasion.

In the Quran, jihad is presented as the obligation to command good and forbid evil, most particularly with respect to the struggle of the faithful against persecution and idolatry. "Let there become of you a nation that shall speak for righteousness, enjoin justice, and forbid evil" (*sura* 3:104). When this struggle for righteousness and justice takes the form of warfare, the Quran speaks of killing (*qital*) in addition to jihad.

Based on a passage in the Hadith of the Prophet, Muslim scholars make a distinction between the "lesser jihad" and the "greater jihad." The lesser jihad is military struggle (war), and the greater jihad is the struggle of believers to live faithful lives, to do good, avoid evil, and to peacefully spread the truth of Allah as revealed to Muhammad. Clearly it is wrong to equate jihad exclusively with the notion of a holy war.

Nevertheless, we must note that "jihad by the sword" is not forbidden, and Muslim jurists agree that military action against unbelievers is justified. But when is it justified? What conditions make "jihad by the sword" a moral and spiritual obligation rather than "jihad by the tongue?"

Among classical Sunni jurists, during the time when Islam was rapidly expanding, jihad by the sword was justified in order to expand Islamic territory, but not to make converts per se. Hence the Sunni jurists developed and elaborated an extensive set of rules governing when it is appropriate to wage jihad by the sword and how to conduct the resulting war. Shiite jurists disagreed with the Sunni position and argued that, at least during the occultation of the Twelfth Imam (see Chapter 9), military action could only be used in defending established Islamic lands, not in capturing new land.

Contemporary Islamic thought on jihad moves in two different directions. One stresses a broad interpretation (the "greater jihad") that enjoins all believers to engage in self-discipline, education, and social reform in order to "command good" and "forbid evil." The second direction stresses jihad by the sword. However, within this second tendency there are disagreements about when jihad by the sword is justified. Some claim that the sword can only be used for defensive wars, not wars of expansion. Others argue that the sword can be used in the struggle to replace secular Islamic states with "true" Islamic states based on the *Sharia*. Osama bin Laden has introduced yet another position. According to him, the sword can be used against civilian populations as well as military personnel of non-Islamic and secular Islamic nations when such nations constitute a threat to the religion of Islam.

It is clear that even if people should believe that the right way to live is that which is commanded by God and is embodied in revelation, there can always be disagreements about the correct interpretations of that "right way." The problem of identifying the specifics of divinely inspired norms persists as long as the situations in which people find themselves change. Still, the divine command theory of ethics and the development of the *Sharia* in Islam, along with parallel developments in Judaism and Christianity, provide a powerful justification for a general set of norms. It is comforting to believe that our way of life is grounded in the wishes of the divine. Still there is always room for disagreement about how best to follow the path God has ordained.

## 11.1.2 Confucian Virtue

Our second case comes from Confucianism, which today numbers a little over 5 million adherents. Confucianism is an English term denoting a wide range of Chinese schools of thought that in one way or another were inspired by and dedicated to the ideas of the First Teacher, also known in English as Confucius. Historians map at least six major transformations of Confucianism. Here we will be concerned only with the beginning, or classical, phase.

The classical era refers to the time when the founders of the Confucian tradition developed and transmitted a body of writings that later scholars used as a source for their thinking. The founders are Confucius (551–479 B.C.E.), Mencius (372–289 B.C.E.), and Xunzi (also spelled Hsün-tzu and pronounced "shuhn-dyuh") who flourished between 298 and 238 B.C.E. The basic literature consists of the *Five Classics* and the *Four Books*. The *Four Books* include *The Great Learning, Doctrine of the Mean, Analects,* and *Mencius.* I will rely heavily on the *Analects,* which are a collection of Confucius's sayings and dialogues with his pupils.

Biographical information is uncertain, but tradition tells us that Confucius was from the nobility and lived at a time when Chinese society was close to chaos and its leaders corrupt and ineffective. When he was three, his father died, and at nineteen he decided to seek a career in government. Ultimately, however, he was to make his name as an educator, not a politician. His reputation in China became so immense that on the popular level he was eventually deified, while among scholars he was venerated as the First Teacher.

What exactly did he teach? Again the evidence is uncertain, but as far as we can tell from the *Analects* he taught *de* (*te*), usually translated as "virtue." This may be a misleading translation because in English, *virtue* is usually associated with morality. This is not the case in ancient China. Virtue (*de*) is a broad concept more akin to excellence and power. People can become excellent at many different things, from sports to study. Not all excellence is moral excellence, but moral excellence is vitally important for living a good life. With excellence comes power, and Confucius was particularly concerned with gaining the power to live life well. D. C. Lau, a noted Confucian scholar and translator of the *Analects,* remarked that the unspoken assumption behind Confucian teaching is "that the only purpose a man can have and also the only worthwhile thing a man can do is to become as good a man as possible."[2]

It seemed obvious to Confucius that good people live good lives and create good societies. Therefore education should focus on developing good people—people whose character exhibits virtue or excellence. In light of this, it is not surprising that one of his central ideas is *ren* (*jen*). *Ren* has been translated in a variety of ways: "human excellence," "love," "benevolence," "humaneness," and "kind heartedness." It is a difficult notion to grasp in a single English word, and Confucius does not give an explicit definition of it. *Ren* is not something we are, but something we can become by cultivating our social, aesthetic, cognitive (thinking), and moral powers. It refers to what we might call "ideal human nature." It is humanity at its best, having realized its full positive potential.

What is such an ideal character like? The ideal character has many qualities such as wisdom, piety, kindness, and respect. A person with these qualities—a person who is a cultivated gentleman, sage, and scholar—acts on the principle of *shu*. (In early Chinese Confucianism, only males had the opportunity to reach the Confucian ideal.) *Shu* means seeing someone else as being like yourself. It is often translated as "reciprocity." In response to a question about whether there was a single principle that one could act on all of one's life, Confucius responded, "Wouldn't it be likening to-oneself (*shu*)? What you do not yourself desire, do not do to others" (*Analects* XV.24). This has sometimes been called the negative Golden Rule, but that is misleading. *Shu* is closely associated with another principle called *chung*, which means doing your best for others. Reciprocity (*shu*) combined with doing your best for others (*chung*) articulates a positive, not a negative, principle for living. These principles of *shu* and *chung* should govern the *five primary relations*: between parent and child, ruler and minister, husband and wife, older and younger siblings, and friend and friend.

There are, however, additional virtues that characterize the good life in its fullest sense. One of these is *li* (pronounced "lee"). *Li* is often translated as "propriety," but it is a broad concept that can mean order, ritual or rite, custom, manners, etiquette, worship, and ceremony.

Humans, Confucius taught, should behave appropriately in all their relationships. The models for appropriate behavior came, according to Confucius, from the traditional rites and customs handed down from the past Golden Age. Confucius thought of himself as a traditionalist, not an innovator. Tradition is important in his view because it provides an external check on what we may subjectively believe to be the right way to act and is a repository of the wisdom of the past with regard to proper conduct.

Confucius's traditionalism is evident in his views of another virtue worth cultivating, the virtue of *xiao* (*hsiao*), which is pronounced "shee-ow". This is the traditional Chinese virtue of filial piety (as it is often translated). This translation is misleading, however, because filial piety usually refers to the obligation sons and daughters have to obey their parents, in particular their father as the head of the household. There can be little doubt that *xiao* has been and is interpreted in this narrow sense. As we might expect, this narrow understanding promoted sexism and child abuse by placing nearly absolute power and authority in the father. However, in its broadest sense, *xiao* involves the practice of kindness, honor, respect, and loyalty among all family members (an ideal seldom achieved in practice).

Confucius placed emphasis on *xiao* because he believed that a strong family is the basis of a strong society. The family is the microcosmic (smaller) version of the macrocosmic (greater) social order. Society ought to be thought of as one large family. It is a short step from this idea to the more radical notion that the whole of humanity ought to be treated like family, with kindness, honor, and respect. We are still a long way from realizing the "family of humanity."

Daoist critics of Confucius accused him of confusing the ritualistic aspects of life with the moral aspects. Confucius's ideas, they argued, made proper manners and blind obedience to elders far more important than any other virtue. Some contemporary critics have even said that Confucius really had no idea of morality, in any modern sense of the word. However, Confucius does talk about *yi* (pronounced "yee" and sometimes spelled *i*), which can be translated as "rightness or what is fitting." D. C. Lau maintains that *yi* should be thought of as Confucius's concept of morality. In one sense, Lau argues, the whole of Confucius's thought should be seen as one long meditation on "what is fitting." If Lau is right, then morality is a central Confucian concern.

Recent commentators argue that we should not ignore the aesthetic dimension of Confucian thought. Ethics has to do with moral value; aesthetics has to do with the value of beauty. The Confucian concern with balance, harmony, and appropriateness reflects aesthetic values, but there is no reason why they cannot also reflect moral values. The division between moral and aesthetic value is something Confucius probably did not recognize. For him to call an action right was not only to pass a moral judgment but also an aesthetic judgment. Moral order is aesthetic order. The good and the beautiful, as Plato would say, are one.

The Confucian vision of the ideal world is one in which the world is like a home shared by all. Trust among all prevails, and "all people love and respect their parents and children . . . there is caring for the old . . . sharing replaces selfishness and materialistic greed . . . and the door to every home need never be locked and bolted by day or night" (*The Record of Rites*, Book IX, one of the *Five Classics*).

---

## Basic Confucian Ideas

1. *Ren* refers to benevolence or acting kindly toward others.
2. *Shu* and *chung* refer to not doing to others what you do not want done to you and doing what is best for others.
3. *Li* refers to propriety, or acting appropriately.
4. *Xiao* refers to familial love and respect.
5. *Yi* refers to doing what is fitting (morality).

---

It is clear that education plays a key role in the process of becoming a virtuous person. Knowledge of the past is a clue to proper action in the present. Since becoming a virtuous person or developing good character is a process, it is something we must learn how to do. Hence, proper instruction and good education are the keys to developing *ren*.

But what about religion? Where does religion fit in? When Western scholars first encountered Confucianism, they wondered about what they had found. Was it a religion, a kind of philosophy, or a form of social ethics? Interestingly, the early Christian missionary-scholars called the most important Confucian texts "classics" rather than "scriptures." This indicates that they felt some uncertainty about how best to describe Confucian literature in Western terms. "Classic literature" might be religious, ethical, political, philosophical, or all of these. By labeling it this way, they avoided a definitive judgment.

There is no doubt that observing the rites and rituals centered on ancestor veneration and honoring rulers were and still are important to Confucianism. The Confucian "family" as we have seen, goes far beyond what we normally think of as the family to potentially include the whole of humanity. Even if we concentrate on the notion of family in the biological sense of people related by blood, this family extends backward and forward in time. In Confucian thought, it includes those who are living, those yet to come, and those who have died. It is not that Confucius believed in life after death. He appears to have expressed agnosticism on that issue. However, rites honoring the rulers and the dead ancestors were important because they reinforced social harmony and promoted the cultivation of virtuous character.

Confucius did speak about the Mandate of Heaven, which allowed rulers to rule. Once the Mandate was withdrawn, the ruler ceased to have a legitimate right to rule. He also spoke of the Dao as a guide to the right path to follow. Among Daoists, the Dao was the way of nature (see Chapter 4), and while Confucians did not often speak of it in this naturalistic sense, it often seems implicit that the right way to live is also the way nature intended humans to live. In other words, the path of virtue is also the path of nature.

This blending of ethics and naturalism does not appear to be very religious to those who think of religion as primarily having to do with supernatural gods. But the Dao is a superhuman force, and if it is also an ethical force, it becomes far more than the usual view of nature as a collective term for processes that are not artificial or created by humans. Humans do not produce the Dao, the Dao produces humans. And the Dao is ethical in the sense that it can be the path to right living.

Tu Wei-Ming, a contemporary scholar involved in the development of what is today known as New Confucianism, addresses what he calls "the intriguing issue of transcendence." Since divine transcendence is associated with such religions as Judaism, Christianity, and Islam, is transcendence at "all relevant to the Confucian mode of being religious?" He writes:

> Confucian religiousness begins with the phrase "ultimate self-transformation," which implies a critical moment in a person's life as well as a continuous process of spiritual cultivation. For us to be actively involved in ultimate

self-transformation, we must make a conscious decision to do so. Since being religious is tantamount to learning to be fully human, we are not religious by default but by choice.[3]

Note that Wei-Ming uses "spiritual cultivation" instead of "moral cultivation." It is clear that, at least for him, Confucianism is more than morality; it is spiritual. The morally right way to live is also a spiritual way to live.

## 11.2 COMPARISON

A comparison of our two cases requires, at the start, a distinction between a **duty ethics** and a **virtue ethics**. According to duty-based ethics (sometimes called deontological ethics), our primary moral obligation is to do our duty. An ethics of duty centers on rules, commands, and prohibitions that spell out what our duties are. According to a virtue-based ethics, our primary moral guides are not rules, commands, laws, and the like, but people who exhibit moral excellence, or an ideal moral character. Duty ethics are based on commands to "do this," while virtue ethics are based on admonitions to "become this."

From what we have learned about Islamic ethics and Confucian ethics, I think it is clear that the most obvious difference between the two centers on the difference between an ethics of duty and an ethics of virtue. Islamic morality is based on law (*Sharia*), and the Islamic tradition has developed an elaborate system of jurisprudence (ways of interpreting and applying law) in order to determine what the law is in this or that situation. Confucianism did not develop systems of law or procedures of jurisprudence. Rather, its focus was and is on education designed to develop the right kind of person. Confucian ethics is confident that the right kind of person (the virtuous sage) will do the right kind of things in any given situation. Islamic ethics is confident that people need rules, laws, and regulations to guide them.

This primary moral difference between Islam and Confucianism is somewhat overstated. There are clear elements of a virtue ethic within Islam, indicated by the reliance on the example of the Prophet and the *Sunna* in general as a source of *Sharia*. There are also clear elements of a duty ethic in Confucianism insofar as developing *ren* amounts to a moral obligation. However, the emphasis on virtue in the Islamic case is embedded in and supported by an elaborate legal system. In Confucianism the emphasis on duty is embedded in a system of education and moral transformation centering on learning what is fitting, on ceremonies, and on cultivating harmonious relationships in the family and in society at large. Islamic ethics seeks to produce the obedient person, and Confucian ethics seeks to produce the wise and virtuous person who practices *ren* (humaneness) naturally and spontaneously.

At the start of this chapter we spoke of the relationships between religion and morality in terms of (1) identifying and legitimating moral norms, (2) motivating and renewing moral commitments, and (3) criticizing some moral norms. Try your hand at comparing Islam and Confucianism with respect to these relationships. I will share some of my ideas about these issues below. Your ideas may be similar to mine, or they may be different. Comparing our different comparisons can be instructive. Answer the following:

1. How do Islam and Confucianism identify and legitimate moral norms?
2. How do Islam and Confucianism motivate people to follow moral norms and to renew their moral commitments?
3. How do Islam and Confucianism criticize some conventional moral norms?

If we examine the ways in which Islam and Confucianism identify and legitimate moral norms, I think we can see some further differences between a duty ethic and a virtue ethic. Islam, as we have seen, recognizes four ways of identifying moral norms; two (the Quran and the *Sunna*) are based on divine revelation, and two (analogy and consensus) are based on human reason and the faith that Allah is rightly guiding the community of believers. Confucianism identifies moral norms by developing a notion of the ideal human being in relationship with the whole human family. The Islamic *Sharia* is ultimately justified by Allah's revelation. Other factors such as human reason play a role (although some Islamic schools have been highly suspicious of its use). Confucianism legitimates moral norms not by appealing to divine revelation of a personal God, but by appealing to the Mandate of Heaven, the Dao, and the harmonious and peaceful society that virtuous people create.

Islam and Confucianism also motivate and renew moral commitments in different ways. Islam motivates much like a military organization motivates its troops. There are rewards and punishments promised in this life and the next as well as powerful processes of socialization instilling in people a sense that a life of submission and obedience is the best way to live. In Islam, one does not submit to human laws and human moral norms, but to divine laws and divine norms. Confucianism motivates primarily by example and social pressure. It offers a model of the virtuous person and says in effect, "Don't you want to live like this?" It instills family values so deeply into the fabric of society that great shame results from acts of disloyalty and failure to obey those whose family status is greater than one's own.

Islam renews moral commitments by offering the possibility of repentance, divine forgiveness, and divine mercy. Allah offers another chance to those who sincerely repent. Confucianism is generally optimistic about human nature or the human heart (although there are those like Xunzi who are not). People are basically good because people have been created by Heaven and it is basically good. It may take a long time to cultivate this basic goodness, and there are bound to be failures along the way. But the message is clear, "Keep trying, keep learning, keep practicing, and someday you will succeed."

How do Islam and Confucianism criticize moral norms? Islam is a prophetic religion born of a radical critique of the prevailing polytheism of its day. Its prophetic history makes it suspicious of human laws and human norms. However, like so many other religions with a strong prophetic foundation such as Judaism and Christianity, as time goes by and power is obtained, a particular set of values, norms, and laws become "the right way" to do things. This "right way" often goes unquestioned until it becomes so abusive or oppressive that calls for reform emerge. Islam can be both conservative and revolutionary.

Confucianism, in contrast, appears to be conservative and traditional. The golden past is sacred. Tradition tells the Confucianist what to do. As Confucius said, he came to teach nothing new but to preserve and pass on the tradition of virtue learned from the sage-kings of the Golden Age. This does not mean that there are no resources within Confucianism for criticism of conventional morality. Recent developments in Confucianism are testimony to its ability to produce change through criticism. However, these "new" movements often claim to be returning to the pure teachings of the past that have become distorted or corrupted. The past, not the future, remains the primary guide.

There is a prophetic motif in Confucianism that we should not overlook. It is the Mandate of Heaven. This mandate permits a ruler to rule as long as he or she rules virtuously. This means the Mandate can be lost. When it is, the people have the right to revolt and overturn the ruling regime. Historically, Confucianism has been so closely tied to government patronage that Confucian-led revolts seldom occurred. The study of the classical literature of Confucianism was required for all government officials, and it was the basis for the civil service examinations in China for centuries. This situation encouraged Confucian support for whatever regime was in power. But, at least theoretically, the prophetic threat of the loss of the Mandate always remained.

I have been using the terms Islam and Confucianism without qualification in developing this comparison, and I must warn you that such unqualified use is misleading. As with all religions, many different and differing views on morality can be found within the ranks of Islamists and Confucianists. However, rather than write each time "some forms of Islam" and "some forms of Confucianism," I have simplified matters for the sake of convenience. Each time students of religion see unqualified words like Islam, Confucianism, Judaism, Christianity, Buddhism, Hinduism, and so on, they should silently add "some forms of."

## 11.3 IDENTIFYING AND LEGITIMATING MORAL NORMS

We have examined how Islam and Confucianism identify and justify moral norms using the ideas of God's commands and the virtuous sage. They do this in other ways as well, and one of the most common ways centers on the idea of natural law.

The central idea of natural law theories is the notion that morality is built into the structure of the universe. If, as Islam claims, an ethical God created the universe, we might expect that such a God used moral norms when creating nature. Confucianism, while not appealing to a moral creator God in order to legitimate its morality, nevertheless refers to the Mandate of Heaven. If a ruler does not rule with justice and mercy, the Mandate of Heaven to rule is lost. Here nature (the Mandate of Heaven) and morality intersect.

Within Christianity, Thomas Aquinas (1225–1274) offered a version of natural law theory that became and in some circles remains a widely influential way for people to identify and justify moral norms. Natural law theory instructs us to ask, "Is it (whatever "it" may be) natural?" If the answer is yes, it is morally good, and if the answer is no, it is morally wrong.

Borrowing from both Stoic philosophy and Aristotle, Thomas argued that all reality can be divided into "natural kinds," and each of these kinds is distinguished from other kinds by a unique essence. This essence tells us what are the natural ends, or outcomes, for each kind. For example, the natural end for an acorn is to develop into an oak tree. The virtue, excellence, or goodness of an acorn is to achieve this outcome. Aquinas was primarily concerned with humans, not acorns, and whether or not their actions fostered or hindered their development toward their natural ends. For example, he argued that suicide is morally wrong because it is contrary to our natural inclination for self-preservation and life. Likewise, monogamy within marriage is morally right because it best promotes the natural human end of reproduction and proper child care.

Perhaps some of the most controversial applications of natural law theory, especially in the modern world, center on sexuality. Roman Catholicism, using natural law theory, has condemned as immoral any use of artificial methods of birth control. Homosexuality has been declared immoral on similar grounds. If the natural end of humans is to reproduce, any sexual activity that is not conducive to reproduction is morally wrong because it is "unnatural." Roman Catholicism takes the same approach to abortion. Because the natural end of a human embryo is to become a human being, aborting that embryo is unnatural because it stops this natural developmental process, just as a squirrel that eats an acorn stops its natural development into an oak tree.[4]

According to Aquinas, natural law is derived from the eternal law of God by which God governs the universe. Only God can know the complete eternal law, but humans, through the use of reason, can derive natural law from this eternal law. Human law is, then, an extension of natural law in particular cases. It follows that the laws by which societies govern themselves should reflect natural law as closely as possible. There will always be disagreements over specific applications, but the general principles should be clear enough. Following this line of reasoning, Pope Leo XIII argued in the encyclical letter *Immortale Dei* of 1885 that since both "nature and reason" command all people to worship God, it should be a public crime for people to act as if there were no God. A state with human laws that shows no concern for religion is, therefore, immoral. It should, Pope Leo concluded, be one of the chief duties of the state to "favor religion, to protect it, to shield it under the credit and sanction of the laws."[5]

Certainly much Islamic thinking about the state and human laws would agree with this natural law approach, and it can be found in other religions as well. As you may recall from your research case "The Primal Man" (Chapter 5), ancient Hinduism regarded the various castes and their duties (*dharma*) as built into the structure of the universe. The notion that duties and castes were natural allowed those in power not only to identify what is moral and what is not, but also to justify it. Hence the *Laws of Manu* (see Chapter 5) asserts that the duty of husbands to control their wives is an "eternal duty." In other words, it is *natural* for wives to be dependent upon their husbands.

It is clear that notions of natural law can, at times, conflict with the rule of reciprocity. If we applied the rule of reciprocity to the issues of the relationship between husband and wife or to matters relating to sexuality, we could come to very different conclusions from those resulting from natural law theory. The rule of reciprocity requires equal treatment of men and women, it requires equal treatment for the theistic and the atheistic citizens of the state, and it requires equal treatment for heterosexuals and homosexuals. Natural law theory, at least for some people, runs counter to that conclusion. Is there some kind of deep contradiction in religious ethics? Can we support the Golden Rule and notions like "do what is best for others" together with notions like natural law?

## 11.4 WHAT IS MORALITY?

We have already defined morality as a set of norms or rules designed to regulate and govern the conduct of humans with one another, with other living creatures, and with their environment. While this definition was useful for beginning our discussion, we need to revisit the issue on a deeper level. What is it about certain norms and rules that make them moral rather than mere custom? Traffic rules regulate our lives with others, and they should be obeyed, but are traffic rules on the same footing as rules like "Be honest"? What makes some rules moral and others not?

In his book *Religion and Moral Reason*, Ronald M. Green writes:

> Religion's deep structure has three essential elements: first, a method of moral reasoning involving "the moral point of view"; second, a set of beliefs affirming the reality of moral retribution; and third, a series of "transmoral" beliefs that suspend moral judgment and retribution when this is needed to overcome moral paralysis and despair.[6]

We will discuss the last two elements in the following section. Here we will concentrate on the first element. But before we turn to that, we need to say something about Green's notion of a "deep structure."

Green argues that there is deep structure below the surface of religious differences that accounts for both the similarities and differences we find among religions. In other words, there is something like a religious grammar (a set of rules) that influence, if not determine, what appears on the surface, just as there are linguistic grammars that influence how different languages are spoken and written. Green suggests an analogy with an ocean archipelago. Viewing the surface of an archipelago, we see apparently disconnected islands. But under the ocean we find that these islands are surface projections or atolls of an interconnected, largely submerged land mass.

Without necessarily endorsing the claim that there is such a deep structure (a claim that would be very difficult to prove), we can grant that much religious reasoning exhibits a moral point of view. We might say then that the religiously transmitted norms and rules that regulate our conduct with others are moral insofar as they embody this moral viewpoint. However, what is the "moral point of view"?

Green suggests that the moral point of view is a "radical impartiality" that is utilized when we make moral decisions. This means that before we make a decision that is truly moral we must look at the situation not only from a self-serving or egocentric standpoint, but also from a universal, impartial, and fair standpoint. To be impartial is not to favor one party over another. What counts morally is not what we desire, but what would be right for any person to do. This is why, Green argues, so much of morality counsels self-discipline, delayed gratification, self-sacrifice, and self-denial. It is not that our own self-interests are not important or even that they are less important than the interests of others; it is that when it comes to morality, our own self-interest is not the only thing to be considered.

Green thinks that the impartiality required by the moral point of view is captured in versions of the Golden Rule found in most major religious traditions. To do unto others as you would have them do unto you requires the ability to transcend self-interest and take into account the point of view of someone else. This rule requires consistency in our actions and prohibits us from doing things we would not want others to do to us.

The idea of impartiality is built into Islamic notions of morality. The best judge is the impartial judge. The *Sharia* emphasizes the need for objective judgment, and the Hadith holds up the decisions of Muhammad in resolving disputes as the models of impartiality and fairness.

The Confucian principle of *shu* (reciprocity) recognizes the need for impartiality in moral judgment. Confucius also captured the fairness and balance of interests required by moral judgment when he said that the virtuous "man does not set his mind either absolutely for anything or absolutely against anything. The sole measure of them all is morality and justice" (*Analects* IV). This idea is reinforced by Mencius, who writes, "Try your best to treat others as you would wish to be treated yourself, and you will find that this is the shortest way to benevolence (*ren*)" (*Mencius* VII.A.4).

Of course it is often very difficult to be truly impartial in our judgments. Self-interest and prejudice can creep in at any point. Confucius recognized this when he claimed that becoming truly virtuous was not an easy thing to do. And Islam recognizes this in its claim that only Allah is a truly impartial, fair, and unbiased judge. Only the divine can have a perfectly moral point of view. By basing morality on a divine command or on the judgment and actions of the truly virtuous person, both Islam and Confucianism recognize the need for impartiality. Who could be more impartial than God or a perfectly virtuous person?

The problem with the Golden Rule is that it is possible to imagine someone who is prepared to do what we normally take to be immoral and gladly permit others to do the same. For example, a person who is terminally ill who steals money in order to go out in a blaze of self-indulgence might well say that anyone else in the same situation is entitled to do the same. Confucius understood the limitation of *shu* (reciprocity) and added the principle of *chung*—doing what's best for others. Allah is not only a just God, but a merciful one as well.

There is more to the moral point of view than impartiality. Justice, the impartial application of law, must also be tempered by mercy and compassion. Impartiality sounds cold and impersonal. Religions also speak of love, compassion, and mercy. Sometimes we need to go beyond being fair in order to do what is best for others.

## 11.5 RETRIBUTION AND GUILT

It is time to turn our attention to the second deep structure identified by Green as a component of religious moral reasoning—"a set of beliefs affirming the reality of moral retribution."

Retribution conveys the idea of recompense, return, and just deserts. It takes many different forms in religion, many of which we have already discussed, such as the law of karma and judgment day. It is intimately tied to the ideas of merit, reward, and punishment. It permeates much religious thought. How many of us believe that God will reward us with eternal life if we are morally good, or with eternal punishment if we are morally bad? How many of us think that judgment day is "payback time"? How many of us cheer at the movies when the good guy wins the girl and the bad guy gets killed? How many of us have said on one occasion or another, "What goes around, comes around"? If a villain has committed a horrible crime, we expect him or her to meet a horrible end. Why?

One reason is that we want to see justice done. It gives us a sense of cosmic satisfaction. Another reason runs deeper than satisfaction. It derives from the moral point of view. If being moral requires self-sacrifice, why make that sacrifice? Why should we sacrifice our self-interest and desire just so someone else is treated fairly? In short, why be moral? In particular, why be moral if morality requires the subordination of our own pleasures, our own desires, and our own short-term joys in order to be fair to others? Others may not be moral at all. They may not live their lives according to a moral point of view, and who is to say that they are any worse off?

Retribution tries to answer the question, Why be moral? Whether it takes the form of karma, judgment day, or the threat of the removal of the Mandate of Heaven, retribution means that the righteous will be rewarded and the unrighteous punished. Those who risk their lives, those who sacrifice their lives, and even those who lose their lives for the sake of righteousness will someday gain an even better life.

It is not surprising that religions, which identify the moral point of view with self-sacrifice, should also develop theories of retribution. It is also not surprising that this way of answering the question, Why be moral? is plagued with ethical difficulties. Our discussion of merit and faith in Chapter 10 already exposed this problem. If the moral attitude is one of impartiality and compassion for the other, and if we should do what is morally right because it is right, then fear of punishment or hope of reward should not motivate our desire to be moral. If retribution is the only answer religions offer to the question of why be moral, that very answer violates the moral point of view by appealing to self-interest.

We are now in a better position to understand why religions also offer, to use Green's terms, "a series of 'transmoral' beliefs that suspend moral judgment and retribution when this is needed to overcome moral paralysis and despair." This is the third deep structure of religious morality that Green identifies, and we can approach it by discussing impurity, shame, and guilt—the sorts of things that might cause "moral paralysis and despair."

## Deep Structure of Religious Moral Reasoning

1. Developing a moral point of view
2. Believing in moral retribution
3. Overcoming moral paralysis and despair

Most religions have elaborate systems of purity. William Paden defines systems of purity as "the many ways that religious systems deal with negativity."[7] Impurity is the opposite of purity, hence to understand impurity we must understand its opposite. The purity/impurity opposition also implies other concepts such as pollution, danger, and **taboo**. Most dictionary definitions define *purity* as free from mixture or contact with that which weakens, impairs, or pollutes. For example, material that is mixed with some foreign substance that weakens it is often called impure. Religious taboos are intended to prevent some kind of contamination, some sort of mixture that weakens the power of the sacred. The food taboos found in many religions are, in part, based on the idea that certain foods should not be mixed. If they are, eating them makes one impure.

Why should mixing certain things cause impurity? Mary Douglas argues in *Purity and Danger* (see "Suggestions for Further Reading") that elaborate rules about purity and impurity result from beliefs about the danger of crossing boundaries between categories that people think superhuman powers have separated and made discrete. For example, among animals that live in water, it is forbidden, according to the Hebrew Bible, to eat finless creatures with legs because they differ from the "natural" (ordained by God) prototype of the fish (a swimmer with fins, not a walker without fins). It is also forbidden to eat rock badger, hare, and pigs because they lack what was common to *ungulate* species (those that both chew the cud and have cloven hooves). The Hebrews were pastoralists, and so it was natural for them to think that God ordained the sorts of ungulate animals associated with pastoral pursuits (sheep for example) as the proper animals for consumption.

Impurity or pollution is closely associated in most religions with ritual impurity. It often comes into play when some ritual rule has been violated, but it can also happen naturally. So a woman during menstruation or childbirth is often considered impure, or a priest may be forbidden to conduct a sacrifice if he or she has been contaminated by contact with something impure.

Practically anything can be designated as pure or impure in the different religions. What is impure in one tradition, might be pure in another. This is one reason why it is so difficult for outsiders, who have their own systems of purity, to understand the taboos of other societies. These taboos often seem overly scrupulous or even ridiculous to outsiders. This is because the rules of purity/impurity must anticipate the detailed and complex nature of human experience. For example, rules for the Islamic fast during Ramadan must take into account possible circumstances that would make the fast valid or invalid. One possible circumstance is one in which food gets caught between the teeth during the permitted evening meal. Let us say that food is still there when the next day's fast begins. This is a potentially dangerous situation. So the faithful are advised that they need not pick their teeth after the evening meal if they know that the food lodged there is not likely to become dislodged and swallowed during the day. However, if they do know that the food is likely to become dislodged and swallowed during the day, they should pick their teeth. If they do not, and if the food does become dislodged and swallowed during a fast day, the fast is invalid.[8]

Other kinds of negativity pose problems for religious ethical systems. These include shame and guilt, two common experiences of people who try to lead an ethical life. Dietrich Bonhoeffer, a Lutheran pastor and theologian, was arrested on April 5, 1943, by the Nazi Gestapo for his involvement in a plot to kill Hitler. He was eventually hanged. In Berlin, between 1940 and 1943, he began to write a book now available under the simple title *Ethics*. In a section on "Shame" Bonhoeffer writes, "Man is ashamed because he has lost something which is essential to his original character, to himself as a whole."[9]

Some scholars have argued that notions like impurity and shame are premoral because they are based on beliefs that are not yet fully moral. They do not reflect what Green calls "the moral point of view." These scholars usually suggest that the concept of morality only enters the picture when we begin to speak of guilt. Guilt is not the same as shame. Guilt is the consciousness of having violated a moral duty. It is the awareness that we have not measured up, not followed the Golden Rule, or not followed some other moral injunction. In short, guilt is what we feel when we know we have not lived up to the moral point of view, and shame is what we feel when we have lost something, such as honor or innocence.

I do not think it is useful to label impurity and shame as premoral concepts and guilt as a moral concept. Religious views of morality are always embedded, as we have seen, in a much larger context containing beliefs about gods, spirits, ancestors, creation, afterlife, ritual practices, and much more. It does not help in understanding the relationship between religion and morality to impose on religions sharp distinctions between the moral and the nonmoral when, in fact, such distinctions are often not sharp and the boundaries are blurred in religious belief and practice. When sharp distinctions are imposed, they often arise from identifying (as Green does) an ethics of duty and related notions of obedience and guilt as the true expression of a so-called moral point of view. In fact, many different viewpoints, such as an ethics of virtue and concerns with purity and impurity, can also express a moral point of view.

It seems to me that shame and guilt are closely tied to the idea of impurity. The violation of taboos and ritual requirements leads to impurity, the loss of something precious leads to shame, and the violation of moral rules leads to guilt. However, when making the distinctions among shame, guilt, and impurity, one thing is clear—human beings are prone to failure.

A sense of deep failure leads to despair, the total lack of hope. It is, as the philosopher Soren Kierkegaard said, "the sickness unto death."[10] Despair can lead, as Green observes, to "moral paralysis." Religions have devised many different ways to deal with human failure and renew human energies and commitments. This too is part of the "deep structure" with which Green is concerned.

Let us use the word *profanity* not in its popular sense of saying "dirty" words or cursing, but to indicate a number of different but related ideas concerning failure and negative experiences such as impurity, shame, guilt, and despair. If we do, then we can follow Paden when he claims that three typical religious patterns for dealing with "profanity" stand out. "These ways are: (1) avoidance of profanity, (2) purification of profanity, and (3) transcending the oppositions of profanity/purity."[11]

### 11.5.1 Avoidance

Religious laws and rules often tell the faithful what *not* to do. Lay Buddhists, for example, vow to follow the five precepts to *refrain* from (1) harming any living being, (2) taking what is not given, (3) misusing the senses, (4) engaging in wrong speech, and (5) taking drugs or drinks that cloud the mind. In the Quran (17:21–37) the so-called Ten Commandments of Islam tell believers not to squander wealth, kill one's children for fear or want, commit adultery, kill any person Allah has forbidden the believer to kill, and interfere with the property of orphans.

This section of the Quran is called the "Ten Commandments" of Islam because it is similar to (but not identical with) the Jewish and Christian Ten Commandments found in Exodus 20. In the Exodus version, the last five of these commandments forbid killing, adultery, stealing, bearing false witness, and coveting or desiring what belongs to others.

These rules take a negative form because they tell the faithful what to avoid, and avoidance is one of the primary ways to escape impurity, shame, guilt, and despair. If we have done nothing wrong in the first place, we need not worry about retribution. If we avoid breaking the rules, we have managed to live free from the danger of despair, we have maintained our integrity and innocence, and we have successfully kept what is sacred pure.

### 11.5.2 Purification

Few if any of us are successful in keeping all the rules. Hence there must be ways of dealing with infractions after they occur. Religions develop many different ways for dealing with profanity and repurifying that which has become polluted by sin and evil. Paden writes:

> At one extreme is the gentle practice of the Tenri Kyo religion of Japan: impure "dust" is "swept" away in rhythmic, ritual gestures of the hands and arms. At the other extreme are public tortures and executions, demonstrating that the horror and absoluteness of the crime—that is, an act of sacrilege that defies the foundations of the world—requires a commensurate horror and absoluteness of destruction.[12]

In between these extremes we find acts of "soul-searching," confession, fasting, prayer, repentance, acts of restitution, bargaining with the divine, self-mutilation, and sacrifice. As we noted in Chapter 6, sacrifices often occur in situations of danger or its threat. Impurity, shame, guilt, and despair are all situations of danger that bring with them the threat of retribution. Sacrificial offerings to overcome profanity must involve something valuable to the believer. Religious suicide and human sacrifice are extreme forms. Others range from making blood offerings (oxen, chickens) to nonblood offerings (grains and cereals).

In some cases, various sorts of sufferings are thought to be the way superhuman powers purify the soul. The sufferings of war, persecution, imprisonment, sickness, poverty, and the like can purify and restore lost righteousness. The bad karma we experience in this life of suffering helps us to learn, and when we return in our next life, we hope to do a better job at keeping the rules and treating others with compassion. Before we turn an indifferent face to the beggar, remember that we were once like that beggar and may be again in the future. Perhaps empathy and compassion are the ultimate reasons for doing to others as we would have them do to us. Retribution and fear of punishment become secondary motivations when we realize that "there but for the grace of God go I." Our suffering can sensitize us to the suffering of others.

### 11.5.3 Beyond Morality

The third way, in addition to avoidance and purification, of dealing with profanity Paden calls "transcending the purity/profanity opposition." To follow this way is to overcome the division between purity and profanity by realizing that these categories are in fact made by humans and projected onto nature. Once this relativity is fully seen, there appears what we might call a "higher" purity that involves an insight into the unity of opposites. St. Paul writes in the New Testament, "There is nothing unclean of itself" (Romans 14:14).

This idea of the unity of opposites is extended by mystics to all dichotomies: good/bad, supernature/nature, hope/despair, I/you, forgiveness/guilt, and all other polarities. Reality is not, in itself, divided into contending opposites; humans who have not realized a "higher" point of view just think it is. Left-handed tantric yoga found in both Hinduism and Buddhism dramatically expresses this insight into the unity beyond opposites by deliberately advocating, for the adept, participation in what is normally considered unclean and immoral behavior such as drinking wine, eating meat, and engaging in illicit sexual intercourse. This *antinominian* (antilaw) attitude can be found in many religions. It arises from the idea that the saved or the liberated are truly free from the laws and rules that constrain others. They are, if you will, free to do what is right (whatever that may be) because they have become purified within.

The *Bhagavad Gita* says that "When he has no lust, a man walks safely among the things of lust and hatred" (43:2). The author of Titus, a book found in the New Testament, writes, "To the pure all things are pure" (Titus 1:15). When profanity is overcome within, it is already overcome without. Those with a clean mind cannot defile themselves, whatever they may do. A Zen story illustrates this idea:

> Tanzan and Ekido were once traveling together down a muddy road. A heavy rain was falling. Coming around a bend, they met a lovely girl in a silk kimono and sash, unable to cross the intersection.
>
> "Come on, girl" said Tanzan at once. Lifting her in his arms, he carried her over the mud.
>
> Ekido did not speak again until that night when they reached a lodging temple. There he no longer could restrain himself. "We monks don't go near females," he told Tanzan, "especially not young and lovely ones. It is dangerous. Why, did you do that?"
>
> "I left the girl there," said Tanzan. "Are you still carrying her?"[13]

Paden comments on this story, "The point is for those still struggling with the world and with the pure/impure contest inside themselves, the outside world continues to mirror these distinctions."[14]

**Typical Religious Patterns for Dealing with Profanity**

1. Avoidance of profanity
2. Purification of profanity
3. Transcending the oppositions of profanity/purity

## 11.6 SUMMARY

How should we live? We can think of different religions as offering complex answers to this basic human concern. This question cannot just be asked and answered once. It is a question we must continually ask and answer as we and our world change. Insofar as the question about how we should live implies a moral lifestyle as part of the answer, we need to understand that central to morality, be it religious or not, is a distinction between what *is* the case and what *ought* to be the case. How people in fact behave is often very different from how they ought to act. There is a gap between the ideal way of life and the actual circumstances of human existence. Religions seek to close this gap by bringing together as close as possible what people do and what they ought to do.

Our preliminary definition of morality focused on the idea of culturally transmitted norms intended to regulate human action. When we asked how religion and morality were related, a complex picture emerged concerning the ways in which religion identifies, legitimates, and criticizes moral norms, along with its ability to motivate humans to follow moral norms and renew their commitment to moral norms when it weakens.

Our first case study focused on Islamic controversies about the divine command theory of ethics. According to this theory, what is morally right is what God commands, and what is morally wrong is what God condemns. In other words, God's will is the basic foundation of all morality. This theory generates a dilemma that is revealed by the question, "Is something morally good because God commands it, or does God command something because it is morally good?" The Asharite theologians argued that since God determines all things because he is all-powerful, it is his command that makes something good or bad. The Mutazilite theologians objected to this viewpoint, arguing among other things that human freedom, which the Asharites appear to deny, is essential to morality. The Asharite view reduces morality to blind obedience, thereby ignoring the role of human intentions and the consequences of human action in determining whether an action is morally right. The divine command theory also runs the danger, according the Mutazilites, of establishing morality on an arbitrary foundation.

*Sharia* is the name for the totality of divine law in Islam. It contains both religious and moral duties. The Quran, *Sunna,* analogical reasoning, and the consensus of the rightly guided community of believers constitute the four sources of *Sharia.* There have been and still are controversies over whether religious law (*Sharia*) or secular civil law ought to be used to govern Islamic societies. The *Sharia* is not fixed, but is dynamic and changing in order to respond to changing circumstances.

We examined Islamic interpretations of jihad (struggle) in order to illustrate the diverse and changing Islamic views of one part of the *Sharia.* Central to understanding jihad is the distinction between the greater jihad and the lesser jihad. The former refers to the struggle that humans must make to submit to Allah's will, and the latter refers to military struggle or holy war. As the terms *greater* and *lesser* imply, jihad is first and foremost a moral and spiritual struggle. Also, "jihad by the tongue" is often praised as greater than "jihad by the sword."

We turned our attention to Confucianism in the second case study. Confucian ethics focuses on developing virtue or excellence in all areas of life. *Ren* (benevolence, humaneness) is a central virtue indicating the sort of character the good human being ought to develop. The principles of reciprocity (*shu*) and doing what is best for others (*chung*) guide the virtuous in their dealings with others.

The virtues of *li* (propriety), *xian* (filial piety), and *yi* (doing what is fitting) extend the notion of virtue to the family, the state, and ultimately, the whole human race. There is also an aesthetic dimension to the virtuous life. It is more than morality, it is also a beautiful and pleasing way to live.

The concept of the Mandate of Heaven indicates a religious dimension to the Confucian ethic, and according to Tu Wei-Ming, a contemporary Confucian thinker, Confucian religiousness is nothing less than "ultimate self-transformation." Confucianism builds moral and spiritual development into the heart of its ethical vision.

Our comparison of Islamic and Confucian views revealed the difference between an ethics of duty and an ethics of virtue. A duty ethic conceives of moral rightness as obedience to one's duties as set forth in some divine law. An ethics of virtue emphasizes morally right actions as stemming from a virtuous person. An ethics of duty says, "Do this," and a virtue ethic says, "Become this."

Lest our contrasts become too misleading, we noted that the idea of virtue is also found in Islam, and the idea of duty is also found in Confucianism. However, in general, it appears that Islamic ethics seek to produce an obedient person, and Confucian ethics seek to produce a wise and virtuous person. Are these really different or just different ways of saying the same thing?

Real differences between Islamic and Confucian ethics can be found. Islam identifies and legitimates moral norms by appealing (although not entirely) to divine revelation. Confucianism legitimates morality by developing notions of the ideal human being living in an ideal society, by appealing to the Mandate of Heaven, and by recognizing that the Dao (Way of Nature) is also the Way of Virtue.

Islam motivates by an elaborate system of rewards and punishments, and Confucianism motivates by appealing to the example of the virtuous sage and social (especially family) pressure. In Islam, moral failure centers on guilt and disobedience. In Confucianism, moral failure leads to shame and dishonor.

As a prophetic religion, Islam is ever ready to criticize the imperfect laws of humans for their imperfection in relation to the divine law. Confucianism is conservative in its moral emphasis, but is not without the prophetic ability to criticize inadequate human laws, as the concept of losing the Mandate of Heaven indicates.

We examined Thomas Aquinas's theory of natural law as one important and widespread example of how what is moral and what is not might be identified. The central idea of natural law theories is that morality is built into the natural structure of the universe. It is part of how the universe operates. Aquinas's theory involves the idea that the universe is divided, by the Creator God, into natural kinds, each of which is distinguished by a unique essence. This essence tells us the natural end of each natural kind. What is morally right is what promotes the true end of a natural kind, and what is morally wrong is what does not allow the essence of a natural kind to flourish. Immorality is unnatural.

There is a possible contradiction between using natural law theory and using concepts like the Golden Rule to identify moral rightness and wrongness.

For example, some might argue that homosexuals are to be treated differently from heterosexuals because homosexuality is "unnatural." If human laws are to be derived from natural laws, then laws making homosexual practices illegal are justified. However, on the basis of reciprocity and fairness, we might argue that homosexuals should have the same rights as heterosexuals.

In Section 11.4 we characterized the moral point of view as one of impartiality. The Golden Rule combined with the idea of compassion exemplifies this moral viewpoint. We used Ronald Green's ideas about the "deep structure" of religious moral reasoning to guide our discussion. According to Green, religions must develop a moral point of view, affirm the reality of retribution, and provide ways to overcome moral failure in order to successfully answer the question about how we should live.

Retribution is one answer religions give to the question of why we should be moral. It is, however, not a good answer because it appeals to self-interest. We should do what is morally right because it is right, not because of our hopes for a reward or fear of punishment.

Our attention shifted to ways of overcoming the danger of moral paralysis brought about by impurity, shame, guilt, and despair. The idea of taboo is often associated with notions of purity and impurity. Taboos try to prevent mixing things that should not be mixed. They prevent the divisions that the divine establishes between natural kinds from being blurred or crossed.

Some people label ideas of pollution and shame (the loss of something valuable) as premoral and notions of guilt arising from disobedience as moral. This distinction is not very helpful because it obscures the fact that religious morality is always embedded in a larger system of beliefs that blur distinctions between what is premoral and moral. It also too narrowly focuses on an ethics of duty (obedience) as most truly expressing a moral point of view when, in fact, many different ethical viewpoints, such as the ethics of virtue, can also express a moral point of view.

William Paden identified three patterns found among religions for dealing with profanity (pollution, shame, guilt, and despair). Religions tell us to avoid it, to purify ourselves of it should we be unable to avoid it, and to transcend it by exposing the relativity of the distinctions between purity and impurity, right and wrong, good and bad.

Avoidance strategies usually rely on prohibitions ("don't do that!"). Ways of purification (if you did do that) such as prayer, confession, sincere repentance, and ascetic acts of self-denial and sacrifice seek to renew moral strength. Suffering can also lead to purification by reinstating the moral viewpoint through compassion.

Transmoral beliefs about the possibility of overcoming the dichotomies that we use to divide the world into manageable bits provide yet another way to deal with impurity. From a higher, mystical viewpoint, we can see the unity of all opposites and realize that moral distinctions are culturally relative and created by humans. For the spiritually enlightened, profanity is finally and completely overcome in the mystical realization of the unity of all opposites.

## 11.7 RESEARCH CASE—JAIN NONVIOLENCE

A man falls into a deep well. He grabs the branch of a tree growing from the side of the well and hangs on for dear life. Looking below he sees in the pit beneath poisonous snakes waiting for him. Looking up he sees two mice, one black and one white, gnawing at the branch he is desperately clutching. He soon realizes that when they gnaw through he will fall. He is in a dangerous predicament and begins to search for a way out. A beehive on the tree that is now shaking begins to drop bits of sweet honey near him. Forgetting his terrible situation he reaches for the sweet drops of honey, loses his grip on the branch, and falls.

Jainas ("jinas"—followers of or children of the victor or *jina*) tell this parable to illustrate an important point about how humans should live. The man in the well represents the soul, which can fall to its death at any moment. The mice symbolize our lives. The white mouse represents the days, and the black mouse represents the nights. Time is slowly eating away at our lives, and most of us, instead of seriously seeking to escape our danger, reach for fleeting experiences of enjoyment and pleasure (the drops of honey). By doing so we lose our chance to get on the right path that will lead us out of the cycles of rebirth and suffering.

We will return to the issue of the "right path," but first some contextual information will aid our understanding. Jainism is a religion originating in India. Jainas date the start of their religion in a distant past when the first of twenty-four great people, or saints, became Tirthankaras or "ford finders." This title indicates that these great saints found the place to cross the river of life, with its countless cycles of rebirth, to the other side, the side where rebirth ceases.

There is no historical evidence for the existence of all twenty-four of these saints, but the last two, Parshava and Mahavira, are historical figures. Many historians credit Mahavira with founding Jainism, but he was probably developing and passing on the teachings of his predecessor, Parshava.

Mahavira (great hero) lived at about the same time as Siddhartha Gautama was developing Buddhism and in the same geographical region of north India. Hence it is not surprising that there are strong parallels between Jainism and Buddhism. In fact the life story of Mahavira as told by Jainas has a remarkable similarity to the life story told by Buddhists about Shakyamuni. However, each of the main branches of Jainism has a different version.

Mahavira's birth, like the birth of many religious founders, is portrayed as miraculous.

[When] the Venerable Ascetic Mahavira was born, . . . [there] rained down on the palace of King Siddhartha [his father] one great shower of silver, gold, diamonds, clothes, ornaments, leaves, flowers, . . . sandal powder and riches.[15]

In his search for enlightenment, he renounced secular life and undertook a life of ascetic practices. Mahavira's renunciation was marked by pulling out the hair on his head (a practice still followed by those who become monks or nuns) to indicate that he did not hold his body in high regard. His enlightenment was marked by gaining great powers of wisdom and insight.

When the Venerable Ascetic Mahavira had become a Jina [victor] and Arhat [saint], he was a Kevalin [liberated one], omniscient and comprehending all objects; he knew and saw all conditions of the world, of gods, men, and demons: whence they came, whither they go, whether they are born as men or animals or become gods or hell beings . . . he the Arhat for whom there is no secret, knew and saw all conditions of living beings in the world, what they thought, spoke or did at any moment.[16]

His first sermon after his enlightenment was on *ahimsa*, which is usually translated as "nonviolence," but literally means "desiring to do no harm to others." Even though the teaching of *ahimsa* is found in Buddhism and Hinduism, it has become a distinctive hallmark of Jainism. No other religion has devoted as much time and attention to *ahimsa*. The universe is filled with various forms of life, and violence to any in thought, word, or deed stains one's soul.

Sometime after Mahavira's death, his disciples, like so many other disciples, split into differing groups, which in turn split into subgroups. The two main groups are the Digambara (sky-clad) and the Shvetambaras (white clothes). As we might guess from these names, a major issue that divided the community was the wearing of clothes. The Digambaras advocate the practice of nudity, and the Shvetambaras advocate wearing white clothes.

To the outsider this may seem like a trivial issue, but behind it stands a debate about what true renunciation involves. This is important because renunciation is part of the "right path" that leads to liberation from the bondage of rebirth. It also has important social implications.

Apparently Mahavira willingly ordained women as ascetics, and evidence indicates that at the time of his death, women ascetics outnumbered men by a ratio of two and a half to one. The Shvetambaras hold that the nineteenth Tirthankara, named Malli, was a woman. The Digambaras claim Malli was a man. They argue further that it is improper for women to go around nude; therefore, women cannot achieve liberation until they are reborn as men. The Shvetambaras not only claim that one of the Tirthankaras was a woman, but also that women do not have to be reborn as men in order to receive liberation. Indeed, according to the Shvetambaras, women can also be teachers of the right path.

In order to understand the right path and the role that the practice of *ahimsa* plays in it, we need to know something about Jain metaphysics. According to Jainism, all of reality can be divided into three basic categories: matter, sentient beings (beings that can sense), and that which is neither material nor sentient. Matter falls into the category of *ajiva* (non-soul), while sentient beings are *jivas* (souls).

The universe consists of three levels: heaven, earth, and below the earth. Each of these is divided into numerous subcategories arranged hierarchically. *Jivas* can take the form of a celestial or heavenly being (god), a human being, an animal, a plant, or a demigod inhabiting the underworlds. Transmigrating souls can move in and out of these different forms. The goal of life is for a *jiva* to rise to the crescent-shaped apex of the universe beyond the highest heaven. Here the Tirthankaras dwell in purity, their *jivas* permanently liberated from the cycle of rebirth. They dwell even above the gods, their souls perfectly clear of any material stain.

Jainism, like Buddhism and Hinduism, teaches that karma keeps us trapped in the cycle of rebirth. However, Jainas understand karma quite differently from Buddhists and Hindus. Karma is material in nature and its particles become attached to *jivas* anytime they do anything. Some actions produce a greater amount of karma than others. Killing, engaging in violence, or desiring to do harm produce a very large amount of karmic material. The soul becomes darker and heavier the more karma particles it accumulates, sinking, eventually, to the very bottom of the universe. Bondage to matter must be broken if souls are to ascend to a life of purity and bliss, free from all suffering and concern. But since karma is accumulated no matter what a sentient being does, how on earth (pun intended) can the soul ever free itself from this horrible bondage?

It is here that the idea of the right path comes in. There are three jewels: *right insight* (viewpoint or faith), *right knowledge*, and *right conduct*. Right insight is a flash, a glimpse that the soul has of its true destiny. This insight starts it on the path of liberation. Right knowledge is coming to know the true nature of the universe and human life. Right conduct consists of five basic principles, the first of which is the most important. These are *ahimsa* (desiring no harm), truthfulness, nonstealing, sexual purity, and nonpossession.

For the purposes of this case, our interest centers on the ethic of *ahimsa*. This ethic automatically means that all Jainas are vegetarians, and the taking of animal life is taboo. Even taking plant life is considered undesirable, and should be done sparingly. Matters of diet become significant because the devotee must avoid harming souls wherever they may be found. Killing and eating meat, fish, and fowl is, of course, completely out of bounds. Certain forms of vegetables, such as eggplant and root vegetables (potatoes and onions), are to be avoided as well because they are teeming with microcosmic life-forms. Water should be strained and boiled before drinking, and monks and nuns should sweep the ground on which they walk and recline, lest any life-forms such as ants might be killed. Meals are to be eaten before sunset to avoid lighting lamps and thereby attracting insects to their deaths. Some ascetics avoid bathing in order not to harm any life-forms living on their bodies or in water.

*Ahimsa* has implications concerning acceptable occupations. Hunting, fishing, and butchering are clearly unacceptable, and farming, while allowed, is dangerous. Hence many Jainas become doctors, lawyers, and merchants. Even though there are strict rules about wealth and possessions, the latent function of *ahimsa* has resulted in a prosperous community because the acceptable professions often attract wealth. The *Acaranga Sutra* on Good Conduct says:

> the sage who walks the beaten track (to liberation), regards the world in a different way. 'Knowing thus (the nature of) acts in all regards, he does not kill,' he controls himself, he is not overbearing.[17]

We have been talking about *ahimsa* almost exclusively in terms of not doing physical harm. But the last comment about not being overbearing and the admonitions to practice *ahimsa* in thought, word, and deed point to a broader meaning. The political potential of *ahimsa* was realized when Ghandi started a nonviolent campaign, which resulted in overthrowing the British colonial system in India. Martin Luther King, Jr., adopted it as an effective tool in the fight to overturn segregation laws. Today many Jainas and others attracted to the *ahimsa* teaching are applying the concept to ecological concerns, environmental issues, and the fight for global peace and justice. Not doing harm has become more than just a part of a right path to individual spiritual well-being.

There are a little over 4 million Jainas in the world today. Most live in India, but there are significant immigrant communities in England and North America. Although the Western world knew next to nothing of Jainism until it was introduced at the World's Parliament of Religions in 1893, it is drawing increased attention as we struggle in the twenty-first century to find ways to preserve all forms of life on this earth in the face of a looming ecological catastrophe. Vasudha Narayanan, a scholar of Jainism observes:

> Many Jains now give broader scope to the interpretation of non-violence and associate it with contemporary issues such as civil rights, national security and nuclear warfare. It is in these areas that the Jains see the large-scale challenge of violence. They see their tradition as one that offers a vision not just for the liberation of the soul, but for the survival of human beings, and indeed, this planet.[18]

## QUESTIONS ON THE CASE OF JAIN NONVIOLENCE

1. Compare the case of Jain ethics to the first case on Islamic *Sharia*. What are the differences and similarities?

2. Compare the case of Jain nonviolence to the second case on Confucian virtue. Do you think there are more differences than similarities? Why or why not?

3. If souls are not physical realities and cannot be killed because they are eternal, why should Jainism be so concerned with physical harm such as killing? Answer this question first from an insider's viewpoint and then from an outsider's viewpoint.

4. Even though these were not discussed in this case, do you think Jainism has mechanisms for dealing with violation of ethical rules? If so, what do you think they might be like? How would you go about checking your hypothesis?

5. Do you find a "moral point of view" expressed in the ethic of *ahimsa*? Is *ahimsa* ultimately motivated by selfish concerns about karmic impact on one's own *jiva*?


## SUGGESTIONS FOR FURTHER READING

In addition to the material found in the notes, the reader may wish to consult the following for more information.

Berthrong, John H. *Transformations of the Confucian Way.* Boulder: Westview Press, 1998. This book provides a developmental survey of Confucianism from its beginnings through the modern age.

Carmody, Denise Lardner, and John Tully Carmody. *Christian Ethics: An Introduction through History and Current Issues.* Englewood Cliffs, NJ: Prentice-Hall, 1993. The authors present a clear and concise overview of Christian ethical thought.

Chidester, David. *Patterns of Action: Religion and Ethics in Comparative Perspective.* Belmont, CA: Wadsworth Publishing, 1987. Although somewhat dated now, this textbook broke new ground when it came out by bringing a comparative perspective to the study of religious ethics, thereby showing its relationship to ritual, myth, sacred cosmos, and other issues.

Cort, John. *Jains in the World: Religious Values and Ideology in India.* New York: Oxford University Press, 2001. Cort discusses Jain ideology, asceticism, temple worship, celebrations, and much more.

Dalai Lama. *Ethics for the New Millennium.* New York: Riverhead Books, 1999. Building on the Tibetan Buddhist notion of *shen pen kyi sem,* meaning "the thought to be of help to others," His Holiness the Dalai Lama discusses the foundation of ethics and the relationship between ethics and the individual.

Denny, Frederick Mathewson. "Law and the State in Classic Islamic Formulations." In *An Introduction to Islam.* 2nd ed. New York: Macmillan, 1994. Denny gives a clear overview of Islamic law.

Douglas, Mary. *Purity and Danger: An Analysis of the Concepts of Pollution and Taboo.* London: Routledge and Kegan Paul, 1966. Douglas's chapters on ritual uncleanness, Leviticus, and boundaries are particularly helpful.

Fingerette, Herbert. *Confucius—The Secular as Sacred.* New York: Harper and Row, 1972. This is an illuminating interpretation of Confucius and his ideas.

Green, Ronald M. *Religious Reason: The Rational and Moral Basis of Religious Belief.* New York: Oxford University Press, 1978. This advanced and tightly argued book relies heavily on Kant, who tries to show that the basis of religious moral views is rational.

Humphrey, Caroline, and James Laidlaw. *The Archetypal Actions of Ritual: A Theory of Ritual Illustrated by the Jain Rite of Worship.* Oxford: Clarendon Press, 1994. The authors argue that ritual actions are meaningless in themselves. Meaning is attributed to such actions by religious authorities and/or individual participants. This interesting theory is illustrated by a careful study of Jain worship rituals.

Jaini, Padmanah. *Gender and Salvation: Jaina Debates on the Spiritual Liberation of Women.* Berkeley: University of California Press, 1991. Jaini traces the ins and outs of the debate about women and liberation in the Jain tradition.

Kessler, Gary E. "How Are Religion and Morality Related?" In *Philosophy of Religion: Toward a Global Perspective.* Belmont, CA: Wadsworth Publishing, 1999. This is an introductory overview of some issues and a collection of essays dealing with various topics, such as the divine command theory, liberation theology, and women's rights.

Lovin, Robin W., and Frank E. Reynolds, eds. *Cosmology and Ethical Order: New Studies in Comparative Ethics.* Chicago: University of Chicago Press, 1985. The editors argue that it is a mistake to isolate ethics from its cosmological background and that a comparative perspective is essential for understanding different religious ethical systems.

Morgan, Peggy, and Clive Lawton, eds. *Ethical Issues in Six Religious Traditions.* Edinburgh: Edinburgh University Press, 1996. This helpful collection of essays discusses how Hinduism, Buddhism, Sikhism, Judaism, Christianity, and Islam deal with different ethical issues ranging from marriage and the family to global issues of poverty and ecology.

## INTERNET RESOURCES

http://www.cs.colostate.edu/~malaiya/jainhlinks.html   This page contains a comprehensive index of links to sites on Jainism. Topics range from the fundamentals of Jainism, to Jain songs and prayers, to Jain texts.

http://www.princeton.edu/~humcomp/alkhaz.html   Al-Khazina is an interactive database for the study of Islamic culture developed for use in university courses on a wide range of topics.

http://acc6.its.brooklyn.cuny.edu/~phalsall/texts.html   This site provides access to electronic texts in Chinese studies, including classic Confucian texts.

## CHAPTER 12

# Institutionalized Religion

T O INSTITUTIONALIZE IS to establish. Sociologists of religion are particularly interested in how and why religious groups establish themselves and what effect this has on both religion and society. How do religious ideas and practices become embodied in groups? How do these groups function? How do they maintain authority, motivate people, and inspire appropriate kinds of behavior?

All groups, religious or not, have certain characteristics. Sociologist Robert L. Johnstone defines a group as

> two or more interacting people who (1) share common goals or aims that stem from common problems and a desire to resolve them; (2) agree upon a set of norms they hope will help them achieve their common goals; (3) combine certain norms into roles that they expect persons within the group to fill and carry out in the interests of the group; (4) agree (often only implicitly) on certain status dimensions and distinctions on the basis of which they create one another; and (5) identify with the group and express or exhibit some degree of commitment to the group, what it proposes to do, and how it proposes to do it.[1]

According to Johnstone, groups that hope to function successfully must meet the challenges posed by five functional prerequisites. We can identify these as (1) recruitment and reproduction; (2) socialization; (3) production of satisfactory levels of goods and services; (4) preservation of order; and (5) preservation of a sense of purpose.[2]

Members of groups die or leave, so groups need a more or less steady supply of new members. This is often achieved in religious groups by encouraging members to have large families and/or by encouraging members to recruit new members. New members must be socialized into the group. They must be trained and educated in the beliefs and practices of the group. New members must be brought to believe sincerely that what the group teaches is not only good for them and their children, but also good for others. Hence groups must provide the sorts of goods and services that people want or have become convinced that they need. There are many different ways to preserve and create order. All of them involve such things as the adoption of codes, laws, rules, constitutions, governance structures, and systems of authority.

The last functional prerequisite that Johnstone identifies (maintaining a sense of purpose) is, perhaps, the most important. We have been stressing how religion provides meaning and purpose to human life by creating a sense of identity and a sense of belonging to something larger than ourselves. If religious groups fail to maintain a sense of common purpose, they fail to provide that meaning, identity, and belonging that people want. If humans are, as some claim, basically social animals, then people not only *want* their groups to maintain a sense of common purpose, but also *need* them to do so.

---

## Five Functional Prerequisites of Groups

1. Recruitment and reproduction
2. Socialization
3. Production of satisfactory levels of goods and services
4. Preservation of order
5. Preservation of a sense of purpose

---

In this chapter we will examine certain aspects of religion that are of particular interest to sociologists. We begin with two case studies. One focuses on Tibetan Buddhism, a religion whose existence is increasingly precarious in its homeland. The other examines a new religious movement that failed tragically, ending in mass suicide, the ultimate antisocial act.

We shall also be concerned with examining some types of religious organizations, the dilemmas faced as religions become larger and more successful, types of authority, the role that scriptures play in maintaining a group, and how gender roles are played out in religious groups. Religions, of course, do not exist in a social vacuum. They are parts of a larger society that affects religious groups, and religious groups affect that larger society. Insofar as that larger society thinks of itself as a nation and of its members as citizens, we can call it a civil society. Civil societies develop what sociologists call **civil religions,** involving beliefs and practices designed to unite all of the different groups within a society into a functioning whole. I am writing this section on Memorial Day, a time when the "civil religion" of the United States honors its military dead as martyrs to a higher cause—the preservation of the whole society.

We close the chapter with a research case on Shinto, the indigenous religion of Japan. This case provides a chance for you to exercise your new skills in the sociological analysis of religion.

## 12.1 TWO CASE STUDIES

### 12.1.1 Tibetan Buddhism

Tibet, an inner Asian land located west of China on the Himalayan plateau, is overwhelmingly Buddhist. The basic ideas and practices of Buddhism were introduced in Chapter 8 and revisited when we studied the paths of merit and faith in Chapter 10.

Not much is known about Tibet before the seventh century. According to early chronicles, kings, the first seven of whom were believed to have descended from the heavens by means of a ladder or cord, ruled Tibet. These kings created a system of law and social order that they believed reflected the cosmic order. The king, as a descendent of heaven, was not only the protector of the cosmic and social order, but also its manifestation on earth. The welfare of the people depended on the welfare of the king.[3]

This cult of divine kingship included the belief that the king had a great power of special significance. The king was the embodiment of the essence of the divine ancestor, which was reborn in each successive king. The king ruled along with a head priest representing the priestly class and a chief minister representing the clan nobility. Power was distributed in a hierarchical fashion connecting heaven, king, priest, nobility, and finally, peasants.

The first Tibetan king to support Buddhism was Tri Songdetsen (754–797). He invited to Tibet the Indian Buddhist abbot Shantarakshita and the great master of tantric meditation Padmasambhava. The first Buddhist monastery was established at Samye about 779.

Teams of translators set about translating Buddhist scriptures into Tibetan. Some of the texts they translated are called *tantras*. The tantras set forth a broad range of techniques for attaining enlightenment designed to shorten the eons-long path described in earlier Buddhist literature. These tantras often recommend actions that run directly counter to the conventional rules for proper monastic conduct, including eating meat and having sexual intercourse. *Left-*

*handed* tantra takes these techniques literally, while *right-handed* tantra understands them symbolically. When the translators came to the Sanskrit word for *teacher* (guru), they translated it with the Tibetan word *lama*. Henceforth Buddhist monks who attained the rank of teacher were called lamas.

Although Tibetan Buddhism derives many of its monastic rules and practices from Theravada (Way of the Elders) Buddhism, Tibetan Buddhists also drew on the ideas associated with Mahayana (Great Vehicle) Buddhism. One of the most important features of Mahayana is its emphasis on the bodhisattva as a person who makes a vow to become a buddha in the future in order to lead all beings out of the samsaric realm of suffering. To become fully enlightened, a bodhisattva must develop infinite compassion.

Avalokiteshvara ("ah-wah-loh-ki-tesh'wah-rah"), who is said to be a manifestation of the compassion of all buddhas, is highly revered in Tibet. His famous mantra *om mani padme hum** is widely used in meditation and prayer. As followers of Avalokiteshvara, Tibetan Buddhists refer to their type of Buddhism as the Buddhism of compassion. Tibetan Buddhists also refer to themselves as followers of Vajrayana (Diamond Vehicle). This vehicle emphasizes the tantric approach to the Mahayana path. It is also called the Thunderbolt Vehicle because, it is said, it can cut the length of time required to achieve buddhahood (which is traditionally reckoned as $384 \times 10^{58}$ years) to three years and three months!

The monastery was an institution of great power and influence before the Chinese communist takeover in 1959. The largest Buddhist monastery in the world, with some ten thousand monks (in 1959), was Drepung. The power and influence of monasteries extended to both the political and economic spheres. The three most important monastic seats around Lhasa, the capital city, could exercise near veto power over major government policies. Monasteries owned large tracts of productive land and acquired substantial wealth.

The Dalai Lama ("dahl'ee lahm'ah") is a title for the most influential spiritual leader (and at one time, political leader) of Tibetan Buddhism. The faithful consider him to be an emanation of Avalokiteshvara. Some schools of Tibetan Buddhism regard each Dalai Lama to be a reincarnation of the previous one, thereby continuing a lineage that allegedly extends back to the creation of the Tibetan people by the Bodhisattva of Compassion.

Monks, whether novice or ordained, were held in great respect and had high social status. Becoming a monk provided one of the few paths to social advancement. Monks who made it to the higher levels of scholar, teacher,

---

*The exact meaning of this mantra is in dispute. Some regard it as meaning something like "O you who hold the jewel and the lotus [have mercy upon us]." If it does mean this, it probably is a prayer addressed to Avalokiteshvara since "Jewel Lotus" was one of his/her many names. For a full discussion, see Chapter 4 of Lopez's book, listed in the "Suggestions for Further Readings."

or meditator attracted substantial patronage. Tibetans saw (and still see) Buddhism as symbolic of their country's identity, and they viewed the institutions of monastery and of monk as the manifestation of Tibetan spirituality. These two institutions validated Tibetan identity as a spiritual people.

In precommunist Tibet, a substantial part of the male population were monks (10 to 15 percent by some estimates), and a smaller part of the female population were nuns (perhaps 3 percent). The nuns lived in six hundred covenants, the largest of which was home to about one thousand women. While monks could advance to full ordination, nuns could not (although recent efforts have been made to change this situation). Being a nun carried little status, and parents usually did not encourage their daughters to pursue the life of a nun. Regardless of low social status, becoming a nun provided an opportunity (for many, the only opportunity) to escape bad marriages or avoid having children by never marrying.

Despite the lower status of nuns and the obvious patriarchal nature of traditional Tibetan society, there were and still are many important female divinities. The goddess Tara is one of the most commonly invoked deities. It should also be noted that nuns did become meditation masters and played important roles as mediums conveying messages from various deities. Avalokiteshvara is represented in both male and female form.

Given the importance of monastic Buddhism in Tibet, it was only natural that as the monarchy declined, political authority shifted to the lamas. Monarchs can pass their power on to their biological descendents, but monks cannot. So by the fourteenth century a form of succession developed in which political and religious power was passed on via the institution of the *incarnate lama,* or *tulku.* Incarnate lamas are technically buddhas because they are manifestations of the third buddha body called the "emanation body." Their rebirth is considered entirely voluntary, and hence their return is celebrated as an expression of great compassion.

Tibetan Buddhism adopted the practice of identifying successive rebirths of great lamas. This institution of the incarnate lama has become a central part of Tibetan society because it assures that power and authority can be passed from one generation to the next. Potential incarnate lamas must pass a test by recognizing personal items of the previous lama. This test is an impressive way of reinforcing the truth of reincarnation and hence, the truth of Buddhism.

The thirteenth through the fifteenth centuries saw the founding of a number of different monastic lineages. Here, we will be primarily concerned with the Geluk lineage.

The Geluk lineage traces its line of authority to Tsong Khapa (1357–1419), a monastic reformer and a creative interpreter of Buddhist philosophy. His disciple, Gendundrup (1391–1474), was identified as the first Dalai Lama. The Gelukpas established monastic universities throughout Tibet. It is this lineage that eventually came to dominate much of the religious and political life of Tibet. The Mongols, after their conversion to Tibetan Buddhism, became powerful patrons of the Geluk lineage and, in 1642, established the fifth Dalai Lama as ruler of Tibet. Now religious and secular power was combined into a single authority.

In the early 1950s the Chinese communists invaded and occupied Tibet. The atheism of communism came into immediate conflict with the faith of the Tibetans. A popular uprising against the Chinese occupation forces began on March 17, 1959. It was ruthlessly put down, and the fourteenth Dalai Lama was forced to flee. He escaped to India, and many of his followers fled to India as well. Today over 100,000 Tibetans live in exile, and Tibet itself remains a Chinese colony.

Since 1959 there has been violent suppression of the Tibetan religion, which peaked during the Cultural Revolution when thousands of monasteries and temples were destroyed. It is estimated that between 1959 and 1979, one million of the six million ethnic Tibetans have died as a result of Chinese policies. From the Chinese point of view, their invasion and occupation of Tibet is a liberation of the Tibetan people from centuries of feudal and religious domination. The people see it very differently.

Since 1979 the Chinese have relaxed their more oppressive policies due to international attention and their own desire to attract the tourist dollar. Some monasteries and temples have been rebuilt, and some Tibetans have returned to the monastic way of life, although their numbers are carefully regulated by the Chinese. The Tibetan community in exile is expanding and attracting both European and American converts. The present (fourteenth) Dalai Lama won the Nobel Peace Prize and gives talks worldwide on the inner peace that Buddhist practice can give.

At one time, Westerners saw Tibet either as a backward place dominated by crude superstitions and magical practices or as an ideal community (Shangri-La) of happy people uncorrupted by the modern world and possessing ancient wisdom of great value. Contemporary scholarship is painting a more balanced and complex picture.

Past monastic practices in Tibet pursued a program of "mass monasticism." The monasteries enrolled as many monks as possible and expelled as few as possible. Many monks were illiterate and followed no rigorous course of study. Quantity, not quality, was emphasized. Monastic leaders thought that having as many monks as possible was a sign of the truth of Buddhism. This policy led to corruption and lax standards. From time to time there were attempts—some successful, some not—to reform the monastic system. Today the situation is very different.

As monasticism is revived in Tibet, the Chinese have been careful to stress the religious rather than the political nature of Tibetan Buddhism. Monks are forbidden to have any political power or influence. The exiled Tibetan community has come into close contact with other religions, cultures, and democratic rather than theocratic political systems. The Dalai Lama stresses that he is a simple Buddhist monk committed to the practice of compassion. It will be interesting to see what happens to Tibetan Buddhism in general and the monastic system in particular if the fourteenth Dalai Lama is ever allowed to go home.

I visited Drepung monastery in 1999. There were about six hundred monks living there and three or four very elderly nuns living in shacks outside the walls. Children can no longer be enrolled, and the communist government forbids enrollment below the age of eighteen. Nevertheless, I did see some monks who appeared younger. The government does not support the monastery, so it has had to devise its own means of raising funds from various sources, including tourist money and alms from lay Tibetans. Money is not distributed equally, but according to points earned by monks in different work units.

The immediate future of the monastery will, to a large extent, depend on whether the monks are willing to concentrate on religious matters alone and forgo political activities. Ninety-two monks from Drepung alone were arrested for participating in ten antigovernment demonstrations between 1987 and 1993. The monks in this monastery and others have a long history of involvement in politics. The Chinese government's attempt to persuade and intimidate Drepung's monks in order to uncouple religion from nationalistic politics has not yet worked as well as the Chinese would like. What has motivated the monks in the past has been a combination of religion and nationalistic concerns. A crucial question is whether strong motivation can be maintained on religious grounds alone.

Modern secular societies tend to view religion as somehow separate from the other structures of a society. Thus they insist on the separation of religion and politics (church and state). This insistence is not always realistic. Religion is not just a private affair divorced from other aspects of society. The long and continued involvement of religion in public life provides strong counterevidence to the secular demand for absolute separation.

## 12.1.2 Jonestown

Around 5:00 P.M. on November 18, 1978, in Jonestown, Guyana, 918 people died. According to their leader, the Reverend Jim Jones, these people committed an act of "revolutionary suicide." As the news reports of the tragedy spread across the globe, people were understandably shocked and dismayed. How could this happen? Why did it happen? The media was quick to use the word *cult* to characterize what Jones and his followers called the Peoples Temple.

The word *cult* had become a dirty word with the public. It suggested brainwashing, kidnapping, weird rituals, bizarre beliefs, fanatical followers, and crazy leaders. Once the label was in place, the standard assaults against founders of new religious movements or alternative religions (terms more neutral than *cult*) soon followed. Jim Jones was portrayed in the news as a "fake," a "fraud," a "sexual pervert," and a "crazy man." How could there be any other explanation?

The student of religion is challenged by such extreme cases to make sense of them from a scholarly viewpoint. Media reports on religion are seldom well informed and often misleading. As students of religion we must probe behind the standard media accounts and ask questions that lead to a deeper understanding. If Jim Jones was so obviously insane, why did these people follow him even unto death? On a tape recording of the final minutes of the tragedy, a man who is apparently a member of the Peoples Temple says, "And I'd like to say that I thank Dad [a title of affection for Jim Jones] for making me strong to stand with it all and make me ready for it. Thank you."[4] Why would a crazy man who is telling his followers to commit revolutionary suicide be called Dad and thanked?

The facts of the case of Jim Jones and Jonestown are easy enough to document since they are a matter of public record. What is not easy to understand is the event Jones called "revolutionary suicide," a term he borrowed from Huey Newton of Black Panther fame.

The story begins when James Warren Jones was born on May 13, 1931, in Lynn, Indiana. Lynn is a small farming community and a seat of both Christian fundamentalism and Ku Klux Klan activity. Jones's mother had Cherokee blood, and his family was considered poor white trash. He apparently felt alienated from society because of the social status of his family. They lived on the margins of Lynn society. According to some, this early experience of alienation became an ongoing problem in Jones's life and explains his moves from one place to another seeking acceptance from society as a whole.

In 1951, Jones, who had married, moved to Indianapolis and, in 1952, became pastor of a Methodist church and director of a racially integrated community center. His outspoken views in favor of the civil rights movement and his public support of Martin Luther King, Jr., resulted in an invitation to leave. While in Indianapolis Jones became interested in communism and its vision of a just, classless society. He found an affinity between socialism and the Christian concern for social justice.

In 1956 he started the Peoples Temple Full Gospel Church, an integrated but mostly black congregation. At the Peoples Temple, he preached what he called "apostolic socialism" citing Acts 4:32–35, for support, which says:

> Now the company of those who believed were of one heart and soul and no one said that any of the things which he possessed was his own, but they had everything in common.
>
> And with great power the apostles gave their testimony to the resurrection of the Lord Jesus, and great grace was upon them all. There was not a needy

person among them, for as many as were possessors of lands or houses sold them, and brought the proceeds of what was sold and laid it at the apostles' feet; and distribution was made to each as any had need.

Jones and his congregation strove to live according to the Marxist maxim (a maxim they also considered Christian), "From each according to his ability, to each according to his need." With his message of apostolic socialism Jones combined a ministry of faith healing and revival-style preaching. He explained his ability to heal by claiming that he was a manifestation of the "Christ Principle."

> I have put on Christ, you see. I have followed after the example of Christ. When you see me it's no longer Jim Jones here. I'm crucified with Christ, nevertheless I live, yet not I, but Christ that lives here. Now Christ is in this body.
>
> You will not get Christ's blessing in Jim Jones' blessing until you walk like Jim Jones, until you talk like Jim Jones, until you act like Jim Jones, until you look like Jim Jones. How long will I be with you until you understand that I am no longer a man, but a Principle. I am the Way, the Truth, and the Light. No one can come to the Father but through me.[5]

Jones warned people that a race war, genocide, and finally, nuclear war was at hand. He predicted a nuclear holocaust to occur on July 15, 1967. He labeled American capitalistic culture "Babylon." There is no evidence that he was not sincere in what he preached or that he personally enriched himself. The evidence does indicate that he was so convinced of the looming catastrophe that he began searching for a place his congregation could move in order to escape nuclear war. His plan was to survive the war and, after Babylon had been destroyed, emerge to rebuild a Christian socialist society.

In 1961, the Peoples Temple became affiliated with the Disciples of Christ, and in 1964, Jones was ordained a minister in that denomination. His millenarian beliefs and his dualistic views of a coming battle between the forces of good (Peoples Temple) and the forces of evil (Babylon) reinforced his belief that nuclear war was at hand. This belief led him to move to Ukiah, California, one of the places that had been identified by *Esquire* magazine as "safe" from nuclear attack.

By 1967 Jones had established an important religious and civic presence in California. He became chairman of the Ukiah Legal Services Society and foreman of the Mendocino Grand Jury. By 1972 he had founded churches in San Francisco and Los Angeles. He published a widely circulated newspaper and had a half-hour radio program. In 1973 he leased 27,000 acres of undeveloped land in Guyana, South America, which was another place identified by *Esquire* as "safe" from nuclear attack.

His combined congregations in California grew so large that the *Sacramento Bee* reported, "Peoples Temple ranks as probably the largest Protestant congregation in Northern California."[6] Jones was named by *Religion in Life* as one of the one hundred outstanding clergymen in the United States. In 1976 he received the Humanitarian of the Year award from the *Los Angeles Herald*. In 1977 he was given the Martin Luther King Humanitarian of the Year award and became chairman of the San Francisco Housing Authority.

What was not reported in the papers, at least not at that time, was the fact that Jim Jones was having sexual relations with a number of young white women and with some men. In 1972 Grace Stoen, a member of Peoples Temple, gave birth to John Victor Stoen, and her husband, Tim Stoen, acknowledged that Jim Jones was the father. Tim Stoen stated in an affidavit:

> The child, John Victor Stoen, was born January 15, 1972. I am privileged beyond words to have the responsibility for caring for him, and I undertake this task humbly with the steadfast hope that said child will become a devoted follower of Jesus Christ and be instrumental in bringing God's kingdom here on earth, as has been his wonderful natural father.[7]

Eventually Grace and Tim Stoen defected separately, leaving the child with the Peoples Temple. The child became the focus of a bitter custody battle, and the Stoens used the press and government agencies to spark investigations of the Temple. Sensationalized news stories from defectors began to appear, and soon both the Treasury Department and the Internal Revenue Service started an investigation, thereby confirming Jones's belief that the Peoples Temple was being persecuted. Jones sensed it was time to leave, and in the summer of 1977 he, along with over one thousand members of the Temple, moved to Jonestown, their "promised land" deep in the heart of the Guyanese jungle.

The defectors and parents of Peoples Temple members formed a group (primarily whites) and named themselves Concerned Relatives. Their stories of sexual, financial, and physical abuses appeared in an article in *New West* (August, 1977).[8] The Stoens initiated legal proceedings to gain custody of John Victor. In 1978 they filed suit, asking for damages of over $56 million. Other lawsuits by other defectors followed. The Social Security Administration asked the U.S. embassy in Guyana to check on the members of Jonestown who received social security checks. Consul McCoy visited Jonestown three times between 1977 and 1978. He interviewed seventy-five people, none of whom wanted to leave. McCoy later said, "Anyone who says it was a concentration camp is just being silly. For the old people, and the people coming from the ghetto, it was relatively better."[9] In spite of positive reports, the U.S. Postal Service stopped delivering or rerouting social security checks. Since the Temple held all assets in common, this threatened the economic survival of Jonestown. Options began to narrow.

In a book by Catherine Wessinger, Rebecca Moore is quoted:

> Jonestown residents were caught in a "vise" consisting of lawsuits filed by Tim Stoen and Concerned Relatives, investigations and actions by federal agencies

that threatened the continued existence of Jonestown, dismay caused by internal dissension, highly negative press stories, and fears that their status in Guyana was precarious because of the Guyanese political situation. The Jonestown residents had no place to go to escape the multiple pressures. Jim Jones could not return to the United States, where lawsuits and a criminal complaint were pending against him. African American residents of Jonestown did not see returning to racist America and ghetto life as a viable option. The white members did not want to be disloyal to the blacks and their shared ideal of multiracial justice and harmony.[10]

Jones's increasingly radical millenarianism did not help matters. He declared the so-called deity of traditional Christianity to be a "Buzzard God" and asserted he was a messiah sent by the True God, the "Principle of Socialism," to rescue people from their bondage to capitalism. He claimed he was previously incarnated as Moses and then again as Lenin. He claimed the King James Version of the Bible was written by white men to justify the oppression of people of color and to subordinate women. He declared that the United States was the Antichrist and that a pitched battle of good versus evil would soon begin.

In November of 1978 Congressman Leo Ryan went to Jonestown at the urging of the Concerned Relatives. He brought with him some of the people the members of Jonestown hated most: representatives of the American government, of the press, and of the Concerned Relatives. After visiting Jonestown, Congressman Ryan informed Jones that his report would be basically positive. He saw neither evidence of force being used to keep people there nor any evidence of "brainwashing." He recommended that Jonestown increase its contacts with the outside world. A man wielding a knife attacked Ryan, and he and his party rapidly departed for the airstrip with those members of Jonestown that decided to go with him.

At the airstrip, Ryan's party was attacked, and he along with four members of his party were killed by some members of Jonestown. About an hour later, Jones began the "White Night"—an event that had been previously rehearsed. The White Night referred to mass suicide. Most died by taking a fruit drink mixed with cyanide and tranquilizers. It appears that most died voluntarily. Two hundred and sixty small children and infants had been given poison, many of them by their parents. Livestock, dogs, and fishponds had also been poisoned along with the supply of drinking water. Most of the dead were American citizens, most were black, and most were family groups.

The decision to commit mass suicide was not the decision of Jim Jones alone, as the tape of the last minutes shows. Christine Miller, a sixty-year-old black woman argued with Jones, claiming that suicide was not a proper response. Jones's power and influence had been declining since the move to Jonestown. His healing power had been replaced by medical health care. The mostly young white women who formed the inner circle of leaders used their administrative skills to run Jonestown. As Jim Jones's mental health deteriorated, the community's will to succeed as a socialist collective became stronger. Once it was clear that they could not succeed, most decided to die for their ultimate concern rather than let their ideal die.

There had been warnings. In the summer of 1978 a member of Jonestown named Mike Prokes wrote to the *San Francisco Examiner,* "We have found something to die for, and it's called social justice. We will at least have had the satisfaction of living that principle, not because it promised success or reward, but simply because we felt it was the right thing to do."[11] Before Ryan's trip to Guyana, defectors, including Grace Stoen, briefed the U.S. State Department on the possibility of mass suicide in Jonestown. In the end, these warnings did not stop the tragedy.

Annie Moore, a nurse, apparently was the last person to die. She wrote a final letter that concluded:

> Jim Jones showed us all this—that we could live together with our differences, that we are all the same human beings. Luckily, we are more fortunate than the starving babies of Ethiopia, than the starving babies of the United States.
>
> What a beautiful place this was. The children love the jungle, learned about animals and plants. There were no cars to run over them; no child molesters to molest them; nobody to hurt them. They were the freest, most intelligent children I had ever known.
>
> Seniors had dignity. They had whatever they wanted—a plot of land for a garden. Seniors were treated with respect—something they never had in the United States. A rare few were sick and when they were, they were given the best medical care . . . We died because you would not let us live in peace. Annie Moore.[12]

Those are some of the facts. What do they mean? How can they be explained? The tendency of both popular and a few scholarly explanations is to focus on Jim Jones. He is the culprit that explains it all. He suffered from extreme alienation, an overinflated ego, paranoia, obsessions with sex, and much more. The bulk of the press made him out to be a "wrathful, lustful giant" with extraordinary powers to brainwash people.

From a sociological viewpoint, I think this explains very little. It certainly does not explain why hundreds of adults voluntarily followed Jones into death. They were not zombies who had lost their will. They argued with Jones and with each other about the best course of action. Our focus needs to be on the community and the racist, capitalistic society it was fleeing.

Catherine Wessinger, using Tillich's idea of religion as an ultimate concern (see Chapter 3), argued that the collective had become, for most of the members of the Peoples Temple, their ultimate concern. An ultimate concern is something for which people are willing to lay down their lives. We do not find it incomprehensible when people willingly lay down their lives for their nation (soldiers do it all the time) or their families. The Peoples Temple was family and nation for the citizens of Jonestown. The story about how it became that for these people is long and complex. It has to do with the ideology Jones preached (millenarianism and apostolic socialism), U.S. racism, idealist fantasies of a perfect society, and the natural desire of people to believe that they have given their lives to a righteous cause.

Jonathan Z. Smith offers some "partial" explanations. He points out parallels between the history of religion and Jonestown. The members of Peoples Temple were not the first, and would not be the last, to commit mass suicide in the name of religion. Jim Jones even reminded a member of that during the final minutes, when a member claimed that this had never been done before. It has been done before, Jones emphatically asserted. Indeed it had, and it usually happened when people found themselves in desperate situations and believed the pure community they had been building had become corrupted. Paradise, utopia, the perfect society in the making had been invaded and profaned by the arrival of Congressman Ryan and others. People from the polluted, racist, capitalistic "outside" had crossed over the boundary to the pure, nonracist, socialist "inside." Jones actually uses the word *invasion* to characterize Ryan's arrival.

If we couple the violation of boundaries with the sense that there are no good alternatives, we can see how desperate people might take their own lives. Some of their members had killed Ryan and others. They knew it was only a matter of time before the law would show up. At one time they had hoped to go to Russia if Guyana did not work out. On the tape of the final minutes we hear Jim Jones saying, "It's too late for Russia." "There's no plane." So "Let's get gone. Let's get gone. Let's get gone."[13]

The causes of this tragedy are much more complex. But Wessinger's and Smith's theories are a step in the right direction. They do not rely on simplistic explanations that focus on one person as the culprit that caused all this. They help us make the bizarre and shocking more familiar. They help us understand that perhaps we too, if we had the same experiences and were in the same situation, might also opt for "revolutionary suicide."

## 12.2 COMPARISON

I think we will find it helpful, as a way of organizing our comparative discussion, to focus on the five functional prerequisites of groups discussed in the introduction to this chapter. Once again I ask you to try your hand at comparison based on the information you have. Note the differences and similarities between Tibetan Buddhism and Jonestown with respect to

1. Recruitment and reproduction
2. Socialization
3. Production of goods and services

4. Preservation of order
5. Preservation of purpose

Again, you may compare your comparison to mine, noting the differences and similarities. Since the information you have is limited, there are bound to be differences because my account draws on additional information.

*Recruitment and Reproduction*   With respect to recruitment and reproduction, I think it is clear that monastic communities like the Tibetan Buddhists that require vows of celibacy cannot fill their ranks by reproduction. The only option available is recruitment. In the precommunist days (what I will call traditional Tibet), recruitment was no problem when it came to monks because of the high social status enjoyed by monks and the willingness of most Tibetan families to send their sons off at an early age to become monks. In occupied Tibet we might think enrollment of new monks would be more difficult, but it is not. Though monks have been killed and imprisoned, children are prohibited by law from joining, and caps are placed on enrollments, still, all available positions are filled.

For the Tibetan Buddhist diaspora (those spread around the world), adding new members, including both monks and nuns, has proved not to be a problem, especially in Europe and the United States. The Dalai Lama is immensely popular and attracts new members by his evident spirituality and wisdom. Also, the International Campaign to Free Tibet is a popular cause, attracting those who are interested in righting what they see to be a social injustice.

The Peoples Temple relied on both recruitment and reproduction. If the Peoples Temple had survived the White Night, there would have been another generation ready to fill its ranks as adult members. Its most successful recruitment came among families, African Americans, and whites who were concerned about issues of social justice and racism. The social situation in the United States in the 1960s and early 1970s created favorable conditions for recruitment. People were concerned about civil rights and nuclear war. There were also a number of communal movements interested in experimenting with socialism. Jones himself had great *charisma* (a quality of persons that attracts others), and the close bonding that occurred among members attracted many who were lonely and isolated.

The Peoples Temple and Tibetan monasticism differ dramatically with respect to recruitment and reproduction. One is a monastic movement and the other is not. One can rely on both recruitment and reproduction to fill its ranks, the other can rely only on recruitment. We can only speculate on how long the Peoples Temple could have kept going if the tragedy at Jonestown had not happened. It is clear at present that Tibetan monastic Buddhism is so ingrained in Tibet that if Tibet did become a free nation, it would flower once more. It is hard to say whether communist "reeducation" programs will have a major impact on Tibetan religious attitudes over the long haul. Perhaps the greatest threat comes from the Chinese resettlement programs in which ever more Chinese are being relocated in Tibet and more and more Tibetans are being forced to move outside their traditional homeland.

*Socialization*   How did these two groups socialize their members into the ideology and practices of the group, and how well did they do it?

In traditional Tibet, the socialization process began early, and therefore had a greater chance of success. If someone has almost complete power and influence over a child, getting him or her to accept the ideology and practices of a group is simply a process of gradual education. In contemporary Tibet, socialization may prove more difficult because new monks must be eighteen to be admitted. Yet the socialization process has already begun in the home, and the motivation to fight for the nation in addition to the religion provides a fertile field supporting the socialization process.

Renunciation also plays a major role in the socialization process. A monk takes vows to renounce the world outside the monastery. These vows, while they do not require complete separation from family and friends, isolate monks from their previous lives and focus their attention on building new bonds with the new community they have joined.

The socialization process in the Peoples Temple was much more difficult than it was in traditional societies that support monastic ideals. The appeal to Christian teachings helped. Early members were predisposed to join Protestant Christian churches because of the religious environment in which they grew up. The added message of socialism and antiracism was also appealing, not only to the ethically concerned and marginalized members of American society, but also to the ethically sensitive and perhaps somewhat guilt-ridden whites. There were education classes and, of course, Jim Jones's preaching, but the most effective form of socialization appears to be the close bonds—indeed, family-like atmosphere that pervaded the group. Jim Jones was called Father and Dad. The sexual bonds that formed between Jones and the "inner circle" of white women also provided a powerful means of socialization. Near the end, when Jones was sinking deeper into paranoia, this inner circle helped keep Jonestown running.

When the end neared, what alternatives did people have? If they gave all their money and property to the group, if they broke with former family and friends and moved to a foreign land, how could they exit? Members of the Peoples Temple, though not monks and not taking vows of renunciation, did in their own way renounce the outside world. And equally important, the outside world renounced the Peoples Temple.

Americans like churches, but they do not like cults. Label something a cult and it immediately becomes strange, different, even somewhat sinister. Once the press used that word for the Peoples Temple, their acceptance by and even success with the general population of California began to diminish. No longer were they a well-intentioned group fighting for social justice and a truly integrated religious community. Now they were dangerous. Now they might not even be "Christian" anymore. As the hostility and suspicion of those outside grew, the fear and desperation of those inside mounted. In the end, there was little left of their former lives in capitalist, racist America that members found attractive.

Both the monastic system of Tibet and the Peoples Temple used similar socialization processes, relying heavily on education and renunciation. The main difference is the attitude of the society at large. Tibetan monasticism has been and still is strongly supported by the general population, but communal and utopian movements in America (of which there have been many) have always been looked on with a suspicious eye. Social status in America is definitely not increased by joining a fringe movement.

*Production of Satisfactory Levels of Goods and Services* The third functional prerequisite of a successful group is producing satisfactory levels of goods and services. There are two levels of goods and services: economic and intellectual/emotional. In traditional Tibet, the monasteries were very wealthy, but individual monks were often quite poor. They were given insufficient funds to live on, so they had to devise ways to supplement their income. Shelter was usually provided, and some food, but the monasteries spent much of their money on religious festivals and other related activities. In contemporary Tibet, individual monks are much better off, getting sufficient or nearly sufficient funds from the money-making enterprises of the monastery. However, goods and services are not distributed equally, but divided according to "work points" earned.

On the emotional and intellectual level, communal life and strong bonds of friendship unite the monks. In traditional Tibet, few monks entered the rigorous education program, but one was available. There were various sorts of degrees possible, ranging from what we might call undergraduate through graduate levels. Buddhism is an intellectually and emotionally challenging religion. Its philosophy and theology are complex and difficult to grasp, there is an almost endless amount of literature to master, and its meditation practices can be very difficult. The faithful engage in relentless self-examination and are constantly seeking personal and moral improvement.

The Peoples Temple was a socialist commune, so all resources were held in common. They were not distributed according to work done, but according to need. At its beginning and at its end it was financially unstable. But it enjoyed several years of prosperity in California. Few appeared to complain about the lack of material goods.

For most members, the intellectual and emotional needs, not economic needs, were primary. Emotionally, the Peoples Temple was able to provide a sense of family. People saw themselves as related in a grand project to create a perfectly integrated society. Their kinship was in their common cause. Although Jones's theology appears to be rather simplistic, and little emphasis was put on philosophical or theological education, many of the white members were college educated. However, it was not the intellectual challenge that attracted them and kept them in the Temple, it was the emotional satisfaction they received from the belief that they had dedicated their lives to a righteous cause.

Both Tibetan monasticism and the Peoples Temple were successful in meeting their members' needs for goods and services. Both were antimaterialistic, so economic demands were not great. Buddhism offered more of an intellectual and emotional challenge to those who wanted to advance to higher degrees; even so, the Temple had an air of social experimentation about it, along with a millenarian spirit that Tibetan monastic Buddhism lacked. However, the Chinese occupation has made monastic life more precarious and thereby more precious.

*Preservation of Order*   The fourth prerequisite requires rules, regulations, organization, and structure. The structure of Tibetan monasticism is hierarchical, with the abbots and *tulkus* enjoying more power than other monks. Like all monastic orders, it had its rules and regulations about work and religious practice. Some people worked in the kitchen, some in the fields, others on construction, and some studied. Drepung had its own judicial system. Expulsion was always possible for major offenses but, in traditional Tibet, seldom used.

The Peoples Temple maintained order to the end. People lined up by families to receive their toxic cocktail. Children were poisoned first, then the adults. The bodies of families were found lying together on the ground. It appeared to be for the most part a very orderly process. Four individuals, including Jones, died of gunshot wounds, and approximately seventy bodies had puncture wounds, which suggests the poison may have been injected. Whether it was injected voluntarily or not could not be determined.

An inner circle of Jones's advisors maintained order in the Temple and in Jonestown. They managed the affairs of the community, from financial to medical. The inner circle was mostly white and mostly female. There appears to have been a constant fear of defection, the worst of sins. Things began to fall apart when the Stoens left. More followed, and eventually, near the end, a few of the inner circle left too. The boundaries between the order inside and the order outside were clearly drawn. To step from the outside in, caused joy. To step from the inside out, threatened not only disorder, but also the very existence of the community.

Tibetan monasticism was far more highly organized than Jonestown. It had to be because it was much larger. Even so, both were hierarchical (in spite of Jones's egalitarian preaching), and both were organized in ways that facilitated getting work done. The members of the Temple would regularly meet (often in all-night sessions) to discuss problems in the community, courses of action, and how to improve their communal life. Jones created order by having what, in effect, amounted to town meetings. The organization of Jonestown appears far more democratic than the organization of Tibetan monasticism, an organization that is feudal in comparison.

*Preservation of a Sense of Purpose* The ideologies and practices of both groups reinforced a shared sense of purpose. This sense of purpose was threatened when the communists invaded Tibet and the Ryan investigative group invaded Jonestown. Invasion, perceived or real, always threatens the expectation that common goals will be reached. In the case of Tibetan monasticism, the invaders demanded that the purpose change. The monks are to abandon, under penalty of law, all political and nationalistic causes. From now on, the monasteries are to pursue exclusively religious goals. Only the future will show whether this revised purpose can be maintained. It is very difficult to separate religion from politics, especially in a nation where the two have been entwined for centuries.

Some might claim that the mass suicide at Jonestown shows that in the end, the Peoples Temple failed in maintaining a sense of purpose. That is certainly true for the defectors. But it may not be entirely true for those who died. They clearly believed that they were leaving this earth to continue the cause elsewhere. The world was not ready for them and their ideals, so they simply had to go somewhere else, just as the community had moved from place to place on this earth. Unfortunately, we know little about their views of the afterlife. In 1973, Jones used the word *translation* to talk about being "translated to a distant planet." The language of death used by Jones and others near the end was spatial—"Let's get gone," "stepping over," "you have to step across," "this world was not our home." Whatever the specifics of their view of life after death, it seems clear that they expected to continue their grand experiment in integrated socialist living someplace else. Most probably died with their sense of purpose in tact.

## 12.3 TYPES OF RELIGIOUS ORGANIZATIONS

We can divide religious organizations into two broad categories. The first we might call natural and the second voluntary. *Natural* religious organizations (perhaps a better word is *group*, or *community*) are those based on kinship (family, clan, tribe), geography (region, nation), race, or culture. In such groups there is little differentiation between religion and the general sociocultural life of the community. These groups often trace their origins back to a sacred ancestor or deity. People are born into the religion by being born into the tribe or nation. Religion is not something someone decides to join.

In natural religious communities, rules regulating marriage, initiation rites, and ritual attention to ancestors are particularly important. Marrying within the group is important because it is the primary means by which this kind of religious group grows and continues. The rites of passage associated with initiation are significant because these mark the transition not just from childhood to adulthood, but from a marginal member of the group to full membership. Attention to matters relating to the ancestors is essential because continuity with the past can secure continuity with the future. Each individual is part of a larger community extending backward and forward in time. Native American religions and tribal religions of Africa and Australia are good examples. However, as we will see later in the chapter when we consider civil religion and state Shinto, the nation can function as a sort of very large tribe binding people who may differ in many respects into an interconnected whole.

*Voluntary* religious organizations are those in which the common bonds between members are not based on kinship, race, or national identity but on commitment to a common teaching. Religion is no longer sustained by procreation, but by recruitment. People need to be convinced by the beliefs and practices of the group in order to become members. Often the word *conversion* is used to characterize this process. Voluntary religious organizations establish missions, often seeking to convert those who are part of natural religious groups to their church or sect.

Sociologists have labored mightily over what has come to be called the "church-sect continuum." The words *church* and *sect* have theological meanings. They also have popular meanings that associate the word *church* with something positive and the word *sect* with something negative. The sociological meaning of these terms should not be confused with either the theological or popular meanings. Sociologists use these terms to distinguish different kinds of organizations or groups.

Precisely what is the difference between a church-type of organization and a sect-type is a matter of dispute. Of the many variables or characteristics to consider, it is difficult to say which are decisive. If we focus on only one variable—the relationship between voluntary religious organizations and the larger society of which they are a part—we can say that typically church-type organizations *accept* the larger society and sect-types *reject* it. But this way of distinguishing between these two types is not entirely satisfactory because denominations also accept the larger society, and so-called cults (I use the word here in a neutral, not a negative sense), or new religious movements (NRM), often reject it. How can we distinguish a church from a denomination and a sect from an NRM (cult)?

Sociological information indicates that a denomination shares some characteristics with both the church-type and the sect-type of organization. Like a church, but unlike a sect, a denomination is usually accepting (for the most part) of the larger society. Like a sect it may have originated in a protest

FIGURE 12.1 The Church-Sect Continuum

movement against the church-type. When the church-type of organization loses it religious monopoly on society, denominationalism usually results. So when the Roman Catholic Church lost its religious dominance of Europe, Protestant denominations like the Lutheran and Reformed arose.

A *denomination* is an official organization that unifies different congregations under a particular set of doctrines and practices. Often these congregations share a similar history, and their members sometimes share a similar ethnic origin. Within the denominations, schisms (divisions) often occur over a variety of different issues. Sociologists call these splinter groups sects. Sects develop because some members come to believe that the denomination has gone too far in its acceptance of the values of the larger society. Hence sects reject the values of the larger society. If we view these relationships visually, they would look like the illustration in Figure 12.1.

As you move to the left on this continuum, the degree of acceptance of the values of the larger society increases. As you move to the right, the degree of acceptance decreases and the degree of rejection increases.

If we add NRM, or cult-type of organization, to this mix, then a cult would be a new religious movement or an alternative religious movement in some society. These movements often begin as small spiritual groups not yet sufficiently institutionalized to be considered a church, denomination, or sect. Something that might be a well-established church or sect in one society might be viewed as a cult or alternative religious movement in another. So Tibetan Buddhism might be viewed as an alternative religious movement in American society and a church-type in Tibet.

We must remember that all organizations, including religious ones, are dynamic. They change over time and in differing circumstances. For example, Jim Jones was an ordained minister of an established Protestant denomination (Disciples of Christ) in Indiana, but his organization became a sect when it moved to California. By the time the move to Guyana occurred, it had become an NRM and presented a radical alternative to mainstream Christianity called "apostolic socialism." The change in title from the Peoples Temple Full Gospel Church to simply the Peoples Temple signals this transformation.

Movement can take place in the opposite direction. Some sects can become denominations, and some cults can also move in that direction. Also, some sects remain sectarian in their outlook. In other words, they become institutionalized as a sect (Figure 12.2).

Scholars continue to debate exactly what factors cause movement along the continuum and off of it. Why do some sects become institutionalized as

FIGURE 12.2 Expanded Church-Sect Continuum

sects and remain steadfastly at odds with the society over certain major issues? Why are different social classes attracted to some organizational types and not others? For example, church-type and denomination-type organizations tend to attract middle- and upper-income groups, while the sect-type tend to attract lower-income groups. We have much to learn about how sects and cults form, how they evolve, the role of power or the lack of it in these processes, and the relationship of all of this to social class. There is already much empirical research available for those who wish to pursue these topics in more detail.

## 12.4 THE DILEMMAS OF INSTITUTIONALIZATION

Among the novels by Fyodor Michaelovitch Dostoevsky (1821–1864), the great Russian novelist, is one titled *The Brothers Karamazov* (published in 1880). Within that novel is a section called the "Grand Inquisitor," which Sigmund Freud called "one of the peaks of the literature of the world."[14] Dostoevsky imagines that Christ has returned during the Spanish Inquisition and that he is arrested and questioned by the Grand Inquisitor of the Roman Catholic Church. The Inquisitor, who recognizes Christ, asks him why he has come back and informs him that his return is dangerous to the stability of the church he has founded. The Inquisitor tells Christ, "I swear, man is weaker and baser by nature than Thou hast believed him!" The Grand Inquisitor also says to the returned Christ, "We [the Roman Catholic Church] have corrected Thy work and have founded it upon *miracle, mystery* and *authority.*"[15]

Max Weber gave the subject of Dostoevsky's literary essay a sociological term. He called it the "routinization of charisma." In time, the original creative surge of the founder of new religious movements is made "routine." Weber thinks this is necessary if the movement is to survive. It must institutionalize and thus create a bureaucracy.

Thomas O'Dea, a sociologist of religion, has noted that the routinization process typically presents religious organizations with **five dilemmas**.[16] The first he called the "dilemma of mixed motivation." In its beginning stages, a new religious movement exhibits a kind of single-minded focus on what it takes to be its main goal and message. As it grows in size and as subsequent generations move into leadership positions that carry rewards, power, and honor, people may begin to ask why people want positions of leadership. Do they seek these positions because of their concern for the mission of the group or because of the prestige associated with leadership positions? Perhaps their motivation is mixed. We might wonder about the motivation of Dostoevsky's Grand Inquisitor. The Inquisitor acknowledges, in the course of his inquisition of Christ, that Christ came to give humans freedom. But freedom, he says, is too much for ordinary humans to bear. So instead of freedom, the church has given them what they want and need—miracle, mystery, and authority.

O'Dea's second dilemma is the "symbolic dilemma." Religions must convey their messages in symbols. Rituals often embody these symbols in concrete action. Initially the rituals remind the early members of important and meaningful experiences. Over time, as the group grows and becomes more routinized, the rituals and symbols may seem increasingly meaningless and strange. Ritual activity becomes a matter of mere formality, taking on a hollow, sometimes even magical, tone. Often the symbols become so dead and the ritual activities so formal, that sectarian movements develop with the goal of revitalizing the beliefs and practices of the group.

The third dilemma centers on problems associated with developing an "administrative order." As an organization grows in complexity, new offices and positions need to be created. A bureaucracy forms. Bureaucracies need to elaborate policies and rules to cover new situations. However, the more they do that, the more flexibility they lose. So the Grand Inquisitor represents an elaborated bureaucracy with its own policies and procedures. He no longer has the flexibility of allowing Christ to go free, even though he recognizes him. It is his responsibility to question and, if necessary, punish those deemed dangerous to the Roman Catholic Church.

The "dilemma of delimitation" refers to the conflict between the need for concrete and specific rules of behavior and the moral spirit of the religion. New situations arise, new rules must be created to apply to these new situations, and soon legalism sets in, making general guidelines hard-and-fast laws. The focus shifts from the "spirit of the law" to the "letter of the law." The Zen story of Tanzan and Ekido recounted in Chapter 11 illustrates this dilemma. Because monks are not to touch females, Ekido would not help a girl across the mud. Tanzan did, recognizing that the spirit of the law (to help others in distress without attachment) was more important than the letter of the law—do not touch a female if you are a monk.

The last dilemma O'Dea refers to as the "dilemma of power." Voluntary religious organizations normally want people to join and to remain adherents because of a sincere conviction that their beliefs are true. However, these organizations are sometimes tempted to use manipulative methods, even coercion, to gain and retain members. The later days of the Peoples Temple are a good example. As defections increased, Jones and other members of the group began to feel ever more threatened. The greater the perceived danger from a declining membership, the greater the manipulation by those in charge. Also, some religions have resorted to coercion (more or less extreme) rather than conversion in order to build their numbers. The hard sell of some televangelists and door-to-door proselytizers is another example of the "conversion vs. coercion" power dilemma.

The success of religious organizations often depends on how well they solve these five dilemmas. Success, however, does not always smell so sweet when compromises have to be made.

> ### Five Dilemmas of Institutionalization
>
> 1. The dilemma of mixed motivation
> 2. The symbolic dilemma
> 3. The dilemma of administrative order
> 4. The dilemma of delimitation
> 5. The dilemma of power

## 12.5 TYPES OF AUTHORITY

What is the probability that some group of people will obey specific commands? Why should any of us believe or do what someone else tells us to believe or do? Why do people sometimes sacrifice their own self-interest in order to obey others? There are many kinds of authority, but here I wish to focus on the different types of authority enjoyed by religious leaders.

According to Max Weber, there are three basic types of religious authority: charismatic, traditional, and legal-rational. Jim Jones is an example of a charismatic leader. His authority was a product of a particular type of relationship that he was able to establish with people by the sheer force of his personality. He was able to inspire loyalty in people. He had a certain quality that enabled him to attract devoted followers and inspire high levels of emotion and commitment.

Weber notes that charismatic authority is revolutionary. It is based on a break with tradition. It provides a new vision of the way the world should be. A religious leader whose authority is based in charisma can get people to change their customary beliefs and do things that their tradition has told them not to do. Jim Jones was able to inspire belief in apostolic socialism among people who had been socialized into capitalism, and he was able to get them to follow him even when it involved a high cost—their own lives. The Jesus portrayed in the New Testament had charismatic authority, as did Buddha,

Moses, and Muhammad. All leaders of new religious movements rely on this kind of authority to get something that is religiously novel started.

Once a religion is up and running and once it survives long enough, traditional authority replaces charismatic authority. Traditional authority is recognized on the basis of what is customary, or traditional, in some group. This sort of authority is usually informal in the sense that there is no formal rule or law authorizing a person or group to exercise authority. For example, it is customary and traditional in Tibet to recognize the authority of certain Buddhist lineages, but there is no law that requires it.

Traditional authority is closely related to what Weber labels legal-rational, but a legal-rational authority is one based on formalized rules, regulations, and laws. These have been thought out and are the result of conscious calculation—hence Weber calls them "rational." For example, professional clergy such as ministers, rabbis, and priests have legal-rational authority because they occupy an office or position that is established as authoritative by the formal rules of some particular religious group.

Professional clergy also enjoy traditional authority because it is customary to see them as authorities in certain matters. There are, of course, many different kinds of clergy, and it is possible for new positions to be created by legal authority that are not necessarily traditional. So when some religious groups began to ordain women as professional clergy, a new position of authority for women was created by new rules, but it was not traditional in many religious organizations to ordain women.

Some religious leaders can have all three types of authority. Martin Luther King, Jr., was a charismatic religious leader who was also head of the Southern Christian Leadership Conference (SCLC) and a Baptist minister. His positions as head of SCLC and as a minister were based on legal-rational authority. But his clergy status was also based on traditional authority because in the black community it is traditional to acknowledge the authority of Christian ministers.

Whatever type of authority a religious leader may enjoy—charismatic, traditional, legal-rational—in the end, some group of people must acknowledge the authority of another group by following their commands. If no one followed, no one could lead.

---

**Types of Authority**

1. Charismatic
2. Traditional
3. Legal-rational

## 12.6 SCRIPTURE

Scriptures are social events. Communities of faith create holy writings for communities of faith. Once sacred scriptures exist, they become another source of authority that influences in turn the communities of faith that produced them. Such communities also continue to shape their scriptures by adding or subtracting material and by evolving new interpretations to fit changing circumstances.

Scriptures function in many ways, but one important way involves establishing a worldview. This worldview, or way of seeing the world and its history, provides a map for understanding life—its origin, meaning, and purpose. This worldview becomes a framework for interpreting subsequent events. For example, numerous Christian groups have been searching for "signs" of the end times in order to prepare for the Second Coming of Jesus. Without a worldview that incorporates the notion that history will at some point come to an end, being on the lookout for signs of the last days makes little sense.

Before written documents, oral traditions (some of which end up in scriptural collections) shape and are shaped by developing communities of faith. Before there was writing, stories, sayings, sermons, prophesies, myths, hymns, moral rules, ritual instructions, and the like existed only when spoken and heard in a communal setting. Even after scriptures (what is written) had come into existence, they were often known only when heard because the majority of believers were often illiterate. Only the elite could read and write. Even when literacy became widespread, the oral/aural (spoken)/(heard) mode persisted as scriptures were read, chanted, sung, and memorized in ritual settings. Whether scriptures are oral or written, communities are quite literally created when people recognize a common source of authority.

In 1987, the national television network of India presented in serialized form the *Ramayana*—a sacred text of epic poetry recounting the exploits of Rama ("rah'muh"), an incarnation of the god Vishnu. This series turned out to be immensely popular. There was an estimated audience of over 100 million, and much of India came to a standstill as people stopped what they were doing to watch an episode. For a moment in time, the diverse people of India became a single community.

Each year the towns and villages of India produce a play reenacting the story of the *Ramayana*. These performances (called *Ramlila* or "play of Rama") last anywhere from nine to thirty days and, in the richer villages, can be very elaborate productions. Because of these ritualized presentations, many Hindus are able to memorize and recall many verses without ever having read the text itself. Through the play, the audiences of the Ramlila become bound in a community of common experience and knowledge. The influence and authority of the *Ramayana* is thereby reinforced. It is quite natural to think that this scripture must be significant if all these millions of people take it seriously (or should I say playfully?).

Hearing is so important in the formation of Hindu scriptures that all the vast amount of sacred literature produced over many generations is divided into two types: *sruti* (that which is heard) and *smriti* (that which is remembered). The classification *sruti* is reserved for all texts that have a nonhuman origin, and the classification *smriti* is used for all texts that have human authors. The four Vedas (*Rig, Sama, Yajur,* and *Atharva*) are *sruti* texts. They are the most sacred texts and became the **canon** (rule or standard) for classifying all other literature as sacred. If an epic poem like the *Ramayana,* for example, acknowledges the authority of the Vedas and claims its teachings are consistent with Vedic teaching, it is admitted into the canon of sacred scripture, even though it has a human author. The Vedic canon was closed (meaning nothing more could be added) about the fourth century B.C.E.

If texts classified as *smriti,* or remembered, have human authors, who are the nonhuman authors of *sruti* texts like the Vedas? Many of us would probably say, because of the influence of Jewish, Christian, and Islamic traditions on our society, that God or gods reveal the Vedas to humans. While we can say that the Vedas are revealed, they have no authors, divine or human.

The Vedas embody the *Vac,* which is the eternal sacred and cosmic word/ sound that brings into being the entire creation. The sounds that the words of the Vedas embody are eternal. The Vedas have no beginning or end. Seers who have developed special spiritual abilities at the beginning of each world cycle hear these sounds. The eternalness and authorless nature of the Vedas enhances their authority because there are no possible changes that might occur, and there is no author (divine or human) that might make a mistake in the course of revealing their content. The Vedas can be trusted because they have none of the defects associated with texts produced by humans. Their authority is eternal and absolute. Some scholars believe that the *sruti* theory of the Vedas was developed in opposition to the canons of Buddhism and Jainism since neither of these religions recognized the authority of the Vedas.

The Christian Bible is made up of two major divisions called the Old Testament and the New Testament. The Old Testament consists of many of the texts found in the Hebrew scriptures, or Tanakh, whose canon took shape over many centuries and combined both oral and written material from different historical periods and different authors. Hebrew scriptures contain twenty-four books divided into three main parts: the Law, the Prophets, and the Writings. The Protestant version of the Old Testament is nearly identical to the Hebrew scripture but, because of different ways of dividing the books, consists of thirty-nine books. The versions of the Old Testament found in Roman Catholic and Eastern Orthodox traditions include seven more books as well as additions to the books of Esther and Daniel.

The Christian recognition of the sacred authority of the scriptures of another religion (Judaism) testifies to the strong bond between these religions. It is rare when one religion accepts as authoritative the scriptures of another tradition. However, this acceptance of Hebrew scriptures did not come without a fight. A priest named Marcion (*ca.* 140) developed an early version of the Bible that completely excluded the Hebrew scriptures. Marcion was a dualist, and he sharply distinguished between the god of judgment, punishment, and wrath and the god of mercy, forgiveness, and love. Marcion identified the first god with the Hebrew deity and accordingly rejected Hebrew scriptures. He identified the second god with the Christian deity and therefore created the first New Testament, consisting of an abridged version of the Gospel of Luke and an edited version of Paul's letters. His charismatic movement produced many early martyrs.

Another group of Christians, the group that finally emerged as the victors over rival Christian groups like the Marcionites, accepted the Hebrew scriptures as they were constituted about the end of the first century and fought against Marcion's interpretation of the Christian message. However, they accepted the Hebrew scriptures only as an *old* testament to the acts of God. They claimed that there was now a *new* testament to the acts of God that made the meaning of the old clear. This new interpretation centered on the recognition of a human being named Jesus as a messiah or christ sent by God in the last days before the establishment of God's kingdom.

The New Testament canon contains twenty-seven books—four gospels witnessing the religious significance of the life and death of Jesus the Christ, the Acts of the Apostles who were the first followers of Jesus, twenty-one Letters, and a book called Revelation. The story of how this particular collection came to be is complex and cannot be recounted in much detail here. Suffice it to say that different churches recognized different books as sacred, and out of the vast amount of material and after much struggle and political infighting, a canon was settled on by representatives of those churches that had the most power. The fact that some Syrian churches omit the letters of Second Peter, Second and Third John, Jude, and Revelation testifies to the fact that the canon of the New Testament is not completely fixed. However, the New Testament as it is generally known in Protestant, Roman Catholic, and Eastern Orthodox Christianity became authoritative by the end of the fourth century. This brief history of the formation of the Christian canon demonstrates clearly the way in which scriptures are creations of communities of faith.

Note that all the books included in the New Testament identify human authors. From a Hindu point of view, they would all be *smriti*, not *sruti*. However, in the Gospel of John, Jesus is identified with the *Logos*, the word by which God created the whole universe. Like the Hindu *Vac*, this creative Logos is eternal and cosmic. This idea opened up the possibility of understanding the Bible to be the word of God in a derivative sense. The Logos is the true "Bible" or divine word, and the human Bible testifies to it insofar as its various human authors testify correctly.

Perhaps the constant battles Christians have fought about what writings should be included in the canon and about how best to interpret them arise, in part, because "what is remembered" by human authors can be mistaken. The insistence of some Protestant groups on the dictation theory of revelation, the inerrancy of scripture, and its literal interpretation testifies to the fact that it is always difficult to claim absolute authority for texts written by humans on the basis of what they remember. The notion that God through the Holy Spirit literally dictated the words of scriptures to the human authors, and the claim that what the authors heard was accurately written down is, from the Hindu perspective, an attempt to move a *smriti* text closer to a *sruti* text. However, unlike Hindu notions of *sruti* and the eternal *Vac*, the eternal Logos heard by the authors of the Christian New Testament has a divine source.

The stories of how the scriptures came to be in religions other than Hinduism and Christianity are different. But most, if not all, when viewed from a sociological perspective, constitute stories of conflict, struggles for power, and the creation of communities.

## 12.7 GENDER

We begin with some definitions. First let us take *sexism* to mean discrimination against persons because of their sex, and any ideology that maintains that one sex (be it male or female) is superior to the other. Sexism manifests itself in subtle and not so subtle ways. One of the more obvious ways involves sex roles. Sex roles encompass tasks assigned on the basis of sex, rather than ability. For example, women might be forbidden to be priests in some religion just because they are women, regardless of their abilities to perform successfully in that role.

Another way sexism manifests itself is in concepts of gender. While the word *gender* is often used to refer to biological qualities designated by the terms female and male, it can also be used to refer to the nature of females and males. In this sense, gender refers to concepts of femininity and masculinity. Every society creates concepts of gender—that is, concepts of femininity and masculinity based on some socially constructed notion of the nature of males and females. For example, women might be thought of as nurturing and nonaggressive by nature. These qualities become feminine qualities, and if a female acts contrary to gender stereotyping, she is often thought of as odd or overly masculine. When she is a child, her playmates will often call her a tomboy. Likewise men might be thought of as unemotional and aggressive by nature, and if a male acts contrary to gender expectation, he may be called a sissy. We are all socialized at a very early age to accept the gender ideas of our society uncritically and to engage in gender stereotyping.

I have referred occasionally throughout this book to the relationship be-tween gender and religion. With respect to females, these references have more often than not shown that women have been and still are portrayed in negative ways, especially in patriarchal religions that insist on the superiority of males. The examples of sexist attitudes found among religions that we have noted can, unfortunately, be multiplied by the thousands. This situation is more than unfortunate because such negative notions of females are given di-vine sanction in sacred texts and religious teachings. In other words, the hu-man origin of gender concepts is obscured by claiming this is the way the gods intended things to be. Restricting female opportunities and placing them un-der the dominance of males now becomes not something that humans invented and hence can be changed, but something the divine invented and hence can-not be changed. By obscuring the cultural origin of gender, religious promo-tion of sexist views becomes doubly harmful. If a female wants to be a priest, or a rabbi, or a Quranic scholar, she may be told that such a desire is an affront to God and amounts to sin. Not only does she want something her society does not want her to have; she wants something that God does not want her to have.

In Hinduism, Judaism, Christianity, Buddhism (the list could go on), women are frequently portrayed as sources of pollution, especially during menstruation. In traditional Hinduism, women could not be educated in the Vedas, they were instructed to view their husbands as gods, and to serve their sons with absolute devotion. Traditional Hinduism taught them and still teaches them that their highest goal in life is to marry and give birth to a son. When their husband dies they are to throw themselves on his funeral pyre as a supreme act of devotion. This practice (called *suti*) is no longer legal, but it still sometimes occurs in rural regions and was practiced in India until the nine-teenth century.

In Orthodox Judaism, women were and are forbidden to study Torah, to become rabbis, or to assume any religious roles reserved for males. To this day many Orthodox Jewish men speak this prayer in the morning, "Blessed art thou, O Lord our God, King of the Universe who has not made me a woman." An infamous saying in I Timothy 2:11–15 (a letter attributed to the Apostle Paul but most likely not written by him) set the stage for twenty centuries of the subordination of women in Christianity. The author of Timothy says:

> Let a woman learn in silence with all submissiveness. I permit no woman to
> teach or to have authority over men; she is to keep silent. For Adam was formed
> first, then Eve; and Adam was not deceived, but the woman was deceived and
> became a transgressor. Yet woman will be saved through bearing children, if she
> continues in faith and love and holiness, with modesty.[17]

The gender bias is clear, and the author backs his sexism with his interpreta-tion of Torah, thereby invoking divine sanction for his views.

As we have already seen, some Buddhist groups taught that women could not be enlightened as long as they remained women. Nirvana was possible only after women were reincarnated as men. Buddhist monks had fewer monastic rules to follow than nuns did. Nuns, no matter how old or experienced, were instructed to serve the youngest and newest monks. They were told that they were on the bottom of the monastic hierarchy.

These examples of giving sacred justification for female subordination are not the whole story. The relationship between gender and religion is far more complex than these few examples illustrate. We need to distinguish religion in the texts from religion in the real world. The texts may say one thing, but practices may be quite different. For example, some Southern Baptist women have told sociological interviewers that while the Bible does teach that women should be subordinate to their husbands, this particular teaching does not really apply to them or to their situations.

There is an increasing amount of data on gender and religion, but how to interpret that data is often problematic. For example, in Hinduism, goddesses are worshiped and often given more powers than the many gods. Some Hindu tantric texts assert gender equality and teach the complimentarity of feminine and masculine forces in both the universe and in society.

Reform Judaism, in contrast to the Orthodox variety, encourages women to study Torah and ordains them as rabbis. There is a long and influential tradition in Judaism that emphasizes verse twenty-seven in the first chapter of Genesis and claims it supports gender equality. The verse reads, "So God created humans in his own image, in the image of God he created them; male and female God created them."

As noted above, some scholars maintain that Paul is not the real author of the first letter to Timothy and hence did not pen the sexist words quoted earlier. They certainly seem to be incompatible with what he wrote in Galatians 3:28 about there being "neither Jew nor Greek, . . . neither slave nor free, . . . neither male nor female in Christ." Evidence indicates that women played an active leadership role in the early church, and that Jesus most likely treated both men and women equally. Today many Protestant denominations ordain women, and even in the Roman Catholic Church, women are becoming "pastoral associates." They perform practically every function of a priest except celebrating the mass.

Nancy Schuster Barnes, a Buddhist scholar, maintains that "Doctrinally, Buddhism has been egalitarian from its beginnings. The same teachings were given by the Buddha to his female and male disciples, the same spiritual path was opened to all, the same goal pointed out."[18] She goes on to argue that sometime between 300 B.C.E. and 200 things began to change. Monks challenged the spiritual capacities of women, and male Buddhists made an effort to prove that women were inferior to men.

Still, there have been and are religions in which women serve in leadership positions. There are also religions founded and developed by women. According to Susan Sered, the existence of religions in which women are dominant raise at least two questions.[19] First, how might religions founded by or directed by women be different from male-dominated religions? Second, how might male-dominated religions change as women assume a greater leadership role?

Sered has tried to answer these two questions by collecting data on several groups in which women have dominated in the past or do now dominate the spiritual scene. Among the many groups she studied are ancestral cults among Black Caribs in Belize, matrilineal spirit cults in Thailand, Christian Science, Shakerism, and Korean shamanism.

She selected these groups because they are all dominated by women, there is no discrimination against women with respect to leadership opportunities, members are self-aware that their group is primarily "a women's religion," and there is also awareness that the group is independent of larger, male-dominated religions. She found three sets of factors that, when they combine, are likely to influence the development of women's religions (a religion dominated by females).

The first condition she calls "gender dissonance." This is an experience "in which culturally accepted notions of gender are either highly contradictory and/or rapidly changing."[20] The second condition is that there is a strong and noticeable cultural emphasis on the maternal role. The last condition is the existence of a high degree of personal, economic, and social autonomy or independence for women.

### Three Conditions Influencing the Rise of Women's Religion

1. Gender dissonance
2. Focus on women's maternal roles
3. A high degree of autonomy from men

Women's religions exhibit, according to Sered, three kinds of developments. First, emphasis will be placed on activities and issues that traditionally fall to women as bearers and caretakers of children. Second, explicit attention will be paid to the issue of patriarchy and its effect on women's lives. These two kinds of development are not particularly unexpected. What is unexpected is the third feature of women's religions. Sered found that the effects of gender on the form and content of the religions studied are not all that different from men's religions. Religions, whether dominated by men or women, will "worship supernatural beings, perform rituals of thanks and appeasement, utilize techniques that induce altered states of consciousness, and provide devotees with persuasive explanations for the ultimate conditions of existence."[21]

## Three Characteristics of Women's Religions

1. Focus on women's issues surrounding the role of being mothers
2. Explicit attention to the issue of patriarchy
3. In form and content similar to male-dominated religions

Statistics from the General Social Survey Cumulative File (1972–1996) indicate that women attend religious services more often than men, and women report stronger affiliation to their religious groups than men. For example, 69.9 percent of women report attending religious services more frequently than once a year compared to 58.2 percent for men. In terms of affiliation, 47.2 percent indicate a "strong affiliation" compared to 35.8 percent of men. Such figures lead to the question, why do women invest more time and energy than men in an institution that devalues them?

There is no simple answer to this question, but a careful consideration of more detailed data indicates at least four typical patterns of response by women to male-dominated religious traditions: abandonment, radical transformation, reshaping, and reframing.[22] According to Lori Beaman, the first response ("abandonment") is based on the assumption that no matter how many changes male-dominated religions make, women will always be treated as second-class citizens. Mary Daly argues that "a woman's asking for equality between men and women in the church would be comparable to a black person's demanding equality in the Ku Klux Klan."[23] According to Daly, the Christian church (as well as other patriarchal religions) is inherently patriarchal and can only serve the interests of men. Abandonment does not deny women's spirituality, and Daly encourages women to create spiritual communities more responsive to the needs of women.

So the first answer to the question about women's involvement in patriarchal religions is that many women have abandoned them, and probably more will continue to do so as a wider range of spiritual options becomes available. However, what might those options be?

This question leads to a discussion of the response Beaman calls "radical transformation." This refers to the alternative spiritual communities women have created that are women-centered and nonhierarchical. An example is a religious movement called Wicca—a goddess-centered spirituality. The goddess is recognized as a positive creative power in humans and in nature. At the heart of many types of Wiccan groups is a celebration of life, especially the life of women, along with a strong emphasis on the central role of the "feminine principle" in life processes. This response goes beyond simple abandonment and seriously attempts to provide a spiritual alternative to male-dominated religions.

In both these cases (abandonment and radical transformation), women leave traditional patriarchal religions and strike out on their own spiritual journeys. But what about the women who stay? What do they do?

"Reshaping" refers to the attempt to modify religious organizations and ideology to reflect the equality of women and men. Increasingly, women are assuming leadership roles in male-dominated religions. They are becoming ministers, bishops, and theologians in ever greater numbers. Antoinette Brown, a Congregationalist, was the first woman ordained to the ministry in the United States. That was in 1856, and she opened the way for others. In 1980, 5.6 percent of all clergy were women. By 1990, 11.3 percent of all clergy in the United States were women. About eighty denominations now ordain women. As of 1993, 4 percent of all rabbis were women, and since the Vatican Council, which concluded in 1965, women have been assuming ever greater positions of leadership in the Roman Catholic Church. Women hold nearly half of professional-level staff positions in Catholic dioceses.

While the gains have been slow in coming and there is still a long way to go, it appears many women remain loyal to traditional patriarchal religions in the hopes of reshaping them in the direction of greater equality. However, there is yet a fourth response to traditional male-dominated religions that Beaman calls "reframing." What is that like? Beaman writes:

> *Reframing* involves the reinterpretation of religious teachings or policy that are at first glance oppressive to women. Research on this strategy examines women's involvement in numerous conservative religious groups, including orthodox Judaism, charismatic Catholicism, and evangelical Christianity. It seeks to explain why women accept patriarchal dogma such as the admonition to women to submit to their husbands. Carolyn Peevey and her colleagues argue that many women in fact reframe such dogma in their everyday lives so as to emphasize partnership with their husbands. Such reframing highlights women's agency and autonomy and minimizes men's headship and dominance. Reframing thus involves a reinterpretation of church teachings by women to maximize their equality at an everyday level, and, unlike reshaping, reframing does not involve a struggle for change at a structural level.[24]

Recall the Southern Baptist woman mentioned earlier. She affirmed that she believed what Paul taught about men being the head of the family, but added that she did not think it applied to her because in her marriage she often shared in and even made decisions for the whole family. That is only one of many forms of reframing.

These responses, or "strategies," as Beaman calls them, are not mutually exclusive. There is a fine line between abandonment and radical transformation, and women often engage in both reshaping (changing religious organizations) and reframing (changing the interpretation of religious teachings).

**Female Responses to Patriarchal Religions**

1. Abandonment
2. Radical transformation
3. Reshaping
4. Reframing

If you know women who are involved in conservative forms of Christianity, you might conduct an informal experiment. Ask them what they make of verses like I Timothy 2:11–15, quoted earlier, or I Corinthians 11:3:

> I want you to understand that the head of every man is Christ, the head of a woman is her husband, and the head of Christ is God.

or I Corinthians 11:7–10:

> For a man ought not to cover his head, since he is the image and glory of God; but woman is the glory of man. [For man was not made from woman, but woman from man. Neither was man created for woman, but woman for man.] That is why a woman ought to have a veil on her head.

Knowing that they are deeply involved in conservative forms of Christianity, what would you predict their responses might be? How would you classify their responses given Beaman's typology?

This is only a brief introduction to the complex relationship between gender and religion. It is difficult to know whether cultural or religious factors play a greater role in shaping people's views, but if I might venture a guess, I think the role of women as leaders of the world religions will continue to increase. What do you think?

## 12.8 CIVIL RELIGION

A few years ago, some scholars did a study of a society called Setats Detinu. They were not interested in the many different sects that divided people (called Setatdetinuians, or Nuians for short) who lived in Setats Detinu, but were particularly interested in the religious beliefs that appeared to unify the people and promote social solidarity. They were interested in identifying what the French philosopher Rousseau called civil religion. In his book, *The Social Contract*, Rousseau identified the beliefs of modern forms of civil religion as belief in the existence of God, in the life to come, in the reward of virtue and the punishment of vice, and the exclusion of religious intolerance.

The scholars hypothesized that they would find these same beliefs in Se-tats Detinu (hereafter SD for short), and they further predicted that these beliefs would be so vaguely defined that few of the many different sects could make much objection to them. However, key terms in these beliefs could not be so vague that they were meaningless. For example, the god in which the citizens of SD believed was not any old god or god in general, but a god that took a particular interest in their country, their history, and their destiny. Because religions are more than beliefs, the scholars fully expected to find key ritual and festive events that celebrated the founders, saints, saviors, and martyrs of the civil religion of SD.

One of the first things the scholars noted was that this civil religion had a scripture that originated when the country came into existence. It was called *S.D. Noitutitsnoc,* and another document called *Sthgir Fo Llib* also served a sacred scriptural purpose. The Nuians also had a trained group of specialists who interpreted these scriptures and applied them to contemporary problems and concerns. The people who developed these sacred documents, such as Nosreffej, were called founding fathers (there seemed to be no founding mothers), and one founding father in particular was held in high sacred esteem because he made it possible for SD to come into existence. His name was Notgnihsaw. Monuments to these people can still be seen today.

In talking to the citizens and in reading about the history of SD, the scholars discovered there had been a crisis that almost tore the country apart. One Nuian was pitted against another in bloody battle. The country survived, thanks to the work of a savior named Nlocnil. Monuments to him can also be found to this day, and his birthday, along with Notgnihsaw's, had been widely and reverently celebrated at one time. Today, however, the practice is waning, having been replaced by a sort of generic birthday celebration for all the leaders. This, the scholars noted, paralleled a larger movement toward generics in this society.

Speaking of generics, the scholars noted that on some of their money, the Nuians had inscribed "In God We Trust." Although few interviewees could give a precise definition of this god, some appeared to know that it was the god who called their forefathers out of bondage in another country to conquer, inhabit, and civilize the wild native people that inhabited the country they invaded. This god protected the Nuians, took a special interest in their wars, and told them that he had a special purpose for them. They were to carry the message of freedom around the world and promote something they called ycarcomed. This god had called them to this destiny just as he had called them to conquer the new land. It was, as one informant put it, their "manifest destiny."

There were also yearly festivals or holy days on which rituals were performed celebrating the birth of their nation (called Yluj fo Htruof), giving thanks for the blessings of their god (called Gnivigsknaht), and remembering the holy martyrs who had given their lives in the service of their country and its god (called Yad Lairomem).

I could go on with this description, but by now most of you have probably guessed that I am describing American civil religion. (The names I have created are common words spelled backwards. Thus Setats Detinu is United States, Notgnihsaw is Washington, Yad Lairomem is Memorial Day, and so on.) The sociologist Robert Bellah pioneered the study of American civil religion in a groundbreaking article published in 1967 titled "Civil Religion in America." Many studies have followed and not a little controversy over whether this civil religion should be called a religion and whether it is a good thing or a bad thing.

Bellah argues that American civil religion is a religion because it embodies the idea of transcendence characteristic of most religions. In other words, there is a divine being and a reality that goes beyond (transcends) this earthly reality. He also acknowledges that while the ideology of civil religion has been used and can be used to justify war crimes (such as the genocide practiced on Native Americans and the enslavement of Africans), there are checks and balances that remind people of the dangers inherent in their myths. In other words, Bellah claimed that at times (such as the Civil War), civil religion could be prophetic and hence critical of such practices as slavery.

Martin Marty, a historian and Christian theologian, has called what Bellah dubbed civil religion, the "religion of democracy" or "state Shinto." (See the research case in this chapter.) He claims American civil religion amounts to idolatry because it makes democracy ultimate and religion its "hand-maiden."[25] Every nation has some sort of civil religion, and an interesting question to pursue is whether all civil religions, by their very nature, provide ideologies that justify a nation's history and future.

As studies of American civil religion increase, new evidence is marshaled, definitions are refined, and interpretations improved. We will not follow the ins and outs of that literature here. However, I hope that what I have said will whet your appetite for more. We all should be interested in finding out more about a religion hitherto largely hidden from view that most of us may belong to by virtue of being citizens, be it American civil religion or the civil religion of some other nation.

## 12.9 SUMMARY

Religion is a social phenomenon. Some religious groups are founded, others are not. Groups are formed around common goals and an agreed upon set of norms that provide roles (such as priest), assign status distribution (clergy/laity), and create group identity. In order to function successfully, groups must find ways of adding new members (recruitment and reproduction), of socializing members, of creating a satisfactory level of goods and services, of preserving order, and of maintaining a sense of common purpose.

We examined two cases: Tibetan Buddhism and the Peoples Temple. After providing historical context and background information, we focused on the institution of the monastery and the mass suicide in Jonestown.

The Tibetan identity as a spiritual people is manifested, the Tibetans believe, in monastic institutions. Different monastic traditions have different histories, and their power varies. Identifying reborn lamas is a way of reinforcing and validating the truth of Buddhism. The Gelup lineage gained state power along with spiritual power, and Tibet was a kind of theocracy until the Chinese communist invasion. Today the Chinese government is encouraging the lineages to abandon the quest for political power and to concentrate on spiritual power alone. The future of Buddhism in Tibet may well rest on the ability to make this shift. Outside Tibet, the exiled community is flourishing and keeping alive the hope that someday there will be a return to an independent Tibetan nation.

While we do not have a full explanation of the mass suicide in Jonestown, scholars of religion can provide better explanations than the popular press. We noted such factors as millenarian beliefs, a dualistic ideology, and growing alienation from mainstream Christianity and the larger American society that led to the tragic end of this new religious movement. In the end, when their boundaries were violated by outside investigators, the members of the group felt trapped, and their hostility toward defectors and others was turned into self-destruction.

The five functional prerequisites of group life organize our comparison of these two cases. The monasteries of Tibet had to rely on recruitment to continue, and the Peoples Temple had to rely on recruitment to get off the ground. Reproduction played a role in Tibetan society as a whole (but not among the monks and nuns) to increase numbers, and it played a similar role in the Peoples Temple. However, this new religious movement did not last long enough for a new generation to take over leadership positions and further refine the ideology and practices.

Socialization processes in both cases involved education. In the case of Tibetan monks, vows of renunciation served to bind people to the group, and a renunciation of the larger American society and its capitalistic ideology, along with the teaching of apostolic socialism, helped to socialize the members of the Peoples Temple.

Providing goods and services includes the satisfaction of both economic requirements and emotional needs. Money in the Tibetan monasteries is not distributed according to need, but according to work. In the Peoples Temple, resources were allocated according to need. On the emotional level, both Tibetan monastic Buddhism and the Peoples Temple managed to create and sustain groups whose members shared a common purpose. The future of monastic Tibetan Buddhism appears to depend on its ability to sustain emotional satisfaction as it shifts focus to spiritual, not political goals. Even at the end and in the face of pending mass suicide, most members of the Peoples Temple seem to have continued their belief in a common goal that if not achieved in this life, would be achieved in the next life.

Order was preserved in Tibet's monasteries by traditional rules and regulations governing monastic life enforced by a hierarchical structure. The Peoples Temple seems to have been egalitarian in its ideals, but hierarchical in structure. There was a stronger democratic element in the Peoples Temple than in Tibetan Buddhism.

Our cases reveal that the Peoples Temple was able to keep alive a common purpose, perhaps with the help of strong beliefs about a life after death in which their work could still be carried out. Tibetan Buddhism is facing a crisis of purpose today. With the communists insisting that there can no longer be a political purpose for Tibetan Buddhism but only a spiritual one, much depends on the success with which this reduction of purpose can be brought about. The exile community, however, still keeps political hopes alive for a free Tibet.

We divided religious organizations into two broad types: natural and voluntary. While voluntary organizations require personal commitment, in natural organizations someone is a member by virtue of being born into a clan, tribe, or nation.

We examined the church-sect continuum by emphasizing the traits of accepting or rejecting the larger societies. Sects tend to reject the larger society, and church-type organizations tend to be more accepting. In the middle, we located denominational organizations that unify different congregations under a common umbrella. New religious movements, or cults, as some would call them, tend to be on the rejecting end of the scale, but often differ from sects insofar as they do not originate in schisms.

We discussed Weber's notion of the routinization of charisma and used the story of the Grand Inquisitor to illustrate the five dilemmas that result from successful growth: mixed motivation, symbolic, administrative order, delimitation, and power. As religious groups attract new members and as their ranks swell, it is inevitable that organizational complexity increases. Eventually, keeping the organization going becomes crucial.

If we focus on religious leadership, we can distinguish three types of religious authority: charismatic, traditional, and legal-rational. It is possible that one person enjoys all three types of authority.

Scripture is a social event. It is created by communities and for communities. The Hindu canon is divided into two types of scripture: *sruti* (what is heard) and *smriti* (what is remembered). *Sruti* scriptures like the Vedas have no human or divine authors, while *smriti* scriptures such as the Ramayana have human authors. Christianity created a canon consisting of an Old Testament and a New Testament. The Old Testament is an adaptation of Jewish scriptures. While all of the books in the Christian Bible have human authors, Christians believe that these authors were inspired by the Logos, or eternal word of God. There is no single agreed upon theory of inspiration, although the so-called dictation theory is popular with conservative groups. Although the Vedas have neither a divine nor human author, they record the eternal *Vac*, or creative sound of the universe, much like Christian scriptures are thought to bear witness to the Logos.

In Section 12.7 we turned our attention to issues of gender. After defining sexism and gender, we examined cases of sexism found in Hinduism, Judaism, Christianity, and Buddhism. A distinction between religion in the texts and religion in the real world allowed us to see that the relationship between religion and gender is complex. Though there are differences between male-dominated religions and female-dominated religions, there are also similarities in teaching and practices. When three factors come together (gender dissonance, emphasis on the maternal role, and a high degree of female autonomy), female-dominated religions flourish. Women's response to patriarchal religions ranges from abandonment and radical transformation to reshaping and reframing.

We developed the notion of civil religion by a fanciful scholarly study of a country called Setats Detinu (United States). We discovered that this civil religion had founders (Jefferson, Washington), saviors (Lincoln), martyrs (soldiers who died in war), and heroes (founding fathers). There are scriptures (Constitution, Bill of Rights), and specialized interpreters (Supreme Court and lower judicial systems) who apply and make sense of this scripture. Basic beliefs center on the existence of God, life after death, reward for virtue and punishment for vice, and the rejection of religious intolerance. The basic ideology centers on the special status of the United States (its history and destiny) and its values of freedom and democracy. While Robert Bellah sees prophetic possibilities in civil religion, Martin Marty labels it little more than "state Shinto."


## 12.10 RESEARCH CASE—SHINTO

[At one time] the Sun Goddess [shocked by the misdeeds of her brother, Valiant Male Kami], opened the heavenly rock-cave door and concealed herself inside. Then the Plain of High Heaven became completely dark, and all manner of calamities arose.

Then the 800 myriads of kami gathered in a divine assembly, and summoned Kami of the Little Roof in Heaven and Kami of the Grand Bead to perform a divination. They hung long strings of myriad curved beads on the upper branches of a sacred tree, and hung a large-dimensioned mirror on its middle branches . . . Kami of Heavenly Strength . . . stamped on an overturned bucket which was placed before the rock-cave. Then she became kami-possessed, exposed her breasts and genitals. Thereupon the 800 myriads of kami laughed so hard that the Plain of High Heaven shook with their laughter.

The Sun Goddess, intrigued by all this, opened the rock-cave door slightly . . . Then Kami of Heavenly Headgear said, "There is a kami nobler than you, and that is why we are happy and dancing." While she was speaking thus, Kami of the Little Roof and Kami of the Grand Bead showed the mirror to the Sun Goddess. Thereupon, the Sun Goddess, thinking this ever so strange, gradually came out of the cave, and hidden Kami of Grand Bead took her hand and pulled her out. Then as the sun Goddess reappeared, the Plain of High Heaven was naturally illuminated.[26]

This ancient myth of Japan needs to be put in context. It is from the *Kojiki*, which was first put together in 712. The *Kojiki*, along with the *Nihongi* (720), constitute two of the most highly revered books of Shinto. I say "highly revered" because Shinto has no official scripture. The major theme of the *Kojiki* is the origin of kingship. Book One contains a creation myth. According to this account, Japan originates through the activity of two married kami, Izanagi and Izanami, who are descendents of the first five heavenly kami. Izanagi and Izanami also create many other kami. The Kami of Fire kills Izanami, and her husband descends to the underworld to find her. When Izanagi returns to earth, he needs to be purified, and the result is the birth of Amaterasu, the Sun Goddess mentioned in the story. She is the ancestor of the imperial family of Japan, and Book Two recounts the story of how her great-grandson becomes the first emperor of Japan. In this way the imperial line is placed in a context that goes all the way back to the sacred beginning of Japan.

Literature on Japanese religion usually describes Shinto ("shin-toh") as the native religion of Japan. It has no founder and arose spontaneously out of people's response to the forces of nature that were called kami ("kah-mee"). This description is partly true, but in fact there is no name for the ancient religion of Japan because it was so intermixed with the culture that no name was needed. Without a name, it was not even singled out as a religion. It was part of everyday life. The name Shinto, which means the "way of the kami," came about when Buddhist missionaries from China brought the "way of the Buddha" to Japan. Only when this happened did the need for a name for the indigenous "religion" of Japan arise. Interestingly, the Japanese *to* is derived from the Chinese *dao* (the way of nature celebrated in Daoism—see Chapter 4).

The word *kami* is often translated into English as "god." This too is misleading. Kami are sacred and hence possess extraordinary powers that pervade everything in heaven, earth, and the underworld. They are associated with the sun, thunder, rain, wind, animals, ancestors, and great people such as the emperors. In ancient Japan the word *kami* is used as an adjective, not a noun, to designate anything mysterious, superhuman, or sacred. In other words, kami are any power deemed worthy of worship and to whom prayers and offerings can be made because they have some sort of power over human affairs.

Scholars today distinguish many different kinds of Shinto, including Folk or Popular Shinto, Domestic or Home Shinto, Sect Shinto, State Shinto, Imperial Household Shinto, and Shrine Shinto. Shinto exhibits great variety, and the use of one word to refer to this variety should not fool us into thinking that there is only one kind of Shinto.

*Popular Shinto* refers to the kind of Shinto practiced in the everyday life of the Japanese people, and *Domestic Shinto* refers to the practices that center on the home altar. *Sect Shinto* is the name for a number of different splinter groups that became independent religious organizations. In pre–World War II Japan, there were thirteen official sects.

*State Shinto* was banned in 1945 by the new constitution that Japan had to accept as part of the conditions of surrender to the American occupying forces. It was mandated because many believed that State Shinto promoted the worship of the Japanese nation and the emperor, which in turn supported the military regime that led Japan into World War II. *Imperial Household Shinto* refers to rites conducted at the three shrines within the palace grounds. These shrines are for the exclusive use of the imperial family. *Shrine Shinto* is the most prevalent type of kami-based faith and, as the name implies, indicates the ritual practices conducted at the many Shinto shrines throughout the country.

Seasonal festivals are celebrated at local shrines, and they typically have something to do with agriculture, the primary financial base of the countryside (although this is changing as Japan becomes ever more urban). Also, priests conduct worship services at the local shrines, which typically consist of purification rites, an offering to the kami, prayer, and a symbolic feast. Usually, purification of pollution and evil is accomplished by individual worshipers symbolically rinsing the mouth and pouring clear water over the fingertips. The minimum requirement for worshiping the kami is periodic presentation of offerings. Many believe that the kami and particularly the ancestral spirits will be unhappy and bring misfortune if a devotee fails to observe this duty. As a rule the formal prayers recited by the priest open with words of praise for the kami and include petitions for favors, thanksgiving, a recitation of gifts offered, and the status and name of the priest. They usually close with words of awe and respect. At the end of a worship service, ceremony (like a wedding), or festival there is a sacred feast (often symbolic) called the *naorai*, which means "to eat together with the kami."

Our discussion will concentrate mostly on State and Shrine Shinto. However, we do need some general knowledge of the historical development of Shinto. No religious faith stands still. It is dynamic and changing, filled with new developments, interpretations, literature, rites, and much more.

During the early period, reverence for the forces of nature and shamanistic practices were widespread. Nature kami, both male and female, abounded. There were no shrine or temple structures, but different areas in nature were sites of religious practice. Many of the shamans were female, and they often interpreted the will of the kami for the people. Today, girls serve as ceremonial assistants to male priests.

Two centuries before the Heian period (794–1185), Chinese culture and religious practices entered Japan. During this period Confucian family values, Daoist views on living in harmony with nature, and Buddhist beliefs and practices became mixed with Shinto so closely that it became almost impossible to separate them.

The Kamakura period (1185–1333) saw struggles for political power emerge among the *shoguns* (regional rulers) as the power of the royal court weakened. Political instability and the struggles of this feudal age made eschatological forms of Buddhism attractive. People came to believe that they were living in the end times and the world would soon end with a great catastrophe.

The Tokugawa period 1600–1868 saw the emergence of a strong central government emphasizing the need for peace, law, and order. During this period several different religious trends developed. The ritual practice of the imperial court, which maintained a formal schedule of complex rituals honoring both the buddhas and the kami, became increasingly important. Both Shinto and Buddhist priests serviced many of the shrines, and hence the shrines became both Shinto and Buddhist places of worship.

During the Meiji period Japan developed into a modern nation-state. A constitutional government was created with the emperor as its head. It provided for a legislature and the separation of religion and the state. A new capital was founded in Tokyo, and a formal tax system was established. This period is usually called the Meiji Restoration because the leadership of Japan wanted to restore both imperial rule and a purified Shinto. Tax money was used to support Shinto shrines, and Shinto became the official "religion" of the Japanese nation. There was an intensified campaign against Buddhism, and the government decreed that Buddhist statues and priests had to be removed from Shinto shrines.

However, Buddhism was so entrenched in Japanese culture that this purification effort failed to be totally effective. Between 1872 and 1875 the government had a Department of Religion that included both Buddhism and Shinto. In 1882 the government formally recognized State Shinto, and to get around the part of the constitution that recognized the separation of religion and the state, the government proclaimed that legally State Shinto was not a religion. Shinto was now described as the embodiment of the values and traditional institutions of the Japanese people. In creating State Shinto and proclaiming that it was not a religion, the government had to create Sect Shinto as a religion. The government did this by setting the official number of sects at thirteen. These sects were not supported with tax money. Thus the illusion was created that religion and the state were officially separate.

In one sense this was not an illusion. The government-supported State Shinto bore little resemblance to traditional Shinto. Because of the word *restoration*, many people both inside and outside Japan have been convinced that the official Shinto of the Meiji period was simply a continuation of past practices and beliefs. This is not so. State Shinto supported patriotism to the nation as represented by the emperor, who was proclaimed chief priest. During most of the previous history of Shinto, Japan was not a nation-state. It had no central national government, and various clans governed the provinces. The allegiance of the people was more to their clans and local villages than to a centralized government.

Shrine Shinto was completely transformed by these new developments. The state underwrote the construction of new shrines, promoted the cult of the kami of the Ise shrine as the highest ancestors, and created a cult of the war dead associated with the ritual activities of various shrines. The effect on popular Shinto by this massive state intervention was immense. It produced a unified institutional and symbolic system where there had been only localized and diverse cultic life at largely independent shrines.

Helen Hardacre, author of one of the best books on State Shinto, argues:

> The creation of even the semblance of a comprehensive, national organization for Shinto dates to 1900. Before that the worship of its deities, the kami, was carried out on a localized basis, and its priests were organized not in a national priesthood . . . but in independent sacerdotal lineages managed by a small number of large shrines . . . or by purely local arrangement and on a rotating basis among male members of the community. Thus in an institutional sense, Shinto has no legitimate claim to antiquity as Japan's "indigenous religion," however frequently the claim is made.[27]

Some people are under the impression that Shinto was a key player in the growing militaristic state, and that it bears major responsibility for promoting the nationalistic and patriotic values and attitudes that eventually led to the Second World War. This is not the case. The military power that came to control the government used Shinto to promote its imperialistic ambitions. However, it must be noted that practically all of the religious traditions in Japan supported the war effort. The Shinto priests of the various local shrines offered no objections. Sect Shinto offered no objections, nor did the various Buddhist sects.

Hardacre remarks:

> the creation of a cult of the war dead . . . tapped Japan's oldest and most affectively laden area of religious life, the cult of the dead and the ancestors. The people sought religious explanations for the multitudinous deaths in war of Japa-

nese youth. Officiating at public memorial rites, Shinto priests . . . inevitably affirmed and glorified Japan's wars. Thus it was not that Shinto itself became an "engine of war," . . . but that it idealized as the highest good a role as the state's obedient servant. And its greatest service to the state has concerned memorialization of the war dead.[28]

After Japan surrendered to the Allies in 1945, American soldiers occupied Japan. A military government was set up, but one of its purposes was to create a new democratic constitution and return home rule as soon as possible. The separation of "church and state" was an important part of this new constitution. However, the provisional, occupying government of Japan understood religion to be something like a church, and so, in adopting the idea of the separation of church and state, they were not sufficiently sensitive to the Japanese religious scene. The Japanese interpreted the idea of separation to mean the cessation of using public money to support the various Shinto shrines and sects (an interpretation approved by the occupying forces), but what should be done when other circumstances arose?

On January 7, 1989, Emperor Hirohito died. Normally, Crown Prince Akihito would be enthroned the next day. But this ceremony was delayed until 1990 while debates raged about how Article 89 of the Japanese constitution should be interpreted. That article explicitly states that "no public money or other property shall be expended . . . for benefit or maintenance of any religious institution or association." Article 89 would appear to prohibit funding for the traditional Shinto enthronement ceremony. There was no purely secular ceremony to mark royal succession. A solution was reached when the government cleverly divided the occasion into a religious part that was paid for out of the royal family funds and a public secular ceremony funded out of the public purse. So the public enthronement ceremony got state support, but the "Daijosai" rite did not. The Daijosai is the occasion when the new emperor assumes spiritual power by spending part of the night in a Shinto shrine. Though the Daijosai was funded out of the imperial court budget, we might wonder whether these careful distinctions between secular and sacred made any real difference since the court budget comes from public funds.

In postwar Japan the political culture has become more pluralistic, and there have been a number of protests against the state's past and present attempts to control Shinto and manipulate religion in support of the interests of the state. The Union of New Religions has been one voice in opposing any state support of Shinto. Shrine Shinto has had to make it on its own without state support, and the lack of state support has not destroyed it, as many predicted. In 1946 the Association of Shinto Shrines was founded. It invited all the local shrines to affiliate, and most of them did. The association is administered by a board of councilors, composed of representatives from forty-six regional associations. The association has six departments, which provide a number of services to member shrines including mutual aid, teaching, and research. This association is closely connected with Kokugakuin University, which is the only Shinto institution of higher education in Japan. In sociological terms, Shrine Shinto reinvented itself as a denomination.

On the local level, priests and committees made up of representatives of the worshipers manage the shrines. Usually they are incorporated, own their own land and buildings, and raise their own funds. Also, many new religions have developed in postwar Japan that mix elements from various sources and help fill the shelves of the new religious marketplace that has taken root after state support ceased. Religiously Japan is now a free market.

## QUESTIONS ON THE CASE OF SHINTO

1. Is Shinto a civil religion in Bellah's sense of the term? If you cannot decide, what further information would you need to settle the issue?
2. Write a three-paragraph interpretation of the meaning of the myth of the Sun Goddess that opened the case. Compare your interpretation with another student's and discuss the differences.
3. Given the fact that goddesses have been and are worshiped in Shinto, that in the early period many shamans were females, and that in recent times the priesthood has been reserved for males, would you say Shinto is sexist or not? What further information would you need to settle the issue?
4. In what ways do you think Shinto functions to provide meaning and purpose to the lives of the Japanese? In your answer, be sure to note the different kinds of Shinto and how they might function to provide meaning and purpose.
5. Do you think the Allies were right to insist that State Shinto be abandoned? In general, do you think conquerors have the right to change the religion of the countries they conquer? Why or why not?

## SUGGESTIONS FOR FURTHER READING

In addition to the material found in the notes, readers may wish to consult the following for more information.

Bellah, Robert. "Civil Religion in America." *Daedalus*, 96 (Winter 1967). In this journal, published by the American Academy of Arts and Sciences, Bellah explains his understanding of American civil religion and presents the evidence that supports his claims.
———. *Tokugawa Religion: The Values of Pre-Industrial Japan.* Glencoe, IL: The Free Press, 1957. A classic sociological study of Tokugawa Shinto. The problem Bellah sets for himself is to answer the question, "was there a functional analogue to the Protestant ethic in Japanese religion?"

Boyarin, Daniel. "Gender." In *Critical Terms for Religious Studies*, edited by Mark C. Tylor, 117–135. Chicago: University of Chicago Press, 1998. Boyarin presents a study of the concept of gender in relationship to religion that summarizes and integrates a number of different theories.

Carmody, Denise. *Women and World Religions*. Nashville: Abingdon, 1979. Carmody synthesizes a lot of information from around the world into a readable book. The student is also directed to an ongoing series edited by Arvind Sharma and Katherine K. Young, called *The Annual Review of Women in World Religions*, published by the State University Press of New York.

Chidester, David. *Salvation and Suicide: An Interpretation of Jim Jones, the Peoples Temple, and Jonestown*. Bloomington: Indiana University Press, 1991. This well-written and detailed account is sympathetic (some would say too sympathetic).

Coward, Harold, ed. *Experiencing Scripture in World Religions*. Maryknoll, NY: Orbis Books, 2000. This helpful collection of essays focuses on the role of scripture in Judaism, Christianity, Islam, Hinduism, Sikhism, and Buddhism.

Goldstein, Melvyn C., and Matthew T. Kapstein, eds. *Buddhism in Contemporary Tibet: Religious Revival and Cultural Identity*. Berkeley: University of California Press, 1998. This collection of essays provides a wealth of information on what is going on today with respect to religion in Tibet.

Hamilton, Malcolm. *Sociology and the World's Religions*. New York: St. Martin's Press, 1998. This book brings together and summarizes a vast range of sociological research on both tribal and world religions.

Lopez, Donald S., Jr. *Prisoners of Shangri-La: Tibetan Buddhism and the West*. Chicago: University of Chicago Press, 1998. Lopez focuses on the myths created by Western culture about Tibet that either romanticize it or demonize it. He argues for a more balanced and realistic view.

Mills, Jeanne. *Six Years with God: Life Inside Rev. Jim Jones's Peoples Temple*. New York: A & W Publishers, 1979. This critical account is by a one-time insider. It details the manipulation that caused some people to substitute self-sacrifice for self-esteem.

Nelson, John K. *A Year in the Life of a Shinto Shrine*. Seattle: University of Washington Press, 1996. This study provides detailed information on what goes on in a Shinto Shrine during a one-year cycle.

Ono, Sokyo. *Shinto: The Kami Way*. Rutland, VT: Charles E. Tuttle, 1962. This book provides a brief overview of Shinto by a former professor at Kokugakuin University, which is closely connected to the Association of Shinto Shrines. It has apologetic undertones but provides a good example of Shinto's self-understanding today and valuable information from a well-educated insider's point of view.

Powers, John. *Introduction to Tibetan Buddhism*. Ithaca, NY: Snow Lion Publications, 1995. Powers discusses the Indian background, Tibetan history and culture, doctrines and practices, and the various schools of Tibetan Buddhism in a clear and sympathetic way.

Reader, Ian. *Religion in Contemporary Japan*. Honolulu: University of Hawaii Press, 1991. The goal of this book is to provide an account of the ways in which religious themes find their way into the lives of the Japanese people. The focus is on religion "at the ground level."

Roberts, Keith M. *Religion in Sociological Perspective.* 2nd ed. Belmont, CA: Wadsworth, 1990. This introductory textbook covers many traditional topics in the sociology of religion along with summaries of empirical research.

Willis, Janice, ed. *Feminine Ground: Essays on Women and Tibet.* Ithaca, NY: Snow Lion Publications, 1987. This collection of essays by different authors provides important information about women in contemporary Tibet.

## INTERNET RESOURCES

http://www-rohan.sdsu.edu/~remoore/jonestown   This site about Jonestown is sponsored by the Department of Religious Studies at San Diego State University. It provides pictures, articles, archival material, three different versions of the so-called Death Tape, and much more. You will also find a link to the New Religious Movements Web site at the University of Virginia.

http://dir.yahoo.com/society_and_culture/religion_and_spirituality/ You will find many links to information about religion at this Yahoo site. Click on "Sociology of Religion" for links to sites providing information about the social scientific approach to the study of religion. Type in "Tibetan Buddhism" for links to Web information on that religion. Also type in "Shinto" for links to additional information on Shinto. Some of these sites represent an outsider's perspective, and some represent an insider's perspective. See if you can tell the difference. Note the sorts of things you looked for in order to make this distinction.

# PART III

# Postliminaries

## CHAPTER 13

# Religious Diversity
# and Truth

W E EMERGE FROM liminality. We are no longer in the threshold; we have crossed the threshold and entered a new world. Why a *new* world? Presumably we know more about religion now than we did before. We also may think differently about religion than we did before. We have acquired new skills, new ways of thinking, new ideas, and learned about new approaches to the study of religion.

I hope this book has answered many of your questions about different religious beliefs and practices. But I am sure it has left you (I know it has left me) with even more questions. Some of these may have to do with religious conflict and rivalry. Some questions may concern how the various religions might be related. Other questions may have to do with religious truth. We need to pay attention to what Mark Twain half humorously and half seriously said in *Letters from Earth:* "Man is the only animal that has a True Religion—several of them."

People who study comparative religions experience what some have called "the shock of recognition."[1] They discover similarities between their own religion and other religions. It seems that in some sense religions are not all that different. We recognize ourselves in what others believe and do. So are all religions equally effective paths to salvation?

Recognition of similarities is often accompanied by "the shock of difference."[2] There is no denying religious diversity. After our initiation into the academic study of religion, we can see that the often-repeated judgment that "all religions are the same" is too superficial given the evidence. Also, it is not fair to others or to ourselves to pronounce all religions the same and to act as if religious differences were not real differences or not very important. What are we to make of this situation? Can all religions be true if real differences separate them?

In this concluding chapter, we will tackle some of these questions. We will explore some of the reasons for religious conflict and competition. We will examine some of the many ways we have been socialized to think about the relationships among religions, and we will examine the question of religious truth. We will also return to the topic of religious tolerance introduced in the first chapter. And we will extend our abilities to understand and interpret religion by looking at the case of a relatively recent religious development called Baha'i. Baha'i advocates religious harmony and peace. What compels it to do so? Why does this message arise at this time in history?

## 13.1 WHY CAN'T WE ALL GET ALONG?

Rodney King asked the above question with respect to race relations, and we can ask it with respect to the relationships among and within religions. Why have religious wars been fought? Why have tens of millions of people been slaughtered in the name of some god? Why does such religiously inspired carnage continue?

Religious conflict is caused by many factors, including nationalistic expansionism, economic inequities, political instability, and long-standing ethnic hatred and prejudice. However, there is no denying that religious beliefs and prejudices have played and continue to play a major role in human conflict. There is the Catholic-Protestant guerrilla war in Northern Ireland, where, as of this writing, attempts at peace appear to have broken down once more. There is the Palestinian and Israeli conflict in the Eastern Mediterranean, where, although not all Palestinians are Muslim and not all Israelis are devoted Jews, religious factors are involved. In the former Yugoslavia, the Christian (Eastern Orthodox) Serbs have murdered their Muslim neighbors under the banner of "ethnic cleansing." We can grant that the political ambitions of Slobodan Milosevic were a key factor in this conflict, but that does not mean that religious tensions did not contribute to the sickening slaughter. The Nazis were far from Christian in their ideology, but most of gentile Germany was either Catholic or Protestant, and in spite of Jesus' admonition to love your neighbor, many of them proceeded to cooperate in and support the mass extermination of Jews. Now various groups seek to cloak their terrorism in terms of a Muslim/Judeo-Christian holy war.

A sociological theory, called *conflict theory*, postulates that conflict arises in cases of power differences. In other words, conflict between and within groups amounts to a struggle for power, wealth, prestige, and privilege. Religions are in competition. The more religions there are, and the more religions are forced by historical, political, economic, and geographical factors to interact, the more likely it is, according to conflict theory, that they will fight (often violently and viciously) over power, wealth, prestige, and privilege.

Conflict arises out of other sources besides the competition for power and influence. Conflict often stems from a sense of threat. The Peace of Westphalia in 1648 brought to a close thirty years of religious and political conflict among Christians. According to some estimates, the population of Europe was reduced from 16 million to less than 6 million due to war, disease, and economic collapse brought about by thirty years of religious warfare among Protestant and Catholic Christians.

In order to try to end the fighting, a policy called **secularization** was introduced. At that time, it was a name for the process of transferring lands and possessions from religious control to civil control. Since that time, the word has been used in a variety of different ways. One way it is used suggests that secularization marks a gradual process of the loss of social and public influence of religious organizations in the modern and postmodern age. Another way suggests that secularization marks a change in traditional religious patterns that involves the increased privatization of religious choice and commitment.

Although scholars disagree about whether secularization marks a decline of religion or a change, most do agree that the sources of secularization can be identified as an increased reliance on human reason as the judge of truth that characterized the modern age and the expansion of scientific modes of thought. And the postmodern age has called into question the presumably unbiased and objective character of human reason by showing that it is tainted by political, economic, and sexist agendas as well as the modern inclination to trust science and technology to solve all problems.

If modernism threatens religion by its elevation of science and human reason to the throne of power and judgment, postmodernism also threatens it by questioning whether there exists any final, absolute, and objective standard of judgment. Historically, at least in many religions, the divine was granted the role of final judge; not only the final judge, but the absolutely objective judge of what is true and what is false. It now appears that this so-called objective judge may be little more than a partisan of the religion that claims power in the name of the divine. The threat to traditional religion is real, and the natural human reaction to threat is to become defensive. So reactionary fundamentalist movements crisscross the landscape of our time, indicating their willingness to fight, even to kill, to preserve what they take to be the traditional and divinely ordained order of things.

The perceived threat of secularization and postmodernism to traditional religious power leaves many ready to fight. As we come into closer contact with cultures and religions very different from our own, we become even more defensive. We live in an age of increased diversity and increased contact between different cultures and religions. By some counts, 2 million Muslims have migrated to the United States. There are now fifty Muslim mosques in Chicago alone. Approximately 100,000 Sikhs live in Toronto. Christianity has spread to the most remote corners of the world. We live in a global religious village. Diane Eck, chair of the Pluralism Project at Harvard University, writes:

> It is precisely the interpenetration and proximity of ancient civilizations and cultures that is the hallmark of the late twentieth century. This is the new geo-religious reality. The map of the world in which we now live cannot be color-coded as to its Christian, Muslim, Hindu identity: each part of the world is marbled with the colors and textures of the whole.[3]

There is not only a geo-religious global community in the making, but also a massive economic globalization occurring in which multinational corporations control one-third of the world's wealth, handle 70 percent of its trade, and fan out in all directions seeking cheap labor. As massive wealth accumulates in the hands of a few, the gap between rich and poor increases. This gap transcends national boundaries, and the poor of New York join the poor of Southeast Asia. Population growth is out of control, the environment is deteriorating at an increasingly rapid rate, and religions appear not only unable to do anything to stop the massive exploitation of people and the environment, but also increasingly defensive and threatened by processes that seem to be beyond anyone's control.

Although we cannot divorce religious developments from this larger setting, we must return our focus to religious conflict. Will this increasing proximity of diverse religions create a climate in which religious conflict will increase? Or will it slowly begin to dawn on people that even if there are many reasons why we cannot get along, we have little choice but to try.

## 13.2 EXCLUSIVISM, INCLUSIVISM, AND MORE

If we lived in a world in which there was only one religion, the question of how the different religions might be related, or which, if any, are true, simply would not arise. If we lived in a world in which religions did not recommend different paths to salvation, promote differing views of reality, and, in some cases, condemn rivals as immoral, demonic, and heretical, we might assume that religious cooperation would replace religious conflict. We do not live in such a world. We live in a world in which some religions have claimed to be the only ones that are true. Not all religions have claimed this, and different elements within religions have held different positions at different times, but the claim to exclusivity in matters of faith is common enough that it deserves a closer look.

## 13.2.1 Exclusivism

In its extreme form, **exclusivism** is the position that one religion is true both in the sense of teaching the truth about ultimate reality and in the sense of providing the only valid way to salvation. Because it would be very odd if not illogical to claim there is one true religion and it is *not* their own, people who support exclusivism mean that their own religion is the only one that is true. It follows that all other religions are false, and the people who profess them are destined for a bad end.

Although some people think that exclusivism is both a natural and logical position to assume when thinking about the different world religions in the context of a concern about truth, it is not. Some religions that focus on worshiping the spirits of nature and the ancestors of their tribe or clan need not be (and often are not) exclusivistic. Just as different people can have different ancestors, so different religions can worship different spirits. A polytheism that recognizes many different gods need not be exclusivistic. Neither is henotheism necessarily exclusivistic because while people may believe that they are obligated to worship one of the many gods, other people have no such obligation. Even monotheism need not be exclusivistic, at least with respect to other monotheistic religions. The Quran recognizes all true believers in one divine being as religiously correct, whether or not they are Muslims.

Within Christianity exclusivism has not always reigned supreme, but Christianity in much of its history has tended toward exclusivism. The reasons for Christian exclusivism are both historical and theological. There were, as we have seen, many different early groups claiming to follow the way of Jesus the Christ. As the new religious movement that was eventually designated by the name Christianity developed into a successful missionary movement, it had to face the dilemmas of institutionalization discussed in Chapter 12. What was unique about its message? Why should someone abandon his or her traditional religious beliefs and practices to join this new way? Why is the Christian conception of the divine better than other conceptions?

We can add to all of the above the political pressures that arose once Christianity became the state religion of the Roman Empire. The Emperor expected this new religion to provide a clear, unified, and distinctive message that would support the unity of the empire. So, what is distinctive about the Christian message? Different Christian groups fought bitterly over the answer to this question, and the turning point came at the Councils of Nicea and Chalcedon. Participants at these councils had to answer the question, "Is Jesus one of many different manifestations of the divine, or is Jesus the one and only unique incarnation of the divine?" The faction supporting uniqueness won the day. So bishops meeting at Chalcedon proclaimed that to be a true Christian and to be saved, one must recognize that "Jesus of Nazareth is unique in the precise sense that while being fully man, it is true of him and him alone, that he is also fully God."[4] As a result, those Christians who think that there is one and only one incarnation of the divine, and it is Jesus of Nazareth, feel obligated to reject the idea of multiple incarnations. The Hindu notion that Krishna, Rama, Jesus, and others are all incarnations of the divine, for example, becomes incompatible with Christian teaching. If we assume that only one religion can be true, then either the Christians are right or the Hindus are right. There can be no middle ground.

It appears to be a short step from exclusivism to religious intolerance, contempt for the religious practices of others, self-righteous pride, and a refusal to engage in serious dialogue with those of other faiths. Preaching for purposes of conversion is preferred over dialogue. Such things as intolerance, contempt, unjustified pride, and disrespect for others raise serious questions about the morality of exclusivism. It is easy to see how exclusivism can promote or at least support religious conflict. It is also easy to see how such a position leads to suspicion and skepticism on the part of others concerning any and all exclusivistic claims. As the philosopher and theologian John Hick remarked:

> However, a "hermeneutic of suspicion" is provoked by the evident fact that in perhaps 99 percent of cases the religion to which one adheres (or against which one reacts) is selected by the accident of birth. Someone born to devout Muslim parents in Iran or Indonesia is very likely to be a Muslim; someone born to devout Buddhist parents in Thailand or Shri Lanka is very likely to be a Buddhist; someone born to devout Christian parents in Italy or Mexico is very likely to be a Catholic Christian; and so on.[5]

It seems to be arbitrary for people to claim that the particular religion into which they happen to be born is the one and only true religion. Why has God seen fit to bless them with the saving truth by accident of birth while excluding the majority of the human race from such a blessing?

Exclusivism need not, however, be either immoral or irrationally arbitrary. Alvin Plantinga, a Christian philosopher, argues that religious exclusivism is not necessarily responsible for immoral attitudes toward others, nor is it necessarily guilty of any faulty reasoning.[6] In response to the charge that there is something morally suspect about religious exclusivism, he replies that people would not be immoral *just because* they believed that they had really good, knockdown arguments supporting their beliefs, which others, assuming they were in a position to hear and understand, would come to agree with. For example, if a scientist believes that her theory about some physical event is the only correct theory and rejects rival theories, we normally would not accuse her of being immoral. Likewise, to reject what other people believe religiously is not necessarily to hold them in contempt, to be intolerant of their right to believe, or to be prideful.

To Hick's suggestion that the accident of birth makes exclusivism intellectually arbitrary, Plantinga responds that there is no reason why the fact that someone is brought up to believe certain things to be true necessarily implies that they are false or that the person is not justified in believing them. If that were so, people brought up to believe that all religions are the same, or that they are all in some sense true, or that none of them is true would be as arbitrary in their belief as the exclusivist. Plantinga adds that some exclusivism in all our beliefs, religious or otherwise, is inevitable if we think, quite reasonably, that ideas that contradict true beliefs must be false beliefs.

Plantinga does not directly address the issue of whether exclusivism necessarily shuts off religious dialogue and hence the possibility of understanding other religious viewpoints. But he does address the issue of learning about religions other than our own. He admits that such learning may be dangerous for exclusivists because it may lead to a lessening if not an abandonment of their faith. But he quickly notes that things do not have to go this way. There are several possibilities. "A fresh or heightened awareness of the facts of religious pluralism could bring about a reappraisal of one's religious life, a reawakening, a new or renewed and deepened grasp [of one's own religious convictions]."[7]

There have been responses to Plantinga's response to those who condemn exclusivism on moral and intellectual grounds. The philosophical and theological debate is far from dead. In some circles, however, there has been a shift in thinking about the relationships among religions. This shift in thinking is called inclusivism.

## 13.2.2 Inclusivism

There are different kinds of **inclusivism,** but, as the name implies, all varieties wish to acknowledge the possibility of salvation in different religions. At the same time, inclusivists wish to assert the superiority of their own religion. How can they recognize the validity of other religions and also insist on the superiority of their own? Different religions have different ways of doing this.

Some early Christians, for example, claimed that the divine revelation to the Jews as found in the Old Testament is true and valid, but it must be interpreted in light of the new revelation of the divine in Christ. They argued that the New Testament completes and makes plain the Law and the Prophets contained in the Old Testament. The Christian scripture includes the Jewish scripture, and hence Christianity includes the truth of Judaism. Nevertheless, it goes beyond that truth by acknowledging a new revelation of the incarnation of God in Jesus, a revelation only "foreshadowed" and "anticipated" in Jewish scripture.

This same kind of argument is repeated in many religions. Muslims argue that Muhammad is the "seal" of the prophets, completing and perfecting the divine revelations given to Moses and Jesus. While Islam did not incorporate Jewish or Christian scripture in its own holy book, the Quran, it did recognize Jews and Christians as "people of the book."

Those who claim to be the last prophet always run the risk of someone else coming along later who claims to be the last prophet whose revelation includes, but supercedes, all previous revelations. The history of the development of much of the world's scriptures could be written in this manner. Each new revelation not only rejects the absoluteness of the old revelations (often thereby increasing the skepticism of outsiders), it also seems arrogant to those who follow what is now "old." Anyone who claims to have the final word on something automatically implies that what another holds dear should not be held so dearly.

Other types of inclusivism see their own religious ideas as hidden, concealed, or implicit in the religions of others. Of the many examples of this sort of inclusivism in the religions of the world, we will concentrate on the views of a Roman Catholic theologian named Karl Rahner (1904–1984) because they have been and still are influential among many Catholic thinkers as well as others. Rahner argued that if we truly believe that God intended his saving grace for all humanity and that the truth of salvation is revealed most perfectly in Christianity, then we must recognize what he called "anonymous Christians." In other words, Buddhists, Hindus, Muslims, Jews, and others who have truly and genuinely responded to God's saving grace are, in effect, Christians, even if they do not think of themselves that way. The Christian church should not think of itself as the exclusive community of those who are saved, but as the historical vanguard expressing explicitly what is hidden in other religions. Rahner writes:

> Until the moment when the gospel really enters into the historical situation of the individual, a non-Christian religion . . . does not merely contain elements of a natural knowledge of God . . . It contains also supernatural elements arising out of the grace which is given to men as a gratuitous gift on account of Christ. For this reason a non-Christian religion can be recognized as a *lawful* religion.[8]

By a *"lawful religion"* Rahner means a historical religion that God has included in the divine plan of salvation. All lawful religions, because they occur within a historical and institutional setting, are liable to error and corruption. When religions fail to promote social justice and support or engage in destructive conflicts with others, they exhibit their human origins and frailty. This does not mean that God cannot use them to dispense grace and forgiveness. Indeed, if there were no human sin in institutional religions or elsewhere, there would be no need for grace. It does mean, however, that Christians (and others) should abandon the either/or mentality that claims a religion must either come from God or it must be a fake, a mere human invention.

Rahner's brand of inclusivism has been criticized from many sides. Christians argue that it fails to appreciate what is radically new in Christ and undermines Christian missionary work. Others argue that Rahner's position is paternalistic, arrogant, and imperialistic. In effect, it says to the devout of any religion other than Christianity that they are deceived because they think they are Buddhists (or whatever the religion might be), but in reality they are anonymous Christians. This hardly seems the best way to promote serious and honest dialogue among the world's faiths.

Rahner denies that his position undermines missionary work because if a missionary converts a non-Christian to Christianity, he turns an anonymous Christian into someone who now consciously knows what he or she truly is. This knowledge is an advance over their previous state. Rahner responds to the charges of arrogance and paternalism by maintaining that non-Christians may indeed think his brand of inclusivism is presumptuous. But they must understand that a Christian has no other choice than to see all genuine acts of divine grace as manifestations of the grace of Christ, even if others do not see them that way. Rahner concedes, as he must, that it is only fair that other religions might refer to Christians as "anonymous Muslims," or "anonymous Buddhists," and so on.

Whatever the defects of Rahner's version of inclusivism, his ideas have helped reflective Catholics to move beyond a parochial understanding of the Catholic dogma, "There is no salvation outside of the church" (*Extra ecclesiam nulla salus*). While Protestant versions of Christianity have always rejected the Roman Catholic version of this doctrine, their rejection has been related to internal fights for autonomy from the dominance of Roman Catholicism. In effect, at least among some Protestant groups, a variation of the old Catholic exclusivism that they fought so hard to overcome has become reinstated as exclusivism with respect to other religions. "There is no salvation outside of the church" is transformed into "There is no salvation outside of Christianity." Rahner's inclusivism is clearly a challenge to any and all forms of exclusivism.

## 13.2.3 Pluralism

If exclusivism holds that there is one and only one true religious path to salvation, and inclusivism holds that different religions may contain in a hidden way the true path that is most clearly expressed in only one, **pluralism** holds that there are many different true paths to salvation expressed in the many diverse religions of the world.

Perhaps the most influential advocate of pluralism writing today is John Hick, a Protestant philosopher and theologian. Hick believes that historical circumstances are now leading to a revolution in human thought about religions comparable to the Copernican revolution in astronomy in the sixteenth century. Before Copernicus's theory of the sun as the center of our solar system won wide acceptance, the Ptolemaic view of the earth as the center prevailed. "Ptolemaic" thinking about religion holds that one or another of the world's religions is at the center of religious truth. So Christianity (if I am a Christian), or Islam (if I am a Muslim), or Hinduism (if I am a Hindu), and so on is the "true center," and all other religious traditions circle around that "sun."

Just as Ptolemaic astronomy was geocentric, so Ptolemaic religion is ethnocentric since accident of birth mostly determines our religious outlook. "Copernican" thinking about religion recognizes a new center around which all religions revolve. Hick refers to that center as the Real.

What is the Real? Hick uses a distinction from the philosopher Kant between *noumena* (things-in-themselves) and *phenomena* (things-as-they-appear) to develop the idea. Just as noumena cannot be grasped by human thought because they do not appear to thought as do phenomena, so the Real-in-itself transcends our limited human ways of talking and thinking. However, the Real-as-it-appears in the various religions can be thought about and experienced.

Hick formulates the pluralistic hypothesis as follows: "the Real (to select this term from several equally available ones) in itself is present to us, or impinges upon us, all the time and that when this impingement comes to consciousness it takes the form of what we call religious experience."[9] These historically and culturally conditioned experiences give rise to different concepts of the Real. Even though the Real-in-itself is beyond human thought, the Real as experienced in time and space is thought of differently in different human communities. In some it is named YHWH, in others Krishna, in still others Dao, or Allah, or God, or the Holy Trinity, or "that which nothing greater can be thought," or Zeus, or kami, or—I could go on and on, but you get the idea. Each finite religious tradition generates its own names and, along with those names, different conceptions of the Real.

Hick thinks that most of these conceptions fall into two camps. One camp thinks of the Real in personal terms. It is conscious, has a will, cares about people, and, in short, exhibits personlike characteristics. The other camp thinks of the Real in nonpersonal terms. It is the Absolute, the Principle, the Infinite, the Eternal, and so on. Hick contends that even though these two camps center on different conceptions of the Real, they are not mutually exclusive. They are, Hick argues, complementary.

The task of demonstrating how they are complementary is not easy. But Hick is encouraged by the fact that all the different religions that fall into the personal camp or the nonpersonal camp have developed systems that promote human spiritual and moral transformation. Hick writes that these "fruits . . . prove a common criterion by which to recognize the salvific transformation of human existence from natural self-centeredness to a new orientation centered in the Real, a transformation which takes different concrete forms with different religious cultures."[10]

This version of pluralism allows for real differences among the religions, but it argues that such differences should not lead to religious intolerance. There are many religious questions to which humans do not have definitive answers, such as whether there really is life after death or whether there is some purpose to human existence. Different religions make claims to have the answers, and their answers often conflict. But neither our ignorance of the answers nor conflicting claims to truth prevent moral and spiritual transformations from taking place in many different religious traditions. Therefore we should tolerate and live in harmony with the conflicting truth-claims.

What about the Real itself? Do we know that it exists? How could we know it if it is beyond the limits of human thought? Hick responds by saying that the existence of the Real as the center of all the religions is a *postulate* that the pluralistic hypothesis must make. If it does not, then we are left with the unattractive alternatives of exclusivism, inclusivism, or of regarding all religious experience as illusory.

Arvind Sharma, a professor of comparative religion at McGill University, has compared Hick's pluralism with the pluralism of the Hindu school of Advaita (nondualistic) Vedanta. As you may recall, Shankara, one of the leading thinkers of this school, claimed that Brahman (Being-in-itself or the divine-in-itself) is not different from Atman (consciousness-in-itself). You may also recall that Hinduism is a convenient word to use for a plurality of religious traditions that developed and took root in India. The religious world in which Advaita developed was already diverse, and most Indians had learned to live more or less in harmony with a wide variety of religious beliefs and practices.

Sharma points out that Hick's distinction between the Real as experienced nonpersonally and the Real as experienced personally is similar (although not identical) to Shankara's distinction between *nirguna* Brahman (the divine without qualities) and *saguna* Brahman (the divine with qualities). The divine with qualities is called Ishvara, or Lord. It is this Lord that is worshiped in the many devotional sects of Hinduism by many names such as Rama, Krishna, Shiva, the goddess Kali, Ganesha, and so on. If Shankara had been aware of the many non-Indian devotional traditions such as Judaism, Christianity, and Islam, all of whom worship a personal divine being, he would have called them worshipers of *saguna* Brahman, or the Lord, as well.

If nondualism is correct, then in the final analysis for Advaita, *nirguna* Brahman and *saguna* Brahman are identical. Hick's claim that they are complementary conceptions of the Real-in-itself would appear to imply a subordination or at least a dualism that Advaita denies. This is one of Sharma's arguments.

Sharma finds other differences between Advaitic pluralism and Hick's pluralism as well. But in spite of the divergences, he concludes that there is a "strong family resemblance" between the two. This family resemblance becomes apparent, Sharma thinks, by the Advaitic statements found in the *Yogavasishtha:*

> Many names have been given to the Absolute by the learned for practical purposes such as Law, Self, Truth.

It is called Person by the Samkhya thinkers, Brahman by the Vedantins, pure and simple consciousness by the Vijnanavadins, Sunya [Nothing] by the Nihilists, the Illuminator by the worshippers of the Sun. It is also called the Speaker, the Thinker, the Enjoyer of actions and the Doer of them.

Shiva for the worshippers of Shiva, and Time for those who believe in Time alone.[11]

### 13.2.4 Pluralistic Inclusivism

If exclusivism, inclusivism, and pluralism provide us with genuinely different options when thinking about religions, and all of these are contested theories, might there be other more attractive options? Schubert Ogden, a Christian theologian who has been active in Christian-Buddhist dialogues, has maintained that there is a fourth option. It is, he asserts, better than those we have so far examined. He calls it **pluralistic inclusivism.**

Ogden argues that both exclusivism and inclusivism boil down to a kind of monism because they hold that only one religion is true or only one religion is fully and completely true. Pluralism offers a genuine option to monism with its claim that many religions are true. He rejects monism as false, and he is skeptical of the pluralistic theory. Therefore he offers a fourth option, which asserts that many religions can be true. This theory is more reasonable for Ogden because it does not require us to prove that one religion is actually true or superior, nor does it require us to prove that many religions are actually true. It requires only that we show that many religions can be true.

Ogden thinks there are good theological arguments based on the Christian tradition supporting this fourth option. Given a Christian understanding of God as love and as the creator of all humanity, it is inconsistent with that understanding to make it impossible for non-Christians to be saved. He writes that "God must be their [non-Christians'] Savior as surely as God is their Creator and Consumator; for God *is* love, and there is no way for a God to love sinners except to do all that could conceivably be done to save them from their sin."[12]

To his credit, Ogden recognizes that if it is possible to give Christian theological reasons to support his pluralistic inclusivism, then other religions can give their own reasons based on their own traditional beliefs and values. "But if the Christian witness is true that it is just this love of God that is the strictly ultimate reality with which every human being has to do as soon and as long as she or he exists humanly at all, then not only Christianity but other religions as well can validly claim to be formally true."[13] By "formally true," he means *can be* true rather than *actually is* true.

All Christian theologians would not draw the same conclusion as Ogden does from the claim that God is love and the creator of all humanity, but it is not my intent here to enter into Christian theological debates. We can ask, however, whether Ogden's pluralistic inclusivism is a more reasonable option than the other three positions. Personally, I think it would be very difficult to show that it is *more* reasonable, but it is certainly a reasonable option. But does it get us very far along the road of understanding how religions are related with respect to the question of truth? All four positions (exclusivism, inclusivism, pluralism, pluralistic inclusivism) presuppose that religions (one or more) can satisfy what philosophers call truth-conditions. To prove Ogden (or any of the others) wrong, we have to prove that it is impossible for any religion to be true. This is a tall order. However, it does open up a fifth option.

### 13.2.5 Naturalism

We will call this fifth option **naturalism** for lack of a better term. Perhaps it is not true that one religion among the many is true (exclusivism). Perhaps it is not the case that one religion among the many is truer than the others (inclusivism). Perhaps it is not the case that in some sense many religions are true, even though very different (pluralism). Perhaps it is not the case that many can be true (pluralistic inclusivism). Perhaps it is the case that none of them is true (naturalism).

To call this view naturalistic is misleading. If naturalism is opposed to supernaturalism, then we must recall that not all religions are supernaturalistic. There can be superhuman forces that are fully natural. We can make the case that many religions worship the forces of nature personified as spirits, ancestors, gods, goddesses, demons, and the like. Some religions, like Advaita Vedanta, oppose any and all dualisms as absolutely real. Such religions would reject the distinction between nature and supernature.

The name naturalism is also misleading because it obscures an important fact. People can reject any and all organized religion as false and still seek an authentic spirituality. Recall the discussion in Chapter 3 that it is possible to be religious without belonging to a religion. Paradoxically, people might deny there is any truth to religion (by which they mean organized religion) and affirm there is truth in seeking and expressing their authentic spirituality. It is also possible to deny that religions are true, and yet find moral value in them. We must keep these qualifications in mind. Nevertheless it is convenient to have a word for this position, so I will stipulate that for our purposes here, we will use naturalism in a very narrow sense to refer to the position that all religions are mistaken in significant ways in their basic or fundamental beliefs, practices, and moral vision.

There is, it seems to me, no conclusive way to prove naturalism true or false. There may well be powers or forces far beyond human comprehension. It may well be that such powers impinge on human existence in a variety of important ways. We are just not in a position right now to know. Perhaps we never will be. Perhaps naturalism, like secularism, is more of a general cultural attitude than a precise position subject to rigorous proof. The task of showing to everyone's satisfaction that all religions are mistaken in core beliefs, practices, and moral vision is probably impossible.

So we seem to be left with something like this: while it is possible that one or more religions can be true, it is also possible that no religions can be true. Both positions appear to be reasonable.

---

**Possible Truth-Relations among Different Religions**

1. Exclusivism—one and only one of the many religions is true.
2. Inclusivism—truth is most clearly and fully expressed in one religion, but other religions also contain truth, although in a partial or hidden way.
3. Pluralism—in spite of their differences, all religions contain valid experiences of ultimate reality.
4. Pluralistic inclusivism—many religions can be true.
5. Naturalism—no religions are true.

---

## 13.3 DIFFERENT PATHS, SAME GOAL?

I often hear my students say, when we discuss the relationship among various religious traditions, something to the effect that all the different religions in the world are just different paths to the same goal. Sometimes they invoke the metaphor of a mountain (recall our discussion of sacred mountains) and imagine each religion struggling to carve out a way to the top by different routes.

The image of different religions as so many different routes to the same place was popularized by the ideas of Sarvepalli Radhakrishnan (1888–1973). He was a scholar and a statesman, serving from 1962–1967 as president of India. As an adherent of Advaita Vedanta, he was fond of quoting the Vedic verse, "The real is one, the learned call it by various names."

The various names are, according to Radhakrishnan, intellectually produced symbols. The real vitality of religion is in personal spiritual realization, not creeds or dogmas. Although he concedes that creeds have instrumental value, they are not absolute. "The name by which we call God and the rite by which we approach Him do not matter much."[14] A religious path or tradition is valid to the degree that it leads its followers to spiritual realization.

It is not surprising that Radhakrishnan advises religious tolerance and respect for differences. We should not, he asserts, seek to convert Buddhists to Christians or Hindus to Muslims, but to help all the diverse traditions of faith rediscover their basic principles of compassion and human service. The solution to the problems raised by religious diversity is not to collapse all the different paths into one, but to respect difference and diversity.

So far Radhakrishnan sounds like a pluralist. But when we ask more precisely what this spiritual realization is at the end of our climb up the mountain, the answers we get sound more and more like the traditional views of Advaita Vedanta reworked for modern consumption. Spiritual realization amounts to the unitive mystical experience as understood in the nondualistic traditions of India. If we make it to the top, we will realize that at the deepest levels of ourselves, we are united with the One Absolute Reality. In other words, we will experience the unity of Atman and Brahman. Radhakrishnan quotes with approval the Maitri Upanishad:

> Some contemplate one name and some another. Which of these is best? All are eminent clues to the transcendent, immortal, unembodied Brahman; these names are to be contemplated, lauded, and at last denied. For by them one rises higher and higher in those worlds; but where all comes to its end, there he attains to the Unity of the person.[15]

There may well be some truth to the metaphor of "different paths, same goal," but it is often too tempting to place our own religious conception of truth on the summit. A genuine pluralistic attitude is betrayed by the thought, "when all the others get to the top, they will find out that my religion was there all along."

We can be misled by metaphors and often are. Perhaps the image of different paths up a mountain to a single summit is misleading. Perhaps there is more than one summit or goal. Perhaps there are no paths, but only socially constructed lifestyles that people find themselves born into or choose. Perhaps there are only different religious constructions of reality that bear little if any resemblance to what is "out there." If the "out there" is what is "true" apart from differing social constructions, differing human experiences, and differing religious beliefs, then what is it? Is there any hope of ever finding it?

## 13.4 WHAT IS TRUTH?

We have been using the words *true* and *truth* vaguely. It is time for some clarification. In particular it is time to confront more directly the question of whether there are any criteria we can use to determine what is true or false religiously. If the idea of truth has something to do with verification, how might we verify the truth of religious claims?

The question of truth becomes particularly important when we look at religious diversity and the conflicting claims made by religions. Some teach a doctrine of the soul, some do not. Some teach that there is an eternal hell, others do not. Some teach that there are many gods, others do not. We could pile example on top of example. By what criteria can we sort all of this out?

We can think of true religions as ones whose core beliefs are true and not false and whose practices are effective. We should add that their core experiences provide knowledge rather than illusion and that they have the power to bring about authentic moral transformations. In the case of salvation religions, we must note that if they are true, they must make salvation a real possibility for people by putting them in touch with whatever has saving power. If we mean by true religion something like the above, we can see that the task of verification is immense. Given what we have learned about the diversity of beliefs, practices, experiences, morality, and conceptions of salvation, it is not at all clear how we might proceed.

---

## Characteristics of True Religion

1. Core beliefs are true.
2. Practices are effective.
3. Core experiences provide knowledge.
4. Authentic moral transformation is possible.
5. Salvation is possible.

---

### 13.4.1 The Proposals of D'Costa and Ward

Gavin D'Costa, professor of religion at the University of Bristol, England, asserts that there are at least four possible options for judging the truth-claims of religions: (1) judging other religions by one's own religious standards, (2) judging other religions by their own criteria, (3) not judging at all, and (4) finding and applying religiously neutral, objective, and commonly acceptable standards of truth.[16] Options 1 and 2 appear hopelessly biased, option 3 begs the question about criteria of religious truth, and there are good reasons to believe that option 4 is not possible.

D'Costa concentrates most of his attention on option 4 because that seems the most reasonable way to proceed. He argues that those who attempt to find neutral and objective criteria are caught on the horns of a dilemma. The problem is this: the more specific the criteria are, the less likely they are to be neutral, and the more general and abstract the criteria are, the less likely they are to be useful.

To illustrate what D'Costa means, let's look at several specific examples of attempts to find religiously neutral criteria. An example that D'Costa himself uses and criticizes comes from Keith Ward, Regius Professor of Divinity at the University of Oxford. Ward has proposed that we can derive neutral criteria of judgment from certain common features of human life. Because all humans seek happiness, we can consider happiness a universal, common, and basic value of all people. People cannot seek happiness in isolation from other values. These other values consist of knowledge, choice, freedom, and justice. We must seek knowledge in order to know how to obtain happiness, and we must make choices between competing goods based on our knowledge. The ability to make meaningful choices requires the freedom to do so. It is pointless to tell people to make a choice and then deny them the freedom to do it. Justice is important in the pursuit of happiness because it tells us that we should be fair. For example, if pursuing $x$ is good for my happiness, then (all factors being equal) it is only fair that someone else can pursue that good as I have pursued it.

Armed with this set of basic values we can make judgments not only about competing religious views, but also about any kind of worldview, be it religious or secular. Does it promote happiness and knowledge? Does it offer meaningful choices? Does it permit freedom of choice? Does it promote justice?

D'Costa points out that these basic values are abstract. Exactly what counts as happiness or knowledge? What precisely is justice? Even in their abstract form, these "common and universal values" sound very much like the sorts of things advocated primarily by Western philosophers. Are they really neutral, common, and universal? If we try to make these abstract values more concrete, in order to make them more useful for discriminating among religions, their neutrality and universality rapidly begin to fade.

Take happiness, for example. Happiness can be found in many different ways, and many different things make people happy. Does anything go? If it does, then the criterion is useless. If some things are not allowed (such has pursuing happiness by inflicting suffering and pain on others), we need to specify what they are. As we do so, we narrow the playing field, so to speak, and we will most likely narrow it in terms of what our own cultural and religious traditions value. As we become more specific, we need to provide justifications. Why, for example, is pursuing happiness by pursuing wealth less good than, say, pursuing justice? Once we get into matters of justification, even more of our religious baggage is likely to be brought into play.

D'Costa's critical analysis amounts to a claim that option 4 (finding and applying religiously neutral standards) is not a real option. It always ends up suggesting standards that in one way or another derive from the individual's own tradition. D'Costa, however, does not find this overly disturbing because he thinks humans cannot help but make judgments about what is true and false using the standards of their own traditions. There is no view from nowhere (just as there is no view from everywhere), so where we must start, even if it is not ideal, is where we are culturally and religiously. This need not result in exclusivism because other religious traditions or parts of them may be perfectly acceptable given our own standards.

The line of reasoning D'Costa develops leaves many questions unanswered, and it is open to charges of ethnocentrism as well as religious imperialism. By what right do we impose our religious criteria of truth on others? To argue that we cannot do otherwise does not establish our *right* to judge, only that we may have fewer options than we think. Before we can judge whether something is true, we have to know what it means. How can we be sure we know what other religions mean by their assertions? Are their beliefs and practices fully translatable into our language? Perhaps some religions are so different from one another that using criteria from our own religious tradition may be like judging the adequacy of jet engines by comparing them to apples. Then again, what are the truth-criteria of our own religions? Religious disagreements occur not only between religions but also within religions, and the issue of truth-criteria is a lightning rod for disagreements.

Standards of truth always have a context. They do not exist in a vacuum. If by "neutral" criteria D'Costa means something like a set of truth standards that have no context, presuppose no framework, and make no assumptions, it is no wonder he finds Ward's proposals inadequate. It is easy to find the suggestions of others inadequate if, at the start, we set the standards too high. Any proposed standard would be inadequate because there are no such things as *absolutely neutral* standards of judgment. We may think it is valuable to work toward absolute religious neutrality, but it is an ideal that we will probably never reach. Does that mean it is not worth trying? It is important to set high standards for athletic competition and for education. If we set impossibly high standards, no one will try. But it does not follow that we should set no standards at all, even if they are less than ideal.

One major problem with D'Costa's proposal that we should use the standards of our own religion to judge the truth-claims of other religions is that it cuts off religious dialogue. Why should we seriously engage someone else with a different religious viewpoint in discussion about any topic, including the topic of appropriate standards, if we already know how we are going to decide the case? Would this not be like a judge who says, "I do not have to listen to the lawyers' arguments about which laws apply and which do not because I already have all the knowledge of legal standards I need to make a judgment."

If we are serious about engaging in meaningful conversation with people from other religious traditions, perhaps we should assume at the outset that all religious knowledge is partial, including our own. No single tradition contains the whole truth. By talking we might discover in what ways our knowledge is limited and partial. By conversation our different views may even start to converge.

Hans-Georg Gadamer (1900–2002), a German philosopher, proposed that we think of truth as a "fusion of horizons." Just as horizons mark the limits of our sight, so intellectual horizons mark the limits of our thought. Those horizons can only become enlarged and perhaps even fused with the horizons of others by authentic and open dialogue. If Gadamer is even partially right, any view of religious truth that prematurely cuts off religious dialogue and the opportunities to learn from each other is already too limited to be of much help in the search for truth.

## 13.4.2 Why Judge at All?

Our focus on standards of judgment for evaluating religious truth has set to one side a more serious consideration of D'Costa's third option—why judge religions at all? Many scholars of religion argue that it is enough for the objective, outside scholar to describe, interpret, and develop explanatory theories. While scholars must and should evaluate different scholarly theories, they should not move beyond that into what we called first-order evaluation in Chapter 2. These kinds of evaluation are matters for theologians, not historians and social scientists.

This strikes me as reasonable advice to the would-be scholar of religion. There are many pressing issues and problems for the student of religion. Describing, interpreting, and explaining are difficult enough. Why jump into the thick of religious debates about who really has the truth?

There may be no absolutely compelling reason to do so. Being nonjudgmental in these matters is often recognized as a virtue. However, if the scholar moves beyond history and social science into philosophy of religion, issues surrounding the different truth-claims are appropriate, even if difficult to deal with. Many of the distinctions, theories, and arguments we have been looking at in this chapter stem from philosophically trained scholars. We should note that many scholars try to appeal to views most people would find reasonable whatever their personal religious convictions may be. Ward's appeal to what is common to all people is a case in point. Appeals to the particular and specific religious doctrines (for example, Ogden's appeal to Christian views of God as love), while not ruled out of bounds, are often muted and usually accompanied, as they must be, with the right of others to appeal to specific ideas derived from their religious traditions.

## 13.4.3 Language Games

There are always other possibilities, and one D'Costa does not mention is the possibility that religions are not true or false but better or worse. We do not think of civilizations as true or false, so why should we think of religions that way? Think of religions, some philosophers advise, as "language games." Just as different games have their own rules and it would be inappropriate to judge, say, a game of tennis by the rules of chess, so the religious language game, or at least some of the language games religions play, should not be judged by inappropriate rules. If the religious language game is primarily symbolic, metaphoric, and poetic, why use rules of truth or falsity? Perhaps it is more appropriate to think in terms of spiritual and moral qualities. Radhakrishnan states that we should "frankly recognize that the efficiency of a religion is to be judged by the development of religious qualities such as quiet confidence, inner calm, gentleness of the spirit, love of neighbour, mercy to all creation, destruction of tyrannous desires, and the aspiration for spiritual freedom, and there are no trustworthy statistics to tell us that these qualities are found more in efficient nations." [17]

Note Radhakrishnan's use of the word *efficiency* in this context, rather than truth. Note as well that while there are no trustworthy statistics on these matters when we compare religions to nations, there are also no trustworthy statistics when we compare religion to religion. The historical record indicates that ability of religions to produce moral transformations in people is ambiguous.

Changing direction away from the focus on true and false to morally better or worse may be attractive in many ways, but most religions claim to teach more than morality, and for most believers matters of truth are important. However, even if we think the focus should shift from truth to moral value, the controversy over criteria errupts again. Now, rather than a controversy concerning criteria of truth, it is about what criteria to use to judge moral value.

Whether we judge religious claims to truth or not, I think we can agree that we need to practice the virtues of fairness and tolerance.

## 13.5 CRITICAL TOLERANCE AND THE PRINCIPLE OF CHARITY

We spoke briefly about critical tolerance in the first chapter. It is time to return to that theme. Our first discussion was in the context of beginners in the field of the academic study of religion. It was part of the preliminaries. We have now passed into the postliminary stage. While all of us have much more to learn about religions and their study, we are more informed now than we were before and hence in a better position to look at the issue of critical tolerance with more understanding.

We learned in the first chapter that tolerance does not imply that we should never make critical judgments, be they positive or negative. Religious toleration does not compel us to accept as true everything others do or believe with respect to religious matters. The concept of tolerance, or toleration (I use the terms interchangeably for the most part) presupposes some disagreement. [18] If tolerance demanded that we accept uncritically what others do and believe, it would banish disagreement and replace it with acceptance. However, if I truly respect the views of others as well as my own, and I truly disagree with them, then I need to practice critical tolerance. This does not have to imply an attitude of resignation in which I "put up" with others, even though I prefer not to. None of us want others merely to put up with us; we want others to respect us and take our views seriously. Critical tolerance does that.

Edward Langerak, professor of philosophy at St. Olaf College, Minnesota, presents a thesis in his essay "Disagreement: Appreciating the Dark Side of Tolerance" that captures part of what I mean by critical tolerance. He writes:

> My thesis is that, although we do need a conceptual framework that allows us to respect many of the views we regard as wrong, it also must allow us to judge that these respectable views are disagreeable and even that sometimes actions based on them should not be tolerated.[19]

Tolerance does not demand that we accept all religious views, let alone practices, but it does demand that we make a sincere effort to understand. What is a sincere effort to understand? Philosophers often appeal to the principle of charity, which states that interpreting what people mean should be done in such a way as to maximize the truth of what they claim. In other words, we need to put the best construction we can on what others mean. In popular speech, this means giving someone the "benefit of the doubt." For example, I may think that ancestor worship goes a bit too far, but it would be wrong to represent it as stupid, unreasonable, and even dangerous. I can understand the importance of respect for ancestors and the sense of debt we feel to those who have gone before.

## 13.5.1  The Blind People and the Elephant

It may be helpful to consider a parable attributed to Buddha about the blind people and the elephant. His disciples, having heard a number of sectarians arguing about what is true, asked what is to be made of all this quarreling among religious sects. Buddha replies by telling a story about a king who once faced a similar situation. The king asked his servants to bring to the palace an elephant and all the blind men they could find. He then told the servants to tell these blind men that an elephant is present and allow them to feel it. Some felt its thick legs and said that an elephant is like a pillar. Some felt its tusks and said an elephant is like a plough. Still others felt its body and said that an elephant is like a granary. Soon the blind men were arguing among themselves about what an elephant is like. The king said that the religious sectarians were like the blind men. Each blind man has partial knowledge of the elephant. But because they do not realize their knowledge is partial, they argue. Partial knowledge, Buddha pointed out, leads to disagreements, bigotry, and even fanaticism.

This parable advises that we should think of all the different religious views as partial views. They all have some value, and they all capture part of the truth. None, however, are completely true. This parable may also imply that just as sight is beyond the capacity of those who are blind, knowing the whole of religious truth (the elephant) may well be beyond the limits of human intellectual abilities. Many religions do claim that ultimate reality is, in the final analysis, a mystery.

This story supports the practice of religious toleration, but it is critical toleration. While each blind man argues about what the elephant is like, it has not occurred to him that his experiences may be limited and not reveal the whole truth. The critical principle implied here is that religions do not contain the complete and final truth, even if they think they do. This principle advises humility about our religious claims to truth and a recognition of human fallibility. It tells us to be suspicious when some religion stakes its claim to the whole truth.

### 13.5.2 The Elephant Principle

If we resist the temptation of claiming that our religion "sees the elephant," and if we think the whole elephant is beyond the human intellect, how can we hold that all religious views are partial? We can only know some view is a partial view if we compare it to a whole view. But such comparison is impossible if no one sees the whole elephant. Perhaps we should not read too much into this parable. After all, it is only a story. Even so, the story appears to suggest a paradox. We cannot know that all views are partial unless we know the entire truth. But if we claim to know the entire truth, we violate the claim that all religions teach part of the truth. So what are we to do? We appear to be caught in yet another dilemma.

Perhaps we cannot do much better than to adopt the principle that all religions have a partial grasp on truth. Jainism suggests that we adopt this principle, but just because Jainism or some other religions suggest it is not reason enough to adopt it. It seems that the only justification for adopting the notion that all religions contain some of the truth is pragmatic. This view encourages religious toleration, explains why religions may disagree, and promotes inter-religious dialogue. If we talk to others who disagree, if we study their religious beliefs and practices, if we listen with the principle of charity to their myths and legends, we may learn something of real value that we did not know before. We can even learn something from atheism and agnosticism if we listen. We do not have to agree in order to learn.

Valuable social benefits also result from adopting the principle (should we call it the Elephant Principle?) that all religious and antireligious views are partial. Adopting such a principle not only promotes dialogue, but also a religiously tolerant society in which "the religious beliefs, or rejection of religion, of the citizen are not allowed to affect their legal right to live, marry, raise children, worship, pursue careers, own property, make contracts, participate in politics, and engage in all the other activities normally open to citizens in that society."[20]

## 13.6 SUMMARY

We have covered a lot of ground in this chapter—ground that has required us to do some careful thinking. We began by trying to explain religious conflict by using a theory from the social sciences called, appropriately enough, conflict theory. The theory derives from Karl Marx, who focused on class conflict in terms of the struggle for wealth. This theory has been considerably broadened since Marx proposed it (although Marx's original insight is preserved). The core of the theory is that conflict arises when power is unequally distributed. The struggles for wealth, power, prestige, and privilege explain some aspects of religious conflict. Competition among religions for allegiance and influence also plays an important role. In addition, threat (real or imagined) from the processes of secularization or other hostile forces can encourage religious conflict.

Secularization can be understood in at least two different ways: loss of religion's influence in the public realm or the increased privatization of religious matters. Modernism's willingness to rely increasingly on human reason, especially in the form of science, as the final arbitrator of truth, and postmodernism's critical questions about how we might fairly discriminate true from false or right from wrong, have contributed to the decline of religious influence in the public arena. Religious fundamentalisms can be seen, at least in part, as reactionary movements resulting from the threat of secularization.

Globalization not only spreads secularization, but also increases the gap between rich and poor, thereby creating a context of increased conflict, including religious conflict. It seems that religions are left with few options: either they continue fighting and increase the conflict, or they figure out ways to get along.

With respect to issues of truth and salvation, we examined five positions or options: exclusivism, inclusivism, pluralism, pluralistic inclusivism, and naturalism. Exclusivism maintains that only one religion is true. Inclusivism recognizes truth in other traditions while maintaining the superiority of one religion. From a pluralistic perspective, all religions are true and valid responses to the Real-in-itself. Pluralistic inclusivism postulates that many religions can be true and effective means to salvation. Naturalism, the last position we examined, maintains that no religions are true and that they do not provide valid paths to salvation.

Christianity's exclusivism stems from its strong Christocentric claims that Jesus is the One Way to God. While Alvin Plantinga does not defend this One Way doctrine, he does defend the rationality of an exclusivistic position. Exclusivism, he argues, is not necessarily immoral or irrational. If he is right, then Christian exclusivism, Muslim exclusivism, Hindu exclusivism (the list could go on) can be defended on the same grounds.

Karl Rahner's views on inclusivism guided us as we examined this position. Rahner has gone far in breaking the exclusivistic attitude of traditional Roman Catholicism by showing that there may well be salvation outside of the church. Many scholars have found his inclusivism morally suspect because of its paternalism and offensiveness to those of other faith communities. Few Christians would like to be called hidden Buddhists, and few Buddhists would like to be called hidden Christians.

John Hick's version of pluralism suggests that we think about a revolution in religious thinking equivalent to the Copernican revolution in astronomy. It may well be that no single religion, even our own, is at the center of the religious universe, but that all of the world's religions revolve around the Real-in-itself. The time has passed when we can place one religion on the central pedestal and imagine all the others circling about it. The time has come for every religion to recall its purpose—to testify to and live the values of one ultimate reality, the sun of the religious universe.

Although Hick is a Christian, some of his ideas on the topic of religious pluralism can be found in the Hindu Advaita Vedanta tradition. Two different views of ultimate reality appear contradictory. The personal view of the ultimate appears incompatible with the nonpersonal view. Advaita reconciles these two ideas in a way similar to Hick by distinguishing between *nirguna* Brahman and *saguna* Brahman. However, Shankara's distinction appears to privilege the nonpersonal view of absolute reality by making *nirguna* Brahman superior to *saguna* Brahman.

The Christian theologian Schubert Ogden supports pluralistic inclusivism. According to Ogden, both exclusivism and inclusivism express a monism with respect to the question of the truth-value of different religions. Pluralism, with its claim that many religions are true, offers a distinctly different option. There is, however, another option—namely, to claim that many religions can be true, although they may not be.

Our discussion of the fifth option that no religions are true (an option we called naturalism for lack of a better name) ended our consideration of the different positions that have been taken with respect to the relationships among religions when it comes to matters of truth and salvation. Naturalism seems as difficult to prove correct as any of the other positions.

Section 13.3 raised the question of whether all religions amount to different paths to the same goal, just as there are different paths to the summit of a mountain. Radhakrishnan's version of Advaita Vedanta provided us with one example of this position. But Radhakrishnan's version sometimes sounds more like inclusivism than genuine pluralism because the summit turns out to be as Advaita describes it. All paths lead to *nirguna* Brahman.

Why should we allow the metaphor of different paths to the same goal to control our thinking in this matter? Why not think of different paths leading to different summits? The religious scene may be more like a mountain range with many peaks than a single mountain with one peak. Perhaps the paths lead nowhere and amount to socially constructed views of reality that correspond to no reality outside the construction.

Pontius Pilate asked Jesus at his trial, "What is truth?" We asked the same question again and suggested that the task of verifying religious truth is immense given the diversity and complexity of religious ideas and practices. We attempted to define a true religion as (roughly) one in which the core beliefs are true, the practices are effective, the core experiences provide knowledge and have the power to produce moral transformations, and salvation is a real possibility. How on earth (pun intended) are we ever to sort through such complexity in our search for true religion?

Gavin D'Costa argues that we have four choices: use the truth criteria of our own religion, judge other religions by their own criteria, avoid the issue (don't judge at all), or find some religiously neutral and commonly accepted standards of evaluation. Keith Ward suggests that we make the fourth choice. He offers the criterion of promoting happiness, choice, knowledge, freedom, and justice as our guiding standard when it comes to judging religious truth. D'Costa finds fault with Ward's suggestions on the grounds that the more abstract the criteria are, the less useful they are, and the more specific they are, the less neutral they are. D'Costa thinks that we have no better option than the first choice (use the truth criteria of our own religion) because the other three options fail in different ways.

There are various problems with D'Costa's argument, not the least of which is what seems to be an imposition of impossible standards of neutrality in order to discredit the fourth position. Also, D'Costa's position does not encourage genuine religious dialogue as a learning experience. Religious truth, if there is any, may only be found when horizons fuse in the process of open discussion and dialogue.

But why should we judge at all? Historians and social scientists have little need to enter into first-order religious debates about the truth of different religious positions. Description, interpretation, explanation, and the evaluation of other scholarly theories are enough to keep them occupied. However, philosophers often go where others fear to tread. They cannot and do not ignore the question of truth.

Philosophers also suggest that the focus on truth-value when it comes to religious matters might better be replaced by a focus on moral value. The religious language game may not play by the rules of the true/false language game. The suggestion that we focus on moral value, while helpful, leads eventually to controversy over what moral criteria to use.

Our return to the theme of critical tolerance led us to note that tolerance should not be confused with acceptance. It is appropriate to disagree and still respect those with whom we differ. If tolerance should not be confused with acceptance, it also should not be confused with a resigned attitude of "putting up with" what we really do not want to "put up with." Critical tolerance demands that we respect those with whom we sincerely disagree.

The principle of charity makes it clear that tolerance also demands that we make every effort to understand those with whom we disagree. We have an obligation to put the best possible interpretation on the views of others who differ with us religiously and in other ways.

The parable of the blind people and the elephant supports the value of religious dialogue because it implies that all religious views are partially true. It gives us some basis on which to proceed as we continue the search for truth, as well as a negative principle: be suspicious of any religion that claims the whole truth.

The parable of the blind people and the elephant raises the question of why we should think all religions, or nearly all, contain a partial grasp of the whole truth if none of us can see the whole elephant. The following dilemma came into view: It seems we cannot know all views are partial unless we can see the entire picture. But if we claim to see the entire picture, we violate the claim that all or most religions teach part of the truth.

We concluded that it would be appropriate to accept the principle that all or nearly all religions contain partial truth. This view encourages religious toleration, promotes interreligious dialogue, and creates religiously tolerant societies.

## 13.7 RESEARCH CASE—BAHA'I

The Baha'i Faith upholds the unity of God, recognizes the unity of His Prophets, and inculcates the principle of the oneness and wholeness of the entire human race. It proclaims the necessity and inevitability of the unification of mankind . . . enjoins upon its followers the primary duty of an unfettered search after truth, condemns all manner of prejudice and superstition, declares the purpose of religion to be the promotion of amity and concord, proclaims its essential harmony with science, and recognizes it as the foremost agency for the pacification and the orderly progress of human society. It unequivocally maintains the principle of equal rights, opportunities, and privileges for men and women, insists on compulsory education, eliminates extremes of poverty and wealth, abolishes the institution of priesthood, prohibits slavery, asceticism, mendicancy, and monasticism, prescribes monogamy, discourages divorce, emphasizes the necessity of strict obedience to one's government, exalts any work performed in the spirit of service to the level of worship, urges either the creation or the selection of an auxiliary international language, and delineates the outlines of those institutions that must establish and perpetuate the general peace of mankind.[21]

Baha'i ("Bah-hi" or more properly "bah-hah'ee") is a young religion, but like so many others it has roots in the older traditional religions, especially Islam. Here we will examine its history as well as its beliefs and practices.

*History*   The story begins with the founding of an Islamic messianic sect of Shia Islam in Iraq and Iran in 1844. The founder and leader of this movement was called the *Bab* (gate), and his followers were known as the Babis. The Bab was said to be the gate between men and the hidden twelfth Imam. The Bab was to prepare the way for the Imam. The Baha'i faith originated in the 1860s as a faction within Babism.

The first Baha'is were followers of Mirza Husayn Ali Nuri (1817–1892). He was an Iranian Persian born to a noble family in Tehran, and he came to be known as Baha Allah (glory of God). Some of the Babis recognized Ali Nuri as a prophet whose arrival was foretold by the Bab, although other Babis, including Ali Nuri's half-brother Mirza Yahaya, rejected this assessment. Mirza Yahaya became known as Subh-I Asal (dawn of eternity), and he led a faction of the Babis that refused to recognize Ali Nuri as Baha Allah.

Why did some Babis follow Ali Nuri and not his brother? We must backtrack a bit, and pick up the story in the "Black Hole" of Tehran. When a wave of religious persecution against the Babis swept Iran after an attempt on the shah's life in 1852, Ali Nuri was thrown into the Black Hole, a notorious prison in Tehran. There he had several deeply moving and transforming religious experiences. In one he heard a voice telling him that God will use him to bring "life to the hearts of the sages." He described another experience as feeling like a torrent of water was running from the top of his head to his chest. It was, he said, like a powerful river emerging from the earth and cascading from the summit of a lofty mountain.

When Ali Nuri was released from prison in 1853, the government confiscated his property, and he was banished along with his family and others to Baghdad. There he began to have increasing influence in the Babi community of exiles. The Persian consul asked the Ottoman police to remove Ali Nuri to Istanbul. Shortly before he left, some claim he declared himself to be "one whom God shall manifest," which is the figure the Bab said would come after him. He did this in spite of the fact that in late 1847 the Bab himself claimed to be the hidden Imam who would appear in the person of the Mahdi. The new message for Muslims was that Muhammad was not the last prophet. Needless to say, this did not sit well with orthodox Muslims.

After several months in Istanbul, the exiles were sent to Edirne in Turkey, and there Ali Nuri, now called Baha Allah, openly declared his prophetic mission and sent letters to various world leaders, including Pope Pius IX. Further troubles between the government and the Baha'is as well as the Azalis (Babi followers of Nuri's half-brother) led to banishment to Palestine. Baha Allah arrived in Acre in 1868, and to this day Baha'is consider Palestine as the Holy Land.

Baha Allah's most important work is known as the *Kitab al-aqdas* (The Most Holy Book). When he died, he designated his eldest son, Abbas Effendi (1844–1921) to be the infallible interpreter of his books and called him the "center of the covenant." Abbas Effendi received the title Abd al-Baha (servant of the glory) and became the leader of the Baha'is.

Abd al-Baha became a world traveler and persuasive missionary, traveling to Egypt, Europe, and America between 1910 and 1913 preaching the message of Baha'i. These missionary activities were consciously and carefully planned and were designed to market Baha'i as a new world faith, "destined to supersede all established religions." The early converts were largely drawn from Westerners interested in psychic phenomena, theosophy, and what we today would call "New Age" teachings. After Abd al-Baha died, he was buried next to the Bab in a shrine on Mount Carmel. In his will, he appointed Shoghi Effendi Rabbani (1899–1957) "guardian of the cause of God" and infallible interpreter of his own, plus his father's, writings. Shoghi Effendi was the eldest son of Abd al-Baha's eldest daughter and the author of the statement with which we began this case.

Shoghi Effendi studied at Oxford and assumed a leadership role at the administrative center of Bahaism in Haifa. He married Mary Maxwell, a Canadian, in 1936. He was responsible for creating the main administrative structure of Baha'i as well as modernizing and internationalizing the Baha'i message.

He died in 1957 without designating a successor or leaving children. To make matters worse, he had excommunicated all his living male relatives. Both he and his father, Abd al-Baha, had been explicit about the need for the Guardianship to continue through the "hereditary principle." They predicted that if this did not happen, the Baha'i faith would be "mutilated." These events provoked a crisis within the movement over authority. The way through the crisis was eventually found by utilizing the administrative system of National Assemblies that Shoghi Effendi had organized. In 1963 these National Assemblies elected the Universal House of Justice, which assumed international leadership of the movement. Members are reelected every five years and still administer the Baha'i movement. When the principle of heredity failed, what we might call the "principle of bureaucracy" carried the day. Baha'i had become a well-organized movement, and authority was passed from family descendents to the administrative mechanisms created by Shoghi Effendi.[22]

Baha'i is organized in pyramid fashion. Each local Baha'i community elects a nine-person local assembly. Each country has a National Spiritual Assembly whose members are elected at a national convention. An international convention elects members to the Universal House of Justice. Even though the history of this movement indicates it has been plagued by factionalism, this administrative structure has proved effective in keeping the Baha'is relatively unified. In addition, severe persecution by other religions has helped to unify the faithful. The largest Baha'i community is still in Iran. Since the 1979 Iranian revolution, the old persecution of the Baha'is by the orthodox Muslims has been renewed. In 1983 the revolutionary government of Iran banned all religious and testimonial activities of the Baha'is.

*Beliefs and Practices*   Our focus here will be on contemporary beliefs and practices. Baha'i theology has changed in many ways since its early days, as it has become more international and distinguished itself more sharply from Shia Islam. It consciously presents itself as a distinct world religion with roots in the messages of many different religions. The Baha'i Guardianship is placed directly in a long line of prophets extending back to Adam and including Noah, Abraham, Moses, Zoroaster, Buddha, Krishna, Jesus, and Muhammad. The Bab brought the old prophetic cycle (called the Adamic Cycle) to a close and began a new prophetic cycle called the Baha'i Cycle or Cycle of Fulfillment. This cycle is to last for 500,000 years, and then another new cycle will start.

At the heart of this vision is a view of revelation usually called *dispensationalism*. Religious revelation and hence religious truth is relative to different times and cultures. The essence of God is the Logos, and the Logos is one, but there are many manifestations of the Divine Logos. The divine goal is to create ever wider unity among people. Abraham unified a tribe, Moses unified a people, and Muhammad unified a nation. Jesus purified individuals, thereby preparing them for even greater unity. The task of Baha Allah was to unify the entire human race.

Each of the prophets accomplished his tasks, and the religions they spawned are not failures, but successful parts of a much larger scheme. In a sense, each of these prophets was the "final" prophet, but they were final in the sense of definitive for their time and place. So Muhammad is truly "the seal of the prophets" as Muslims claim, and Jesus is the final manifestation of God as Christians assert. However, every prophet is the seal or final manifestation of those who preceded them. They are not final in the sense that there will never be any more prophets or any more revelations.

This dispensational view of revelation allows Baha'is to accept all religions as true but none as the complete and final truth. In a sense, this is a version of inclusivism since each prophet includes the truth of the previous prophets. However, we might say it is an inclusive inclusivism. The voyage of the human soul is an infinite voyage toward the infinite unknowable essence of God.

According to Abd al-Baha, there are five types of spirits: animal, vegetable, human, faith, and the Holy Spirit. God gives the spirit of faith, and this spirit, added to the human spirit, makes eternal life possible. Faith is essential to Baha'i spiritual life. Faith, along with hope, is what keeps humanity moving toward God.

The idea of the eternity of the soul means, for Baha'is, the eternal journey toward God. Both a heavenly paradise and an eternal hell are meant symbolically. Heaven symbolizes believers on the right path to God, and hell symbolizes the unbelievers who knowingly reject the option of faith and perform evil deeds. The path to hell leads to total annihilation unless the soul believes the divine message concerning the eventual unification of the whole human race and begins to take that path toward a new society of unity and peace.

The long passage with which this case opened is a condensed summary by Shoghi Effendi of the primary teachings. If you read it carefully, you will find an interesting mixture of progressive views (such as equality of women and men along with the desire to reduce the gap between the poor and rich) and conservative views (strict obedience to one's government). The roots in traditional Islamic teachings are obscured. Since the majority of converts today are from non-Islamic backgrounds, few realize the essentially Islamic vision that informs Baha'i thinking. Both Islam and Baha'i share the idea that history is a process directed by periodic divine interventions whose purpose is to reveal God's will in the form of *Sharia*, a comprehensive legal, moral, and social system designed to shape and regulate human behavior at all levels. The Universal House of Justice is today responsible for developing this new *Sharia* for a unified world and unified human race that Baha'i will usher in.

The Islamic (also Jewish and Christian) ideas of covenant and "rightly guided" leaders are also obscured by Shoghi Effendi's summary of Baha'i teachings. The Madhi is the rightly guided leader of Islam, and the exclusivism of Shi'ite sectarian movements often stemmed from each sect claiming to have leaders that are rightly guided by God. This is one reason why fights over how the authority is passed on continually plagued traditional Islam as well as the Baha'i movement. A corollary of this idea is the use of excommunication and shunning of those who fail to recognize and obey the correct leadership. The Baha'is faced a crisis in leadership with the death of Shoghi Effendi in part because he had excommunicated male members of his family who rejected his authority. The Universal House of Justice has inherited the mantle of being rightly guided.

Traditional Islamic views have been greatly modified and modernized. Also, the history of the movement has been officially rewritten to incorporate Babism. Abd al-Baha characterized Baha'ism and Babism as opposites. Whereas Babism was militant, exclusivistic, willing to use violence, and generally opposed to modern progressive ideas, Baha'i was pacifistic, inclusivistic, opposed to violence, and receptive to at least some elements of modern thought. Shoghi Effendi conflated Babism and Baha'i, giving the impression that what they taught was largely the same. This served his purposes well because linking a movement closely with past movements often bolsters subsequent religious authority.

Today, as Third World converts along with Western progressive social activists fill the ranks, the admonition to obey one's government without question is sounding more and more outdated. The Universal House of Justice has recognized this, and just as past leaders have incorporated modern elements into a traditionally Islamic framework, so the present leadership is developing more social activist projects, including medical, agricultural, and literacy projects in cooperation with the United Nations.

The ritual practices of Baha'i are not elaborate. They are derived from Islam, and center primarily on ritual prayer, annual fasting, and pilgrimage. All of these are *obligatory* for faithful Baha'is. Other practices, such as rites of passage, are *prescriptive*.

Ritual prayer is private, and the believer has three alternatives: to pray once in twenty-four hours, or once at noon, or three times a day. The believer is to face in the direction of the tomb of Baha Allah in Acre. Fasting takes place once a year in the last month of the solar year (March 2–20). Unless ill or pregnant, believers fast from dawn until dusk for nineteen days (there are nineteen solar months divided into nineteen days). The pilgrimage is not well defined. At first, only male Baha'is were to go to the homes of the Bab in Shiraz, Iran, and to Baha Allah in Baghdad. These have become increasingly difficult (the Bab's home was destroyed in 1979), so pilgrimages to "lesser" sites have evolved. These include the tombs of the Bab and Baha Allah outside Haifa and most recently the grave of Shoghi Effendi in London. Fairly elaborate rituals are performed at these pilgrimage sites.

There is no priesthood, nor are there any sacraments. Recently, semiprofessionals, both men and women, have been appointed to protect and to spread the faith. While these individuals may be thought of as a kind of clergy, they do not perform ritual functions. Nineteen times a year on the first of each month, Baha'is come together for the Nineteen-Day Feast. These feasts, which are usually held in homes of members, involve the reading of prayers and sacred texts, discussion of administrative issues, and the sharing of food and drink. Like Muslims, Baha'is are forbidden to drink alcohol.

Although there are no mosques, there are seven temples that are showpieces used largely for public gatherings. The temples are presently located in the United States (Wilmette, Illinois, near Chicago), Germany, Australia, India, Panama, Uganda, and Samoa.

The primary rites of passage are naming ceremonies for babies, marriage, and funeral rites. Circumcision is allowed, but not mandatory. Marriages can be arranged and often are in places like Iran. However, they do not have to be. Only the consent of both parties and all living parents is required. Burial is carried out according to a complex set of regulations, and cremation is considered undesirable, but not strictly prohibited.

In origin, Baha'i belongs to the world of nineteenth-century Iran. But at significant stages of its development it has responded positively to many Western ideas and values. Its leaders, since about 1920, have faced squarely the dilemmas of institutionalization and have carefully planned and organized in order to make Baha'i a world religion. Few religions have so self-consciously managed their development. Rational organizations, conscious articulation of goals, and rational planning to achieve them sound more characteristic of businesses than religions. But as Max Weber predicted, everything in the modern world, including religion, becomes increasingly subject to rationalization and the forces of routinization.

## QUESTIONS ON THE CASE OF BAHA'I

I have directed you enough. Instead of focusing on the answers to questions I ask, analyze this case on your own. Carefully reread the case, and as you read, jot down any questions or ideas that occur to you. These can be descriptive, interpretive, comparative, explanatory, and evaluative questions. They can be questions requiring more information or parallels to other cases we have already studied. Jot down tentative answers to your questions, and check out your ideas by gathering additional information or rechecking ideas and cases from elsewhere in this book. I have provided a few hints at possible lines of development in the case itself. Use your questions and notes as background information for writing a five- to seven-page paper on the case of Baha'i.

You have two choices for your paper. The first is a comparative study in which you select another religion and compare and contrast it with Baha'i. Create a useful typology for comparison to focus your research and structure your paper. For example, your typology might be drawn from any of the many typologies found in previous chapters or some combination thereof. You may find it more useful to create your own, letting it develop out of the Baha'i case.

The second choice involves creating a hypothesis and testing it against the evidence. In this paper, state a hypothesis, summarize what some of the literature has to say about the answer, explain what sort of evidence (such as statistical, historical, testimonial, primary, secondary, etc.) you gathered, whether the evidence proved or disproved the hypothesis, and areas for further research. A hypothesis is a one-sentence statement that is provisional and is adopted to explain certain facts. In other words, it is a tentative explanation that needs to be tested in light of the evidence. Examples of some possible hypotheses are (1) Baha'i is primarily Islamic in spite of its claim to be a new world religion; (2) Baha'i has failed to satisfactorily solve the dilemma of administrative order; (3) Baha'i's revisionist history with respect to the Bab is intended to create more plausible credentials for the faith. These are some of mine, and you *cannot* use them! Create your own. Have fun.

## SUGGESTIONS FOR FURTHER READING

In addition to the material found in the notes, readers may wish to consult the following for more information.

Baha'u'llah. *The Seven Valleys and the Four Valleys*. Translated by Marzieh Gail. Wilmette, IL: Baha'i Publishing Trust, 1945. This is a book of mystical meditations by Baha Allah using Sufi images and symbols.

Bausani, Alessandro. "Baha'is." In *Encyclopedia of Religion*, vol. 2, edited by Mircea Eliade, 40–42. New York: Macmillan, 1987. This article provides a brief overview of Baha'i history, practices, beliefs, and organization.

Coward, Harold. *Pluralism: Challenge to World Religions*. Maryknoll, NY: Orbis Books. 1985. Coward describes the views about religious diversity and conflicting truth claims found in Judaism, Christianity, Islam, Hinduism, and Buddhism. He closes with a helpful chapter on religious diversity and the future of religion.

Dean, Thomas, ed. *Religious Pluralism and Truth: Essays in Cross-Cultural Philosophy of Religion*. Albany, NY: State University of New York Press, 1995. Dean has edited a collection of essays by well-known scholars on four themes relating to problems associated with cross-cultural truth in religion.

Hick, John. *An Interpretation of Religion: Human Responses to the Transcendent*. New Haven, CT: Yale University Press, 1989. In this book Hick develops his version of pluralism in some detail, including the development of an "ethical criterion."

Hick, John, and Askari Hasan, eds. *The Experience of Religious Diversity*. Aldershot, England: 1985. This book is a collection of essays by scholars and representatives of different religious traditions on the issues that relate to questions of truth.

Locke, John. *A Letter Concerning Toleration*. Edited by James Tully. Indianapolis, IN: Hackett Publishing, 1983. In 1689 the British philosopher John Locke published this letter in which he presents the case for what amounts to the separation of church and state. He maintains that the secular magistrate of the state is to act for the good of the whole of society as he sees it and is not to determine that good by appeal to any particular religious doctrine. This idea was revolutionary for Locke's time, but was attractive to a Europe that had recently been nearly destroyed by vicious and prolonged religious warfare.

Maceoin, Denis. "Baha'ism." In *A New Handbook of Living Religions*, edited by John R. Hinnells, 618–643. London: Penguin, 1998. Maceoin provides reliable information on history and beliefs as well as a review of sources and recent scholarship. I am greatly indebted to his discussion.

Neville, Robert Cummings, ed. *Religious Truth: A Volume in the Comparative Religious Ideas Project*. Albany, NY: State University of New York Press, 2001. These essays by different scholars explore the idea of truth as found in Chinese, Hindu, Buddhist, Jewish, Christian, and Islamic religions.

Panikkar, R. *The Intrareligious Dialogue*. New York: Paulist Press, 1978. Panikkar focuses on different models of religious dialogue and sets forth some "rules of the game." He argues that defensiveness and attempts to prove others wrong based on one's own faith do not contribute positively to religious dialogue.

Schuon, Frithjof. *The Transcendent Unity of Religions*. New York: Harper and Row, 1975. Schuon argues that there are two levels to religion: the exoteric, or outer face, and the esoteric, or hidden face. Outwardly religions are different, but inwardly they are all united in a unity that transcends difference and discord.

Smith, Wilfred Cantwell. *Towards a World Theology*. Philadelphia: Westminster Press, 1981. It is time, Smith argues, to go beyond sectarian theology and develop theological ideas in a global context.

———. *Questions of Religious Truth*. New York: Scribner, 1967. Smith argues that religions are not true or false, but better or worse.

Wentz, Richard E. *Why Do People Do Bad Things in the Name of Religion?* Macon, GA: Mercer University Press, 1987. Wentz tackles this difficult and important question by distinguishing between religion and religious.

Wilson, Bryan. *Religious Toleration and Religious Diversity* Santa Barbara, CA: The Institute for the Study of American Religion, n.d. Wilson provides a concise overview of the nature of religious diversity and the development of tolerance in society.

## INTERNET RESOURCES

http://www.mideastinfo.com/Religion/bahai.htm   This site provides links to information about Baha'i. Much of it is apologetic, so use with care. This is a good place to find primary sources.

http://www.fas.harvard.edu/~pluralsm/   Here you will find information about the Harvard pluralism project, information on different religious groups, and links to other sites.

http://www.wcc-coe.org/wcc/what/interreligious/index-e.html   This is the Web site for the World Council of Churches, which deals with interreligion relations and dialogue.

# Notes

## Chapter 1

1. Some of the material in the first three chapters was first published in Gary E. Kessler, *Ways of Being Religious* (Mountain View, CA: Mayfield Publishing, 2000). Reprinted by permission of The McGraw-Hill Companies, Inc.
2. F. Max Müller, *Lectures on the Science of Religion* (New York: Charles Scribners, 1872), 10–11.

## Chapter 2

1. Clifford Geertz, "Religion as a Cultural System," in *Anthropological Approaches to the Study of Religion*, ed. Michael Banton (London: Tavistock, 1966).
2. Gary Kessler, *Philosophy of Religion: Toward a Global Perspective* (Belmont, CA: Wadsworth Publishing, 1999), 3.
3. Donald S. Lopez, Jr., ed., *Buddhist Hermeneutics* (Honolulu: University of Hawaii Press, 1988), 8.
4. Karl Marx and Friedrich Engels, *On Religion* (New York: Schocken Books, 1964), 42.

## Chapter 3

1. William P. Alston, "Religion," in *The Encyclopedia of Philosophy*, ed. Paul Edwards (New York: Macmillan, 1967), 7:141–142.
2. Benson Saler, *Conceptualizing Religion: Immanent Anthropologists, Transcendent Natives, and Unbounded Categories* (New York: Berghahn Books, 2000), 9.
3. Mary Daly, *Beyond God the Father* (Boston: Beacon Press, 1973), 19.
4. Paul Tillich, *Christianity and the Encounter with World Religions* (New York: Columbia University Press, 1963), 4.
5. Melford E. Spiro, "Religion: Problems of Definition and Explanation," in *Anthropological Approaches to the Study of Religion*, ed. Michael Banton (London: Tavistock, 1966), 96.
6. Edward Evans-Pritchard, *Witchcraft, Magic and Oracles among the Azanda* (Oxford: Clarendon Press, 1976); Keith Thomas, *Religion and the Decline of Magic* (New York: Macmillan, 1986).
7. Claude Levi-Strauss, *Structural Anthropology* (New York: Basic Books, 2000).
8. Mary Douglas, *Purity and Danger: An Analysis of Concepts of Pollution and Taboo* (London: Routledge, 1966).
9. Quoted in Lawrence S. Cunningham, et al., *The Sacred Quest: An Invitation to the Study of Religion* (Englewood Cliffs, NJ: Prentice-Hall, 1995), 13. Also see James G. Frazer, *The Golden Bough* (London: Macmillan, 1990), 50.

## Chapter 4

1. Translation by Wing-tsit Chan, *A Source Book of Chinese Philosophy* (Princeton: Princeton University Press, 1963, 1991), 139.
2. Isabelle Robinet, *Taoism: Growth of a Religion*, trans. Phyllis Brooks (Stanford, CA: Stanford University Press, 1997), 26.
3. It is customary to capitalize the word *God* when speaking of monotheistic conceptions of the divine and not to do so when referring to gods and goddesses. However, some

think this practice conceals a prejudice and argue that, in fairness to others, the word should not be capitalized or capitalized all the time. This issue is complicated by the fact that *God* can function as a proper name in English. For the most part I have opted to follow the custom of capitalizing God when it refers to one supreme deity and to use lowercase when referring to more than one divine being.

4. Anselm, *Proslogion*, trans. Robert Van Voorst, in *Readings in Christianity*, 2nd ed. (Belmont, CA: Wadsworth, 2001).

5. *The Bhagavad-Gita: Krishna's Counsel in Time of War*, trans. Barbara Stoler Miller (New York: Bantam Books, 1986), 100.

6. J. R. Walker, *The Sun Dance and Other Ceremonies of the Oglala Division of the Teton Dakota* (American Museum of Natural History, Anthropological Papers, vol. XVI, part II, 1917), 152–153.

7. *Authorized Daily Prayer Book*, trans. S. Singer, 9th American ed. (New York: Hebrew Publishing Company, 1912), 89.

8. *The Book of Common Prayer* (London, 1855).

9. *Upanishads*, trans. Patrick Olivelle (Oxford: Oxford University Press, 1996), 153.

10. Ludwig Feuerbach, *The Essence of Christianity*, trans. George Eliot. (Gloucester, MA: Peter Smith Publishers, 1854).

11. Peter L. Berger, *The Sacred Canopy: Elements of a Sociological Theory of Religion* (Garden City, NY: Doubleday & Company, Inc., 1967), 28.

12. Bruce Bryant Friedland, "Ganesha Ritual a Milestone for Hindus," *Jacksonville (FL) Times-Union*, 9 September 1999.

13. Robert L. Brown, ed., *Ganesh: Studies of an Asian God* (Albany, NY: State University of New York Press, 1991), 3.

## Chapter 5

1. From Barbara C. Sproul, *Primal Myths: Creating the World* (San Francisco: Harper & Row, 1979), 92.

2. There are two versions of the giving of the commandments at Sinai, and the golden calf episode is mentioned in the second version, which starts at Exodus 24:9. It is instructive to compare Exodus 19–24:8 (the first version) with Exodus 24:9 and following.

3. Louis Ginzberg, *The Legends of the Jews*, vol. III (Philadelphia: The Jewish Publication Society of America, 1911), 90–94.

4. Mircea Eliade, *Myth and Reality*, trans. Willard R. Trask (New York: Harper and Row, 1963), 5–6.

5. *Averroes on the Harmony of Religion and Philosophy*, trans. G. F. Hourani (London: Luzac Oriental, 1961).

6. Michael Ruse, "Introduction," in *Religion and Science*, Bertrand Russell (New York: Oxford University Press, 1997).

7. Peter Berger, *The Sacred Canopy: Elements of a Sociological Theory of Religion* (Garden City, NY: Doubleday, 1967), 25.

8. *The Rig Veda: An Anthology*, trans. Wendy Doniger O'Flaherty (London: Penguin Books, 1981), 31.

9. *The Laws of Manu*, trans. Wendy Doniger with Brian Smith (London: Penguin Books, 1991), 13.

10. Ibid., 197.

11. Bruce Lincoln, *Myth, Cosmos, and Society: Indo-European Themes of Creation and Destruction* (Cambridge: Harvard University Press, 1986), 164.

## Chapter 6

1. Burton Watson, trans., *Hsün Tzu: Basic Writings* (New York: Columbia University Press, 1963), 94–95.
2. Evan M. Zuesse, "Ritual," in *The Encyclopedia of Religion*, ed. Mircea Eliade (New York: Macmillan Publishing Company, 1987), 12:405. My definition is a modified form of Zuesse's definition.
3. Theodore Gaster, *Thespis: Ritual, Myth, and Drama in the Ancient Near East*, 2nd rev. ed. (New York: Gordian Press, 1975), 26.
4. Henri Frankfort, *Kingship and the Gods: A Study of Ancient Near Eastern Religion as the Integration of Society and Nature* (Chicago: University of Chicago Press, 1948/1978), 319.
5. J. B. Pritchard, ed., *Ancient Near Eastern Texts Relating to the Old Testament*, trans. S. Sachs, 2nd ed. (Princeton: Princeton University Press, 1955), 334.
6. Jonathan Z. Smith, *Imagining Religion: From Babylon to Jonestown* (Chicago: University of Chicago Press, 1982), 93.
7. The Rev. Richard E. Power, *Our Mass: A Manual for the Dialogue Mass* (Collegeville, MN: St. John's Abbey, 1956), 44–45.
8. For more information on *Black Elk Speaks*, see "Suggestions for Further Reading." Black Elk has sparked considerable controversy in the scholarly world. He participated in the Roman Catholic Church until his death and made a conscious connection between the seven major rituals of the Lakota Sioux and the seven sacraments of the Church. Some have argued that he was a genuine Christian who was only culturally attached to the Lakota religious tradition; others argue the reverse. For a careful discussion of the issues, see William A. Young, *Quest for Harmony: Native American Spiritual Traditions* (New York: Seven Bridges Press, 2002), 209ff.
9. Joseph Epes Brown, recorder and ed., *The Sacred Pipe: Black Elk's Account of the Seven Rites of the Oglala Sioux* (Norman, OK: University of Oklahoma Press, 1953, 1989), xix. The quotes that follow are taken from this source starting with page 116.
10. Bruce Lincoln, *Emerging from the Chrysalis: Studies in Rituals of Women's Initiation* (Cambridge: Harvard University Press, 1981), 106.
11. Ibid., 108
12. Nahum N. Glatzer, ed., *The Passover Haggadah* (New York: Schocken Books, 1953), 25. The quotes relating to the seder that follow are all taken from this source.
13. E. M. Broner, "Honor and Ceremony in Women's Rituals," in *The Politics of Women's Spirituality: Essays on the Rise of Spiritual Power within the Feminist Movement*, ed. Charlene Spretnak (Garden City, NY: Doubleday Anchor, 1982), 237–238. Miriam, the sister of Moses, helped lead the Hebrews out of exile. She was a prophetess in her own right and is the first woman in the Bible to be given that title.

## Chapter 7

1. This quote and most of the other information about Kilimanjaro come from Edwin Bernbaum's beautiful book, *Sacred Mountains of the World*. See the list of suggested readings for more information.
2. Mircea Eliade, *Patterns in Comparative Religions*, trans. Willard R. Trask (New York: New American Library, 1963), 220. The original source referenced by Eliade is *The Native Tribes of Central Australia* (London, 1899), 337.
3. Diane Eck, *Darśan: Seeing the Divine Image in India* (Chambersburg, PA: Anima Books, 1981), 3. This book is a "must read" for all those who would mistake bowing to images of the divine as mere idol worship.
4. Alan Watts, *Myth and Ritual in Christianity* (Boston: Beacon Press, 1969), 86. Watts's book is an informative study of Christian symbolism covering art, architecture, the

church year, and much more. His approach is heavily influenced by Carl Jung's theory of archetypes.

## Chapter 8

1. Today this site is marked by the Dome of the Rock located on top of the ruins of the Jewish Temple.
2. This and the following quotes come from *The Translation of the Meanings of Sahih al-Bukhari*, trans. Muhammad Muhsin Khan (Chicago: Kazi Publications, 1979), 5:144.
3. I rely here on the work of Glock and Stark. See "Suggestions for Further Readings" at the end of the chapter.
4. *The Life of the Buddha as It Appears in the Pali Canon, the Oldest Authentic Record*, trans. Nanamoli (Kandy: Buddhist Publication Society, 1972), 21.
5. *Buddhist Scriptures*, trans. Edward Conze (Middlesex, England: Penguin Books, 1959), 49.
6. Ibid., 50–51.
7. Ibid., 52.
8. Friedrich Schleiermacher, *The Christian Faith*, trans. H. R. Mackintosh and J. S. Stewart. 2nd ed. (Edinburgh: T&T Clark, 1928), 4.
9. Not all students of Schleiermacher would agree with Otto's interpretation. But I must pass over the ins and outs of this debate here. Suffice it to say, scholars dispute Otto's "subjectivistic" interpretation of Schleiermacher.
10. Again I am relying on Glock and Stark's typology.
11. This category comes from Glock and Stark.
12. Kieran Kavanaugh and Otilio Rodríquez, eds, "Introduction," in *The Interior Castle*, Teresa of Avila (New York: Paulist Press, 1979), 2.
13. Quoted in Alison Weber, *Teresa of Avila and the Rhetoric of Femininity* (Princeton, NJ: Princeton University Press, 1990), 160.
14. Ibid.
15. *The Book of Her Life, Spiritual Testimonies. Soliloquies*, trans. Kieran Kavanaugh and Otilio Rodríquez. In *The Collected Works of St. Teresa of Avila*, vol. 1 (Washington, DC: Institutes of Carmelite Studies, 1976), *Life*, chap. 27, no. 4.
16. Ibid., *Spiritual Testimonies*, 14.
17. Weber, *Teresa of Avila*, 11.
18. Ibid., 164–165.
19. Ibid., 165.

## Chapter 9

1. Elie Wiesel, *Night*, trans. Stella Rodway (New York: Farrar, Straus, and Giroux, 1960), 40.
2. Ibid., 42.
3. See E. E. Evans-Pritchard, *Witchcraft, Oracles, and Magic among the Azande* (Oxford: Oxford University Press, 1937).
4. *Upanishads*, trans. Patrick Olivelle (Oxford: Oxford University Press, 1998), 142.
5. William Theodore de Bary, ed., *The Buddhist Tradition in India, China and Japan* (New York: Vintage Books, 1972), 25.
6. Ibid.
7. R. A. Nicholson, ed. *Selected Poems from the Divant Shamsi Tabriz* (Cambridge: Cambridge University Press, 1898/1977), 125.
8. David Hume, *Dialogues Concerning Natural Religion* (Oxford: Oxford University Press, 1935), 244.
9. J. L. Mackie, "Evil and Omnipotence," in *Philosophy of Religion: Toward a Global Perspective*, ed. Gary E. Kessler (Belmont, CA: Wadsworth Publishing, 1999), 226.

10. William Rowe, "The Problem of Evil and Some Varieties of Atheism," in Kessler, 240.

11. Alfred North Whitehead, the "father" of process philosophy would disagree with the idea of mutual transference of energy, but Charles Hartshorne, a student of Whitehead, endorses mutual transference.

12. Schubert Ogden, "Evil and Belief in God: The Distinctive Relevance of a 'Process Theology,'" *The Perkins Journal* (Summer 1978): 33.

13. Mary Baker Eddy, *Science and Health with Key to the Scriptures* (Boston: The First Church of Christ, Scientist), 472–473.

14. Elie Wiesel, *The Trial of God* (New York: Random House, 1979), 157.

## Chapter 10

1. William James, *The Varieties of Religious Experience: A Study in Human Nature* (New York: Simon & Schuster, 1997), 393.

2. *Hymns of Guru Nanak* (New Delhi: Orient Longmans, 1969), 25.

3. From the *Khalsa Consensus Translation*, Dr. Sant Singh Khalas (http://www.sikhs.org/english/frame.html), 176.

4. Quoted in W. Owen Cole, "Sikhism," in *A New Handbook of Living Religions*, ed. John R. Hinnels (Cambridge: Blackwell, 1997), 331–332.

5. "Salvation," in *The HarperCollins Dictionary of Religion*, ed. Jonathan Z. Smith (San Francisco: HarperCollins, 1995), 954.

6. Roy C. Amore, "Puñña," in *The Perennial Dictionary of World Religions*, ed. Keith Crim (San Francisco: Harper & Row, 1981), 585.

7. Daniel Boucher, "Sutra on the Merit of Bathing the Buddha, in *Buddhism in Practice*, ed. Donald S. Lopez, Jr. (Princeton, NJ: Princeton University Press, 1995), 67.

8. Gregor Rippel, *The Beauties of the Catholic Church*, trans. F. J. Shadler (New York: Fr. Pustet & Co., c.1881), 404.

9. Donald K. Swearer, "A Modern Sermon on Merit Making," in *Buddhism in Practice*, Lopez, 401.

10. From the *Shinshu Shogyo, Zensho II*, cited in *Shinran's Gospel of Pure Grace*, Alfred Bloom (Tucson: University of Arizona Press, 1965), 32. Bloom's study of Shinran is one of the best available.

11. Martin Luther, *Lectures on Romans*, trans. Wilhelm Pauck, in *The Library of Christian Classics* (Philadelphia: The Westminster Press, 1961), XV:137.

12. Martin Luther, "A Treatise on Christian Liberty," in *Luther's Works*, eds. H. T. Lehmann and H. J. Grimm (Philadelphia: Fortress Press, 1957), XXXI:371.

13. Jacques Malan, "The Possible Origin of Religion as a Conditioned Reflex," *American Mercury*, 25:314.

14. Tony K. Stewart, "The Goddess Sasthi Protects Children," in *Religions of India in Practice*, ed. Donald S. Lopez, Jr. (Princeton, NJ: Princeton University Press, 1995), 354.

15. Walter Burkert, *Creation of the Sacred: Tracks of Biology in Early Religions* (Cambridge: Harvard University Press, 1996), 169.

16. Instructions given by Ibn Abi Zayd al-Quayrawani (922–996). See Gary Kessler, *Western Ways of Being Religious* (Mountain View, CA: Mayfield, 2000), 194.

17. Hew Mcleod, "Sikh Hymns to the Divine Name," in *Religions of India*, Lopez, 129.

18. See D. G. Dawe's discussion of "Salvation," in *The Perennial Dictionary of World Religions*, ed. Keith Crim (San Fransico: Harper & Row, 1989), 643–646.

19. From *The Buddhist Traditions in India, China and Japan*, ed. Wm. Theodore de Bary (New York: Random House, 1969), 21.

20. From *Buddhist Texts through the Ages*, ed. Edward Conze (New York: Harper & Row, 1954), 202–203.

21. D. T. Suzuki, *Zen Buddhism* (New York: Doubleday, 1956), 84.

22. D. T. Suzuki, *Introduction to Zen Buddhism* (London: Rider, 1949), 97.

23. Sallie King, "Awakening Stories of Zen Buddhist Women," in *Buddhism in Practice*, Lopez, 520–521.

## Chapter 11

1. "Acquisition," in *The Word of Islam*, ed. John Alden Williams (Austin, TX: University of Texas Press, 1994), 153.

2. *The Analects*, trans. D. C. Lau (London: Penguin Books, 1979), 12.

3. Tu Wei-Ming, *Centrality and Commonality: An Essay on Confucian Religiousness* (Albany, NY: State University of New York Press, 1989), 116.

4. Aquinas himself permitted the aborting of embryos and fetuses up to the time of "quickening" (the time when the mother can feel the fetus move). He did this because he thought the function of the soul was to make matter alive, and hence the soul did not enter the fetus until it exhibited movement. Today the Roman Catholic church has taken a more radical position, declaring that human life begins at conception.

5. Clyde L. Manschereck, ed., *A History of Christianity* (Englewood Cliffs, NJ: Prentice-Hall, 1965), 376.

6. Ronald M. Green, *Religion and Moral Reason* (New York: Oxford University Press, 1988), 3.

7. William Paden, *Religious Worlds: The Comparative Study of Religion* (Boston: Beacon Press, 1994), 141.

8. Ayatollah Khomeini, *A Clarification of Questions*, trans. J. Borujerdi (Boulder: Westview Press, 1984), 212.

9. Dietrich Bonhoeffer, *Ethics*, trans. Eberhard Bethge (New York: Macmillan, 1955), 20.

10. Soren Kierkegaard, *Fear and Trembling* and *The Sickness unto Death*, trans. Walter Lowrie (Garden City, NY: Doubleday & Company, 1954).

11. Paden, *Religious Worlds*, 152.

12. Ibid., 154.

13. Paul Reps, *Zen Flesh, Zen Bones: A Collection of Zen and Pre-Zen Writings* (Garden City, NY: Doubleday, n.d.), 18.

14. Paden, *Religious Worlds*, 158.

15. *Jaina Sutras*, trans. H. Jacobi, Part I (Oxford: Clarendon Press, 1884), 251.

16. Ibid., 263–264.

17. Ibid., 46.

18. "The Jain Tradition," in *World Religions: Eastern Traditions*, ed. Willard G. Oxtoby (Oxford: Oxford University Press, 1996), 172.

## Chapter 12

1. Robert L. Johnstone, *Religion in Society: A Sociology of Religion*, 6th ed. (Upper Saddle River, NJ: Prentice-Hall, 2001), 35.

2. Ibid., 37–42.

3. In addition to the information found in John Power's book *Introduction to Tibetan Buddhism* (see "Suggestions for Further Reading"), I am indebted to the discussion found in the introduction to *Religions of Tibet in Practice*, ed. Donald S. Lopez, Jr. (Princeton, NJ: Princeton University Press, 1997), 3–36.

4. This is part of an extract taken from the transcript of a tape of the final forty-three minutes at Jonestown obtained by the *New York Times* from the International Home Video Club, Inc., New York City, and published in the *New York Times*, 15 March 1979. This extract can be found in Appendix 2 of Jonathan Z. Smith, *Imagining Religion: From Babylon to Jonestown* (Chicago: University of Chicago Press, 1982), 134.

5. Rebecca Moore, *Sympathetic History of Jonestown: The Moore Family Involvement in Peoples Temple* (Lewiston, NY: Edwin Mellen Press, 1985), 155.

6.  Quoted in Jonathan Z. Smith, "The Devil in Mr. Jones," in *Imagining Religion: From Babylon to Jonestown* (Chicago: The University of Chicago Press, 1982), 107. I am indebted to Smith's discussion for much of the background information on Jim Jones and Jonestown.

7.  Moore, *Sympathetic History of Jonestown*, 229.

8.  See Smith, *Imagining Religion*, 107.

9.  Moore, *Sympathetic History of Jonestown*, 288.

10. Catherine Wessinger, *How the Millennium Comes Violently: From Jonestown to Heaven's Gate* (New York: Seven Bridges Press, 2000), 41.

11. John Hall, *Gone from the Promised Land: Jonestown in American Cultural History* (New Brunswick, NJ: Transaction Books, 1987), 254.

12. Quoted in Wessinger, *How the Millennium Comes Violently*, 51–52.

13. Smith, *Imagining Religion*, 133.

14. Quoted in the introduction by Anne Fremantle to *The Grand Inquisitor* (New York: Frederick Ungar Publishing, 1978), viii.

15. *The Grand Inquisitor*, 12, 13.

16. Thomas O'Dea, *The Sociology of Religion* (Englewood Cliffs, NJ: Prentice-Hall, 1966), 90ff.

17. The last verse is controversial. I have followed the translation of the RSV. Others suggest translations like "she will be saved through the birth of the Child [Jesus] and "she will be brought safely through childbirth."

18. Nancy Schuster Barnes, "Buddhism," in *Women in World Religions*, ed., Arvind Sharma (Albany, NY: State University of New York Press, 1987), 105.

19. Susan Sered, *Priestess, Mother, Sacred Sister* (New York: Oxford University Press, 1994). For a more complete discussion of Sered's study, see Johnstone, *Religion in Society*, 248–250.

20. Ibid., 43.

21. Ibid., 8.

22. Lori Beaman, "Gender and Religion," in *Sociology of Religion: A Reader*, eds. Susanne C. Monahan, William A. Mirola, and Michael O. Emerson (Upper Saddle River, NJ: Prentice-Hall, 2001), 115ff.

23. Mary Daly, *The Church and the Second Sex* (New York: Harper and Collins, 1968), 6.

24. Beaman, "Gender and Religion," 117.

25. Martin Marty, *The New Shape of American Religion* (New York: Harper & Row, 1958), 78.

26. *Kojiki* [Records of Ancient Material], trans. Joseph M. Kitagawa, chap. 17, in *The Great Asian Religions: An Anthology*, eds. Wing-Tsit Chan, et. al. (New York: Macmillan, 1969), 232–233.

27. Helen Hardacre, *Shinto and the State, 1868–1988* (Princeton, NJ: Princeton University Press, 1989), 5.

28. Ibid., 161.

## Chapter 13

1.  See James C. Livingston, *Anatomy of the Sacred: An Introduction to Religion*, 3rd ed. (Upper Saddle River, NJ: Prentice-Hall, 1998), 420–421.

2.  Ibid., 420.

3.  Diane Eck, "A New Geo-Religious Reality." Paper presented at the World Conference on Religion and Peace, Sixth World Assembly, Riva del Garda, Italy, November, 1994. Quoted in Mary Pat Fisher, *Religion in the Twenty-First Century* (Upper Saddle River, NJ: Prentice-Hall, 1999), 14. Note that there are two different uses of pluralism relevant to our topic. One is the descriptive use, which refers to religious diversity or variety. It is in that sense that pluralism is used in Eck's pluralism project. Another use of

pluralism is normative. In this sense it refers to a particular theory about the relationship among religions with respect the issue of truth. In order to avoid confusion, I have used the word *diversity* instead of *pluralism* wherever possible to indicate the descriptive sense, and I have restricted the word *pluralism* to its normative sense.

4. M. Wiles, "Christianity without Incarnation?" in *The Myth of God Incarnate*, ed. John Hick (Philadelphia: Westminster Press, 1977), 1.

5. John Hick, "Religious Pluralism," in *A Companion to Philosophy of Religion*, ed. Philip L. Quinn and Charles Taliaferro (Cambridge, MA: Blackwell Publishers, 1997), 610.

6. Alvin Plantinga, "A Defense of Religious Exclusivism," in *Philosophy of Religion: An Anthology*, 3rd ed., ed. Louis P. Pojman (Belmont, CA: Wadsworth Publishing, 1998), 517–530.

7. Ibid., 530.

8. Karl Rahner, "Christianity and the Non-Christian Religions" in *Theological Investigations* (New York: Seabury Press, 1996–1979), 5:124.

9. Hick, "Religious Pluralism," 612.

10. Ibid., 612.

11. Quoted in Arvind Sharma, *The Philosophy of Religion and Advaita Vedanta: A Comparative Study in Religion and Reason* (University Park, PA: Pennsylvania State University Press, 1995), 224.

12. Schubert Ogden, *Is There Only One True Religion or Are There Many?* (Dallas: Southern Methodist University Press, 1992), 99.

13. Ibid., 99–100.

14. S. Radhakrishnan, *Eastern Religions and Western Thought* (Oxford: Clarendon Press, 1939), 317.

15. S. Radhakrishnan, "Religion and Religions," in *Relations among Religions Today*, eds. Moses Jung et al. (Leiden, Netherlands: Brill 1963), 135.

16. See D'Costa, "Whose Objectivity? Which Neutrality?" in *Philosophy of Religion: Toward a Global Perspective*, ed. Gary Kessler (Belmont, CA: Wadsworth, 1999), 562–573.

17. Radhakrishnan, *Eastern Religions and Western Thought*, 323.

18. Nick Fotion and Gerald Elfstrom argue in their book *Toleration* (Tuscaloosa, AL: University of Alabama Press, 1992) that we should reserve the use of *tolerance* to name an accepting attitude, and we should use *toleration* to indicate enduring the disagreeable. They wish to do this because one of the connotations of tolerance is a kind of begrudging endurance that others find offensive. It connotes an attitude something like, "I may not like your religion, but I will put up with it if I have to." While the authors are right about disassociating tolerance from begrudging endurance, their proposal obscures the important role that genuine disagreement plays.

19. Edward Langarek, "Disagreement," in *Philosophy, Religion, and the Question of Intolerance*, eds. Mehdi Amin Razavi and David Ambuel (Albany, NY: State University of New York Press, 1997), 112.

20. J. B. Schneewind, "Bayle, Locke, and the Concept of Toleration," in Razavi and Ambuel, 4.

21. Shoghi Effendi, *Guidance for Today and Tomorrow* (Wilmette, IL: Baha'i Publishing Trust, 1953), 3–4.

22. There was some opposition to the transfer of authority from family to administrative mechanisms. Mason Remey, a Baha'i residing in New Mexico, proclaimed himself the heir to the Guardianship. In 1961 he designated Joel B. Marangella as his successor. Remey's group considers itself the true representatives of the Baha'i tradition, calling itself Orthodox Baha'i. They refuse to recognize the Universal House of Justice.

# Glossary/Index

anthropology of religion (*continued*)
to understand how religion is related to culture. 19–20

anthropomorphic beings: Literally "in human form," this refers to the tendency of many religions to describe the gods in human form. 64

antinominianism, 281

antitheodicy, 209, 210, 211

Anu, 79

Aphrodite, 63

apocalyptic movements: From the Greek word *apocalypse*, which means "revelation," and has come to refer in general to a type of literature or religious movement that alleges to reveal future events related to the fulfillment of religious hopes and dreams. 194, 203

Apollo, 135

apologetics: The activity of offering a defense of one's religion. 5

Apophis, 63

apostolic socialism, 299–300, 304, 328

Aquinas, St. Thomas, 21, 22, 204, 226–227, 273, 284, 380n4

archetypes: The word means "primary model," and Carl Jung uses it to name what he thinks are universal psychological patterns encoded in the collective unconscious of the human race. 178–179, 183
self, 179, 180, 183
universal, 91

architecture, 139–144

arch (*mihrab*), 143

Aristotle, 273

Arjan, Guru, 222

Arjuna, 61

ark (*aron kodesh*), 141

Ark of the Covenant, 141

art
and religion, 137–145, 146

ascent images, 166

ascetic: A person who lives an austere life of self-denial, often involving physical deprivations such as fasting, in order to intensify devotion or enhance spirituality by becoming independent of physical needs and desires.
asceticism, 178, 223, 231, 287

ascetic Protestantism, 233

aseity: The claim that God's existence, unlike the existence of other beings, is uncaused. 67

Ashaglun, 214

Asharites, 262, 283

Ashurbanipal, 79

Ashvaghosha, 161

Association of Shinto Shrines, 335–336

astronomy, 94

*Atharva*, 317

atheism: The view that God does not exist as a being external to the human mind. 7, 71, 73

Athena, 63

Atman, 69–70, 351, 355

atonement theories, 112, 115, 228–229, 252

Auditors, 214

Augustine, St., 205

Aurobindo, Ghose, 96

Auschwitz, 189

Australian aborigines
Dreamtime, 126–127, 130–134, 144, 145, 201
natural religious communities, 310
religion of sanctification, 218
totemism, 63

authority, types of, 314–315

autonomy stage, of ego development, 179

Avalokiteshvara, 295, 296

Averroes, 95

avoidance, 280, 282, 285

*axis mundi*: An "axis of the world" represented by a pole, tree, or mountain connecting the earth with the sky and the underworld. 126, 142, 144, 145

Azalis, 367

Azande, 191, 211

Bab, 367, 368, 371

Babism, 367, 370

Babylon, 79, 88, 112, 213

Babylonian New Year. *See* Akitu festival

Baha Allah, 367, 369, 371

Baha'i, 342, 366–372
beliefs and practices, 369–372
eternity of soul for, 369
history, 367–68
organization, 368
persecution by orthodox Muslims, 368

Baha'i Cycle/Cycle of Fulfillment, 369

Baha'i Guardianship, 369
Bahram I, 214
Bakongo, 64
Bali, 65
baptism, 113, 148, 149
baptismal font, 148
Barnes, Nancy Schuster, 321
basilicas, 142
Beaman, Lori, 323, 324
*The Beauties of the Catholic Church* (Rippel), 238
Bellah, Robert: "Civil Religion in America,"
    327, 330
Berger, Peter L., 73, 191
*Bhagavad Gita*, 61, 282
Bhai Burdas, 223
bhakti yoga, 176, 177, 182, 235
bias
    defined, 7
    in religious definition, 37–40, 47
biblical revelation, 57
Big Bang theory, 94
binah, 141
Bin Laden, Osama, 264, 265
birth control, 273
Black Caribs, 322
Black Elk (Hehaka Sapa), 106–107, 108, 109,
    111, 119, 377n8
Black Hole of Tehran, 367
Black Panthers, 299
Blind people and the Elephant, parable of,
    361–362, 366
blood, 111
blood offerings, 281
*bodhi*, 163
**bodhisattva**: A title for any person who has
    taken a vow to become enlightened (a
    buddha) and lives a life of compassion
    intent on gaining enlightenment for
    himself/herself and all others as well. 162,
    295
Bodhisattva of Compassion, 295
*bodhi* tree, 161
Bonhoffer, Dietrich: *Ethics*, 279
*Book of the Dead*, 249
Borobudur, 139
Brahma, 66–67, 163
Brahman, 69–70, 250, 351, 355
Brahmin, 193
Broner, E. M., 122
*The Brothers Karamazov* (Dostoevsky), 312

Brown, Antoinette, 324
Brown, Joseph Epes: *The Sacred Pipe*, 107
Brown, Robert L., 75
Buddha, 153, 160–166, 214, 286, 369
    on achievement of enlightenment, 237
    charismatic authority, 314
    compared to Muhammad, 166–167, 168
    enlightenment, 170, 172, 173, 236
    enlightenment experience, 178, 180
    as exemplary prophet, 181
    question of divinity of, 167
    refusal to speculate about afterlife, 250
    utilization of trance, 182
Buddhadasa Bhikku, 239, 243
Buddha of Infinite Light, 240
buddhas, 153, 160
Buddhism, 4, 35, 160–167
    canon, 317
    Chan Buddhism, 254
    Chinese Buddhism, 237, 254
    of compassion, 295
    concentration techniques, 176
    doctrine of impermanence, 206
    egalitarianism, 321
    eschatological forms of, 333
    five precepts to refrain from, 280
    foundational experiences, 182
    Four Noble Truths of, 220
    Ganesha, 73
    and Jainism, 286
    karma theodicy, 198–199, 212
    left-handed tantric yoga, 281
    letting go of attachments, 13
    Mahayana (Greater Vehicle) Buddhism, 200,
        254, 295
    making of merit, 236–237, 243
    meditation, 164–165, 180
    notions of afterlife, 250–251, 254
    sexism, 320, 330
    temples, 143
    Theravada Buddhism, 197–198, 254, 295
    Vajrayana (Diamond or Thunderbolt Ve-
        hicle), 254, 295
    women portrayed as sources of pollution in,
        320
Buraq, 157
Burkert, Walter, 245

calendars, 136, 149–150
Calixtus, St., 148

calligraphy, 138, 146

calling, 231–232

Calling on the Name, 246

Calvin, John, 227, 231–232, 233

Cambodia, 254

Canaan, 83, 93

Canaanites, 81

**canon:** Literally "rule" or "standard," it is used as a general term for any authoritative set of sacred or secular writings. 317, 330

capitalism, and Protestantism, 231, 233, 253

cargo cults, 199

Carmel, Mount, 368

Carmelites, 183

carnival rites, 103, 106, 112, 113

castes, 99, 192, 233, 274

*cathedra,* 147

cathedrals, 136

ceremonial space, 144

cessation, 164

Chaco Canyon, 136

Chagga, 128–130, 133, 134

Chan Buddhism, 254

*Chandogya Upanishad,* 69, 192

chanting, 255

Chapter House, 149

charisma, 305

   routinization of, 312, 329

charismatic authority, 314, 329

charity, principle of, 223, 361, 362, 366

Chinese Buddhism, 237, 254

Chinese communists, occupation of Tibet, 297, 309

Chinese popular religion, 4, 201, 250

choir, 147, 148

Christian Bible, 200, 317, 330. *See also* New Testament

*The Christian Faith* (Schleiermacher), 168

Christianity, 4, 56–57, 220, 224–229

   canon, 330

   compared to Sikhism, 229–230, 252–253

   concepts of sin, 225–227

   exclusivism, 345–346, 363

   as form of bhakti yoga, 176

   images of God, 226

   Jewish roots of, 153, 224–225, 252

   *kyrie,* 246

   as messanic movement, 113

   monotheism, 65

   multiple forms of, 225

   and natural law theory, 273

   notions of judgment, immortality, and resurrection, 249–250

   as otherworldly eschatological theodicy, 200

   patriarchalism, 323

   as religion of salvation, 218–219

   sexism, 320, 330

   *See also* Coptic Church; Eastern Orthodox Church; Nestorians; Protestantism; Roman Catholicism

Christian Science, 322

Christmas, 136, 150

Christos, 224

*chung,* 267, 268, 276, 283

churches, 141–143, 146

Church of Jesus Christ of Latter-day Saints, 239

church-sect continuum, 310–312, 329

church-type organizations, 310–312

Cicero, 69

Cipriano de Aguayo, 184

circumambulate, 139

"Civil Religion in America" (Bellah), 327

**civil religions:** A set of beliefs and rituals that unite the diverse elements of a society into a unifying ideology. 294, 310, 325–327, 330

civil rights movement, 28

Civil War, 327

clan totems, 62–63

classification schemes, 25

clergy

   distinction from laity in Catholic Church, 231–232

   professional, traditional authority of, 315

   Protestant, marriage among, 242

   women, 324

Clifford, William K., 70–71

cloven hooves, 278

**cluster definitions:** Definitions of religion that list a set of family traits found in many members of the "family" religion. They differ from essential definitions, which attempt to state the essence of religion. *See* **functional definition** and **substantive definition.** 36–37, 47

coercion versus conversion, 314

collective sacrifices, 116

collective unconscious, 178, 180, 181, 183

colonialism, 199

commemorative ritual, 120

communal revelations, 158

communal worship, 223
communion, 113, 120
**communitas**: A term that indicates the social solidarity that develops during the liminal or transitional phase of a rite of passage. 109–110, 112
comparative religious studies, 13, 14, 16, 19, 23, 27, 29
**comparison**: A fair and balanced account of the similarities and differences among examples of phenomena. 27
compassion, 276, 281, 285, 295
competition, among religions, 343, 363
concentration techniques, 176
Concerned Relatives, 301, 302
confession, 241
confession of faith, 65
confirmation (holy chrism), 148, 149
confirmatory sacrifices, 116
confirming religious experiences, 170, 182
conflict theory, 342–343, 363
Confucianism, 4, 265–270
    blending of ethics and naturalism, 269
    comparison with Islamic on ethics, 270–277, 284
    on impartial moral judgment, 276
    Mandate of Heaven, 209, 271, 272, 273, 284
    morality, 260, 268, 275–276, 283, 284
    notion of family, 267–268, 269
    vision of ideal world, 268
Confucius, 266
congregational structures, 139, 141, 146
consensus, 271, 283
Conservative Judaism, 81, 141
consistency, and truth, 9
Constantine, 65
context dependent, meaning as, 26
contingent being, 58
convents, 144
conversion, 113, 310
    versus coercion, 314
Copernican thought, about religion, 349–350, 364
Copernicus, Nicholas, 94
Coptic Church, 57, 66
Corinthians, Letters to, 325
**cosmogonic myths**: Sacred stories about the beginning of the universe. 86
**cosmological myths**: Sacred stories about the order and structure of the universe. 86
cosmological religious functions, 88

cosmopolitanism, 13
cosmos, 80
Council of Chalcedon, 345
Council of Nicea, 345
covenant, 370
creation myths, 97, 98, 111, 132, 193, 331
critical intelligence, 7–9, 11, 15, 18
critical philosophy of religion, 21
**critical tolerance**: An attitude that endorses freedom of religion but does not necessarily approve of every religious belief and practice. 10–12, 15, 18, 360–361, 365–366
crossing, 148
cruciform ground plan, 142, 147
cud, 278
*cui bono*, 28
*cultus*, 40
cultivation of insight, 164, 165, 181
cultivation of tranquility, 164, 165, 181
cults, 113, 298–299, 306–307, 310, 311, 329
cultural bias, 47
Cultural Revolution, 297
culture, concept of, 19–20
Cyrus, King, 224

Daijosai, 335
D'ai Shan, 126
Dalai Lama, 295
    fifth, 297
    first, 296
    fourteenth, 297, 298, 305
Daly, Mary, 39, 323
Damian, Peter, 57
**Dao (Tao)**: The Way, referring, in the Chinese religion of Daoism, to the ultimate truth, source of all reality, and the Way of Nature. 54–56, 59, 61, 235, 271, 284, 331
*Daodejing (Tao-te-ching)*, 54, 60
Daoism (Taoism), 4, 53–56, 59–60, 69, 268, 269, 331
*dars'an*, 140
*darshana*: In Hinduism, the viewing or seeing of the divine in an icon. It is considered an act of worship. In Buddhism, it refers to a visionary experience. It can also refer to a Hindu philosophical system. 244, 253
Darwin, Charles: *Origin of the Species*, 94
Day of Atonement, 105
Day of Pentecost, 150
days of the dead, 113

*dhikr*, 246
D'Costa, Gavin, 356–359, 359, 365
dead religions, 19
death
    as sacrificial act, 86
    as transcendence of self-consciousness, 220
death/resurrection motif, 112
de Chardin, Pierre Teilhard, 96
deductive (logical) argument, about God and evil, 204
*The Deeds of the Buddha (Buddhacarita)*, 161–162
deep structure
    of religious moral reasoning, 274–277, 280, 285
    of text, 26
**deism**: The belief that God created the universe but does not intervene in its operation. 67, 72
delimitation, dilemma of, 313
Delphi, 135, 136, 146
Demiurge, 87
demonic possession, 227
**demons**: Superhuman beings midway between humans and gods, often described as evil and harmful, but they can also be good and helpful. 64–65
denomination, 310–311, 329
dependency stage, of ego development, 179
**description**: Stating the facts of a case as objectively as possible by classifying some *x* under a category according to some property (*p*) of *x*. 24–26, 29, 30
desire, as cause of suffering, 165
despair, 279, 281, 285
*de (te)*, 54, 55, 266
developmental historical studies (history of religion), 19
devotion, 223–224, 230, 252
*dharma*: In Hinduism, this refers to the sacred law, which specifies caste duties. In Buddhism, it refers to the teachings of Buddha, such as the Four Noble Truths. 192, 193, 211, 274
*dhikr*, 253
*dhyana*: This Sanskrit word can refer to meditation in general or specific meditative states and stages along a meditative path. 164
dictation theory, 330
Digambara, 287

dilemma of power, 313–314
Diocletian, 214
"Disagreement: Appreciating the Dark Side of Tolerance" (Langerak), 361
Disciples of Christ, 300, 311
discipline of action, 176
dispensationalism, 369
dissatisfaction, 219, 233–235, 252
divine command theory, 260, 261–265
Djanggawul, 132
*Doctrine of the Mean*, 266
Dogen, 254, 255
dogmatism, 7
Dome of the Rock, 378n1
domes, 142
Domestic (Home) Shinto, 332
Dostoevsky, Fyodor Michaelovitch: *The Brothers Karamazov*, 312–314
Douglas, Mary: *Purity and Danger*, 45, 47, 278
*do ut des*, 114, 115, 235, 242, 243, 253
dreaming, theories of, 159
Dreaming-places, 131
Dreamings, 130–132, 133, 136, 144
Dreaming-tracks, 131
**Dreamtime**: According to Australian Aborigines, this is a sacred time when everything that exists today was created. 126–127, 130–133, 136, 145, 201
    comparison to Mount Kilimanjaro, 133–134
Drepung, 295, 298, 308
dualism, 72, 255
    Christian, 226
    subject/object, 219–220
dualistic theodicies, 67–68, 72, 191–192, 203, 212
Durkheim, Emile, 63
**duty ethics** (deontological ethics): An ethical system based on the notions of duty, obligation, and obedience to rules. 270, 271, 284, 285

Ea, 79, 80, 86
Easter celebrations, 19, 150
Eastern Orthodox Church, 57, 66
    New Testament, 318
    Old Testament, 317
    sacramental principle, 138
Eck, Diane, 140, 344, 381n3
**ecstatic** experiences: This term refers to those experiences in which individuals lose control of themselves. 155, 158–159

Eddy, Mary Baker: *Science and Health with Key to the Scriptures*, 207–208
Edirne, 367
education
    role in process of becoming virtuous person, 268
    and socialization processes, 328
ego, 88, 179, 182, 219
Egypt
    gods and goddesses, 63
    notion of afterlife, 246, 249
eightfold path: The Buddhist middle way leading to nirvana, which consists of right understanding, right thought, right speech, right action, right occupation, right effort, right mindfulness, and right concentration. 160, 180
Eight-Limbed Yoga, 175, 180
Eisai, 254
elect, 214, 232–233
Elephant principle, 362
Elfstrom, Gerald, 382n18
Eliade, Mircea, 91–92, 132
Elohim, 81, 87
emanation body, 296
emergence, 110
emissary prophets: Those who believe they have been given a divine message along with the assignment of getting others to believe the message. 158, 164, 181
empathy, 281
enlightenment, 163, 166, 181, 237, 255
    Buddha's experience, 170, 173, 178, 180
*Enuma elish*, 79–81
    Akitu festival, 105, 118, 119
    binary opposition in, 92
    comparison with Moses story, 84–86, 88
    as a creation myth, 84, 97, 125
    as a hero tale, 84
    purpose of, 90
environmental issues, 344
Epiphany, 150
Esagila, 103
eschatological myths: Sacred stories about the end of history or the destruction of the world. 86
eschatological theodicies, 193–194, 195, 196–197, 199–201, 211, 212
eschatology: This refers to ideas about "last things," or the end of time. This end may be thought of as otherworldly or this-

worldly and is often associated with judgment, punishment, and reward.
Eshu, 64
essence: That quality or qualities that make something what it is and not something else. 35, 273, 284
essentialism, 35, 47
ethics, 260, 268. *See also* morality
"The Ethics of Belief" (Clifford), 70–71
ethnic cleansing, 206, 342
ethnocentrism, 13, 38, 358
etiological myths: Sacred stories explaining why something came to be or got the way it is now. 86
Eucharist, 120, 148, 242
Euphrates River, 92
evaluation: Second-order evaluation involves value judgments about the quality of some description, interpretation, or explanation. First-order evaluation refers to the formation of value judgments about religious claims and events.
    as goal of religious studies, 28–29, 30
Evans-Pritchard, Edward E.: *Witchcraft, Magic and Oracles among the Azande*, 44, 116
Everest, Mount, 126
evidence, reliability of, 9
evidentialism, 70
evil
    denial of, 207–208, 212
    external, 226
    as punishment for sin, 205
    theological problem of, 68, 189–217
evolution, 90, 94, 96
exaltation, 145
exclusivism: This refers to the idea that one religion is true both in the sense of teaching the truth about ultimate reality and in the sense of providing the only valid way to salvation. 344, 345–347, 352, 353, 354, 363, 370
excommunication, 370
exemplary prophets: Those who have significant religious experiences and see their mission as teaching others how to have those experiences for themselves. 158, 164, 181
Exodus, Book of, 280
experiential dimension, of religion, 46
explanation: There are different kinds: interpretations that deepen our understanding;

Geertz, Clifford, 20
Geluk lineage, 296–297, 328
gender, and institutionalized religion, 319–325, 330
gender, as concepts of femininity and masculinity, 319
gender bias, in definitions of religion, 38–39, 40, 47
gender dissonance, 322, 330
Gendundrup, 296
General Social Survey Cumulative File, 323
Genesis, 85, 87
geocentrism, 94
Ghandhi, Mohandas, 176, 289
gifts, 230, 253
Girard, René, 115
giving (dana), 236
globalization, 13, 14, 16, 344, 363
Gobind Singh, Guru, 221
God
    aseity of, 67
    speculation about nature of, 65–67
    transcendence of, 70
goddesses, 63–65, 179, 296, 321
god-image, 179
God-realization, 224
gods, 63–65
Goethe, Johann von, 13
Golden Rule, 259, 276, 284, 285
Good News (gospel), 225
good works, 240, 242
Gordon, Charles George "Chinese," 195, 196
Gothic, 147
grace, 223, 229, 233, 238, 252
grace through faith, as path to salvation, 239–243
grammar, hidden rules of, 26–27
greater jihad, 265, 283
*The Great Learning*, 266
Greece
    mystery cults, 249
    notion of life after death, 249
Greek Orthodox, 139
Green, Ronald M.: *Religion and Moral Reason*, 274–275, 276, 277, 279, 285
groups, functional prerequisites of, 292–293, 304–305, 327–328
guided evolution, 95
guilt, 279, 281, 284, 285
*Guru Granth Sahib*, 221, 222

guruship, doctrine of, 223
Guyana, South America, 300

Hades, 249
Hadith, 156, 263, 264, 275
*Haggadah*, 120–121
halloween, 113, 150
happiness, 357, 365
Hardacre, Helen, 334–335
Hare (Lord) Kirshna, 176
Hargobind, 221
Harney Peak, 126
*haroset*, 122
Hartshorne, Charles, 379n10
Hasan, 194
Hasidic Judaism, 81
Hatha yoga, 175
healing rituals, 113
heaven, 201, 212, 230, 248, 251, 369
    and hell, symbols of, 20
Heavenly Masters Sect, 53
Hebrew Bible. *See* Old Testament
Heian period, 333
heliocentrism, 94
heliotropism, 243, 253
hell, 200, 212, 230, 248, 249, 252, 369
**henotheism**: The belief that many gods may exist, but people should worship only one of the many. 64, 85
Hera, 63
Her Alone They Sing Over (*Ishna Ta Awi Cha Lowan*), 106–111, 119
    comparison to Akitu, 111–112
**hermeneutics**: A method for interpreting information, particularly textual information, that pays close attention to the context and structure of a text. 26, 29
hero tales, 84, 111
Hick, John, 39, 206, 346, 349, 350, 351, 364
**hierophanic** religious functions: This term is derived from *hierophany*—literally, a manifestation or revelation of the sacred. 88
high altar, 148
higher knowledge, 69
Hinduism, 4, 160, 253, 346
    *Bhagavad Gita*, 61, 282
    bhakti tradition, 221
    Ganesha, 73–76, 192
    goddess worship, 321

Hinduism (*continued*)
 gurus, 223
 importance of hearing in scriptural formation, 317
 individual immortality, 250
 karma theodicy, 192–193, 198
 left-handed tantric yoga, 281
 mantras, 144
 monism, 69
 monotheism, 65
 natural law approach, 274
 puja, 244, 253
 Rig-Veda, 98, 317
 scripture, 329
 sexism, 320, 330
 *sruti*, 317, 318, 319, 329–330
 temples, 140
 *trimurti*, 66–67
Hindu Society, 73, 75
Hira, Mount, 153, 155
Hirohito, Emperor, 335
**history of religions**: Developmental and comparative studies using historical and linguistic techniques to understand religions. 23
Hitler, Adolf, 206, 210, 279
Holocaust, 189–190, 206, 211
holy chrism, 148
holy orders (ordination), 148
Holy Spirit, 65, 66, 150, 201
holy wars, 20, 265, 283
holy water, 135, 147
homosexuality, 273, 285
honesty, 7, 15, 18
human condition, dissatisfaction with, 219, 233–235, 247, 252
humanism, 71–72
human sacrifice, 11, 281
Hume, David, 204
hunting rituals, 112
Husain, 194
hymns, Sikh, 223

**iconoclasticism**: Literally refers to "breaking images," but in religious studies, it usually refers to movements opposed to the use of images in worship. 138, 146
iconoclastic movements, 138–139
icons, 137, 139, 146
*The Idea of the Holy* (Otto), 169–170

identity
 derived from belonging to religious group, 20–21
 as part of larger family unit, 201
**ideological rituals**: Rituals that seek social control by changing the mood, behavior, sentiments, motivations, and values of people, usually for the sake of the community as a whole. 113, 119
**ideology**: Any set of doctrines or beliefs that form the basis of a political, economic, or religious system. 89
idol, 146
idolatry, 138, 225–226, 252, 327
ignorance, as primary problem with humans, 234, 252, 253
*ijma*, 263
images, offerings to, 244
imagination, 10, 11
**imam**: Title for the leader of prayer in an Islamic mosque. 143, 194, 367
immanence, 70, 72
*Immortale Dei*, 273–274
immortality
 individual and nonindividual, 250, 253–254
 as living in harmony with the Dao, 56
 of soul, 249
Imperial Household Shinto, 332
impurity, 277–278, 279, 281, 285
incarnate lama, 296
incarnation, 138
**inclusivism**: A position that does not deny the idea of truth in all religions, but still asserts the superiority of one religion. 347–349, 352, 353, 354, 363, 369
inclusivism, pluralistic, 352–353
incorporation phase, of ritual, 109
India, 98, 192
Indian Ghost Dance, 113
individual immortality, 250, 253
individualism, 232
Indo-European myths, 98, 99
Indra, 163
inductive (evidential) argument, about God and evil, 204–205, 212
indulgences, selling of, 238, 241
initiation rites, 107, 110, 132, 171
 women's, 117, 119
inner worship, 244
Inquisition, 94, 183–184, 312

inquisitions, 20, 228

**insider's view**, of religion: In the study of religion, the view of a religious participant, who seeks understanding in order to increase faith. *See also* **outsider's view.** 3, 4, 5, 15

institutionalized religion
  civil religions, 325–327
  five dilemmas of, 312–314
  and gender, 319–325, 330
  scripture, 316–319
  types of authority, 314–315
  types of religious organizations, 309–312

integration stage, of ego development, 179

intellectual dimension, of religion, 46

*The Interior Castle*, 184, 185

internal sin, 241

International Campaign to Free Tibet, 305

**interpretation**: An account of what something means, involving seeing *x* as a sign of *y*. 26–27, 29, 30

intolerance, religious, 346

introvertive, 172, 173, 182

invigoration, 102, 104, 105, 118

Iranian revolution, 368

Ise shrine, 334

Ishvara, 351

Isis, 63

Islam, 4, 156, 158
  and Baha'i, 370
  bhakti tradition, 221
  comparison with Confucianism on ethics, 270–277, 284
  *dhikr*, 253
  divine command theory of ethics, 261–265, 283
  Five Pillars of Islam, 156, 181, 195
  formal prayer, 245
  foundational experiences, 154, 155–156, 167, 182
  fundamentalism, 264
  iconoclasticism, 138, 146
  on impartial moral judgment, 276
  monotheism, 65
  notions of judgment, immortality, and resurrection, 249–250
  notions of morality, 275
  as otherworldly eschatological theodicy, 200
  sacred spaces, 135
  and science, 95

*Sharia*, 235, 261, 263–264, 265, 270, 271, 275, 283, 370
  two main branches of, 194
  *See also* Muhammad ibn Abdullah

Israelites, 93

Izanagi, 331

Izanami, 331

Jainism, 4, 260–261, 286–290, 362
  and Buddhism, 286
  canon, 317
  karma, 288
  metaphysics, 288
  nonviolence, 289

James, William: *The Varieties of Religious Experience*, 39, 218, 233, 235, 247, 251

James I, 149

Japan
  banishment of State Shinto, 332, 335
  Buddhism, 241, 254, 333
  historical development of Shinto, 331–336
  mythology, 65, 87

*jatis*, 99

Jericho, 93

Jerusalem Temple, 141, 378n1

Jesus of Nazareth, 153, 224–225
  and atonement, 228
  charismatic authority, 314
  as incarnation of divine, 65, 67, 242, 346
  second coming of, 200, 225, 316

Jethro, 81

Jews
  deliverance from Romans, 224–225
  Holocaust, 189–190, 210, 342
  sects, 224

jihad, 195, 264–265, 283
  by the pen, 264
  by the sword, 265, 283
  by the tongue, 264, 283

*jina*, 286

*jivas* (souls), 288

jnana yoga, 176–177, 182, 235

Job, Book of, 209–210

John, Gospel of, 225, 318

John of the Cross, 183

Johnstone, Robert L., 292

Jones, Jim, 298–304, 305, 306, 311, 313–314

Jonestown, 11, 298–309, 328

Jon Frum cargo cult, 199–200

Joshua, 93

Joshua, Book of, 93–94
Josiah, King, 120
jubilation, 103, 104, 105, 118
Judaism
    iconoclasticism, 138, 146
    Kabbalah, 246
    monotheism, 65
    Moses story, 81–84
    notions of judgment, immortality, and resurrection, 249–250
    parent religion of Christianity, 225, 318
    sexism, 320, 330
    Torah, 81, 85, 138, 235, 320
    tradition of gender inequality, 321
judgment, notions of, 250
judgment day, 200
Jung, Carl Gustav, 155, 177, 180, 182, 183, 377n4
justice, 276, 357, 365
justificatory stories, 89

Kaaba, 156
Kabbalah, 246
kaddish, 190, 210
Kamakura period, 333
*kami*, 235, 331
Kant, Immanuel, 350
Karaperamun, 199
**karma**: The word means "action" and is often used to refer to the law of action—namely, that every act produces a result, which ultimately determines a person's rebirth.
    bad, 281
    Buddha's discovery of, 162–163, 165, 181
    Hindu theodicy, 192–193, 211
    Jainism, 288
    and merit, 236
    nontheistic view of, 192–193
    past, 224, 248
    and purgatory, 200
    in Sikhism, 222
    theistic view of, 193
    theodicies, 192–193, 196–199, 205, 212
karma yoga, 176, 177, 182, 235
Kaur, 221
Khadija, 155
Khalsa, 221
Khomeini, Ayatollah, 263
Kibo, Peak, 128–129, 136
*kiddush*, 121

Kierkegaard, Soren, 279
Kilimanjaro, Mount, 127–130, 136, 145
    comparison to Dreamtime, 133–134
King, Martin Luther Jr., 28, 260, 289, 299, 315
King, Rodney, 342
Kingu, 80
*Kitab al-aqdas* (The Most Holy Book), 367
knowledge, 357, 365
**koan** meditation: A technique used in the Rinzai sect of Zen involving a short paradoxical question given by a master to a student and designed to shock the student out of dualistic modes of thought. 254, 255, 256
*Kojiki*, 331
Kokugakuin University, 336
Korea, 254
    shamanism, 322
Koresh, David, 11
Krishna, Lord, 61, 67, 369
*kyrie*, 246

Lahore, 221
Lakota Sioux, 10, 377n8
lama, 295, 296, 328
Lanfranc, 57
Langerak, Edward: "Disagreement: Appreciating the Dark Side of Tolerance," 361
language games, 359–360, 365
Laos, 254
Laozi, 53, 59–60, 72
*Laozi. See Daodejing (Tao-te-ching)*
**latent function**: In contrast to manifest function, this refers to the hidden and often unintended functions of a myth or ritual action. 88
Latin cross, 142
Lau, D. C., 266, 268
lawful religions, 348
*Laws of Manu*, 98–99, 274
laying on of hands, 113
left-handed tantras, 294
left-handed tantric yoga, 281
legal rational authority, 314, 315, 329
Lent, 150
Leo XIII, 273–274
lesser jihad, 264–265, 283
letter of the law, 313
"letting go of attachments," 13
Levi-Strauss, Claude, 44
Levites, 84
Lhasa, 295

*Mysticism: Sacred and Profane* (Zaehner), 172–173
*Mysticism and Philosophy* (Stace), 172
myth: Sacred story.
  defined, 78
  functions of, 88
  as idealization of ritual, 118
  of origin, 125
  popular use of word, 97
  and ritual, 114, 116–119
  and science, 93–97
  theories of myth, 89–93
  types and functions of, 86–89, 97
myth and ritual theory: A school of scholarly
  interpretation and its theories concerning
  a necessary link between myth and ritual.
  90, 104, 118–119, 120

Nabu, 103
Nagasena, 198
Name (Nam) of God, 223, 246, 252
Namrel, 214
Nanak, Guru, 221, 223, 233
Narayanan, Vasudha, 289
narthex, 147
National Assemblies, 368
National Spiritual Assembly, 368
Native Americans
  genocide, 327
  religions, 64, 310
natural evil, 190, 205
naturalism: In a narrow sense, this refers to the
  position that all religions are mistaken in
  important ways when it comes to matters
  of truth. 353–354, 364
natural law theories, 273–274, 284–285
natural religious organizations, 309–310, 329
natural science, 21
natural theology, 96
Nature kami, 333
nature mysticism, 173, 182
nave, 147, 148, 149
Nazis, 189, 342
Nebuchadrezzar, 79
necessary being, 58
nectar (amrit), 221
negative Golden Rule, 267
Neihardt, John G.: *Black Elk Speaks*, 106–107
*nembutsu*, 240–241, 246
Neoplatonism, 69
Nestorians, 57, 66

neurotic behavior, 178
New Age, 172
New Confucianism, 269
New Hebrides (Vanuatu), 199
New Jerusalem, 251
new religious movements, 113, 310, 311, 328,
  329
  charismatic authority and, 315
  routinization of, 312–314
New Testament, 225, 317, 318, 330
  Book of Revelation, 194, 251
  Book of Titus, 282
  Gospels, 227
  Muslim recognition of, 156
  notion of resurrection, 249
  on sin, 227
Newton, Huey, 299
Newton, Isaac, 67
*New West*, 301
Nicean council, 65
Nicene Creed, 65–66
Nietzsche, Friedrich, 245
"Night Journey," 156, 158, 159, 166, 167, 172,
  181, 182
"The Night of Power and Excellence, 155–156
*Night* (Wiesel), 189
*Nihongi*, 331
Nimrod, Naomi, 122
Nineteen-Day Feast, 371
Nineveh, 79
Niño, Rodrigo, 186
*nirguna* Brahman, 351, 364
nirvana: A Buddhist term meaning extinction
  of suffering and release from the cycle of
  rebirth. 160, 237, 240, 250–251, 254, 321
Nisan, 102, 103
Nobel Peace Prize, 297
*nomos*: From the Greek word for "law." It is often used in a general sense to refer to anything that exhibits order. It is sometimes
  used interchangeably with *cosmos*, the
  Greek word for an ordered universe. 190,
  191, 197, 209, 211, 213
nonblood offerings, 281
nondualism, 69
nonpossession, 288
nonstealing, 288
nontheistic traditions, 234
nonviolence
  Jainists, 289

rationalistic theory of myth: A theory that interprets myths in particular and religion in general as prescientific explanations. 90, 94, 97

rationalistic theory of ritual, 117, 120

Re, 63

reading, 9–10, 15, 18

the Real, 350, 351

Real-as-it-appears, 350

Real-in-itself, 350, 363, 364

realized Christianity, 71

reason
    and divine revelation, 57
    reliance on, as threat to traditional religious power, 343, 363

Re-Atum, 87

rebirth. See reincarnation

reciprocity (shu), 267, 274

recompense theodicy, 205, 210, 212

Reconstructionist Judaism, 81

*The Record of Rites*, 268

reductionism: Often used by phenomenologists in a pejorative sense to refer to what they see as inappropriate explanations of religious phenomena in terms of nonreligious factors. 23

Reformed (Discalced) Carmelites, 183

Reform Judaism, 81, 141
    women in, 321

reframing, of patriarchal religions by women, 324

reincarnation, 192, 196, 205, 222, 224, 229, 233, 237, 248

relic, 139

*religio*: Latin word for religion that means either taking care in practicing rites like sacrifice or being under an obligation to practice rites. Combining both meanings, we get "the obligation to practice rites carefully." 37

religion
    ability of to produce moral transformation, 356, 360, 365
    alternative, 299, 311
    and art, 127, 137–145
    benefits of study of, 12–14
    as coping mechanism, 24, 68
    of democracy, 327
    dimensions of, 46
    exclusive, 344, 345–347
    inclusive, 347–349

    influence of social status on, 60
    insider's view of, 3, 4, 5, 15
    as language game, 359–360, 365
    and morality, 259–261
    as opiate, 106, 111
    outsider's view of, 4–5, 15
    philosophy of, 21, 23, 359, 365
    and politics, separation of, 298
    and problem of evil, 68, 189–217
    qualities needed of student of, 6–12
    of salvation: A class of religions that teach that things are not as they should be and need to be transcended; often contrasted with religions of sanctification. 218–219, 230–233, 234–235, 247–251, 251–252, 356
    of sanctification: A class of religions that teach that things are as they should be and the religious task is to maintain this situation. 218–219
    and science, 95–96, 98
    as "social glue," 20
    symbolic theory of, 177
    teaching of vs. teaching about, 4, 16
    use of term in English, 37
    women-dominated, 322
    *See also* institutionalized religion

religion, defining
    confusion of religion and spirituality, 39–40
    freedom from bias, 37–40
    marks of good definition, 33
    precision of definition, 34–37
    types of definitions, 41–42
    usefulness of definition, 33–34
    working definitions, 40, 45–47

*Religion, What Is It* (Tremmel), 48

*Religion and the Decline of Magic* (Thomas), 44

*Religion in Life*, 300

religion-making characteristics, 46

religious architecture, 139–144

religious art, 10, 139

religious authority, types of, 314–315, 329

religious calling, 231–232

religious conflict, 342–344, 363

religious diversity, 341, 344

religious experience: Any kind of experience, from visions and voices to intense feelings of love and devotion, that the person having the experience believes to be religiously significant. 154–155
    debates about the nature of, 168–170

religious experience (*continued*)
types of, 158–160, 169–171
religious experiences
responsive, 170, 182
religious grammar, 275
religious intolerance, 346
religious organizations, types of, 309–312
religious other, 6
religious pluralism, 349–352
religious professionals, benefits from merit schemes, 239
religious studies (religion studies), 3–6
goals and methods, 24–29
map of the field, 18–22
as scholarly language about religion, 22
religious suicide, 281
religious symbol systems, 20
religious truth, 21, 341, 355–359
as partial, 361–362, 366
Remey, Mason, 382n22
*ren* (*jen*): A Confucian concept often translated as "human excellence," "love," "benevolence," "humaneness," and "kind-heartedness." 266–267, 268, 270, 283
renunciation, 244, 287, 306, 328
repetition, in music, 144, 146–147
reshaping, of patriarchal religions by women, 324
resurrection, of spiritual body, 249. *See also* afterlife
retribution, 276–277, 281, 285
revelation
biblical, 57
dictation theory of, 319
dispensational view of, 369
religious experiences of, 158
Revelation, Book of, 194, 251
revitalization rituals: These movements, along with their complex ritual activity, seek to revitalize a culture or a religion seen as dying or in the process of being lost. 113, 119
revolutionary suicide, 299, 304
right concentration in the eightfold path, 164, 165
right conduct, 288
right-handed tantras, 294–295
right insight, 288
right knowledge, 288
right mindfulness in the eightfold path, 164, 165

Rig-Veda, 98, 317
Rinzai Zen, 254
Rippel, Gregor: *The Beauties of the Catholic Church*, 238
rites of passage: Rituals and ceremonies marking the passages or transitions in life such as birth, puberty, marriage, illness, and death.
Baha'i, 371
as ideological ritual, 113
in natural religious communities, 310
phases of, 15
women's, 106–111, 117–118, 119
ritual: This term refers to stylized, symbolic bodily gestures and actions, usually repeated in specified ways on occasions of significance and in special contexts often involving what the participants take to be sacred presences. 35, 313
defined, 101–102
expressive functions, 113–114
and magic, 117–118
and myth, 116–119
prayer, 371
purity, 109, 278
religious functions, 88
and sacred space, 125
salvation, 113, 119
social functions, 113
therapeutic and antitherapeutic, 112, 119
types and functions, 112–114
women's, 122
Robinet, Isabelle, 55
Roman Catholicism, 57, 66
and abortion, 380n4
applications of natural law theory to sexuality, 273
concept of salvation, 242
dispensing of merit and grace, 242
doctrines of hell and purgatory, 201
exclusivism, 364
*Extra ecclesiam nulla salus*, 349
fall doctrine, 226
loss of religious dominance of Europe, 311
mass, 105
merit doctrine, 238
moral theology, 226
New Testament, 318
Old Testament, 317
opposition to heliocentrism, 94
sacramental principle, 138, 148

sacred spaces, 135
sexism, 238
sin concept, 252
women in modern church, 321, 324
Roman Empire, 60, 345
Rousseau, Jean-Jacques:*The Social Contract*, 325
routinization of charisma, 312, 329
Rowe, William, 204–205
royal yoga, 175–176, 177, 182
Rumi, 202
Russell, Bertrand: *Science and Religion*, 95
Russia, 210
Ruwa, 128, 134, 136
Ryan, Leo, 302, 304, 309

sacramental principle: A term used by Paul
   Tillich to refer to the tendency on the
   part of religions to invest material things
   with the quality of being sacred. 138, 146,
   148
sacraments, 44, 148, 149, 230, 242
sacred: A term that is used in a variety of ways,
   but most often refers to that which is set
   apart, extraordinary, and totally different
   from the profane. Derived from Latin for
   that which is done "inside the temple." 56
sacred buildings, 139
sacred mountains, 126, 127–130
sacred power, 60–62, 65, 72
sacred songs, 144
sacred space, 125–127, 128, 145
   establishment of meaning, 134
   features of, 134–137
   Mount Kilimanjaro, 128–130
   paradox of on artistic level, 138, 146
sacred stories, 78–99, 133
sacred time
   Dreamtime, 125–127, 130–133, 136, 145,
      201
   establishment of meaning, 134
   features of, 134–137
   paradox of on artistic level, 138, 146
sacred writings, 10
sacrifice, 146, 281
   animal, 11, 116
   explanations of, 114–116
   human, 11, 281
   as reenactment of primal events, 115
   as substitution, 115
   theories of, 119, 235
   violence as root of, 115

*saguna* Brahman, 351, 364
St. Andrew, Cathedral of, 127, 147–150
St. Peter's Cathedral, Rome, 238, 241
*salat*: The name for Islamic ritual prayer. 245–
   246, 253
Saler, Benson, 38
*salus*, 247
salvation, 247–251
   Calvin's understanding of, 232
   Christian theology of, 228–229
   paths to, 235–247, 253
   praying for, 24
   religions of, 218–219, 230–233, 234–235,
      251–252, 356
   rituals: Rituals designed to change a person's
      identity from a spiritually corrupt, pol-
      luted, sinful, or lost state to a spiritually
      saved state that provides freedom from
      sin, corruption, ignorance, and the like.
      113, 119
*Sama*, 317
*samadhi*, 175, 176
Samhain, 62
samsara: The world of suffering and rebirth in
   which people are trapped by ignorance
   and desire. 162, 165, 192, 211, 237, 240,
   248, 295
sanctification, 170
   religions of, 218–219
sanctioning experiences, 170
sanctuary, 140, 147, 148
Santiago de Compostela, 186
Sasthi, 244
Satan, 65, 203, 226, 227, 229
*satchitananda*, 250
Sat Guru, 223
satori: Japanese Zen term for enlightenment.
   255
Saul, 153
scapegoat: Some object, usually an animal like
   a sheep or a goat, that is made to carry
   the guilt and sins of others.
   theme, 103, 105, 112, 115
schisms, 311
Schleiermacher, Friedrich Ernst Daniel: *The
   Christian Faith*, 168, 182
science
   and myth, 117
   and religion, 95–96, 98
   threat to traditional religious power, 343,
      363

*Science and Health with Key to the Scriptures* (Eddy), 207–208

scripture, 19, 230, 316–319, 329

seasonal pattern, theory of, 118, 120

Second Coming, 200, 225, 316

**second-order activity:** The study or reflection on some first-order activity. The academic study of religion is here characterized as a second-order activity. *See* **first-order activity.** 4, 29

Second Temple, destruction of, 120

Sect Shinto, 332, 333–334

sect-type organizations, 310–312, 311, 329

**secularization:** This word is used in a variety of different ways. One type of usage clusters around the notion that secularization refers to the diminishing role of religion as a serious social influence in the modern and postmodern age. Another type centers on the notion that secularization marks a religious change from traditional public patterns in the direction of increasing privatization. 343

 threat to traditional religious power, 343, 363

Seder, 120–122

self, 88, 219

self-archetype, 179, 180, 183

self-centeredness, movement to God-centeredness, 223, 252

self-consciousness, 252

 alienation within, 219–220

 transcendence of, 202–203, 220, 252

selfishness

 in good works, 242, 243

 and rebirths, 222–223

self-mortification, 178

semantics, 92, 93

**semiotics:** The general study of signs. It is usually divided into three parts: pragmatics (the study of the way people, animals, or machines use signs), semantics (the study of the meaning of signs), and syntax (the study of the relations among signs). 26, 93

sentient beings, 288

separation of church and state, 4

separation phase, of ritual, 109, 110

September 11 attacks, 264

Septuagint, 225

Serbs, 342

Sered, Susan, 322

Seth, 63

sexism

 in institutionalized religion, 319, 320, 330

 in monastic tradition, 237

sex roles, 319

sexuality, applications of natural law theory to, 273

sexual purity, 288

Shakerism, 322

Shakyamuni. *See* Buddha

shamanic ecstasy, 155, 171–172

**shaman:** This is the name for a religious functionary usually found in tribal societies, who engages, with the help of spirit guides, in healing, divining, and other activities important to the community through the means of ecstatic trances and visions. 10, 171, 182

shame, 279, 281, 284, 285

Shangri-La, 297

Shankara, 69–70, 173, 207, 208, 250, 351, 364

Shantarakshita, 294

*Sharia:* This term refers to Islamic law as a whole and derives from an Arabic word meaning "path," or "way." 261, 263–264, 265, 270, 271, 275, 283, 370

Sharma, Arvind, 351

Shasta, Mount, 126

*shaykhs*, 158

Sheol, 249

Shia Islam, 194, 211, 367, 369

Shinran, 239–241, 242, 253

Shinto, 235, 310, 330–336

Shira, 128

Shiva, 66–67, 74–75

Shoghi Effendi Rabbani, 368, 370, 371

shoguns, 333

shrine, 139, 143, 146

Shrine Shinto, 332, 334, 335

*shu*, 267, 268, 275, 276, 283

shunning, 370

Shvetaketu, 69

Shvetambaras, 287

Siddhartha Gautama. *See* Buddha

*siddhis*, 176

signified, 26

sign (signifier), 26

Sikhism, 4, 220, 221–224

 bhakti yoga, 176

 compared to Christianity, 229–230, 252–253

and economic success, 233
   praying on Name (Nam) of God, 223, 246, 252
Silk Road, 214
sin
   Christian concept of, 225–227, 252
   evil as punishment for, 205
   external and internal, 241
Sinai, Mount, 83, 84, 126, 141
Singh, 221
sitting meditation, 254–255
Sitz im Leben: German, meaning "situation or place in life." Technically, it refers to the establishment of the context of a text (where, when, by whom, to whom it was written, and its purpose or function). This information is useful for textual interpretation. 26
Slow Buffalo, 107, 108, 109, 117, 171
Smart, Ninian: Worldviews, 170, 182
Smith, Jonathan Z., 104, 105, 113, 119, 304
Smith, Wilfred Cantwell, 16
smriti, 317, 318, 329
The Social Contract (Rousseau), 325
social control, 230
social dimension, of religion, 46
social functions, of myth, 88
social science, study of religion, 19, 23
society, 20
sociology of religion: This area of religious studies applies standard sociological theories of human social behavior to religion in an attempt to uncover the way social factors influence religious beliefs and practices. 20–21
Socrates, 259
sola fide, 242
Son, second person of trinity, 65, 66
Soto Zen, 254–255
soul, 62, 286, 369
   immortality of, 249
   reincarnating, 212
   transmigration of, 197
soul-making theodicy, 206, 212
soul mysticism, 173, 182
Southern Baptists, 321, 324
Southern Christian Leadership Conference, 315
south transept, 148
Spanish Inquisition, 94, 183–184, 312
Spenta Mainyu, 68

Spinoza, Benedict, 69
spirit of the law, 313
spirit possession, 113, 159
spirituality vs. religion: The development of spirituality is the goal of many religions, but it is not necessary to belong to a religious organization in order to pursue spiritual development. 39–40, 40
spiritual realization, 354, 355
Spiro, Melford E., 41–42, 46, 47
Sri Lanka, 254
sruti, 317, 318, 329–330
Stace, Walter T.: Mysticism and Philosophy, 172, 182
stained-glass windows, 139, 149
Stalin, Joseph, 206
State Shinto, 332, 333–334
"state Shinto" (civil religion), 327, 330
Stoen, Grace, 301, 303, 308
Stoen, John Victor, 301
Stoen, Tim, 301
Stoicism, 69, 273
Streng, J.: Understanding Religious Life, 48
structuralist theory, of myth: A theory of myth in particular and religion in general that claims there are underlying logical structures (often thought to be binary oppositions) that order myths and religion, much like there are underlying syntactical rules that order language. 92
stupa: A Buddhist shrine, generally dome shaped with a towerlike structure on top. Stupas symbolically represent in architectural form key aspects of Buddhism and often contain scripture or serve as reliquaries associated with Buddha. 139, 140, 146
Subh-I Asal, 367
subject/object dualism, 219–220
submission, theodicy of, 209–211
substantive definition: A type of essential definition that focuses on the "what" or content (substance) of religion. See functional definition. 35–36, 47, 48
subtext, 27
Sudan, 195, 196, 197, 199, 212
suffering
   desire as cause of, 165
   overcoming, 166, 198, 295
   problem of, 68, 72
   and purification, 285

**Sufism:** The name for a mystical movement within Islam. 158, 194–195, 201, 246

suicide, religious, 281

suicide bombings, 20

*sui generis*, 23, 30

Sumerians, 79

Sun Goddess, 330–331

*Sunna*, 270, 271, 283

Sunni Islam, 194, 211–212
    jihad by the sword, 265
    sources of *Sharia*, 263

supererogatory acts, 238

**superstition:** A negative term used by one religion to designate the beliefs of other religions as false or wrongly motivated by fear. 42–45, 47

surface structure, 26

*The Sutra on the Merit of Bathing the Buddha,* 237

Suzuki, D. T., 255

symbolic dilemma, 313

**symbolic theories,** of myth: This refers to a theory of myth in particular and religion in general that claims meaning is symbolic, hence hidden beneath the literal surface. 90–91, 94–95, 97

synagogues, 138, 141, 146

**syncretistic:** The adjectival form of syncretism, which refers to a blending of various religious elements. It is sometimes used in a pejorative way to name religions that seem somehow incoherent. However, in fact, all religions are syncretistic to one degree or another. 213

syntax, 92, 93

synthesis, 8

**taboos:** A restriction or prohibition common to a religion or culture intended to protect the sacred and prevent pollution by the profane. 113, 278, 279, 285

Taliban, 11, 138

talismans, 246

Tanakh, 317

tantras, 294

Tanzania, 127

Tara, 296

**teaching of vs. teaching about religion:** The difference between sectarian (teaching of) and nonsectarian (teaching about) instruction pertaining to matters of religion. 4, 16

**technological rituals:** Rituals that have as their goal producing or preventing a change of state in nature so that humans can benefit in some way. 112, 119

televangelists, 314

temple pujas, 244

temples, 139–141, 143, 146

temptation, 226

Ten Commandants of Islam, 280

Ten Commandments (Decalogue), 64, 83, 84, 141, 280

Teresa of Avila, St., 155, 183–186

text, 27

Thailand, 254, 322

thanksgiving, sacrifices of, 115

theistic mysticism, 172–173, 174, 175, 182

theistic traditions, 234

**theodicies:** In its theological sense, a theodicy is any solution to the problem of evil that reconciles the existence of an all-good and all-powerful God with the evil that exists in the world. In its broad sense, it refers to any ideological (religious or secular) explanation of evil and other anomic events. 190–191
    dualistic, 67–68, 72, 191–192, 203, 212
    eschatological, 193–194, 195, 196–197, 199–201, 211, 212
    functions of, 208–211, 213
    of participation, 201–203, 212, 250
    of protest, 210, 211
    recompense, 205, 210, 212
    soul-making, 206, 212
    of submission, 209–211
    types of, 197–203, 211, 212

**theology:** Literally, theology means "talk about God" and hence, the study of God. More broadly, it refers to an activity of insiders who seek to articulate a coherent and systematic account of what they take to be ultimate reality and other matters central to their religious tradition. 21–22

theoretical bias, 38, 40, 47

theory
    evaluation of, 28
    explanation and, 27

**therapeutic and antitherapeutic rituals:** Rituals that seek to produce a change in the state of human health, either to heal the sick or bring sickness to the healthy. 112, 119

Theravada Buddhism, 197–198, 254, 295
thesism, 7
"Thirteen Principles," 65
this-worldly eschatological theodicy, 199–200
this-worldly salvation, 248, 252, 253
Thomas, Keith: *Religion and the Decline of Magic,* 44
Thor, 63
Thryn, 63
Tiamat, 79, 80, 81, 86, 97, 102
Tibet, 294
  Chinese resettlement programs, 306
  community in exile, 297, 298
Tibetan Buddhism, 254, 293, 294–298, 311
  compared to Jonestown, 304–309, 328
  diaspora, 305
  monasticism, 296, 297–298, 305, 307, 309
  preservation of order, 308–309
  preservation of sense of purpose, 309
  production of satisfactory levels of goods and services, 307–308
  recruitment and reproduction, 305
  socialization, 306
Tigris River, 92
Tillich, Paul, 41, 42, 46, 47, 146, 303
*Timaeus* (Plato), 87
Timothy, Book of, 320
Timothy, Letters to, 321, 325
Tirthankaras, 286, 287
Titus, Book of, 282
*to,* 331
Tokugawa period, 333
Tokyo, 333
tolerance, 382n18
  critical, 360–361
  religious, 10–12, 15, 18
Torah: A Hebrew word that has multiple meanings, including reference to the first five books of the Hebrew Bible, to a scroll containing divine law, to revelation in general, to teaching, to the essence of the divine law, and to the source of salvation. 81, 85, 138, 235, 320
Torah scrolls, 141
total depravity, 227
totem: Most often an animal or plant representing the sacred power of a social group, often thought of as the first ancestor. 62–63, 130
Tower of Babel, 85
traditional authority, 314, 315, 329

trance states, 144, 176
tranquility, 164
transcendence, 22
  in Confucianism, 269–270
  of God, 70
  linguistic, 56
  of profanity, 281–282
  of self-consciousness, 202–203, 220, 252
transfer of merit, 237, 238, 239
Transic insight, 165
transition phase, of ritual, 109
transliteration, of Chinese characters, 54
transmoral beliefs, 285
tree of enlightenment, 161
Tremmel, William Calloley: *Religion, What Is It,* 48
*The Trial of God* (Wiesel), 210
*trimurti,* 66–67
Trinitarianism: The teaching that God's nature is a tri-unity rather than a simple unity. 65, 72
Trinity, 65–66
Trinity season, 150
Tri Songdetsen, 294
true religion, 355–356, 365
  neutral criteria for, 356–359
truth
  as fusion of horizons, 358–359
  pursuit of, 8–9
truth-conditions, 353
truthfulness, 288
Tsong Khapa, 296
*tulku,* 296, 308
Turner, Victor, 109
Twain, Mark, 341
Twelfth Imam, 265
Twelver Shia, 194
Tylor, E. B., 62, 72
typologies: A classification system by types used for ordering diverse elements. 25, 26, 29, 86, 97, 112, 172–174

Ukiah, California, 300
*ulama,* 263
ultimate concerns, 35, 41, 42, 303
ultimate truth, 72
unconscious, 178–179, 183
*Understanding Religious Life* (Streng), 48
understanding vs. explanation, 22–24
ungulate species, 278
unidimensional measure, 34

Word (Logos), 69, 225, 318–319, 330, 369
Word (*shabad*), 223
work ethic, 232–233
World's Parliament of Religions, 289
World Trade Center, 191
world transformation, 231
world-transforming Protestantism, 233, 253
worldview, scriptural establishment of, 316
*Worldviews* (Smart), 170
worship
    communal, 223
    inner and outer, 244
    as path to salvation, 243–247, 253
    Shinto, 332
    in Zen practice, 255
Wulamba, 132
*wu-wei*, 55

*xian*, 283
*xiao (hsiao)*, 267, 268
Xunzi, 99, 266, 271

*Yajur*, 317
YHWH: The name of God revealed to Moses by a voice in a burning bush, probably pronounced "Yahweh," but considered by Jews too holy to speak. It is usually translated as "I am who I am." 81, 83, 85, 87, 93, 141, 153, 170, 246
*yi*, 283
Yigdal, 81
yoga: A Sanskrit word referring to different kinds of spiritual disciplines and paths, including the disciplines of meditation (raja yoga), devotion (bhakti yoga), action (karma yoga), and knowledge (jnana yoga). 175–177, 182, 192, 235, 281
*Yogavasishtha*, 351–352
Yoruba, 64
Yugoslavia, 342

Zaehner, R. C.: *Mysticism: Sacred and Profane*, 172–173, 182
Zarathustra (Zoroaster), 67–68, 214
*zazen*: Literally means "sitting meditation" and refers to a technique developed in Soto Zen designed to express the buddha-nature we all possess. 254–255
Zen Buddhism, 220, 254–256
Zeus, 63, 135
Zion, Mount, 141
Zipporah, 81
Zoroaster, 369
Zoroastrianism, 67–68, 203